ACCESS TO THE SEA FOR DEVELOPING LAND-LOCKED STATES

MAP I

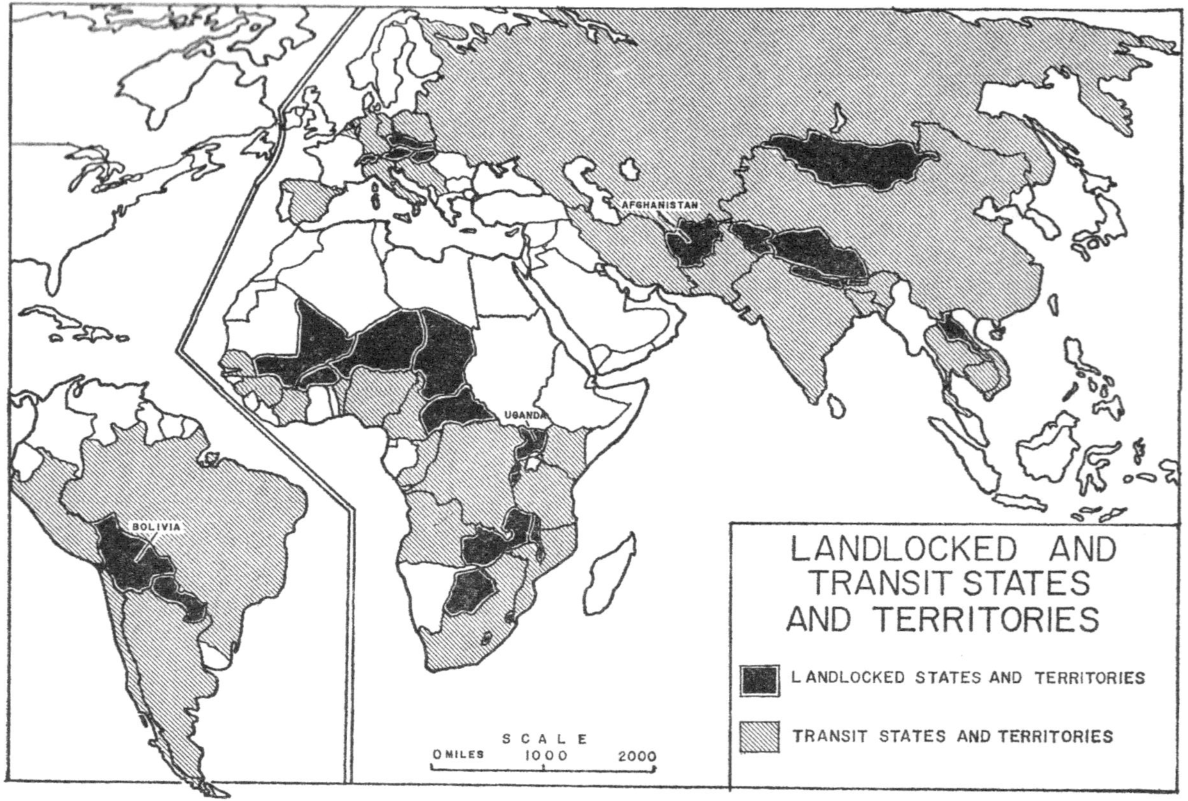
AFGHANISTAN
UGANDA
BOLIVIA
LANDLOCKED AND TRANSIT STATES AND TERRITORIES
LANDLOCKED STATES AND TERRITORIES
TRANSIT STATES AND TERRITORIES
SCALE
0 MILES 1000 2000

ACCESS TO THE SEA FOR DEVELOPING LAND-LOCKED STATES

by

MARTIN IRA GLASSNER

MARTINUS NIJHOFF / THE HAGUE / 1970

ISBN 978-90-247-5022-1 ISBN 978-94-015-1176-6 (eBook)
DOI 10.1007/978-94-015-1176-6

TABLE OF CONTENTS

LIST OF ILLUSTRATIONS

PREFACE

This study is an outgrowth of an interest in the question of access to the sea developed by the author during a ten-month sojourn during 1962 and 1963 as American Vice Consul in Antofagasta, Chile. During this period he had the opportunity to visit Peru three times and Bolivia twice. This experience, supplemented by research in many libraries in New York, Washington and California and by interviews, documents and other reference materials, resulted in a detailed study of Bolivia's campaign for an outlet to the sea. [1]

The present study has drawn some material from the earlier one, but is such an elaborate expansion of it that it might well be considered a wholly new effort. The effort was made because the problem of access to the sea has become more critical since the Second World War as the emphasis on trade and economic development has grown while at the same time many new land-locked states were being born. There have, moreover, been more threatened and actual interferences with free transit during this period than during the preceding half century and more. A thorough examination of the subject seemed in order, then, as an aid to an understanding of the problems involved and as a guide to future attempts to resolve them.

In addition to a general survey of the question, three case studies have been included both as illustrations of many of these problems and as specific situations by which to test proposed solutions. Since Africa, Asia and South America, the three continents on which developing land-locked states are to be found, have different geographic, historical, cultural, legal and economic patterns, one country has been selected from each continent for intensive scrutiny. Bolivia was selected over Paraguay in South America because Paraguay has access to the sea via an internationalized navigable river and thus her land-locked status is somewhat qualified, and also

[1] Martin Ira Glassner, "Bolivia and an Access to the Sea" (unpublished Master's thesis, California State College at Fullerton, August, 1964).

because Bolivia has been waging an intensive campaign for access (or an outlet) to the sea since losing her littoral to Chile at the beginning of the War of the Pacific in 1879. Afghanistan was selected because of all Asian land-locked states, she has the most active foreign trade and other relations and because she is the only state to have actually suffered recently what so many land-locked states fear: severance of her most important access route to the sea.

The choice of an African case study was more difficult. All of the former French and Belgian land-locked territories were eliminated at once both because their foreign economic relations are relatively undeveloped and because of the scarcity of reliable statistics and other materials in English. Of the former British land-locked territories, Zambia seemed most suitable and the collection of materials on that country was undertaken. Before this process had gone very far, Zambia became so involved in the Rhodesian imbroglio that it became impractical to continue. First, Zambia was becoming too much like Afghanistan in respect of access to the sea and the intention was to select cases which would differ substantially from one another. Second, sources of reliable current information on Zambia's foreign trade and transit began to dry up as this material was withheld or falsified for political reasons by all parties concerned. So Uganda was chosen as an alternate because, with Zambia, she has the most extensive foreign trade of all the African land-locked states and because there is no dearth of reliable information on that country. This proved a happy choice, as Uganda illustrates something approaching an ideal situation for a land-locked state, quite the opposite of Afghanistan's and very different from those of most other developing land-locked states, though she is similar enough in many ways that she is not really unique.

This work is a number of things packaged together. It is first of all a study in the political geography of developing countries: their boundaries, internal cohesion, transportation systems, trade routes, relations with their neighbors, and, of course, their access to the sea, which itself has been a subject of study by political geographers for many years. [2]

Second, it is a study in "the codification and progressive development

[2] "Political geography, then, may be defined as the study of areal differences and similarities in political character as an interrelated part of the total complex of areal differences and similarities. The interpretation of areal differences in political features involves the study of their interrelations with all other relevant areal variations, whether physical, biotic, or cultural in origin." Richard Hartshorne, "Political Geography," in *American Geography; Inventory and Prospect,* ed. Preston E. James and Clarence F. Jones (Syracuse, New York: Syracuse University Press, 1954), p. 178.

of international law." [3] It traces the evolution of international law on one issue through several centuries, culminating in a multilateral convention which still has not laid the issue to rest. It is a clear illustration of the immense difficulty of achieving "world peace through law."

Third, it is an illustration of the operations and influence of the developing countries in attacking specific problems of trade and economic development through the United Nations. It illustrates how they disagree among themselves on many issues, how they can win concessions from more powerful states, and how their victories are seldom complete. Here, as in other arenas, they are being tempered in the crucible of experience.

Finally, it is a demonstration of the complexities of even such a relatively small problem in international relations. In order even to understand the problem, to say nothing of solving it, it is necessary to draw from many disciplines – geography, history, economics, law, political science, sociology, even anthropology and psychology. How much more complex are the great issues of war and peace!

A study of this nature reveals clearly that while much progress has been made, much remains to be done, not only in assuring free access to the sea for land-locked states, but in many related matters as well. Among these are the elimination of all artificial barriers to trade and economic development, the wise and equitable distribution and use of the resources of the sea, the inclusion of all states and peoples in the international community on a basis of equality, the development of international law as a means of guiding and regulating behavior of states, and the evolution of forms of political and economic organization which would better serve the needs and interests of the peoples of the world than the present system of numerous "sovereign" states.

It would certainly be presumptuous to expect this study to do more than point up the need for more work on these greater problems, but it might also provide some useful guidelines for chipping away at them bit by bit over a long period of time, which, in truth, is all we mortals can hope to do.

New Haven, Connecticut
August 1968

[3] From the Statute of the International Law Commission, adopted by the General Assembly of the United Nations on November 21, 1947.

CHAPTER I

CHARACTERISTICS OF LAND-LOCKED STATES

The emphasis in consideration of the special problems of land-locked states has shifted markedly since the First World War and even more markedly since the Second World War. Prior to 1914 there were only four independent land-locked states outside Europe: Bolivia (land-locked only since 1879), Paraguay (which had access to the sea via an internationalized navigable river), Ethiopia (which has become a coastal state with the acquisition of Eritrea by federation in 1952 and by absorption later), and Afghanistan (which did not become fully sovereign until 1919). Of these only Bolivia had a substantial foreign trade and she had had adequate access to the sea at least since 1904. Within Europe the land-locked and transit states had managed to devise a system of internationalized rivers, special transit rights, free zones in ports and other arrangements to secure the relatively free flow of goods and people between the land-locked states and the sea. The many serious and vexing problems of access to the sea in Europe had been essentially solved in one way or another by the eve of the Great War. Since then few serious problems of access to the sea have arisen there and these have generally been solved in accordance with long-established principles.

While the principle of access to the sea had been established in Europe, changing conditions in Africa, Asia and South America necessitated increasing emphasis on the importance of such access in the process of economic development and the construction of a legal regime which would meet the needs of the land-locked states and territories in these continents as well as being suitable for the very different conditions prevailing in Europe. These new conditions include a new urgency in programs of economic development, the growing importance of transit trade in the process of economic development, and more frequent actual or threatened interruptions of that trade. Moreover, the number of land-locked states in the world has more than doubled since 1914 and, except for Austria, Hungary and Czechoslovakia replacing Serbia as land-locked states in Europe in 1918, for a net gain of two, all of the new land-locked states are in Africa and Asia. (See Map 1.)

For these reasons, this study focuses on those land-locked states which have relatively recently begun the process of economic development: those of Africa, Asia and South America. It is necessary, however, to include the European land-locked states in an initial survey, since they serve as a useful basis for comparison with "mediterranean" states in other continents.

Definitions

The term *state,* for the purposes of this study, shall include those political units in the world which exercise a large measure of control over their own external affairs and which are recognized as states by a substantial proportion of the international community. Thus, in Table 1, those units listed under "Other Territories" fail to fulfill either or both of these qualifications. Each, however, has a distinctive political and/or cultural character which entitles it to consideration as a discrete political unit. Each, moreover, displays or has displayed in the recent past some of the attributes of sovereignty and may in the future become a *state.* For these reasons they are included in this general survey.

The term *land-locked* means having no seacoast whatever, being completely mediterranean. The term is deliberately defined as narrowly as possible so as to make the examination of land-locked states manageable. It eliminates states such as Jordan, Iraq and Congo (Kinshasa) which have corridors to the sea and coastlines thereon, regardless of how useless the seacoast may be for foreign trade. Such states exhibit many, if not most, of the characteristics of truly land-locked states and much of what is said herein applies to them. However, we are isolating truly land-locked states for study, and examination of *nearly* land-locked states would warrant a separate, and most worthwhile, study. On the other hand, this definition includes those states, such as Paraguay and all but the two smallest land-locked states of Europe, which have access to the sea via internationalized navigable rivers – essentially, long "arms" of the sea. Such states exhibit some of the characteristics of coastal states, but consider themselves land-locked and are here considered land-locked because they do not exercise "sovereign" control over their aqueous highways to the sea. [1]

[1] A practical political guide to which states are land-locked and which are not is

The term *transit state* means in its most general sense any state through which goods or passengers pass in transit to or from another state. In the United Nations Convention on Transit Trade of Land-locked States, however, it is defined as "any Contracting state with or without a sea-coast, situated between a land-locked State and the sea, through whose territory traffic in transit passes." [2] For the purposes of this study, this more restricted definition is quite satisfactory, except for the word "contracting". It should be noted here that there are at present very few examples of land-locked states that are also transit states (Mongolia and Uganda being the most important right now). There is a trend, however, toward land-locked states becoming also transit states; this will be discussed later.

The term *developing* means essentially the same as "underdeveloped," except that it conveys the impression of forward movement, of being engaged in the process of economic development. Some states are "developing" more vigorously and/or successfully than others, to be sure, but that does not concern us here as our only purpose is to distinguish them from the industrialized, "developed" states. Since no generally acceptable definition of "underdeveloped" is available, we may adopt one which suits our purposes. "Economic development" is considered by W. W. Rostow and other economists to mean the improvement of the standard of living until the society reaches a stage of "high mass consumption" of goods and services. The standard of living is typically, inadequately of course, expressed in terms of annual per capita income, and as a general yardstick this serves as well as any and better than most. Using this measurement, then, we may say that a "developing" state is any one in which the annual per capita income (or the gross national product divided by the total population) is below $ 400 regardless of short-term fluctuations in economic indicators, including per capita income. This figure was deliberately set higher than is customary in order to include Mongolia; as it is, it effectively excludes all the land-locked states of Europe and includes all those of Asia, Africa and Latin America, those with which we are concerned anyway because of their special problems.

Finally, this study is concerned with *access to the sea,* and not with transit problems in general. Thus, overland transit between two states through the territory of a third is not considered unless one of the states

which ones participate as land-locked states in United Nations conferences on the subject. Jordan, Iraq and Congo (Kinshasa), for example, do not.

[2] Article 1 (c). The text of this Convention may be found in Appendix II.

is land-locked. Also excluded from consideration are the rights of passage between states or other territories and their exclaves embedded within another country; e.g., the Belgian exclaves in The Netherlands or the former Portuguese exclaves in India. By the same token, states which acquired seacoasts recently, such as Ethiopia, Poland and Serbia, are not included, even though their transit problems may not have been substantially eased by the mere acquisition of a seacoast. The terms "access" and "outlet" to the sea are discussed in greater detail in Chapter VI.

Geographic Characteristics

In terms of physical geography, it is evident that the thirty-five land-locked states and other territories have little in common other than that they have no seacoasts. In area, none can be considered as truly large – none is larger than 600,000 square miles, about the size of Quebec (584,860 sq. mi.) or Saudi Arabia (617,800 sq. mi.). There are fourteen coastal states and one territory larger than the largest land-locked state (Mongolia). However, nine land-locked states have between 200,000 (about the size of Thailand – 198,500 or Central America – 200,412) and 600,000 square miles. Eighteen coastal states and three territories fall into this category. In the category 50,000 (about the size of Greece – 50,547 or Alabama – 51,609) to 200,000 sq. mi. are thirty-two coastal states and five territories and only five land-locked states. Four land-locked states and territories in Africa are smaller than 50,000 sq. mi., while there are thirty-seven coastal states in this category and a large number of territories, some of which are expected to become independent in the near future. Thus, while most landlocked states must be considered small in area, so are most of the coastal states of the world and there is a very wide range of sizes among the land-locked states themselves. Although area is not a distinctive feature of land-locked states, no really large state is land-locked.

All land-locked states are located in the interiors of continents, of course, but some are considerably more "interior" than others. Those states closest to the sea (300 miles or less from their capitals to their principal seaports in a straight line) are mostly located in Europe, smallest of all the continents and the one with the best circulation systems. Only Bolivia, Lesotho and Malawi on the other continents can be considered reasonably close to the sea. But this advantage of closeness to the sea is in large part cancelled out for these states by high transportation costs due to difficult topography, sparsely settled country, or inadequate transportation systems.

The effects of the interior location of most land-locked states are to increase costs of all imported and exported goods and the time needed to transport those goods; to increase risks of loss, damage or pilferage enroute; to necessitate larger numbers of trucks, railway wagons, etc. to haul a given quantity of goods; and to increase maintenance costs of transportation equipment. These effects are felt, of course, by the interior districts of coastal states, and perhaps in greater degree, but here the crucial difference is the need for goods in transit to or from a land-locked state to cross an international boundary, a matter which can be – and has been – very important.

Of all the land-locked states outside Europe, all but two have three or more neighbors with which they must remain on good terms if they are to be reasonably certain of free access to the sea. Broadly speaking, more neighboring states, particularly coastal states, give the land-locked state a wider choice of routes to the sea, but in practice, few really have more than one or two practicable routes, and only Bolivia and Zambia can readily choose between ports on two oceans. [3] Having other land-locked states as neighbors might be an advantage to a mediterranean country since they would tend to be more sympathetic and cooperative in transit matters, but generally the location of more than one political unit between the land-locked state and the sea merely complicates the transit situation.

More important than the number of neighboring countries, land-locked or coastal, is the distance and nature of the terrain between the economic core of a land-locked state and the economic and/or political core areas of its neighbors or between its core and a good seaport. This can be more important even than straight-line distances between one and the other. In some cases, notably in South America and West Africa, the core area of a land-locked state is closer to that of another state or to a seaport than to the extremities of the state itself. This is largely due to the European colonial practice of providing transportation and communications between coastal ports and the interior to facilitate the export of cash crops, minerals, ivory and slaves. This is of considerable help in terms of access to the sea, but it is an overall weakness of too many African land-locked states. This weakness is a distinct handicap in bargaining for the rights to *use* these facilities.

The final aspect of location is the latitude of the world's land-locked states. Most of them are located entirely or largely within the tropics, but

[3] Afghanistan and Rwanda also have some degree of choice in this respect, but the choice is generally exercised, when it is, for political reasons rather than for economic reasons such as costs, delivery time, etc.

TABLE 1. COMPARISON OF LAND-LOCKED STATES AND TERRITORIES

STATES	Date of Indep.	Area [1] (sq. mi.)	Population [1] ('000)	Distance to the sea (miles) [2]	Adjacent Territories (land-locked)	GNP per cap. [1]	Foreign Trade as % of GNP [1]
SOUTH AMERICA							
Bolivia	1825	424,000	3,400	Mollendo 250, Santos 1,550 Antofagasta 800, Arica 200	5(1)	$ 150	45
Paraguay	1811	157,000	2,000	Rosario 550	3(1)	200	25
EUROPE							
Austria	1919	32,400	7,300	Trieste 225, Hamburg 460	6(4)	1,080	47
Czechoslovakia	1919	49,400	14,000	Trieste 325, Hamburg 310	6(2)	900	42
Hungary	1918	40,000	10,000	Trieste 275	4(2)	870	34
Liechtenstein	1866	60	20	Genoa 200, Rotterdam 425	2(2)	–	–
Luxembourg	1839	1,000	330	Antwerp 125	3	1,820	–
San Marino	*1631*	*23*	*17*	*Rimini 10*	*1*	–	–
Switzerland	1648	16,000	6,000	Genoa 175, Rotterdam 375	5(2)	2,150	52
AFRICA							
Botswana	1966	275,000	560	Durban 450 Lourenço Marques 450	3(2)	55	94
Burundi	1962	10,750	3,200	Dar es Salaam 675	3(1)	45	21
Central Af. Rep.	1960	238,000	1,300	Pointe Noire 700	5(1)	75	48
Chad	1960	496,000	3,300	Lagos 900	6(2)	65	19
Lesotho	1966	11,700	860	Durban 200, Cape Town 625	1	55	65
Malawi	1963	46,000	4,000	Beira 300	4(1)	40	46
Mali	1960	465,000	4,600	Dakar 650, Conakry 475	7(2)	60	22
Niger	1960	459,000	3,300	Cotonou 500, Abidjan 725	7(3)	70	27
Rwanda	1962	10,000	3,100	Mombasa 700, Dar es Salaam 750	4(2)	50	29*
Uganda	1962	92,500	7,500	Mombasa 500	5(1)	100	39
Upper Volta	1960	106,000	4,900	Abidjan 525	6(2)	50	21
Zambia	1964	288,000	3,700	Beira 575, Dar es Salaam 1,000	8(3)	200	69*

* % of exports only in monetary sector of GNP

ASIA							
Afghanistan	1747	251,000	15,000	Karachi 650	5(1)	65	22
Laos	1954	91,400	2,000	Bangkok 375, Saigon 575	6	65	26
Mongolia	1924	593,000	1,100	Tientsin 775	2	390	39
Nepal	1768	54,300	10,000	Calcutta 450	3(2)	65	–

OTHER TERRITORIES	Area [1] (sq. mi.)	Population [1] ('000)	Distance to the sea (miles) [2]	Adjacent Territories (land-locked)	GNP per cap. [1]	Foreign Trade as % of GNP [1]
EUROPE						
Andorra	175	11	Barcelona 75	2	$ –	–
Byelorussia	80,000	8,600	Riga 250, Kaliningrad 300	2	–	–
Vatican City	.2	1	Rome	1	–	–
West Berlin	250	2,200	Hamburg 160	1	–	–
AFRICA						
Rhodesia	150,300	4,300	Beira 300	4(2)	220	83
Swaziland	6,700	370	Lourenço Marques 100	2	240	–
ASIA						
Bhutan	19,300	700	Calcutta 375	3(2)	–	–
Jammu and Kashmir	86,000	3,560	Bombay 1,100	5(2)	–	–
Sikkim	2,740	176	Calcutta 350	4(3)	–	–
Tibet	472,000	1,300	Canton 1,200	6(4)	–	–

Notes:

[1] All figures are rounded from latest available statistics and intended for comparative purposes only.

[2] Rounded straight-line distance from capital of land-locked state or territory to most commonly used seaports.

in very few of them is the core area located in a region with a tropical climate, since climate is a function of altitude and physiography as well as of latitude. Only Mongolia and the land-locked states of Europe are located at any great distance from the tropics, a matter of considerable importance in their economic geography.

The topography of land-locked states likewise exhibits only the most general pattern. While nearly all land-locked states have some mountains, Paraguay, Luxembourg, Hungary, Laos, Mongolia and most of those in Africa are mostly gently rolling or nearly flat except for some mountain ranges on their peripheries or mountains scattered within them. All but the smallest of the *European* land-locked states are well drained by many rivers, most of which are navigable and some of which have been internationalized by treaty. The land-locked states in Africa, except for Mali, Niger and Chad, are also well-watered and drained, but only the Central African Republic has the benefit of inexpensive river transport on the Oubangui and Congo. Even this advantage is limited, however, for the Congo River is not navigable below Brazzaville and goods must be shipped by rail between there and Pointe Noire on the Atlantic Ocean. Bolivia and Paraguay both have access to internationalized navigable rivers, but only Paraguay has found it feasible to use hers to any great extent; even here, it is generally cheaper to rail goods between Asunción and Santa Fé or Rosario in Argentina, further down the Paraná River. In Asia, only Laos of the four land-locked states has even a potential water route to the sea and this will not become a reality until the Lower Mekong Project is completed in perhaps two decades. [4] Like size, location, and topography, the climate of land-locked states shows considerable variation, ranging from Mongolia's cool, dry climate to Rwanda's hot, wet regime. Bolivia has great internal climatic variations.

The human geography of land-locked states reveals more common characteristics than their physical geography. In population, all may be considered small countries, though the most populous, Afghanistan and Czechoslovakia, could conceivably be considered as middle-sized. Of the twenty-five land-locked states in the world, however, only two (Botswana and Lesotho), aside from Luxembourg and the micro-states in Europe, have fewer than one million people; most range in size between one and five millon. (Thirteen fall in this category.) The distribution of population

[4] For additional information on this project, see Schaaf and Fifield, *The Lower Mekong: Challenge to Cooperation in Southeast Asia* (Princeton: D. Van Nostrand Co., Inc., 1963) and Sewell and White, "The Lower Mekong," *International Conciliation*, no. 558, (May, 1966).

within each state follows the same patterns as in the coastal states in the same continent. Since only a small proportion of the population in each land-locked state outside Europe may be considered as urban, the dominant occupation is some form of agriculture. Subsistence farming is by far the most common everywhere, with plantation agriculture being important in the more tropical areas and livestock herding in the drier areas.

The political geography of land-locked states, aside from their access to the sea, is complex and fascinating, but only one aspect of it need concern us here: the internal strength of the state as a modern nation-state. It is difficult to measure this and any conclusions must be hesitant and tentative. We have little to guide us except the concept of "the state idea" binding together people of diverse cultures into a nation-state; or a nation, defined in a cultural sense, into a political state. The state idea was a concept originated by Friedrich Ratzel in his *Politische Geographie* and elaborated upon by Hartshorne, who called it the *raison d'etre* of the state. [5] It may fairly be generalized that the land-locked states of Europe are by now true nation-states whose ecumenes are essentially coextensive with their national territories. Outside Europe, possibly only in Paraguay, Lesotho, and Mongolia has the state idea really become a part of the intellectual equipment of the average person. Afghanistan, Nepal and Malawi are probably close to being true nation-states, but in each case there are still areas outside the "effective national territory." It seems unlikely that the remainder of the eighteen non-European land-locked states are even close to becoming nation-states. This lack of cohesion in most of the states certainly contributes to their essential weakness, especially in bargaining for transit rights and facilities. Other factors, to be discussed below, also contribute to this weakness.

Historical Characteristics

In terms of age as independent political units in approximately their present forms, most of the world's land-locked states fall into four categories. The oldest are those which are essentially remnants of fragmented medieval Europe, though formal sovereignty may have been obtained relatively recently. Second are those which emerged from the collapse of the Spanish American Empire: Bolivia and Paraguay. Next are those which emerged a century later as successor states of the old Austro-Hungarian Empire: modern Czechoslovakia, Austria and Hungary. Young-

[5] Richard Hartshorne, "The Functional Approach in Political Geography," *Annals of the Association of American Geographers*, XL (June, 1950), pp. 110–117.

est of all are those former colonies and protectorates of European powers in Africa which have become independent in the mid-twentieth century. This leaves only those in Asia to be accounted for. Each has a distinctive national history, but each, except for Laos, was able to obtain independence and maintain it because of its location between Russia or China on the north and China or Britain on the south.

Functionally, the land-locked states can be categorized as buffer states, refuge states and administrative conveniences. All of the mediterranean states of South America and Asia and the larger ones of Europe may be characterized as being, to some degree, buffer states. The smaller European states, plus Lesotho and Botswana in Africa, are refuges of harassed minorities escaping from the persecution, warfare and political disintegration raging about them. The remainder of the African land-locked states have no real *raison d'etre,* having no long histories as national entities, no ethnic homogeneity, weak economic foundations, few natural boundaries, and no national cultures. They simply happened, largely by chance, as the major European powers carved up the continent for their own benefit. The boundaries separating British, French and German territories resulted largely from their relative military and economic power in the region and the divisions within the respective colonial areas were drawn partly along tribal lines, but mostly for administrative convenience.[6] These have now become states. Whether they have a future remains to be seen. They are, apparently, developing distinctive national personalities and may survive for some time.

Swaziland is scheduled to become independent on September 6, 1968, but otherwise no new land-locked states are likely to be created in the foreseeable future. The Kashmir dispute might be settled eventually by giving that divided land independence; Tibet may once again break away from or be released by China; Sikkim and Bhutan may be guided to complete independence by India – or absorbed by her or China; West Berlin, whatever its fate, is unlikely to become a sovereign state; Andorra and Vatican City have existed so long as quasi-states that there hardly seems any reason for their statuses to change significantly; Byelorussia is considered here only because it is represented at the United Nations and has participated in the UN conferences concerning land-locked states – it is clearly not a state and not likely to become one even if other units of the Soviet Empire do. Finally, Rhodesia, a territory in political limbo,

[6] Indeed, French Equatorial Africa was not divided into Gabon, Moyen Congo, Ubangi-Shari and Chad until 1946! They are now the states of Gabon, Congo, Central African Republic and Chad, respectively.

not really a colony, but not recognized as independent either: it probably will be so recognized reasonably soon and then will probably be the last land-locked state to be formed unless an existing state (USSR, Congo, China) fragments and creates new ones.

Generally, as pointed out by Eric Fischer, the urge of states to have seacoasts works continuously even today, and tends to diminish the number of land-locked states. This works commonly either by the extension of corridors to the sea, a process which has lost favor as nationalism has intensified, or by some kind of federation or merger with coastal states. Bolivia and Peru were briefly federated in the nineteenth century; Austria and Hungary have reached the Adriatic at various times; Serbia became the principal unit in the new state of Yugoslavia; Ethiopia absorbed Eritrea; etc. This process is likely to continue.

> If experience from other continents, where developments had more time to progress, are of [sic] any indication, it appears that the two continents with the oldest organized political life, Europe and Asia, have the lowest percentage of their area or population in land-locked countries. Africa has the largest percentage in both respects. This seems to confirm the view that there is a tendency of land-locked states to be reduced. [7]

That this reduction is unlikely to happen readily, however, is the subject of a detailed discussion in Chapter VII.

Political Characteristics

Of the twenty-five land-locked states in the world, all but six are republics. Of these six, Liechtenstein, a principality, and Luxembourg, a grand duchy, are feudal remnants; Lesotho is still a kingdom while Burundi, which became independent as a kingdom, is now a republic; and only Mongolia of the Asian mediterranean countries is a republic, while the other three are kingdoms.

The old concept of buffer states has lost much of its meaning in a time of intercontinental missiles, ideological warfare, and high-speed communications and transportation. [8] A more logical breakdown of political

[7] Eric Fischer, "Landlocked Countries of Africa," unpublished paper read before the Association of American Geographers in Denver, Colorado, September 1963.

[8] "Buffer states were not only *de facto* not independent but often lacked a *de jure* sovereign status and seldom maintained direct diplomatic relations with the world at large. They were a 'local affair' – a 'private' geopolitical arrangement among the neighboring powers and as such not members of, or protected by, the international community as a whole." Ladis K. D. Kristof, "The Nature of Frontiers

functions today would be according to ideological lineup. Czechoslovakia and Hungary in Europe and Mongolia in Asia are currently aligned with the USSR; Bolivia and Paraguay in South America, and Luxembourg in Europe are clearly aligned with the United States; Austria and Switzerland in Europe and Laos in Asia are neutral by tradition or treaty; Liechtenstein and San Marino in Europe are not tied militarily to either of the superpowers, but are democratic and Western European in culture; Afghanistan and Nepal in Asia and all of the African states in this study profess to be non-aligned and some of them are in one degree or another. All except for Afghanistan and possibly Burundi are largely oriented toward "the West," meaning primarily France, Britain or South Africa.

All of the twenty-five land-locked states are members of the United Nations except Liechtenstein, San Marino, and Switzerland and even they participate in many United Nations activities. Those in South America and Africa are members of their respective regional organizations, the Organization of American States and the Organization of African Unity. All participate in the work of the United Nations Economic Commissions in their regions. All but Liechtenstein and Chad of the states existing at the time participated in the 1965 Conference on Transit Trade of Land-locked Countries at UN Headquarters, along with Byelorussia and the Holy See (Vatican City).

All of the land-locked states may be considered militarily weak, even compared with middle-rank powers such as Canada or Israel. Afghanistan, Paraguay and Switzerland, however, could probably defend themselves quite ably against attack by any but the largest powers. Few, as indicated above, are truly modern, united nation-states in complete control of their national territory and guided by the state idea. Fewer still outside of Europe are economically strong. Thus, while some of the land-locked states are useful to the larger coastal states because of their location, minerals, or votes in the United Nations, in terms of the traditional indicators of national power they are uniformly weak. Their bargaining power in bilateral negotiations with transit states for transit rights derives principally from international law and the possibilities of reciprocity and mutual economic advantages. In multilateral negotiations, they have the additional advantage of being able to present a more-or-less solid front against opposition which is likely to be characterized more by inertia than

and Boundaries," *Annals of the Association of American Geographers,* XLIX (1959), p. 280, n. 59. If this rather strict definition of "buffer state" is accepted, then it is clear that buffer states are no longer being created, with the possible, but doubtful, exception of Laos.

outright rejection of their demands. In general, in all their dealings with transit states, they must rely on persuasion rather than threats.

Economic Characteristics

In economic terms, the land-locked states of the world fall clearly into two categories: developed and developing. Even Hungary, the poorest of the European mediterranean states, has a per capita income more than double that of her Comecon partner Mongolia, the "richest" of the non-European land-locked states. All of the others outside Europe have per capita incomes of $ 200 per year or less, some much less. Compounding this problem is the high proportion of the gross national product (GNP) contributed in all of them by foreign trade, in some cases half or more of it. These countries, in order to remain viable states, must literally trade or die. Moreover, an item which does not appear in Table 1 but which is at times even more crucial than the volume of trade is the composition of the trade; most of the developing land-locked states are essentially one-product countries. This dependence on one or even two commodities subjects them to the vicissitudes of natural and market phenomena over which they have little or no control.

In addition, despite the seemingly low population densities in some of the developing countries, they all have current or incipient population problems. Much of their sparsely settled land is so for very good reasons: poor soils, aridity, high altitude, steep slopes, rugged terrain for transportation routes, lack of exploitable minerals, distance from markets. These handicaps can be overcome, if at all, only with sound planning; heavy investments of capital, technology, skilled labor and good management; and time, all of which are in short supply in these countries. Indeed, some of them, such as Malawi and Nepal, are so poor they must export some of their population as laborers or soldiers in order to earn money denied them by lack of accessible natural resources.

Among the developing land-locked states, few are able to ship the bulk of their imports and exports over one route by one mode of transport without expensive, time-consuming and risky breaks-in-bulk and transshipments, often several of them in one journey. Moreover, with very few exceptions, land-locked states have little or no control over the availability, suitability, or operating efficiency of the transportation systems and port facilities outside their borders upon which they depend for their foreign trade, and they have little leverage in the determination of tariff schedules for their transit goods. This dependence upon other states for transport facilities is a distinguishing characteristic of land-locked states.

Finally, while it can be demonstrated that transit trade can be profitable for the transport systems of transit states,[9] the bargaining power of the land-locked states is reduced considerably in many cases because they compete with their transit states in the production of the same few products, particularly in Africa. As for imports, the profitability of handling transit trade is often reduced by smuggling, either into the land-locked countries, avoiding payment of the established transportation charges, or from the common carriers before they reach the land-locked state. Which of these occurs and in what degree depends on the economic conditions and policies prevailing in both the land-locked and transit states at a given time; in any case, smuggling can seriously injure economies which are frequently fragile to begin with.

Before closing this chapter, it would be well to point out one more characteristic which clearly distinguishes land-locked states from all other states, large or small, rich or poor, strong or weak, old or new. That is the fact that these states are not only dependent upon transit states for their access to the sea, but also that they *know* they are so dependent. There is a distinct psychological factor involved which must always be taken into account when considering land-locked states in terms of history, politics, economics, geography or international law. The urge to the sea, the feeling of national claustrophobia, has been strongest in the large interior states of Europe and in Bolivia, where it has been a preoccupation of at least the country's rulers for nearly a century. It was evident in Ethiopia and is still so to a lesser degree in Afghanistan. It is less conspicuous in Africa, but these countries became truly land-locked *only* upon the attainment of independence and for all of them that was less than a decade ago. Whether a feeling of geographic strangulation will develop among the interior states of this huge continent remains to be seen. Certainly Zambia, Botswana, Lesotho and Malawi are painfully aware of the enormous political liabilities inherent in having their access to the sea controlled by Portugal and South Africa, even though Rhodesia, for the moment, is benefitting from this same arrangement.

To summarize, then, we may say that land-locked states are small, weak, interior states, whose boundaries and even existence in some cases were determined by more powerful neighbors. They are dependent for their foreign trade upon transportation facilities owned and controlled by

[9] For a most detailed study of this and many other relevant matters, see United Nations, Economic Commission for Africa, *Transit Problems of African Land-locked States* (E/CN.14/TRANS/28) (2 February 1966).

other states with whom they must remain on good terms and they are very much aware of the precarious nature of this dependence. They lack seaports, which historically have served as foci of industrial development and exchanges of goods and ideas from near and far. They would much prefer to have such coastal "windows on the world" and not be land-locked at all. Since they are, however, and are likely so to remain for some time, they have been trying by various means to diminish the handicaps inherent in their geographic conditions. It is to these efforts that we now turn our attention.

CHAPTER II

DEVELOPMENT OF INTERNATIONAL LAW WITH RESPECT TO LAND-LOCKED STATES

There seem to be two basic approaches and one lesser approach to the question of access to the sea, all rooted deeply in international law. A fourth approach has developed only since the middle of the twentieth century. They are discussed below in the context of their historical development, but may be summarized here with a few pertinent quotations.

The first approach is that of freedom of transit. The United Nations Economic Commission for Africa, for example, says flatly,

> The problem of the free access to the open sea by a land-locked country is part of the more general one of freedom of transit. The latter comprises in itself the fundamental economic interests and the legal safeguards of the countries concerned. [1]

The second view is that access to the sea derives directly from the "freedom of the seas." As one analyst summed up the argument,

> If the ocean is free to all mankind [*res communis*], it is reasonable to suppose that every people should have access to the shores of the ocean and the right to navigate all navigable rivers discharging into it, since they are "only a natural prolongation of the free high seas". [2]

These two approaches are closely linked; indeed, some writers consider that they are virtually the same or that one is simply an aspect of the other. A third concept, one which has never had great support and which is virtually extinct today, is that transit constitutes a "public law servitude", roughly comparable to an easement in municipal law.

[1] United Nations, Economic Commission for Africa, *Transit Problems of Eastern African Land-locked States* (E.CN.14/INR/44), (Addis Ababa, 6 November 1963), p. 3.

[2] Norman J. G. Pounds, "A Free and Secure Access to the Sea," *Annals of the Association of American Geographers*, XLIX (1959), p. 257.

> ... the right of way under public law provided land-locked States with an unquestionable right of passage over territories separating them from the sea, without need of any treaty or, in theory, even of an international agreement.[3]

There has always been, however, a question whether in fact land-locked states have a permanent and unrestricted *right* of transit across intervening states to the sea.

> The problem of freedom of transit stems from the clash of two principles of international law, namely, the principle of territorial sovereignty of each state and the principle of freedom of communications for all nations as it is embodied in the various international agreements. So, the function of international law was always "to strike a balance reconciling these naturally opposing principles."[4]

The post-World War II period has seen the evolution of a relatively new concept which goes a long way toward striking this balance. It is expressed succinctly in a principle of international law adopted by the 1964 United Nations Conference on Trade and Development and incorporated verbatim in the Preamble to the 1965 Convention on Transit Trade of Land-locked States.

Principle I

> The recognition of the right of each land-locked State of free access to the sea is an essential principle for the expansion of international trade and economic development.[5]

This concept of access to the sea as a matter of concern to the entire international community rather than a particular right of land-locked states has encouraged some progress in the resolution of the problem, yet much remains to be done.

Developments Through the Nineteenth Century

Land-locked territories from ancient times have frequently had to face obstructions, restrictions, tolls or heavy transit dues on goods and persons passing between them and the sea through more advantageously placed territories. As trade grew in importance, the commercial advantages of

[3] George Scelle, *Manuel de droit international public,* 1941, part I, p. 389, cited in E.CN.14/INR/44, p. 4.

[4] E.CN.14/INR/44, p. 3.

[5] United Nations Conference on Trade and Development (UNCTAD), *Report on the United Nations Conference of Plenipotentiaries on Transit Trade of Land-locked Countries: note by the Secretariat* (TD/B/18, 1965) (Geneva/New York, 1967), p. 2.

free rights of way gradually began to loom larger than the need to maintain absolute territorial sovereignty. As early as the eleventh and twelfth centuries, territories in Europe, particularly Italy, began giving treaty rights to land-locked territories and began the internationalization of rivers, the first means of assuring access to the sea for land-locked states. By the late eighteenth century, however, restrictions and heavy tolls on transit were still common. The principle of free transit was reinvigorated by the armies of France which in 1792 reopened the mouth of the River Scheldt, closed by the Dutch in 1648, and by the diplomacy of Thomas Jefferson which resulted in the Treaty of San Lorenzo el Real of 1795. This treaty gave Americans the right to navigate the Mississippi River and other Spanish rivers to the sea, conceding in fact if not in principle Jefferson's claim that "the Ocean is free to all men, and their rivers to all their inhabitants."

At the end of the Napoleonic Wars, the Congress of Vienna codified the principles of freedom of navigation on international waterways that had been established in recent years. Of particular concern at that time were the Scheldt, the Meuse and the Rhine. Throughout the nineteenth century, the principles of free transit through straits, on rivers and overland gradually became firmly established as recognition grew that such transit was necessary for the development of commerce and industry to the benefit of both land-locked and coastal or riverine states.

Possibly the crucial role in this growing liberalization of transit in Europe, however, was played by new forms of transportation, particularly the railroad, which resulted in greater competition, improvement of transit facilities, and the reduction of the advantage enjoyed by coastal and riverine states. By the end of the century, transit duties in Europe had virtually disappeared. In Latin America, the newly independent states generally reacted against the Spanish imperial trade and transit monopolies by throwing open their territories to the ships and traders of all nations. By the First World War, most navigable waterways, natural and artificial, in Europe, East Asia, South America and Africa had been internationalized. But nagging problems remained. Access to the sea was still not accepted as a specific right of land-locked states.

In January 1917 President Woodrow Wilson, addressing the United States Senate, advocated that "every great people" in the process of development "should be assured a direct outlet to the highways of the sea ... with a right comity of arrangement no nation need be shut away from free access to the open paths of the World's commerce ..."[6] Wilson

[6] Quoted by Pounds, *op. cit.*, p. 258.

was thus consistent not only with his own ideas regarding the rights of states and the freedom of man, but with the ideas of a long line of distinguished Americans, including Jefferson, J. Q. Adams, Grant, Calhoun and Clay, all of whom had insisted upon the rights of all to navigate the seas and the rivers flowing into them.

Wilson followed these remarks by including among his Fourteen Points provisions for "a free and secure access to the sea" for Serbia (Point 11) and for Poland (Point 13). [7] Before Serbia could achieve this objective for which she had fought in the First Balkan War (1912–13), she became part of the new kingdom of Yugoslavia, with a long coastline on the Adriatic. Poland became the beneficiary of a relatively new concept, the actual annexation of territory intervening between an inland state and the sea. Such a corridor to the sea would, supposedly, provide greater security for the land-locked state because any attempt to interfere with commerce there by another state would be a violation of national sovereignty and thus more serious than a violation of freedom of transit. Corridors became fashionable during the territorial reorganizations following the First World War, with Finland, Iraq, Transjordan, Palestine and Colombia receiving very short shorelines on the open sea or a navigable river. The scramble for Africa had produced similar corridors in the late nineteenth century, but the most important – and contentious – was undoubtedly the Polish Corridor.

The framers of the Covenant of the League of Nations did not deal specifically with the question of access to the sea, but rather with the broader one of freedom of transit, including that between inland points. Article 23(e) of the Covenant is significant because it was the first attempt to deal with the matter on a world-wide basis. It provided that the Members of the League "will make provision to secure and maintain freedom of communications and of transit and equitable treatment for the commerce of all Members of the League." In pursuance of this provision a series of conferences took place during the 1920's which produced both multilateral conventions and bilateral treaties aimed at the facilitation of free transit. Among these, the most important for our purposes are the Convention and Statute on Freedom of Transit and the Convention and Statute on the Regime of Navigable Waterways of International Concern, both signed at Barcelona on April 20, 1921, along with several other important documents; and the Convention and Statute on the International Regime of Maritime Ports, signed at Geneva on December 9, 1923.

[7] *Encyclopaedia Britannica,* 1965 ed., Vol. IX, p. 671.

The Barcelona Conventions of 1921

Two of the principal means of providing access to the sea for land-locked states – corridors and navigable waterways – have already been discussed. Of these, corridors were considered *ad hoc* arrangements which might be arrived at by negotiation but were not suitable for regulation by the world community. While they may assure a mediterranean state of access to the sea, they raise questions of self-determination for peoples living in such corridors and rights of transit across the corridors themselves. Again, the Polish Corridor is the classic horrible example. [8] None has actually been created, as such, in more than forty years and it seems unlikely that any will in the foreseeable future. [9] Some existing ones, in fact, were eliminated during the period 1939–45. The second – navigable waterways – and a third, overland transit, were considered in great detail by the General Conference on Communications and Transit which met at Barcelona in 1921 under the auspices of the League of Nations.

The practice of granting overland transit rights had, like that of free navigation of international waterways, deep roots in the commerce of Man and the special status accorded the merchant and the caravan in ancient societies. It did not become institutionalized, even on a bilateral basis, however, until the nineteenth century and was not formalized by the world community until the Barcelona Conference. Examples of nineteenth century treaties granting transit rights were those between Portugal and the United Kingdom regarding their respective territories in Africa and between the United States and Canada granting reciprocal privileges in rail transit across southern Ontario between Detroit and Buffalo and the State of Maine between Quebec and New Brunswick. Nevertheless, few of these arrangements concerned land-locked sattes and none was based on mutual acceptance of an inherent right (under natural law or any other regime) of a land-locked state to access to the sea.

The Barcelona Conference, then, adopted the Convention and Statute on Freedom of Transit, commonly known as the Barcelona Convention.

[8] A good theoretical and historical discussion of corridors and transit may be found in Osborne Mance, *Frontiers, Peace Treaties, and International Organization* (London: Oxford University Press, 1946), pp. 6–11. See also Richard Hartshorne, "The Polish Corridor," *Journal of Geography,* XXXVI (1937) for a thorough analysis of this particular problem.

[9] The Jerusalem Corridor, created by the Israelis during their War of Independence in 1948 to link Jerusalem with the sea, conforms in principle with the three alternate corridors proposed by the Palestine Partition Commission of 1938 and may be considered as an exception. Air corridors, such as those of the Western powers into West Berlin, are a special case and need not be considered here.

This agreement obligates the contracting parties to facilitate free transit by rail or waterway on routes convenient for international transit through their territory. The principle of non-discrimination in freight rates on the basis of nationality was defined and a number of other issues were clarified. The complete texts may be found in Appendix I. A one-sentence Declaration Recognizing the Right to a Flag of States Having no Sea-coast was the only document produced by the Barcelona Conference to mention land-locked states specifically. Moreover, the Conference broke little new ground, essentially codifying most of the more liberal provisions accumulated in international law by custom, treaty and interpretation to that date. Nevertheless, by not distinguishing between coastal or riparian states and land-locked states with or without navigable rivers, the international community, backed by the prestige of the League of Nations (which in 1921 was still considerable), did make a tangible and important contribution to the establishment of the rights of land-locked states to access to the sea.

> The system established by the Barcelona Convention on Freedom of Transit provides clear proof of the firm determination of the States represented at the Conference [more than forty of them, thirty-two of which ratified the Convention] to recognize the right of the land-locked countries to transit through surrounding territories, a right supported by strong guarantees regarding equality of treatment and permanent enjoyment, as well as by a machinery for the settlement of disputes to which its implementation might give rise.[10]

The Barcelona Convention, indeed, despite its weaknesses, came to be regarded as a datum plane, a minimum standard to be used thenceforth in negotiations for bilateral and multilateral agreements on transit, including those involving access to the sea. It retained its value and prestige for more than forty years, a not inconsiderable accomplishment in the twentieth century.

During the interwar period other important agreements were negotiated concerning railways, power lines, pipelines, ports and other transport facilities, all in conformity with and tending to reinforce the principles of free transit enunciated in the Barcelona Convention. Aircraft, however, present special problems and air transport is a major class of exceptions to those principles. The major relevant international conventions are the Paris Convention of 1919, the Pan-American Convention of 1928 and the International Air Services Transit Agreement signed at Chicago on December 7, 1944 under the auspices of the fledgeling International Civil

[10] E.CN.14/INR/44, p. 5.

Aviation Organization. While each of these conventions explicitly acknowledges the exclusive sovereignty of each state over its own airspace, each restricts this sovereignty by applying to this "sovereign" airspace the principle of innocent passage hitherto reserved for the high seas – but only for nonscheduled aircraft. Arrangements for scheduled airlines remain a subject for bilateral negotiation.

Nevertheless, it is doubtful whether the special content of air transport agreements can properly be regarded as a departure from or negation of the more general development in the direction of the principle of freedom of transit. The proper explanation of the restrictive tendency of these agreements is that States, while starting historically with an acknowledgement of the principle of freedom of passage, have deliberately abandoned it in relation to air transport. Their reasons for doing so were in part economic and in part related to the special considerations of security involved in permitting unrestricted flight by alien aircraft. Moreover, it remains an open question whether, in the long run, this approach will continue to be found compatible with the general interests of the users of international civil aviation facilities . . . [11]

Developments After World War II

Shortly after the end of the Second World War, the major trading states of the world undertook, on the initiative of the United States, a commitment to reduce tariffs and other barriers to trade for their mutual benefit. The general principles of liberalized trade and the participants' specific undertakings (123 bilateral trade agreements) are embodied in the General Agreement on Tariffs and Trade (GATT), adopted at Geneva on October 30, 1947. Article V of GATT is entitled "Freedom of Transit." While not referring specifically to land-locked states, Article V does reaffirm the principles of the Barcelona Convention by stating, *inter alia,*

2. There shall be freedom of transit, through the territory of each contracting party, via the routes most convenient for international transit, for traffic in transit to or from the territory of other contracting parties . . .

. . . .

6. Each contracting party shall accord to products which have been in transit through the territory of any other contracting party treatment no less favourable than that which would have been accorded to such products had

[11] E. Lauterpacht, "Freedom of Transit in International Law," *Transactions of the Grotius Society,* XLIV, (1958–59). This is probably the most comprehensive discussion in English on freedom of transit.

they been transported from their place of origin to their destination without going through the territory of such other contracting party . . . [12]

Other provisions of GATT include nondiscrimination in "charges, regulations and formalities", prohibition of "any unnecessary delays or restrictions" and similar protection for goods (including baggage) and vessels and other means of transport in transit across the territory of a contracting party. In some respects, particularly in regard to provisions for settlement of disputes, GATT was less extensive and less emphatic than the Barcelona Convention. It amounted, in fact, to little more than a reaffirmation of the general principle of freedom of transit and made some recommendations which applied only to the contracting parties. Simultaneously with GATT, however, the Geneva Conference prepared a draft Charter of World Trade for submission to a plenipotentiary conference which was to take place shortly in Havana. This draft went further, in some respects, than GATT itself with regard to rights of landlocked states.

The purpose of the conference which opened in Havana in November 1947, the month following the adoption of GATT, was to organize an International Trade Organization (ITO) which would supervise a vastly expanded world trading system based on the freest possible trade in accordance with principles of competitive private enterprise. The conference produced a charter which was never ratified by more than one state (Australia, with reservations) and never went into effect. Nevertheless, Article 33 of the Havana Charter of March 24, 1948 is considered to have been a step forward on the road to "a free and secure access to the sea" for landlocked states.

Again, the Havana Charter reaffirmed and in some respects strengthened the Barcelona Convention's provisions for freedom of transit. In seven of its eight paragraphs, Article 33 of the Havana Charter was virtually identical with the seven paragraphs of Article V of GATT. Two differences are significant, however. GATT establishes a multilateral most-favored-nation-system with respect to transit traffic in paragraph 5; the Havana Charter includes this identical provision in its own paragraph 5, but an interpretive note provides specifically that if

a Member grants to a country which has no direct access to the sea more ample facilities than those already provided for in other paragraphs of Article 33, such special facilities may be limited to the land-locked country concerned

[12] UNCTAD, *Texts of International Instruments and Certain Recommendations Relating to Transit Trade* (E/CONF.46/AC.2/2), (25 September 1964), pp. 67–68.

unless the Organization finds, on the complaint of any other Member, that the withholding of the special facilities from the complaining Member contravenes the most favoured nation provisions of this Charter. [13]

The purpose of this provision was to encourage "the conclusion of special arrangements going beyond the normal rules regarding transit between countries." [14]

The Havana Charter contained, in addition, a wholly new provision, not included in either the Barcelona Convention or GATT.

6. The Organization may undertake studies, make recommendations and promote international agreement relating to the simplification of custom regulations concerning traffic in transit, the equitable use of facilities required for such transit and other measures designed to promote the objectives of this Article. Members shall cooperate with each other directly and through the Organization to this end. [15]

This was indeed one of the most constructive and promising work [sic] envisaged for the ITO, inasmuch as it was not enough to propound the principle of freedom of transit. The promotion of adequate administrative and other procedures and measures to achieve freedom of transit was considered equally important. [16]

Since the Havana Charter never entered into force, the Barcelona Convention and Article V of GATT remained the yardsticks by which facilities for transit trade of land-locked states could legally be measured. During the Review Session of GATT in 1954–55, at which many suggested changes in the agreement were considered, no proposals were made to change Article V, nor was any suggestion made to review paragraph 6 of Article 33 of the Havana Charter. Until that time, no complaints had been made to GATT regarding the application of its transit provisions. [17] This is not to say that there had been no violations of these provisions. Pounds cites the refusal of Lithuania to allow Polish goods in transit to cross her territory from 1920 to 1939 as the "only one clear case of a coastal state in modern times regularly refusing to allow an inland state to have access to its coast." [18] This is quite true, since the principle of freedom of transit

[13] *Ibid.*, p. 70.

[14] United Nations, Economic Commission for Asia and the Far East (ECAFE), *Problems of Trade of Land-locked Countries in Asia and the Far East* (ECAFE/I&T/Sub.4/2), (Tokyo, 29 August 1956), p. 7.

[15] E/CONF.46/AC.2/2, p. 70.

[16] ECAFE/I&T/Sub.4/2, p. 8.

[17] *Ibid.*, p. 9.

[18] Pounds, *op. cit.*, p. 266.

had been generally accepted. However, as he himself points out later in his article,

> While there has been no change in the legal status of transit rights during the past twenty years, the actual practice of nations has undoubtedly deteriorated. This has happened in two distinct ways. In the first place, states have used their ability to interfere with the right of transit of goods across their territory as an instrument of national policy ... Elsewhere the threat or even the fear that transit rights would be denied have prevented some countries from making use of rights which were legally theirs ... [19]

Pounds cites only the Egyptian blockade of the Strait of Tiran and "the obstruction and even destruction of pipelines" by other Middle Eastern countries as examples of interference with transit trade as "an instrument of national policy." There had been others, however, notably Pakistan's closure of her border with Afghanistan in 1949 and again in 1953. It was this situation that led to the next step in clarifying, expanding and formalizing the rights of land-locked states to access to the sea.

In January 1956 the United Nations Economic Commission for Asia and the Far East (ECAFE) considered the problems of its land-locked members (Afghanistan, Laos, and Nepal) and after discussion of the issues approved a resolution in which it recommended

> that the needs of land-locked member States and members having no easy access to the sea in the matter of transit trade be given full recognition by all member States and that adequate facilities thereof be accorded in terms of international law and practice in this regard. [20]

This was the first time that a major international body gave special consideration to the "needs" of land-locked states as such. The word "needs" is prominent here, and not "rights," but there is no indication of a necessity for new rules or procedures for the benefit of land-locked states. Significantly, reliance was still placed on existing "international law and practice."

ECAFE did not let the matter rest, however, but produced a report several months later devoted to *Problems of Trade of Land-locked Countries in Asia and the Far East.* This is more evidence of the increasing emphasis upon existing or potential trade problems rather than "rights" of land-locked states. The report contains valuable historical background and texts of existing trade and transit agreements, in addition

[19] *Ibid.*, p. 267.
[20] E/CN.11/425, cited in E.CN.14/INR/44, p. 11.

to a discussion of the "problems of transit trade and their solution." The recommendations, however, were relatively conservative:

(1) The countries who have so far not acceded to the Barcelona Statute of [sic] Freedom of Transit may be urged to do so at an early date ... It may also be hoped that all the countries of the region would eventually join the General Agreement on Tariffs and Trade and thereby also accede to the principles and articles relevant to the transit trade.

(2) The countries be urged to negotiate and conclude bilateral agreements in conformity with the principles of the Barcelona Statute, The Havana Charter and the GATT ... [and] bear in mind ... also the necessity for adopting concrete administrative procedures and practices ... [to] facilitate the implementation of the basic principles of freedom of transit.

(3) ... that the officials and personnel handling or dealing with the various phases of transit trade be imparted proper training ...

(4) ... the countries should include in their economic development plans, plans for improvement of transport, development of new routes ... which will facilitate the transit trade between neighbouring and contiguous countries and which will particularly provide additional transport for the trade of land-locked countries. [21]

In its next annual report the Economic and Social Council of the United Nations endorsed these recommendations as a "constructive step forward." As a result of ECAFE's activities also, Laos became the first and only country to adhere to the Barcelona Convention and Statute (on November 24, 1956) since the Second World War. It was evident that interest was growing in the peculiar problems of land-locked states, particularly as they affected economic development. The 1956 recommendations of ECAFE, modest though they were, sparked a drive in the United Nations to deal with the question in a comprehensive and, hopefully, definitive manner.

We may now return to the question raised at the beginning of this chapter; i.e., whether there is, or was prior to 1958, a "right" of access to the sea for land-locked countries recognized in international law. One authority summarizes the arguments on "The Law Relating Generally to Transit," which, in turn (and quite interestingly), he includes as one of several "Customary Restraints on Sovereignty,"

The authors have divided on the question whether there is or is not a general duty to grant transit rights across national territory to neighbouring States which are unfavourably situated. Those opposed argue that since there

[21] ECAFE/I&T/Sub.4/2, pp. 22–23.

are degrees of economic 'necessity' it is difficult in the abstract to distinguish mere assertions of transit needs from actual dependence upon neighbouring territory, and that it is only when facilities are actually created that the dependency is really established. The other school argues from the thesis of the economic interdependence of States to a juridical conviction in favour of transit rights, pointing out that not only have such rights actually been created in many instances by agreement but that the area of discretion of sovereigns to impede the passage of goods is now so restricted by treaty that an absolute right of exclusion appears antiquated. Opinion over the past fifty years has definitely hardened in favour of the view that at least in some instances States whose economic life and development substantially depends upon a grant of transit rights may legitimately claim them. This dependence is most obvious in the case of land-locked States, and they may offer analogies for other instances.[22]

E. Lauterpacht is among the leading publicists who conclude that some states "may legitimately claim" transit rights. Regarding these rights, he says,

> The existence of a right of transit may be said to be dependent upon two basic conditions. In the first place, the State claiming the right of transit must be able to justify it by reference to considerations of necessity or convenience. Secondly, the exercise of the right must be such as to cause no harm or prejudice to the transit State.[23]

He concludes his essay by noting the widely held belief that the League Covenant, the Barcelona Convention and similar instruments, while recognizing the principle of free transit, in fact create only an obligation on the part of a coastal state (in the case of land-locked states) "to negotiate for and conclude upon reasonable terms a transit agreement when the circumstances . . . so warrant." He rejects this thesis, indicating that the view that these conventions

> create something more than a mere obligation to negotiate is one for which strong justification can be found in considerations of principle. The disposition to question the existence of a right of transit as dependent upon a balancing of interests between the State seeking and the State granting transit stems primarily from a rigid adherence to a positivist approach. Yet it becomes increasingly questionable whether this approach adequately reflects the modes in which the international community allows the law governing its conduct to be made or modified . . .
> At the same time, evidence of the existence of less exacting standards for the

[22] Daniel Patrick O'Connell, *International Law,* Vol. I (Dobbs Ferry, New York: Oceana Publications, Inc., 1965), pp. 613–614.

[23] Lauterpacht, *op. cit.,* p. 332.

establishment of rules of law does not by itself prove the existence of a right to transit in the terms canvassed above. It must, indeed, be conceded that the submission that there is a right to transit in the circumstances and under the conditions set out above is a hesitating one. It depends to some extent upon selective evidence and it involves reliance upon reasoning which is not free of controversial elements. *Nevertheless, the fact is that freedom of transit is one of the most fundamental needs of the community* . . . It should not be regarded as particularly surprising if, in international law, the existence of a definable interest of the community came to be recognized by the acknowledgement of a legal right to freedom of transit. [24]

Indeed, this is precisely what has been happening since the 1950's. It may be quite true, as Professor Pounds says, that "[t]he idea that an inland state has a right of access to the sea springs from the concepts of natural law that were held in the eighteenth century." [25] Since that time, however, more and more stress has been laid upon the economic benefits that would accrue to all if free transit is granted. While much rhetoric today still includes references to custom and "natural law," it is fair to say that "necessity and convenience" provide the strongest support for claims to free transit in the mid-twentieth century. Moreover, the stress has also been shifting somewhat away from lumping access to the sea for land-locked states in with freedom of transit in general and more toward considering this question as related to but distinct from the broader principle because of the greater economic "necessity and convenience" involved.

Finally, the achievement of independence by so many former European colonies in Asia and Africa in the mid-twentieth century, the very factor which has led to this change of emphasis and the stronger demands for special treatment of land-locked states, has also led to a revival of the intensity and respectability of nationalism in the international community. Paradoxically, perhaps, this increased sensitivity to infringements on "territorial sovereignty" has just about killed the argument that free transit constitutes a servitude upon the coastal state and hardened the resistance of the coastal states to granting any more concessions to their land-locked neighbors than absolutely necessary.

A French analyst, Hubert Thierry, wrote in 1958,

Different doctrines tend to grant the existence of a rule of international law assuring a general freedom of access to the sea in favor of enclosed states. Positive law, on the other hand, such as is derived from analysis of conventions relative to freedom of transit, is less liberal toward the enclosed

[24] *Ibid.*, pp. 350–351.
[25] Pounds, *op. cit.*, p. 267.

states or, if one prefers, more respectful of the sovereignty of their maritime neighbors.[26]

He then went on to discuss the concept of an international servitude as "a special concession to the advantage of the land-locked state" and concluded that "it is clear that such a construction does not correspond to the positive law as it is accepted by the maritime states."[27] Not only was the servitude argument dead, but other arguments in favor of free transit for land-locked states were fading in favor of newer, more practical arguments.

The United Nations Conference on the Law of the Sea

At the eleventh session of the United Nations General Assembly in February 1957, six land-locked states requested the inclusion of the question of access to the sea in the agenda of the United Nations Conference on the Law of the Sea, to be held the following year in Geneva. This request was granted, despite the fact that the International Law Commission, an organ of the General Assembly, had not been and was not asked to prepare draft articles on the subject. The Assembly resolution, however, was mildly worded and contained only a hint that existing international law and practice were inadequate.

Shortly before the Conference opened in Geneva, a Preliminary Conference of thirteen land-locked states was held to prepare proposals for presentation to the Conference. After much discussion and many compromises, the Preliminary Conference drew up a list of seven general principles. Among them, these are relevant to the present study:

Principle I The right of each land-locked State of free access to the sea derives from the fundamental principle of freedom of the seas.

. . . .

Principle V The transit of persons and goods from a land-locked country towards the sea and vice versa by all means of transportation and communication must be freely accorded, subject to existing special agreements and conventions.

The transit shall not be subject to any customs duty or specific charges or taxes except for specific services rendered . . .

. . . .

[26] Hubert Thierry, "Les Etats Privés de Littoral Maritime", *Revue Générale de Droit International Public* LXII (October-December 1958), p. 615.

[27] *Ibid.*, p. 616. This article also cites earlier studies of international servitudes. See also Ferenc A. Váli, *Servitudes of International Law: A Study of Rights in Foreign Territory* (2nd ed.; London: Stevens & Sons, Ltd., 1958).

Principle VII The provisions codifying the principles which govern the right of free access to the sea of the land-locked State shall in no way abrogate existing agreements between two or more contracting parties concerning the problems which will be the object of the codification envisaged, nor shall they raise an obstacle as regards the conclusion of such agreements in the future, provided that the latter do not establish a regime which is less favorable than or opposed to the above-mentioned provisions. [28]

These Principles may be considered as expressing the general feeling of the land-locked states regarding transit in 1958. In the Fifth Committee and in the floor debates, the land-locked states "vigorously asserted their claims to free communications with seaports and to enjoyment of equal rights with Coastal States in matters of navigation." [29] They were reasonably successful, considering the give-and-take to which their recommendations were subjected, for even in the Fifth Committee they were a distinct minority of the seventy-three states participating. The Soviets tried to obtain for land-locked states an absolute right of transit, including free access to ports of the coastal states and duty-free entry of goods much like the traditional right of innocent passage through the territorial sea in peacetime. This effort was defeated because most states recognized that the coastal state had to protect its own security.

The general trend noted since the Second World War in discussions of access to the sea was evident at the Geneva Conference also.

All of the proceedings on land-locked states at the Conference hinged on the economic liabilities suffered by reason of inaccessibility to the sea and reflected cooperation in reducing the distinction between maritime and land-locked states. [30]

The final recommendation of the Fifth Committee to the Conference contained some of the elements of the Principles, but in a modified form. It read in part:

II . . . 1. In order to enjoy the freedom of the seas on equal terms with coastal States, States having no seacoast should have free access to the sea. To this end States situated between the sea and a State having no seacoast

[28] United Nations, General Assembly, *United Nations Conference on the Law of the Sea, Official Records, Vol. VII (Fifth Committee: Question of Free Access to the Sea of Land-Locked Countries)* (A/CONF.13/43, 24 February–27 April 1958) (Geneva, 1958), pp. 78–79.

[29] Max Sorensen, "Law of the Sea," *International Conciliation*, No. 520 (November, 1958), pp. 199–200.

[30] G. Etzel Pearcy, "Geographical Aspects of the Law of the Sea," *Annals of the Association of American Geographers*, XLIX, (March, 1959), p. 22.

shall by common agreement with the latter and in conformity with existing international conventions accord:

(a) To the State having no sea-coast, on a basis of reciprocity, free transit through their territory; and

. . . .

2. States situated between the sea and the State having no sea-coast shall settle, by mutual agreement with the latter, and taking into account the rights of the coastal State or State of transit and the special conditions of the State having no sea-coast, all matters relating to freedom of transit and equal treatment in ports, in case such States are not already parties to existing international conventions. [31]

The recommendation of the Fifth Committee was accepted by the full Conference and incorporated as Article 3 into the Convention on the High Seas, one of four conventions produced by the Conference on the Law of the Sea.

This was helpful, emphasizing as it did the economic necessity of free access to the sea and stressing that access to the sea is a corollary of freedom of the seas, but it still did not really break new ground. In Article 3 of the Convention on the High Seas, for example,

[t]he phrase 'in conformity with existing international conventions' was intended to refer to all agreements dealing with the matter, bilateral as well as multilateral, but especially to the Barcelona Convention of 1921, . . . and to the Geneva Convention of 1923 on Maritime Ports. It was apparently hoped in this way to give broader effects to the substance of these agreements, permitting free access to most types of vessels, and at the same time preserve the autonomy of the coastal state by requiring the landlocked state to negotiate an agreement to secure the open access. [32]

The inherently conservative approach of the Fifth Committee and the full Conference on the Law of the Sea is indicated by the following comment:

In summary, the basic premise of all problems concerning landlocked states did not constitute a crusade for obtaining rights, but rather involved the strengthening of existing rights along with the method of operation and the realization of effective agreements. [33]

Even the Rapporteur of the Fifth Committee, Afghanistan's Dr. Tabibi, was rather restrained in his later evaluation of the results of the Con-

[31] A/CONF.13/43, p. 87.

[32] Myres S. McDougal and William T. Burke, *The Public Order of the Oceans; A Contemporary International Law of the Sea* (New Haven: Yale University Press, 1962), p. 113.

[33] Pearcy, *op. cit.*, p. 23.

ference. He commented that while Article 3 of the Convention on the High Seas "firmly established" the legal right of transit for land-locked states, the "practical aspect... remained unsolved."[34] Indeed, a great deal remained to be done; rather than subsiding, pressure for a more definitive solution to the question of access to the sea, particularly for the developing land-locked states, increased after 1958.

The United Nations Conference on Trade and Development

Since 1958 Mongolia and twelve African land-locked states have joined the United Nations and have entered the world trading community as independent entities. The number of land-locked states in the world has more than doubled since 1958. In addition, the interference with and threats to free transit of which Professor Pounds wrote continued, particularly in the case of Afghanistan and Pakistan. This problem received the attention of the first Ministerial Conference on Asian Economic Cooperation held at Manila, December 3–6, 1963. At that Conference, Afghanistan, Laos and Nepal, three land-locked members of ECAFE, "stressed the importance of providing adequate and unrestricted transit facilities for developing their trade..." and the Resolution on Asian Economic Cooperation, the final act of the Conference, included a unanimous agreement to request the ECAFE Secretariat to assist the three countries in preparing a draft convention.[35]

ECAFE followed this up with a unanimous resolution at its next meeting in Tehran in March 1964 stressing the "critical importance" of access to the sea in economic development and

> strongly recommends that the subject be given urgent and sympathetic consideration at the forthcoming United Nations Conference on Trade and Development...[36]

[34] Abdul Hakim Tabibi, *The Right of Free Access to the Sea*, n.p., 1966, pp. 2 and 19. Dr. Tabibi has been the force behind most of the United Nations work on land-locked states. Former Afghan Minister of Justice and member of the International Law Commission, he was Chairman of the Afghan delegation at the 1958 Law of the Sea Conference and at the Tehran meeting of ECAFE in 1964, served as Chairman of the subcommittee on land-locked states of the Fifth Committee of UNCTAD in 1964, and as chairman of the Afghan delegation to the United Nations Conference on Transit Trade of Land-locked Countries in 1965 was again very active. Dr. Tabibi is currently Afghan Ambassador in Tokyo.

[35] United Nations, ECAFE, *Regional Economic Cooperation in Asia and the Far East; Report of the Ministerial Conference on Asian Economic Cooperation, Manila 3–6 December 1963* (E/CN.11/641) (United Nations, 1964), p. 2.

[36] United Nations, *ECAFE, 20th Session 2–17 March 1964, Tehran* (E/CN.11/657) (United Nations, 15 March 1964), p. 2.

Once again, as in 1956, ECAFE, led by Afghanistan, considered seriously the question of access to the sea and prodded the United Nations into action.

The huge United Nations Conference on Trade and Development was held from March 23 to June 17, 1964 in Geneva. The Nepal-Laos-Afghanistan draft convention, cosponsored now by eight African land-locked states, formed the basis of an attempt to obtain from the world community guaranteed access to the sea. Although the question was not included in the original agenda of the Conference, it was assigned for study to a special forty-member subcommittee.

In the subcommittee meetings, the Soviet Union wanted the problem to be handled by the new world trade organization which it was proposing. The United States (only an observer at the subcommittee meetings) felt that "the drafting of a new convention was primarily the concern of land-locked countries and their neighbors, . . ." [37] This was the same position the United States had taken at the 1958 Geneva Conference, but was quite different from her position during and for some time after the War of the Pacific, when she attempted to obtain free transit for Bolivia, which had lost her coastal province to Chile. Czechoslovakia proposed that the Conference adopt the Principles proclaimed by the Preliminary Conference of Land-locked Countries at the 1958 Conference and that a draft convention be referred for action to the proposed new trade organization.

The subcommittee members generally agreed that it was necessary to modernize the Barcelona Conventions, but differed on the method of doing so. Bolivia, Paraguay, the African land-locked states and others wanted a convention completed by the Conference. Chile, Peru, the European states and others felt that the Conference was not equipped with legal experts and background information to conclude such a convention and wanted one prepared by a commission of international jurists and other legal experts. The fundamental difference in approach between Bolivia and Chile is evident. The subcommittee eventually adopted eight Principles and several recommendations which were all adopted unanimously by the full Committee. [38]

The Principles adopted were similar in substance to those adopted by the land-locked states in Geneva in 1958. There were some differences, however, which are pertinent to this discussion.

[37] United Nations, Office of Public Information, Press Release EC/TR/148 (CTD/E/21), 29 April 1964.

[38] The Fifth Committee on Expansion of International Trade and Regional Groupings.

Principle VII In order to accelerate the evolution of a universal approach to the solution of special and particular problems of trade and development of land-locked countries in different geographical areas, the conclusion of regional agreements in this regard should be encouraged by all states.

Principle VIII The facilities and special rights recognized to land-locked countries in view of their special geographical position are excluded from the operation of the most-favored-nation clause.[39]

Among the recommendations adopted were two which would have the Secretary-General

appoint a committee of twenty-four members . . . during 1964 . . . to prepare a new draft convention treating the proposal made by African-Asian land-locked countries as a basic text and taking into account the principles of international law . . .

and have the resultant draft presented "to a conference of plenipotentiaries in the middle of 1965."[40]

The Secretary-General followed these recommendations and appointed a Committee on Preparation of a Draft Convention Relating to Transit Trade of Land-locked Countries. The Committee of twenty-four states, which did not include Uganda, met at Headquarters, New York during October and November of 1964, and again the African and Asian land-locked countries led the discussions, particularly Abdul Rahman Pazhwak of Afghanistan. The Chairman, Mr. Ruegger of Switzerland, recalled in his opening statement that the Committee was to treat as a basic text the Afro-Asian land-locked countries' draft, which largely followed the 1921 Barcelona Convention on Freedom of Transit. However, that Convention was no longer adequate and the Committee was also to take into account the principles of international law included in the 1958 Convention on the High Seas as well as conventions and agreements regarding transit trade currently in force and submissions by Governments. In essence, the objective was "to resolve once and for all the difficulties of land-locked countries . . ." as the Argentine representative expressed it.[41]

[39] United Nations, Office of Public Information, Press Release EC/TR/194 (CTD/E/34), 11 May 1964.

[40] United Nations, General Assembly, Nineteenth Session, Official Records Annex No. 13, *Report of the United Nations Conference on Trade and Development* (A/5906, November, 1965), p. 41.

[41] UNCTAD, Committee on Preparation of a Draft Convention Relating to Transit Trade of Land-locked Countries, *Summary Records of the Second and Third Meetings* (E/CONF.46/AC.2/SR.2 and SR.3), 7 December and 1 December 1964.

The Committee's discussions, as might be expected, were both broad and detailed, ranging from the Committee's terms of reference and the proper degree of adherence to the Barcelona Convention, through the question of including arms and ammunition as "goods in transit," to such details as the proper length of time goods in transit could be stored without charges. Every viewpoint was well represented, including those of the United States, the USSR, and the General Legal Division of the United Nations Secretariat. The Committee had ample background material and recommendations with which to work, most of it provided by the Secretariat and by ECAFE. These documents established a general framework around which the Committee did prepare a Draft Convention on Transit Trade of Land-locked Countries for submission to the Conference of Plenipotentiaries.

After the Committee completed its work, the Nineteenth General Assembly was able, without a vote, to convene the full-dress Conference which was to take place the following summer. An even more impressive array of background documents was assembled, including some from agencies not directly involved, but interested nonetheless. An example is the Final Act of the International Conference on Faciliation of Maritime Travel and Transport, which met in London during the spring of 1965 at the invitation of the Inter-governmental Maritime Consultative Organization (IMCO), submitted by the Observer of the IMCO at the Conference. Included in this Final Act is the Convention on Facilitation of International Maritime Traffic which emerged from the London Conference. This Convention included a provision that the measures adopted "apply equally to the ships of coastal and non-coastal States the Governments of which are Parties to the Convention." [42] While this is essentially a reaffirmation of the Barcelona Convention's provisions, it is an expansion and modernization of them and parallelled the work of UNCTAD itself. It illustrates the world-wide interest in the problems of "non-coastal" states.

The Convention on Transit Trade of Land-locked States

The United Nations Conference on Transit Trade of Land-locked Countries opened at Headquarters, New York on June 7, 1965. It was the first conference convened under UNCTAD, which had been made a

[42] UNCTAD, United Nations Conference on Transit Trade of Land-locked Countries, *Note by the Observer of the Intergovernmental Maritime Consultative Organization* (TD/TRANSIT/R.3) (United Nations, 10 June 1965), p. 2.

permanent agency of the United Nations. By this time, 120 countries had joined UNCTAD; of them twenty-five were land-locked. The Conference on Transit Trade was attended by delegates of fifty-eight countries and observers of ten countries, including Iran and Peru. Since the Committee had left a number of issues unresolved, the Conference had considerable work to do.

The mood of the delegates was serious; there was real pressure to reach agreement and the feeling was repeatedly expressed throughout the Conference that a treaty should be drafted which would last at least twenty-five years. Of course, everyone realized that conditions could change, that everything depended on the parties living up to the provisions of the treaty, and that politics could intervene, but still there was no propaganda or ill will expressed during the Conference, at least in the view of one American participant. [43] The Conference, however, was not without its frustrations and heated verbal exchanges. Perhaps the American view of the Conference was colored by the fact that the United States still had little interest in the subject, was in favor of any agreement that might be worked out as long as it pertained only to goods passing in transit through littoral states and not through distant states (e.g. Japan to Britain through the United States), and in fact made no significant contribution to the work of the Conference. [44]

There were vigorous debates throughout the Conference on everything from whether free access to the sea was an inherent right of land-locked countries which would be reaffirmed in the Convention or whether the task of the Conference was merely to resolve technical problems of transit traffic, to whether the Convention should specify the procedures for clearing in-transit goods through customs. [45] While all speakers paid lip-service to the necessity for the freest possible transit for land-locked countries, it was evident that few delegations were willing to surrender much of their own "sovereignty" in order to achieve this. Moreover, not even the land-locked states agreed among themselves on the urgency for and scope of a new Convention. Broadly speaking, the European land-

[43] These latter observations were made during an interview on July 20, 1967 by Mr. Rowan Gaither of the Office of the Legal Advisor, United States Department of State. Mr. Gaither served on the American delegation to the Conference.

[44] Mr. Gaither also said that the United States signature to the Convention signifies approval, but "we don't feel there's any point in ratifying it because the United States would not be directly affected by it."

[45] The Pakistani delegate insisted at one point, for example, "Abstract considerations relating to the legal rights and obligations of nations should be left to the competent bodies, such as the International Law Commission." TD/TRANSIT/SR.8, p. 15.

locked states had few complaints, while those of Africa, Asia and South America were most vigorous in seeking broader rights and guarantees for the land-locked states. Likewise, some transit states were more understanding and cooperative than others. Generally, those which had good relations with their neighboring land-locked states fell into this category.

Unlike most international conferences, assignment to committees and other functions was not on a regional basis, but by an allocation among the land-locked, transit, and "other" states. This division was blurred, however, by the fact that some of the land-locked states were also transit states, as were some of the "other" states. Moreover, while the great majority of the participants were "developing" countries and the emphasis throughout was on the importance of access to the sea to economic development, the "developed" countries were not always enthusiastic about aiding the developing land-locked states in the matter of free transit. There were, finally, divergences over many provisions based on other considerations, some of a domestic nature, with many states stoutly supporting some proposals while firmly rejecting others. Probably the most detailed analysis of the Convention to date is that by John H. E. Fried, Legal Adviser to His Majesty's Government of Nepal on assignment from the United Nations, and member of the Nepali delegation at the Conference. His conclusions are presented here in full:

1. The main significance of the 1965 U. N. Conference which hammered out this Convention was that the problems which transit involves for land-locked States, their coastal neighbours and "third countries" were for the first time discussed at an international plenipotentiary level. These problems have thus acquired, as it were, "status" on the world scene.

2. Having acquired such status, those transit problems, especially of the developing land-locked countries, will probably appear more frequently on the international scene, for example, UNCTAD. Also, the increasing awareness of transit problems *in general,* which were regulated a generation and a half ago in the Barcelona Statute, may lead to its revision.

3. On the other hand, attitudes of States regarding transit through their territory, seem to have stiffened. This is reflected in the Convention. The Convention reveals stronger insistence on conditions, provisos and escape clauses, compared with such instruments as the Barcelona Statute 1921 or the GATT 1948 – to say nothing of the 1874 Berne Postal Congress which created the great liberal transit system of the Universal Postal Union.

4. The New Convention deals with transit, not only to and from, but also through land-locked States. It has various noticeable and beneficial features. It amply protects countries when acting as transit States.

It contains little which is new, and no radical innovations or breakthroughs.

This is largely due to the fact that conditions of land-locked States differ considerably from each other, as do their relations with their respective neighbours. Hence the need for separate bilateral and, as the case may be, multilateral and regional agreements.

5. The twin notions that transit traffic is a "burden" or "favour" and that only land-locked countries impose such "burden" are unfounded in reality and law. Transit is an obvious and expanding feature of world trade, indispensable for economic development and well-being of all States. All are dependent on the immutable facts of geography, but some much more than others. These inequalities can only be alleviated by a spirit of solidarity.

6. Transit trade offers particularly many illustrations of interplay between international and municipal law. The pertinent domestic laws and regulations of the countries involved and – as cannot be sufficiently emphasized – the manner in which municipal rules are actually applied by officials on the working level – are at least as crucial as are international treaties.

7. For land-locked States, especially those with a small choice of outlets to the outside world, transit trade is a topic of grave concern. The atmosphere and debates at the 1965 Conference showed that clearly. Those matters stare the people of land-locked States constantly in the eyes. They are often felt as reminders that land-locked countries are not truly independent.

The Convention is designed to alleviate such situations. But in order to achieve this, the Convention has to be under-pinned and "filled in", as said before, by separate agreements. The Convention itself envisages that these provide for "greater facilities" than are mentioned in its own, necessarily *general* and cautious provisions.

8. Transit trade problems are getting *more,* not less, important as time goes on, because unhampered, fast, reliable and economical transit is becoming ever more essential for nations and individuals. Unless progress is made in this field, the world will be faced, because of frustrations of land-locked States, with a new source of dissent and complications on an international scale. [46]

The Convention entered into force on June 9, 1967; by July 7, 1967 it had been signed by twenty-nine states, of which three had ratified it, and acceded to by five states which had not signed it. [47] On balance, it is fair to say that while the Convention undoubtedly represents important progress in international law, the developing land-locked states were far from completley satisfied with it. It is the latest, but not the last, word on the subject.

A detailed evaluation of the 1965 Convention appears in Chapter VII. At this point, however, it seems appropriate to examine three case studies of land-locked states which will illustrate some of the real and potential problems faced by such states and serve as reference points for this evaluation.

[46] John H. E. Fried, "The 1965 Convention on Transit Trade of Land-locked States", *Indian Journal of International Law*, VI (1966) pp. 28–30.

[47] United Nations Secretariat, *Status of Multilateral Conventions* (ST/LEG/3, Rev.1) (7 July 1967), p. X–15.

CHAPTER III

AFGHANISTAN

> History shows us that he who holds the Hindu Kush holds the key to India, and that the urge to descend from the highlands and possess the rich lands of the plain is sooner or later irresistible . . . I do not wish this to be held to imply that the Government and people of Afghanistan are at this present time contemplating a descent on the valley of the Indus. I am sure they have no such intention . . . But I am equally sure that there is an impulse stronger than obligations and treaties which will sooner or later, and perhaps sooner than later, bring these highlanders down off their hills to possess themselves of the goods and perhaps of the lands of their neighbours on the plains. They can be prevented by the concerted action of the two Governments concerned, and in no other way. [1]

This gloomy forecast by a British historian and former Minister to Afghanistan may be somewhat overdrawn, but it is by no means purely imaginary. Afghans have, indeed, swept out of their mountains into the Indus valley several times in the past, most recently in 1947 when some of them joined their fellow Pathans in Pakistan in the drive for Kashmir. Moreover, as Afghanistan develops a complex modern economy, however slowly, she may also be developing "an urge to descend from the highlands" all the way to the Arabian Sea. Indeed, it has been suggested that these people, who have fought so frequently and so successfully for their freedom, may have had in mind a seacoast for themselves at the height of their campaign for an independent Pushtunistan during the 1950's. Access to the sea is a sensitive and critical matter for this former buffer between Russia and Britain, now a peaceful battleground between East and West.

The Geographic Setting

Major mountain ranges are often considered by laymen to be excellent

[1] W. K. Fraser-Tytler, *Afghanistan; A Study of Political Developments in Central and Southern Asia* (2nd ed.; London: Oxford University Press, 1953), p. 299.

bases for political boundaries, and in some cases they are. Afghanistan, however, is an exception, for she straddles the mighty Hindu Kush, a range of mountains which rise to more than 24,000 feet radiating westward for more than 700 miles from the great Pamir Knot of Central Asia. This region straddling the Hindu Kush has been of enormous importance through the recorded history of Asia. Indeed, as one writer has described it,

> Among Pakistan's neighbors, Afghanistan is strategically most important. It is a land-locked country whose contacts with the outside world are through the passes which cross into Pakistan. The Hindu Kush, which divides Afghanistan into two distinct parts, also separates Central from Southern Asia. The great conquerors who crossed the Hindu Kush also found their way into the Indo-Pakistan sub-continent. In fact, the Hindu Kush is the first line of defence of the Indo-Pakistan subcontinent. [2]

To the south and north of the Hindu Kush are lower parallel ranges, the Koh-i-Baba and the Band-i-Turkestan, respectively. To the north and south of these ranges are lowlands; the northern, extending into the U.S.S.R., being smaller than the southern, which extends well into Baluchistan in southwestern Pakistan. Other ranges of mountains as high as 15,000 feet, however, bring the mountainous area of the country to more than two-thirds of its total area. While the plains and mountain valleys contain most of the economic activity of the country, the mountains dominate its history, geography and psychology.

The country is drained by many rivers and smaller streams, but only four are considered major ones. The most important, and the only one that is navigable, is the Amu Darya, known historically as the Oxus. This river rises high in the Pamirs, flows westward through northeastern Afghanistan and along the Soviet border, then northward through the Kara Kum Desert, eventually to empty into the Aral Sea. Below Bakhorak the Amu Darya is broad and meandering with many islands. The left, or Afghan, bank is low and subject to flooding; the right, or Soviet, bank is firmer and all of the sizable river towns are on the Soviet side. The Helmand, flowing southwestward from the Hindu Kush and emptying into desert lakes on the Iranian border, is longer and has a greater volume within Afghanistan than the Amu, but is not navigable. It is, however, the focus of a massive multi-purpose river basin development scheme which is already transforming this desert region into fertile agricultural land. The third river is the 650-mile Hari Rud, which flows westward from the

[2] Aslam Siddiqi, *Pakistan Seeks Security* (Lahore: Longmans, Green and Company, 1960), p. 24.

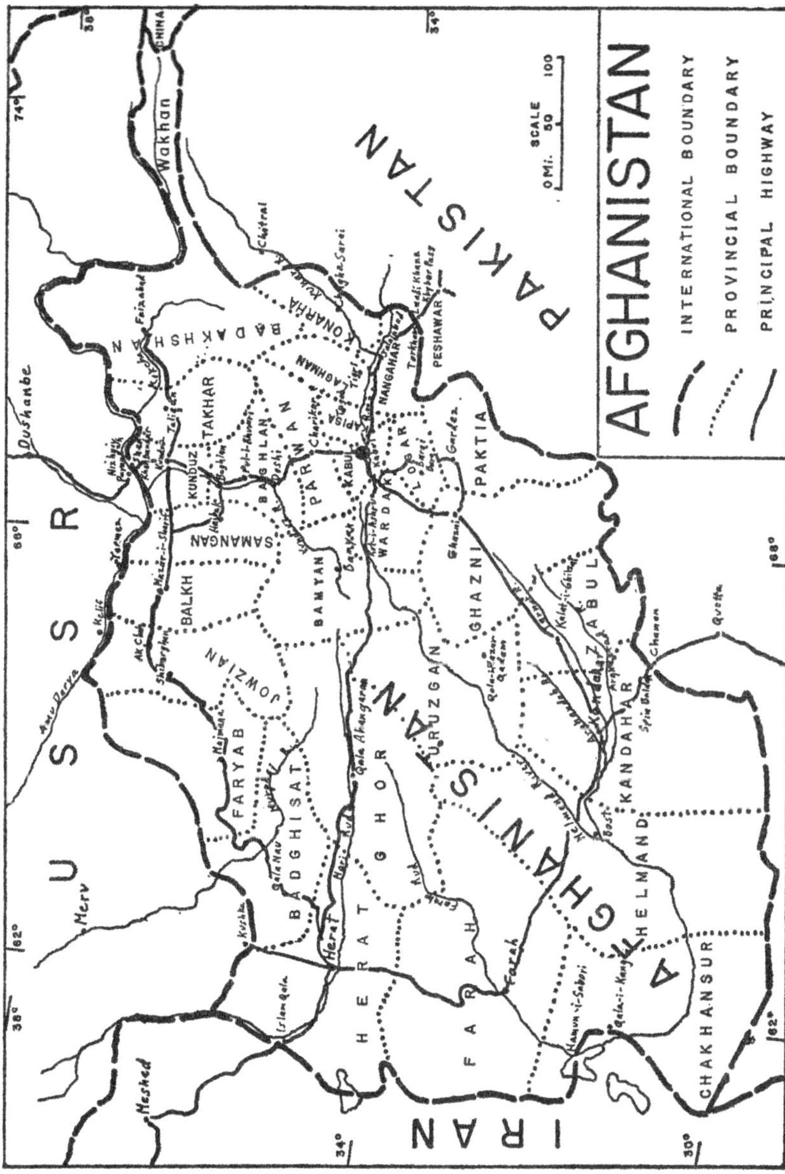
AFGHANISTAN
INTERNATIONAL BOUNDARY
PROVINCIAL BOUNDARY
PRINCIPAL HIGHWAY
SCALE
0 MI. 50 100
U S S R
PAKISTAN
IRAN
CHINA
Wakhan
AFGHANISTAN
BADAKHSHAN
TAKHAR
KUNDUZ
BAGHLAN
SAMANGAN
BALKH
JOWZJAN
FARYAB
BADGHISAT
HERAT
FARAH
GHOR
BAMYAN
PARWAN
KAPISA
LAGHMAN
KONARHA
NANGAHAR
KABUL
WARDAK
LOGAR
PAKTIA
GHAZNI
URUZGAN
ZABUL
KANDAHAR
HELMAND
CHAKHANSUR
PESHAWAR
Dushanbe
Merv
Meshed
Quetta
Herat
Farah
Chaman
Amu Darya
38°
34°
30°
62°
66°
68°
74°

MAP 2

northern flanks of the Hindu Kush and near Herat turns northward to form part of the border with Iran. Finally, the Kabul River flows south then east out of the Hindu Kush to empty into the Indus in Pakistan, some 300 miles away. Below Jalalabad the Kabul flows through a deep gorge so that overland traffic must use the higher Khyber Pass through the mountains.

The climate of Afghanistan may be described as generally dry but variable, since elevation and exposure, as well as the seasons, produce a wide variety of climates. The north is generally colder and drier than the south, the border area being, except in the mountains of the east, a true desert, with less than ten inches of rain per year. It is sparsely populated, though the foothills and valleys further south support considerable irrigated agriculture. Kandahar, near the Registan Desert in the south, is at an altitude of 3,462 feet and receives only seven inches of rain per year. From here westward well into Iran is absolute desert, much of it covered by sand dunes or salt flats. Kabul, the capital, is in the better watered eastern portion of the country, but at 5,995 feet still receives only 13.3 inches of rain and snow per year. In the south and west, temperatures sometimes go well over 100° F, but for the most part the country is cooler and, of course, quite cold in the mountains, the highest of which remain snow-covered the year around. Most precipitation in Afghanistan comes in the winter, and the summers are noted for their strong north and north-west winds which sometimes reach 100 miles an hour. Altogether, the climate is harsh and difficult for humans and most of their economic activities.

Afghanistan is an agricultural country. Some three-quarters of the national income is derived from agriculture, and only after unusually poor harvests is it necessary to import food. Figures on the amount of cultivated land vary considerably, but it probably does not exceed ten percent of the total area of the country, and much of this is irrigated. About half of the total cropland is devoted to low-yielding wheat fields, with cotton as the second crop. Both cotton and sugar beets have grown greatly in importance in the last two decades. Other important crops are fruits, nuts, and sugar cane. About one-third of the people are employed in raising some 65 million head of livestock, about half of which are chickens. By far the most important livestock, however, are the Karakul sheep, which produce both wool and from one to three million skins a year for export.

Mining in Afghanistan is still rudimentary, though the country is known to be rich in minerals. Good quality coal is mined near Mazar-i-Sharif in the north and natural gas from northern fields is now being exported to the

U.S.S.R. Petroleum has not yet been found in commercial quantities, but exploration is continuing. Other known minerals include the rich Haji-gak iron ore deposits in the eastern mountains, gold, copper, bauxite, asbestos, beryllium, sulphur, chromium, talc, lead, zinc, marble and several precious and semi-precious gems. Mining is unlikely to be an important activity for some time.

Industry is similarly only in the first stages of development. Besides shortages of capital, technology, trained administrators and incentive, inadequate electric power and primitive and expensive transport have inhibited growth of manufacturing beyond the handicraft stage. While most of those handicaps are gradually being overcome, industry today still consists largely of relatively small-scale plants processing local products and making basic consumer goods. These are being improved and expanded now.

Afghanistan's foreign trade has been growing in importance, particularly since 1954, when her economic development programs began. Karakul has long been her most important export, not only in terms of annual income ($ 10 million to $ 17 million), but also because it can stand the high cost of air transport when necessary and, since it is sold almost entirely in New York and London, is the country's principal source of hard currency which is badly needed for expanding imports. Rapidly growing in value in recent years have been exports of fruits and nuts. In 1965–66 dried and preserved fruits and nuts alone earned $ 17,877,600, more than the $ 16,084,000 earned by Karakul skins, while fresh fruit exports brought in another $6,130,200. Raw cotton was worth $11,131,800 and carpets and rugs $ 8,940,100. Other important exports are oilseeds, wool, hides and skins and sausage casings. Afghanistan's total exports in 1965–66 came to $ 69,972,100. Her best customers, in order, were the Soviet Union, which took nearly all of her raw cotton and much of her processed fruits and nuts; the United Kingdom, which took more than half of her Karakul; the United States, mostly Karakul and processed fruits and nuts; Pakistan, which bought nearly all the fresh fruit exports; and India, an important customer for fresh and processed fruits and nuts. Germany and Japan are other important trading partners.

Imports, as might be expected, consist of a wide variety of capital and consumer goods and petroleum, by far the single most important import. The U.S.S.R. supplied nearly all of Afghanistan's $ 4,331,200 worth of petroleum imports and nearly all of her $ 3,030,800 worth of sugar imports. Also in 1965–66, $ 3,998,300 worth of cotton fabrics were imported, mostly from India, Pakistan and the Soviet Union, and other products from many countries. The principal suppliers of her $ 56,511,200 worth of commercial imports were, in order, the Soviet Union ($ 18,154,600), Japan ($ 7,969,600), India ($ 4,988,200) and Pakistan, Czechoslovakia, the United States and Germany, each of which supplied just under $ 4 million worth of goods. These import figures, however, can be most misleading unless the loan and grant imports are added to the commercial accounts. Afghanistan's total imports in 1965–66, then, came to $130,984,900, nearly double what she earned from her exports. [3]

Perhaps more important than the statistics, however, are the overall trends in Afghan foreign trade. First, the volume of this trade, commercial and other, is increasing rapidly, thus making access to the sea ever more important for what had until very recently been a remote, isolated and poverty-stricken feudal mountain kingdom. Second, Afghanistan has become increasingly dependent upon the Soviet Union for petroleum and other products, for development aid and as a market for her exports. As recently as May 1967 the Soviet Union contracted to buy from Afghanistan her first non-agricultural or handicraft product – $ 300,000,000 worth of natural gas between 1967 and 1985. [4] This trend is being countered to some extent by growing trade with Pakistan, now that relations between the two countries have improved. In 1963, for example, an important Pakistani trade journal merely listed the categories of products which might be exchanged between the two countries, mostly agricultural products and consumer goods, [5] while in April 1966 the two countries signed a trade agreement in Rawalpindi under the terms of which Pakistan would provide rice, fish, poultry, butter and tea in exchange for Afghan dried fruits, mustard and potato seeds, and goat and sheep skins. [6] While the United States and Britain are valued as importers of Afghan Karakul, prices for this product fluctuate widely and unpredictably and, therefore, dollar and sterling earnings do also. Moreover, these countries demand payment for their exports to Afghanistan in the same currencies, a requirement which Afghanistan is generally hard-pressed to meet. American aid programs are far more important to Afghanistan in both economic and political terms than dollar and sterling trade.

[3] All foreign trade figures are from Royal Government of Afghanistan, Ministry of Commerce Statistical Department, *A Summary of Afghanistan's Foreign Trade in 1344 (March 21, 1965 through March 20, 1966)*, Kabul, August 1966.

[4] *The Kabul Times*, May 14, 1967.

[5] "Pakistan's Trade with the Afro-Asian Countries," *Pakistan Trade*, XIV, No. 12, December 1963, p. 4.

[6] *The Times* of London, April 19, 1966.

Afghanistan for millenia has been a crossroads of history, with various groups of people migrating east and west, north and south through the region. Armies, too, have marched repeatedly through here on the way to or from Mongolia, Russia, Western Europe, Persia or India. All of them have left descendents scattered about the country and, just as the country is broken into several regions and many isolated pockets by mountains, so is the population diverse and insecurely linked by the "state idea."

The largest single ethnic group in the country is the Pushtus, or Pathans, who are known as "true Afghans." [7] They are the ruling group in the country and may constitute a majority. [8] They live mostly in the south and southeast of the country and around Herat and Seistan. They are probably basically caucasoid in origin, speak Pashto or Dari (a dialect of Persian), are mostly Sunni Moslems and are city dwellers, farmers and nomads. Many are still living in tribal groups and those along the Pakistani border have traditionally been brigands, though they are settling down now. The second largest group is the Tadjiks, who live principally in the mountains of the Wakhan Corridor and the cities and towns of the northern plains and adjacent areas of the Soviet Union. They probably constitute about 20 to 25% of the population, speak Persian, are Shia Moslems, and work as merchants and artisans as well as farmers. Many are found in and around Herat and Kabul. Other important groups are the Uzbeks and other Turko-Mongol peoples in the northern and central sections and in the U.S.S.R., who are mostly Sunni Moslems and speak their own Turkic languages. The Hazaras are a largely Mongoloid people speaking an archaic Persian and practicing both the Sunni and Shia varieties of Islam. They live largely in the mountains of Hazarajat south of the main range of the Hindu Kush, and along the Iranian border. There are many other smaller ethnic groups scattered through the country

[7] The name of these people and their language is given variously as Pushtu, Pashto, Pakhtun, Pushtoon, Pathan, Pakhto, Pushtun, etc. Pakhtun is generally preferred in Afghanistan, while in Pakistan the people are nearly always referred to as Pathan. In this paper Pathan is used when referring to those in Pakistan, but Pushtu is used for those in Afghanistan and the proposed state of Pushtunistan because of its greater familiarity to Western readers.

[8] Figures concerning the ethnic composition of the Afghan population are diverse and not very reliable. George B. Cressey, for example, in *Crossroads; Land and Life in Southwest Asia* (Chicago: J. B. Lippincott Company, 1960), p. 564, says the Pathans "make up some two-fifths of the total population," while *The Encyclopaedia Britannica,* 1965 ed., Vol. I, p. 237, says they "form about 60% of the population." Cressey may be nearer the truth, since the Pakistanis often charge that the Pathans are a minority in Afghanistan and the Afghan government is sensitive on the subject.

including Arabs, Kurds, Jews and Hindus. Perhaps 98% of the people of Afghanistan are Moslem and possibly 75% speak Pashto or Dari, the official languages, or both, but it still cannot be said that Afghanistan is a unified nation-state with a true national consciousness despite its more than 200 years of independence.

Only recently have new all-weather and paved highways begun to tie together the regions occupied by these diverse peoples. The lack of good internal transportation systems has long retarded development of the country and contributed to its isolation. Even now there are only some 4,200 miles of motorable roads in the country, of which 2,700 are considered "improved" and 1,500 of them are paved. There are, moreover, very few vehicles to use these roads – 8,500 trucks in 1965, 1,500 buses and 7,000 passenger cars. [9] Progress is being made, however, and the Afghan Government, with American and Soviet help, is making road-building a high-priority aspect of its development program. A circumferential highway around the interior of the country has been completed, including links to cities on the Soviet, Pakistani and Iranian borders. Many other projects are in progress. Afghanistan still has no railroads, though a spur from the Pakistani railhead of Chaman to the Afghan border town of Spin Baldak is now under construction. Another has often been proposed through the Khyber Pass linking Peshawar with Kabul, but the railroad currently terminates at Landi Khana near the Afghan border. No other railroads are even contemplated for the country and Afghanistan may well skip the railroad age altogether.

Ariana Afghan Airlines, however, provides extensive internal service, connecting Kabul, Kunduz, Khost, Mazar-i-Sharif, Kandahar, Maimana, Herat and Faizabad. In 1965 it operated two DC-3's, two DC-6's and one Convair 440. Ariana also operates international services out of Kabul and Kandahar to Rotterdam via Tehran, Damascus and Beirut; from Kabul to Moscow via Tashkent; from Kabul to Delhi via Amritsar; and directly between Kabul and Peshawar. Besides Ariana, the national airlines of Pakistan, India, Iran and the U.S.S.R. fly into Kabul. The Kandahar International Airport, still a magnificent white elephant built by the United States, may yet fulfill its original purpose as the hub of air transportation not only for Afghanistan but for all the surrounding countries if relations improve sufficiently among all of these countries.

Communications are still largely primitive in Afghanistan. At the end of 1964 the country had only 35,000 radio receivers and at the beginning

[9] United States, Bureau of International Commerce, *Basic Data on the Economy of Afghanistan* (OBR 66–34), (June 1966), p. 5.

of 1965 only 8,683 telephones,[10] most of which were in Kabul. If Afghanistan is to be a truly modern, unified state, she will need far better communications.

Historical and Political Background

The earliest recorded use of the term "Afghan" in any form is by a sixth century Indian astronomer, but the history of the region currently occupied by the Kingdom of Afghanistan began much earlier than that. The earliest known occupants of the area were Scythians and Dravidians, though they were probably not the aboriginal inhabitants. Indo-Aryans spread through the region in the second and first millenia B.C. About 540 B.C. the country was conquered by Persia under Cyrus and the conquest was consolidated by Darius I. Under this Achaemenian Empire, there were seven satrapies or provinces, all of whose names are still prominent in Afghanistan and adjoining states – Bactria, Herat, Kabul, Seistan, Kandahar, Merv and Hindu Kush. Alexander the Great conquered the country in 330 B.C. and used it as a base of operations against Turkestan and India. Greek influence persisted in Afghanistan long after the Greek armies withdrew, despite the occupation of the eastern provinces by Indian rulers and the disintegration of political authority in the remainder of the region. During the second century A.D. the country may have been united briefly under the rule of the Kushans, who came from the west to establish an empire that included northern India and all the territory to the frontiers of China.

Invasions from the west and north continued for the next few centuries until the Turks, who had ruled the region for a hundred years, were defeated by the Chinese in 658 and Arab armies reached the area. The Arabs brought Islam with them and by the ninth and tenth centuries it had replaced Buddhism as the dominant religion. By this time, however, the power of the caliphate was waning and many local dynasties rose and displaced the foreign rulers in various parts of the country. One of these was the Ghaznevid Dynasty of the late tenth century, which at the height of its power ruled from Kurdistan to Kashmir and from the Amu Darya to the Ganges. This empire shrank steadily, however, and was dissolved in the twelfth century after more invasions from the north and west. During the next three centuries successive waves of Mongols, Tadjiks, Turks and Uzbeks swept over the region, with periods of rule by local

[10] *Encyclopaedia Britannica Book of the Year 1967*, p. 71.

chieftains interspersed. Near the end of the fourteenth century Timur (Tamerlane) reestablished Mongol rule over much of the country and northern India. Under the Timurids (1404–1507), Afghanistan enjoyed peace and prosperity and a great flowering of the arts. This period came to an end with an Uzbek invasion out of Central Asia. The last important Mongol ruler, Babur, was driven out of northern and western Afghanistan by the Uzbeks; he, in turn, moved eastward and in 1526 took Delhi and established the Mogul Empire. For the next two hundred years, Afghanistan south of the Hindu Kush, including Kabul and Kandahar, was generally tied to India; the western portion, including Herat and Seistan, was under Persian domination; while Balkh and Badakhshan in the north were at times semi-independent but frequently invaded by Uzbeks and Persians.

As the Mogul Dynasty weakened, the Safawid Dynasty of Iran absorbed southern and western Afghanistan, but they, too, were weakening from about 1628 on. Through all of these invasions and occupations, local tribes put up fierce resistance and, while some may have been pacified by isolation or bribery, they were never conquered. Rebellions were frequent, but not until the eighteenth century did Afghanistan emerge as a united nation under Afghan rule. A successful rising against the Persian governor of Kandahar in 1709 may be considered as the beginning of the Afghan national awakening. This was followed in 1716 by the liberation of Herat. The Afghans continued harassing the decaying Persian Empire and in 1722 a small army of them defeated a much larger Iranian force near Isfahan and captured the city.

The Russians and Turks, however, were also invading Iran and, after defeating each of these invaders in turn, the Afghans were themselves weakened by internal dissention and driven out of Iran by a local brigand chief in 1730. After defeating the Afghans again and taking Herat in 1732, this brigand was elected Shah of Iran in 1736 and became Nadir Shah. Nadir Shah continued his eastward march, taking Kandahar after a year's siege in 1738 and the heart of the Mogul Empire at Delhi in the following year. He then returned to Persia and was assassinated in 1747. After his death his empire fell apart. In Afghanistan, a tribal chief named Ahmad Abdali was elected king of the Afghans and changed his tribal name to Durrani. This was the true beginning of independent Afghanistan.

During the next twenty-five years Ahmad Shah liberated all of Afghanistan and went on to conquer all the territory from Meshed to Kashmir and Delhi and from the Amu Darya to the Arabian Sea. After his death about 1773, his successor, less capable and unselfish than he, permitted this empire to disintegrate. This collapse of the Afghan empire was aided greatly by the Persians, once again pushing from the west; the Russians, encroaching from the north; and the Sikhs and British, the former accused by the Afghans of acting as tools of the latter, moving in from the east. Internal strife so weakened the Durranis that by 1835 they had lost control of the country to Dost Mohammed, who established the Barakzai or Mohammedzai Dynasty. Dost Mohammed was defeated by the Sikhs in 1836 in the last Afghan attempt to retake Peshawar, but in the following year was able to resist a new Persian siege of Herat. The British failed to make an alliance with Dost Mohammed against the Russians and used this as a pretext for an invasion of Afghanistan, setting off the First Afghan War (1838–1842). The British succeeded in occupying the major cities of southern and eastern Afghanistan and deporting Dost Mohammed to India, but were finally driven out in a retreat which ended in a massacre. Dost Mohammed was released by the British and returned to rule his country until 1863. Persia, meanwhile, had taken Herat again but the city became Afghan permanently (until now, at any rate) in 1863.

After the death of Dost Mohammed, a weak son succeeded and received a Russian mission at Kabul, which had been capital of the country since the 1770's. The Russians had been advancing through Central Asia, conquering the independent states and Khanates of the Kirghiz, Tadjik, Uzbek and Kazakh peoples. Tashkent and Bukhara were captured in 1865 and Samarkand in 1868. By the following year the Russians had reached the Amu Darya. The British were determined to halt the Russian advance and their growing influence in Afghanistan and invaded for the second time in 1878. The Afghans once again fought well against an invader, but again the British took the major cities. And again, internal dissension among the Afghans (and this time among the British as well) confused the picture, but the British supported Abdurrahman Khan, a grandson of Dost Mohammed, came to an agreement with him, and after defeating a rebel army, left Afghanistan in 1881. Abdurrahman Khan succeeded in bringing peace and unity to Afghanistan, while the British had retreated from their "forward" policy in India vis-a-vis the Northwest Frontier and the Afghan country. The result was that in 1893 the two countries were able to agree on a compromise boundary between Afghanistan and India, later known as the Durand Line. This border was completely illogical, having no basis in ethnology, geography or history; it simply delimited the area of even nominal British control. Though it has been controversial ever since, it has stood as the border between Afghanistan and India, then

Pakistan, and is unlikely to be altered greatly in the foreseeable future.

Abdurrahman Khan ruled his country well and died peacefully in 1901. But he left behind some unfinished business. The agreement establishing the Durand Line also committed each party not to "exercise influence" over the line. It gave the British, moreover, some control over the foreign policy of Afghanistan, for they were still wary of both the Pathan tribes and the Russians. The new king, Habibullah Khan, was a progressive monarch and he laid the foundations for the modern economic infrastructure. He also maintained a strict neutrality through World War I and in February 1919 demanded from the British recognition at the Paris Peace Conference of Afghanistan's "absolute liberty, freedom of action and perpetual independence." Within a few days, however, he was assassinated. After Habibullah's death, his third son, Amanullah Khan, seized the throne. His first act was to proclaim Afghanistan's complete independence. The British reacted violently and the Third Afghan War began in May 1919. Fighting was inconclusive, however, and finally the British recognized Afghanistan's independence in a peace treaty signed at Rawalpindi on August 8.

Another important event of Amanullah's reign was the establishment of more normal relations with Iran, in response to friendly overtures from Reza Shah Pahlavi in 1923. In 1925 the two countries resolved their border dispute and in 1929 King Amanullah and his queen made a state visit to Iran. Since then, relations between the two countries, while not cordial, have been at least reasonably warm and free of serious friction. During the Civil War in Russia following the Bolshevik revolution, fighting broke out between Afghan and Red Army troops, but it never became really serious. In 1921 the two countries concluded a border agreement confirming the Amu Darya as part of the boundary and including some concessions by the Soviets. The concessions were never implemented, however, and the present border was not definitively established until 1946.

Amanullah continued his enlightened rule until he was driven into exile during a civil war in 1929 and replaced by a brigand chief who ruled by terror for nine months. In October 1929 a cousin of Amanullah, Mohammed Nadir Khan, restored peace and began a reign in which he instituted many reforms in education and other activities. The most dramatic of the reforms was his grant to his people in 1930 of a constitution which provided for a bicameral legislature. This was the first formal limitation on the authority of an Afghan King. But this steady progress was again interrupted in 1933 by the King's assassination.

Nadir Khan's only son, Mohammed Zahir, ascended the throne at the age of 19, the first Afghan monarch to be educated in Europe (France). The young king followed his father's progressive lead, but was not a dynamic leader. The country was, in fact, governed successively by his two uncles and his first cousin, who served as prime ministers. Partly, of course, his rule was limited by the constitution, but that did not prevent his royal relatives from ruling quite firmly. Zahir Shah may well have been discreetly biding his time until both he and his people were prepared to take really dramatic steps forward. He did, however, travel to all parts of his kingdom, establishing a real rapport with his people.

Afghanistan remained neutral through World War II, but soon after the war became embroiled in the partition of India and subsequent events. There had long been skirmishes along and raids across the Durand Line and through the turbulent Northwest Frontier Province of India. The British had, in fact, never really attempted to govern this region very strictly and it was largely autonomous "tribal territory." The tribes were mostly Pathan, closely related to the Pushtus of Afghanistan. When the partition of India was proposed in 1947, the Afghans raised the question of a separate sovereign state for the Pathans living on the Indian side of the line.

> Prior to partition the government of Afghanistan suggested that the Pathans be allowed to decide whether to accede to India, accede to Pakistan, or become independent. This suggestion, outlined in diplomatic notes, was later rejected on the ground that the inhabitants of the North-West Frontier Province had already voted in favor of joining Pakistan ... The Afghan government sponsored propaganda calling for the creation of an autonomous state of Pakhtunistan, or Pushtunistan, which would include all the Pathans within Pakistan. Maps of Pakhtunistan depicted an area stretching east of the Indus River and south to the Arabian Sea and may have reflected the wish of land-locked Afghanistan to gain direct access to the sea.[11]

After becoming independent, Pakistan refused to consider the establishment of an autonomous or sovereign Pushtunistan, but continued to administer the mountainous border area rather loosely, as the British had. Afghanistan, however, continued her pressure.

> A silent war developed alongside the loud propaganda war. The Afghan transit trade through Pakistan became a battleground. Beginning in 1947, the Pakistanis subjected Afghan in-transit goods to delays, which forced payment of high demurrage charges; they limited the number of railway cars to trans-

[11] Donald N. Wilber, *Pakistan* (New Haven: HRAF Press, 1964), p. 312. On page 52 of the present work is a copy of such a map.

PUSHTUNISTAN - AN EXTREME PROPOSAL

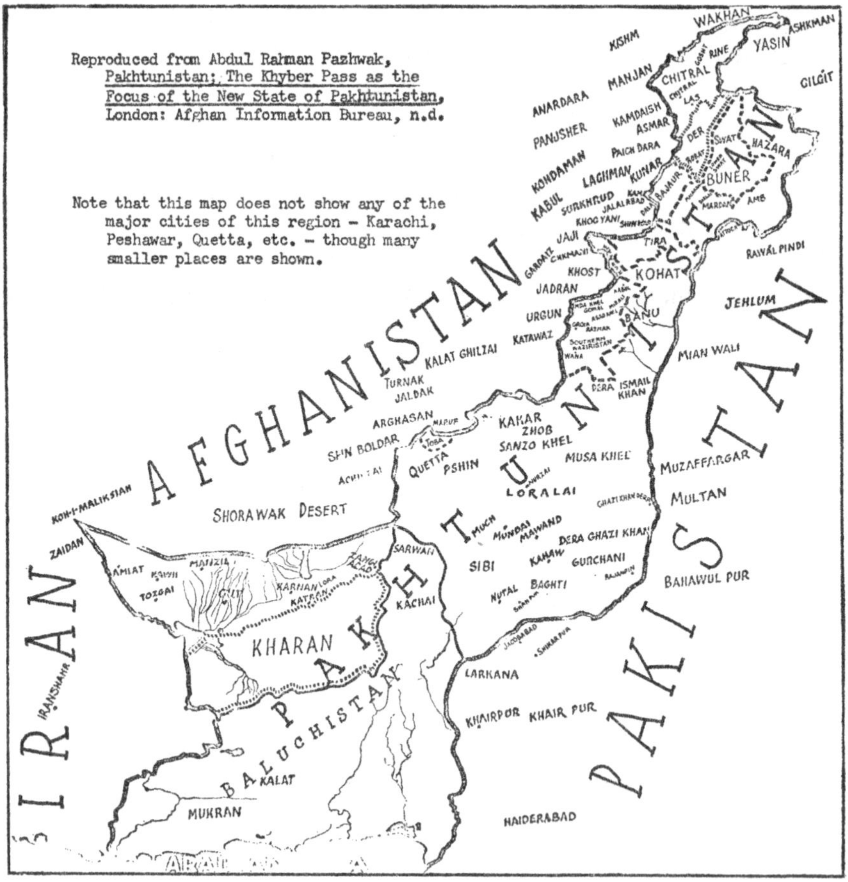

MAP 3

port goods, and often items in transit never reached Afghanistan, or were damaged en route.[12]

After the invasion of Kashmir by tribal groups related to the Afghans, the demand for Pushtunistan intensified. In August 1949 a group of Afridi tribesmen proclaimed the state of Pushtunistan, stretching from Chitral in the north to Baluchistan and from the Khyber Pass to Bolan on the banks of the Indus River. Afghanistan shortly announced that all treaties with the United Kingdom, especially the Durand Agreement, were null and void. Pakistan publicly dismissed all this as of little consequence, but in fact was quite worried.

> [I]n December 1949, they attempted to exert pressure on Afghanistan by halting shipments of petroleum products, on the pretext that the Afghan tankers did not meet safety requirements. At the same time Afghan export and import traffic through Karachi, then Afghanistan's major shipping link with the outside world, slowed to a virtual halt.[13]

This dispute soon quieted down but the Afghans were frustrated, not only by this Pakistani harassment, but by American aid to Pakistan and apparent lack of interest in Afghan problems. Accordingly, for the first time, in July 1950 she signed a four-year barter agreement with the USSR. The Soviets offered petroleum products, cotton cloth, sugar and other important commodities in exchange for Afghan wool and raw cotton on very favorable terms. The agreement also provided for Soviet technical assistance to Afghanistan, especially in petroleum exploration and storage, and Afghan goods were permitted free transit through the USSR.

In 1953 Sardar Mohammed Daoud, nephew of Nadir Shah and cousin of Zahir Shah, became Prime Minister. He was adamant about Pushtunistan and pursued the matter assiduously. In order to strengthen his hand, he appealed to the United States for modern weaponry. The United States, however, was allied with Pakistan which was already criticizing Washington for giving massive economic aid to India. So, not wishing to offend Pakistan further, the United States refused the Afghan request. Daoud then turned to Moscow, which did not refuse his request. The Soviets have continued to supply the Afghan army until today it is virtually completely Soviet-equipped. Despite this, however, Afghanistan was still vitally dependent upon Pakistan for her access to the sea and she had, moveover, still some hope that a Pushtunistan would actually be created.

[12] Louis Dupree, "Afghanistan's Big Gamble," *American Universities Field Staff (AUFS) Report South Asia Series,* 2 May 1960, p. 8.

[13] Arnold Fletcher, *Afghanistan; Highway of Conquest* (Ithaca: Cornell University Press, 1965), p. 255.

Between 1950 and 1955, Afghan transit trade through Pakistan actually increased, while trade with the USSR was mushrooming, and by 1955 80% of Afghanistan's exports and 79% of her imports passed through Pakistan. In 1955, however, there were more riots over Pushtunistan and Pakistan again closed the border, this time for five months.

> The Afghans asked the Americans for assistance in creating a new transit route through Iran to the port of Chahbar on the Persian Gulf. Both Iran and the United States pronounced the idea economically impractical, since 3600 miles of new roads (mainly in Iran) and port facilities would have had to be constructed. The Afghans then simply requested the Russians, and they agreed, to renew the 1950 transit agreement . . . [14]

This agreement provided for Soviet transit through Afghanistan and also marked a massive increase in Soviet aid to Afghanistan. Her problems were far from solved, however. The United Nations Economic Commission for Asia and the Far East (ECAFE) Survey for 1955 remarked,

> In 1954–55, Afghanistan's economy showed signs of improvement . . .
>
> However, there are certain basic problems Afghanistan has to solve before it is able to carry out a large scale expansion in production and trade and substantially increase her standards of living.
>
> Recent developments have brought to full light Afghanistan's special problem of a land-locked country and of few means of communication. [15]

On May 29, 1958 Pakistan and Afghanistan signed a transit agreement in Kabul which provided for improved transportation facilities for Afghan goods. These improvements were to be largely financed by the United States under separate agreements signed with both countries in the following month, and largely followed the recommendations of a survey by the Los Angeles engineering firm of Koebig and Koebig. While this display of mutual goodwill (generated by considerable American pressure on both sides) was heartening, it did not endure, for in August 1961 another dispute broke out between the two neighbors which resulted in their common border being closed again, this time until July 1963.

This dispute was most complex, involving a variety of Cold War issues, Pushtunistan, Kashmir, etc., although the border closure was directly precipitated by a Pakistani demand that Afghanistan close her consulates and trade offices in Pakistan. Pakistan rejected the Afghan demand for recision of the closure order, charging Afghanistan with "aggressive and

[14] Dupree, *op. cit.*, p. 10.

[15] Quoted in *Asian Recorder*, 8–14 June 1957.

hostile activities against Pakistan." [16] Afghanistan retaliated by closing the border on September 3 and breaking diplomatic relations on September 6. Charges flew back and forth with the United States, as an aspiring peacemaker and friend of both, caught in the middle. Louis Dupree reported from Kabul,

> The closing of the Afghan-Pakistani border surprised many observers, who could not believe the Afghans would really do it. Logically, as everyone knows, the border closure would adversely affect the now booming American aid and assistance programs, threaten Afghan merchants and fruitgrowers with loss of this year's fruit crop, and possibly deliver the whole trade of the country into Soviet channels. But here pride overrode practicality as it often does in international affairs. [17]

The Soviets came to the rescue, in part at least, by dramatically airlifting virtually the entire Afghan grape harvest to Soviet Central Asia at their own expense. Some of the grapes and other fresh fruits were flown on to European Russia and Eastern Europe where they commanded premium prices. In November 1961 the Afghans and Soviets signed another agreement increasing Afghan transit facilities in the USSR. All Afghan overland trade was then diverted through the USSR, except for American aid shipments, which continued to pile up in Karachi and Peshawar.

The United States was apparently instrumental in bringing about a new Afghan-Iranian agreement on January 9, 1962 granting Afghanistan some transit facilities in Iran. This does not appear to have been implemented, but it probably influenced Afghanistan to reopen the border for eight weeks beginning January 29 to clear the backlog of American aid shipments. These included medicines, cement, milk powder, wheat and machinery.

Finally, on May 28, 1963, Afghanistan and Pakistan signed an agreement in Tehran re-establishing diplomatic relations and reopening the border. Trade and transit were to be resumed under terms of the 1958 agreement. Pakistan had already extended her railroads from Peshawar and Chaman to the Afghan border, but the Afghans had not yet built their portions. In any case, the border was officially opened on July 20. On July 25 Ariana Afghan Airlines resumed service to Karachi and on July 26 trade across the border resumed after a lapse of nearly two years.

Meanwhile, Prime Minister Prince Mohammed Daoud had been dili-

[16] Government of Pakistan White Paper dated 2 September 1961. Quoted in *Asian Recorder*, 15–21 October 1961.

[17] Louis Dupree, "'Pushtunistan': The Problem and Its Larger Implications," Part I, *AUFS Report*, November, 1961, p. 10.

gently attempting to modernize his country. In 1954 he announced the country's commitment to long-term planned economic development. In the following year he established a planning commission which drew up a five-year development program to commence in 1956. He promoted education, both within Afghanistan and abroad. He sponsored the overseas training of several technocrats who assumed high government positions after their return home. He invited Soviet, Czech, West German and American technicians to help develop the country's infrastructure and build factories. He intensified development of agriculture in the north and work on the Helmand River project, which had been started in 1939, but limped along for years. Some social reforms were also introduced, but they failed to take hold. During the period in the early 1960's when the Afghan-Pakistan border was closed, it became evident that Daoud had served his country well, but was rapidly becoming obsolete. Domestically the country had probably progressed as far as it could under autocratic royal rule before the new generation began disturbances which might endanger both the economy and the society, including the monarchy. In foreign affairs, the dispute with Pakistan over Pushtunistan was obviously damaging the country, and in particular, the border closure was severely hurting the economy and making Afghanistan dangerously dependent upon the Soviet Union. Prince Daoud, it was clear, had to go. He did, more or less gracefully, on March 3, 1963. Afghanistan began a new era.

The departure of the intensely nationalistic Prince Daoud from the government, while making possible the reopening of the border less than three months later, did not mean the end of political tension in the country. Prince Daoud continued to exercise what influence he could from behind the scenes. Early in 1964, however, the forces of moderation prevailed in the country. Relations with Pakistan improved and a draft constitution was drawn up. The new Constitution went into effect on September 20, 1964. Under its terms, the direct relatives of the king are barred from all cabinet posts, judgeships and seats in the National Assembly. The Assembly, while debating the draft, added the proviso that no member of the Royal Family could give up his royal status, thus barring Prince Daoud permanently from an active political role. Afghanistan is now a constitutional monarchy ruled largely by the Loya Jirga, or Great National Assembly, continuing its rapid social and economic development, continuing its policy of strict neutrality and non-alignment, and on reasonably good terms with Pakistan. The Pushtunistan issue, while perhaps not laid to rest permanently, is at least dormant and Afghanistan has experienced no serious disruptions of her access to the sea since 1963.

The United States, The Soviet Union and the Afghan Economy

Afghanistan, as already noted, faces formidable geographic obstacles to economic development. In addition, the fragmentation of the largely primitive, often nomadic and essentially unskilled population into small, widely scattered agricultural and pastoral villages and communities intensifies the difficulties of mobilizing and training manpower for a modern industrial society. Moreover, Afghanistan still has little or none of the economic and social infrastructure so necessary for the creation of such a society. Land tenure systems, labor unions, political parties, banking and insurance, scientific and technical education, etc. are either totally lacking or only rudimentary. Capitalism, as known in Western Europe and North America, has never really developed in Afghanistan. Consequently, capital formation and allocation, investment, foreign trade and nearly all other economic activities are, of necessity, functions of the government. With the development of constitutional government, education, the physical infrastructure, and contacts with the outside world, we may expect some growth of private entrepreneurship. Indeed, there are already some joint state-private enterprises. In general, however, it has been the government which has assumed responsibility for economic development and this situation is likely to prevail for the foreseeable future.

Afghanistan's turbulent history discouraged, if it did not actually prevent, a concerted effort to keep pace with the economic growth in her neighbors to the north and south, to say nothing of the industrialized world, until thc twentieth century. By then, the country was so far behind that catching up has been enormously difficult. Nadir Shah's development plan of 1932, based on the partial industrialization of the country, was fundamentally autarkic and, like those of his predecessors, limited and hesitant. Still, it did represent progress. In 1939 the Helmand River Basin multi-purpose development project began. Work proceeded slowly through the Second World War, but after the war the government began investing heavily in the project. This drew the first important foreign aid to the country in the form of funds from the new World Bank and both funds and technical assistance from the United States. Since then the United States has become the principal supporter of the project. It has already made major contributions to the region – and the country – in irrigation, water supply, hydroelectricity, road building and settling of nomads. One unforeseen and unfortunate side effect of the damming of the Helmand and Arghandab Rivers was the threatened reduction in the flow of water to cultivators in the Iranian province of Seistan. This led to some tension between the two countries, the first since the last major battles over control of Herat and Kandahar. Patient and calm negotiations, however, have led to mutually satisfactory arrangements and the two traditionally hostile neighbors are now on reasonably good terms.

In addition to the Helmand, other development projects were undertaken after 1946 and in 1951 the Afghan Government signed a Point Four agreement with the United States, but not until 1954 did the new, progressive government of Sardar Mohammed Daoud announce its commitment to long-term, planned economic development. In the same year, after the death of Stalin in 1953, the Soviet Union first entered the foreign aid field outside its own immediate sphere of influence. They extended to Afghanistan credit for construction of a flour mill and a bakery ($ 3 million) and for paving streets in Kabul ($ 2 million). A reasonable explanation for this change in traditionally hostile relations between the two countries is offered in the next section.

In 1955 a new planning commission drew up a five-year development program which commenced the following year. The Soviets then began a serious foreign aid drive with a $ 100 million credit for a variety of projects: hydroelectric power stations, automobile repair factory, highway construction, irrigation canal, improvement of the Kabul Airport, preliminary surveys for oil and gas, etc. At the same time the United States began to step up her aid to Afghanistan and the country became one of the very few in the world to receive both American and Soviet large-scale aid. Both countries assign Afghanistan a high priority in their use of foreign aid as instruments of their foreign policies. The literature on the subject is abundant and there is no need to detail it here. Our concern is only with those projects directly related to Afghan transportation and foreign trade; i.e., with her access to the sea.

One of the primary emphases in the first five-year plan was the improvement of the country's still primitive transportation system. Pakistan was having similar problems. The originally inadequate transportation network of West Pakistan was reeling under the blows inflicted by partition and by her own, and later Afghanistan's, development programs. Accordingly, in 1957 Koebig and Koebig was asked by the United States International Cooperation Administration to survey the transportation facilities of Afghanistan and Pakistan. Among its conclusions and recommendations were the following:

2. A bilateral trade agreement between Pakistan and Afghanistan should be negotiated at the earliest possible date in order to insure the most efficient use of transportation facilities.

3. The highway from Spin Baldak to Kandahar in Afghanistan ... should receive an asphaltic road-mix pavement wide enough for two traffic lanes.

4. The road from Kandahar to Kabul in Afghanistan should be rebuilt to a width sufficient for two traffic lanes but with only one paved lane centered on the roadway ...

. . . .

6. The North Western Railway in Pakistan is generally over-loaded, especially with respect to those lines leading to the Afghan border. Improvement of the route from Karachi to Chaman via the westerly side of the Indus River would provide the shortest and most satisfactory route to Afghanistan and would serve to relieve the burden on many of the main lines of the railway. Afghanistan traffic on the long route from Karachi through Peshawar to the border near Landi Kotal should be kept to a minimum.

. . . .

8. The railroad should be extended across the Afghan border from Chaman to Spin Baldak. ... Terminal facilities should be provided on both sides of the border.

. . . .

11. Construction of railways in Afghanistan from Spin Baldak to Kandahar and from Kandahar to Kabul is not economically justifiable at this time or in the near future, and such construction would be a continuing burden on the Afghan people. [18]

The report also recommended many improvements in the West Pakistan railroad facilities and those of the port of Karachi.

This report touched off a massive road-building program in Afghanistan. Both the Soviets and Americans rushed in to cooperate with the Afghans and – oddly, perhaps – tacitly with one another. Both contestants in the waning Cold War met in Kabul, along with aid representatives of many other countries and international agencies, but outside the capital the Soviets concentrated their activities in the region between the Hindu Kush and the Soviet border, while the Americans discreetly stayed outside the Soviet "sphere of influence" and worked in the region from Herat around through the Helmand Basin and Kandahar to Kabul. During the next ten years over 2000 kilometers of all-weather road were constructed. [19] The most spectacular engineering feat, by far, was the construction of a 26-mile tunnel under the 11,000 foot Salang Pass through the Hindu Kush. It was completed by the Soviets in August 1964 as the key link in a new highway from Kabul to Doshi and from Doshi to Sher Khan Bandar (formerly Qizil Qala) on the Amu Darya, principal Afghan port for Soviet trade. The latter segment of the highway was

[18] Koebig and Koebig, *Report on Transportation Facilities of Afghanistan and Pakistan*, Los Angeles, October, 1957, pp. i–ii.

[19] *The Kabul Times Annual 1967*, p. 51.

completed in 1966. Since its opening the Salang Tunnel route has been handling 500–600 overloaded trucks a day, but it is difficult to maintain because of the heavy winter snowfalls. [20]

Americans have already completed a new road between Kandahar and Spin Baldak on the Pakistani border and nearly completed one from Herat to Islam Qala on the Iranian border. One of the earliest projects was the highway connecting Kabul with the Khyber Pass via Jalalabad and Tor Kham. The only section of the planned circumferential highway yet to be modernized is that from Herat to Mazar-i-Sharif. Construction is under way on the easternmost portion of this route, but it has a low priority and may not be completed for some time. Secondary roads through the mountainous interior of the country, particularly a new one between Kabul and Herat through the Hazarajat, are being planned or are under construction.

While roads have received top priority in the Afghan, Soviet and American programs, other modes of transportation have also received attention. After the Soviets improved the existing airport at Kabul, the Americans built a huge new international airport at Kandahar. While something of a prestige project and of little economic value right now, it still may prove valuable if air traffic between the U.S.S.R. and Pakistan and between Turkey and Iran and Pakistan increases as expected. Smaller airports have been built in other cities around the country. Also, at long last, the much-discussed railway extension from Chaman to Spin Baldak across the Afghan-Pakistani border is now under construction, ten years after it was urged by the Koebig and Koebig report of 1957. It is being financed by the United States.

The emphasis on transportation in the Afghan development programs is well justified on purely economic grounds. One observer puts it this way:

> If any single factor of the economy is to be named the main lever of intensified economic activity today, it is undoubtedly transport. Development of roads in recent years has lowered the cost of haulage, widened the market, made mining of coal and movement of labour easy and profitable, and has created an increasing demand for petroleum which again has led to exploitation [sic] for oil. Once the petroleum resources are developed with Russian aid, a transport revolution with a steady supply of petroleum will play somewhat the same role as the railways once played in many developed countries of today . . . [21]

[20] Louis Dupree, "Afghanistan: 1966," *AUFS Report,* July, 1966, p. 20.

[21] Amalendu Guha, "Economic Development of Afghanistan 1929–1961," *International Studies,* VI (April, 1965), p. 439.

But transport has political and strategic value as well, and these factors will be discussed in some detail in the next section.

Afghanistan's foreign trade has been discussed in general terms in the section on The Geographic Setting and more details will be included in the following section, Afghanistan's Access to the Sea. One aspect of her foreign trade, however, is important to discuss in this section on Soviet-American rivalry: the dramatic and immensely significant rise in Soviet-Afghan trade during the last fifteen years. Even discounting Afghan imports of Soviet and Eastern European development aid goods, barter trade with these countries has risen from virtually nil in 1951 to some 43% of her imports and about 28% of her exports. Perhaps more important than the volume of trade is its composition. The Soviet Union and Eastern Europe buy about 90% of Afghanistan's exports of raw cotton and about 80% of her wool exports; they supply some 80% of her petroleum imports, nearly 99% of her sugar imports, more than one quarter of her cotton textiles and nearly half of her motor vehicles. All of these imports and exports are staples not subject to wide fluctuations in demand or price.

The United States and her closest allies play a very different role in Afghan trade. True, the United States and the United Kingdom purchase virtually all of Afghanistan's Karakul exports and Britain and Germany buy nearly 90% of her carpets, but these are luxury products subject to unpredictable fluctuations in demand and increasing competition from other countries. They are difficult to control in quality and increase in supply. Moreover, Britain's total exports to Afghanistan amount to less than the value of Soviet sugar alone, while the most important American export to Afghanistan in 1965–66 was just over a million dollars worth of used clothing! [22]

Clearly it would be in Afganistan's best interests to diversify the products she exports and her trading partners as well. She is attempting to do the former, but there is no evidence that she is planning to open new markets for or find additional suppliers of those products which are so heavily traded with only one or two partners. Meanwhile, the Soviet Union is taking advantage of the situation. Not only is she making a net profit in her Afghan trade (about $ 24 million in 1964), but Afghanistan was virtually tied with Indonesia as the USSR's third most important trading partner in all of non-communist Asia behind India and Japan in 1964. [23] But again, more important than the volume of trade is its composition. As

[22] All figures derived from tables in *A Summary of Afghanistan's Foreign Trade in 1344 (March 21, 1965 through March 20, 1966).*

early as 1960 it was evident that the Soviets were using petroleum exports to Afghanistan as an important instrument of their foreign policy, as, indeed, they were doing elsewhere in the world as well. More than just exports are involved, however.

> To consolidate their position as petroleum suppliers, the Russians have constructed storage facilities at Mazar-i-Sharif, the Afghan highway center nearest to Termez on the Amu Darya, three additional depots (sometimes reported as pumping stations for a prospective pipeline) along the road from the river port of Khelif to Mazar-i-Sharif, and a larger tank farm on the outskirts of Kabul. At Qizil Qala [now Sher Khan Bandar] on the Amu Darya north of Kunduz, they have built a small river port complete with a floating pumping unit to unload oil from barges into the tank farm on the Afghan shore. Finally, Soviet petroleum products move from the railhead at Kushka south along a Soviet-improved road to Herat, where additional storage space is provided. Thus the only region in Afghanistan which now relies on petroleum from Pakistan is that around Kandahar in the south. [24]

The Soviets, however were not forcing anything on the Afghans; rather, they were helping Afghanistan to develop not only alternate transit routes to those through Pakistan, but also alternate trading partners in case of another border closure. Michel puts it this way:

> So long as Pakistan allows relatively unrestricted trade and transit, Afghanistan can maintain a desirable balance between suppliers of petroleum products and can reach her principal fruit markets in India . . . The net effect of Afghanistan's transit arrangements and closer trade relations with the Soviet Union has so far been quite beneficial and has undoubtedly improved Afghanistan's bargaining position, politically as well as economically. By developing an alternate source of petroleum products and manufactured goods, and alternate land and air routes to Europe, Afghanistan has been able to bring pressure on the West, and so on Pakistan, to keep open the routes to Karachi and to her Indian markets. Whether she will ultimately have to "pay the piper" remains to be seen. [25]

This policy did not work very well vis-a-vis Pakistan, since shortly after this article was published the Afghan-Pakistani border was closed again, this time for nearly two years. It did serve, however, to mitigate

[23] Daniel and Lois Dougan Tretiak, "Moscow's Trade with Asia," *Far Eastern Economic Review*, LI (February 3, 1966), p. 205. Original source of the Tretiaks' figures was Vneshniaia Torgovlia Soiuza SSR, Moscow 1965. Moscow made a greater profit only on her trade with India, of all the non-communist countries of Asia in 1964.

[24] Aloys A. Michel, "Foreign Trade and Foreign Policy in Afghanistan," *Middle Eastern Affairs*, XII (January, 1961), p. 12.

[25] *Ibid.*, p. 15.

the effects of the closure to some extent. It has also served to help maintain Afghanistan's traditional neutrality, the foundation of her foreign policy (and survival!), and keep her from getting entangled in the Soviet-American political and ideological struggle.[26] Since 1963, however, the balance has tended to shift too much toward the USSR and the Afghans have been trying to develop *another* alternate source of petroleum – Iran. It is certainly in Afghanistan's best interests to remain on good terms with all of her neighbors.

Afghanistan's Access to the Sea

While most of the great invasions and migrations entering Afghanistan through her long and tortured history have come from the west and northeast, these have also been the directions least favorable to Afghanistan's foreign trade. Long stretches of sparsely settled desert, barren mountains and bleak steppe lie between her and the sea in southwest and central Asia. These regions have had little to offer Afghanistan and could buy little from her. Transit through them is difficult, unpleasant and expensive and is likely to remain rare for many, many years. Most of Afghanistan's foreign trade has been routed through Karachi; indeed, in 1953–54 some 88% of it. The balance goes largely through the Soviet Union, with some at times moving through India or Iran.

Afghanistan's relations with China are cordial, but somewhat distant. The two countries have a common border of about fifty miles at the eastern extremity of the Wakhan Corridor, that geopolitical finger of mountainous territory tacked on to Afghanistan by the British and Russians to complete the kingdom's role as a buffer state between them. Other than that, however, they have little in common. They established diplomatic relations in 1955, exchanged visits of prime ministers in 1957, signed a treaty of friendship and non-agression in 1961 and a border treaty in 1963. The Chinese have been providing some technical assistance and may have some small political influence in Kabul, but the Afghans keep a close watch on the Chinese technicians administering China's $ 28 million development grant. Trade between the two countries is so minimal that it is lumped together in Afghan statistics under the heading of "other barter countries" – other than the USSR and Czechoslovakia. The Wakhan Corridor, moreover, is useless as a transit route. It has only primitive

[26] Afghanistan's neutrality has been preserved so well that, according to *The New York Times* of May 28, 1967, the Soviet and American aid missions there cooperate quietly and sometimes tell the Afghans to take the advice of the other.

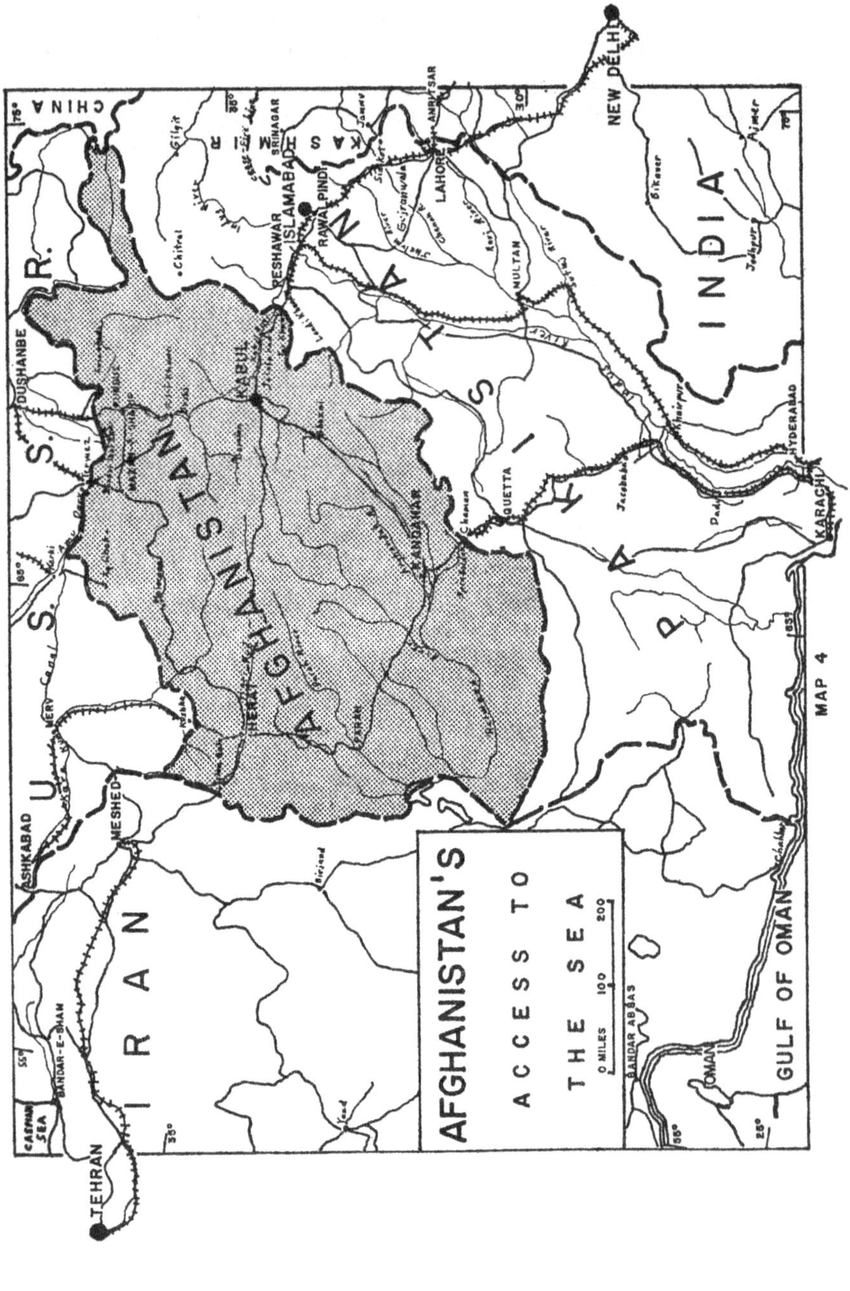
AFGHANISTAN'S
ACCESS TO
THE SEA
0 MILES 100 200
MAP 4
AFGHANISTAN
U.S.S.R.
CHINA
KASHMIR
PAKISTAN
INDIA
IRAN
CASPIAN SEA
GULF OF OMAN
OMAN
TEHRAN
BANDAR-E-SHAH
ASHKABAD
MESHED
MERV
DUSHANBE
HERAT
FARAH
KANDAHAR
KABUL
PESHAWAR
ISLAMABAD
RAWALPINDI
SRINAGAR
LAHORE
AMRITSAR
NEW DELHI
MULTAN
QUETTA
Chaman
HYDERABAD
KARACHI
BANDAR ABBAS

roads which are impassible for any wheeled vehicles in winter, and besides, it leads nowhere. China, for the present at least, may be discounted completely as an Afghan route to the sea.

Afghanistan has managed to remain on good terms with India, despite the former's evident sympathy for Pakistan in the Kashmir dispute. Before the partition of India in 1947, relations between the two countries were governed by the Treaty for the Establishment of Neighbourly Relations between the Government of Afghanistan and the British Government, dated 22 November 1921, and the Anglo-Afghan Trade Convention of June 1923. Neither dealt exclusively with transit, but both emphasized the principle of freedom of transit expressed in the recently adopted Barcelona Convention and Statute. The first treaty exempted most Afghan goods entering Indian ports from customs duties and specified customs clearance procedures. Routes between the ports and Afghanistan were also agreed upon, as well as procedures for inspection and sealing of goods in transit. The second treaty specified the transit routes and administrative procedures in more detail. After partition these treaties became the concern of independent India and Pakistan separately. It was soon found that they were completely inadequate for an Afghanistan which was resuming the process of economic development in a more intensive manner than before the Second World War. Peter Franck commented in 1949,

> Efforts have been made to remedy the worst problem facing Afghanistan's transit trade. The Afghan Trade Convention of 1923, providing that certain goods in transit across India to Afghanistan were not subject to the usual customs regulations, freed government goods required for public services from duties and other formalities. Goods imported for commercial purposes, however, were subject to duty and a series of bureaucratic requirements, although refunds were made in the case of goods transported over the regular routes. By means of this stipulation the Government of India apparently sought protection against shippers who might profit from disposing of their goods in India instead of sending them on to Afghanistan as planned. But this protective device, continued by the dominion governments of India and Pakistan, means that three to six months may elapse before the customs authorities refund the duties on transit goods. A similar regulation has been enacted in connection with goods leaving Afghanistan. [27]

In 1952 India and Afghanistan signed a Treaty of Friendship and Commerce which in Article 15 provided transit facilities for Afghanistan. These facilities were detailed in the Indo-Afghan trade agreement of June

[27] Peter G. Franck, "Problems of Economic Development in Afghanistan," *The Middle East Journal*, July, 1949, pp. 305–306.

1957, and in subsequent agreements in 1959 and 1962. These agreements included provisions for transit by air. In 1964 a new Indo-Afghan Trade Agreement was signed which was to be valid for one year and renewable for another two.

Trade between the two countries, however, rests on more than friendship and treaties, now that they have no common border. It rests also upon free transit across Pakistan. Since partition the railroad connecting Peshawar and the Afghan border with the Indian rail network at Amritsar has been used only sporadically due to the political differences between the subcontinental neighbors. In normal times this does not work a great hardship on Afghanistan, whatever the consequences for India and Pakistan. The Afghans prefer to ship by truck since highway transport between Kabul and Amritsar takes only-one-third as long as rail transport between Landi Khana and Amritsar and truck on the Afghan portion. Goods do not have to be trans-shipped or inspected enroute. The trucks are sealed in Afghanistan and only the seals are inspected in Pakistan. The most important highway used in Afghan transit across Pakistan to India is the old Grank Trunk Road which runs from Peshawar through Lahore and Delhi to Calcutta. Any Afghan goods in transit through India, however, use the port of Bombay. Aside from occasional shipments to or from Japan or other Far East points, this transit route, while available, is little used. Much more important is the trade between Afghanistan and India, for India buys about one quarter of Afghanistan's exports of fruits and nuts and is the source of one half of her cotton textiles and most of her tea.

India suffered so badly from the closure of the Afghan-Pakistani border in 1961–63 that an airlift was organized to exchange Afghan fruits for Indian textiles, tea, spices and machinery. This increased transport costs markedly and still depended on the tolerance of Pakistan, so it was manifestly a temporary expedient. In 1965, when Indian-Afghan trade was again disrupted, this time by the Pakistani-Indian fighting over Kashmir, the airlift was not repeated. After the fighting stopped, Pakistan permitted greatly restricted one-way truck traffic across the border into India. Apparently, since she was by now on better terms with Afghanistan, she did not object to Afghans selling fruit in India but did not want India to be exporting to Afghanistan. While the border was closed Afghan-Indian trade went through Bombay. The restrictions were lifted in July 1966 but they illustrate the tenuous nature of the highway route between India and Afghanistan.

While the histories of Iran and Afghanistan are intimately intertwined and there are many cultural bonds between them, political relations have only recently begun to warm noticably and there is still not much trade between them. The first hesitant step toward normal commercial relations was a barter agreement signed in June 1960. It provided for Iranian textiles, including velvets, to go to Afghanistan and in return Iran undertook to transship and sell overseas Afghan dried fruit. Another agreement was signed by the two countries later in the year which provided for some transit facilities and Afghan purchase of Iranian petroleum. The major agreement, however, is that signed on February 1, 1962 with a five year validity period.

This 1962 agreement was concluded during the longest of the Afghan-Pakistani border closures and the outside pressures on Iran and Afghanistan to reach agreement were considerable. The United States, particularly, urged it upon Iran, partly to provide a route for her aid shipments to Afghanistan which would bypass Karachi and partly to encourage better trade relations between the two monarchies and lessen the dependence of Afghanistan on the USSR both for petroleum and for the transit of her goods. Iran found it difficult to increase trade substantially, however, even after the agreement was signed.

> [B]ut small sales of petroleum soon began and by 1963, after much diligence on the Iranian side and meetings between the Shahs of Iran and Afghanistan, expansion in trade between the two countries was marked. Iran can supply Afghanistan with many goods it has been importing from elsewhere, such as tobacco products; trouble has recently been taken to improve the quality of Iranian cigarettes. The rupture of relations and the closure of the frontier between Afghanistan and Pakistan on 6th September 1961 helped to increase Irano-Afghan trade, although the Shah personally intervened to bring about better relations between Pakistan and the Afghan government. [28]

The 1962 agreement provided reciprocal free transit rights and warehouses and storage facilities for Afghan transit goods in Khorramshahr, Bandar Shahpur and Meshed. The main rail route for this transit trade is between Khorramshahr, at the head of the Persian Gulf, and Meshed. Goods must be hauled by truck over a poor road through very difficult terrain. The road now under construction between Herat and Islam Qala is supposed to be extended to Meshed, but construction in Iran is proceeding slowly and the road will probably not be completed for another two years. Meanwhile, the route between Khorramshahr and Afghanistan is both expensive and risky. The Iranian port of Bandar Abbas between

[28] Donald N. Wilber, *Contemporary Iran* (New York: Frederick A. Praeger, 1963), p. 491.

the Persian Gulf and the Arabian Sea has been used for Afghan transit trade at times, but it has inadequate port facilities and poor communications with the interior. Traffic using Bandar Abbas must go through Tehran enroute to or from Meshed, another difficult and expensive route. Iran is now favorably disposed toward developing the tiny port of Chahbar near the Pakistani border for Afghan transit trade and building a road northward to Afghanistan. It would not pay for itself, but it would help to open up a desolate part of Iran and, since Afghanistan would be the principal beneficiary, she might be willing to help pay for it. A railroad through eastern Iran is not even contemplated at this time. All in all, Iran provides a most unattractive and impractical outlet to the sea for Afghanistan, though it serves in emergencies and may improve in the future.

Trade between the Soviet Union and Afghanistan, as already noted, was minimal until after 1951. Afghan transit trade across Soviet territory, if there was any, was certainly negligible. In effect, article 6 of the Soviet-Afghan Friendship Treaty of February 1921 in which "Russia agrees to the unimpeded and customs-free transit through its territory of all categories of goods bought by Afghanistan either in Russia itself through government bodies, or directly abroad" [29] remained dormant.

After Soviet-Afghan trade began to grow and the USSR became interested in courting Afghanistan, the two countries signed a transit agreement. This agreement of June 1955 revived Article 6 of the 1921 treaty and greatly elaborated it. They extended most-favored-nation transit treatment to each other, waived customs duties for transit goods and made some provisions for expediting transit trade. The treaty was to have a five year duration. Three months later a one-year supplemental agreement between the state transit agencies of each country detailed the procedures for handling transit trade. (The agreement contained an automatic three-year extension clause.) This agreement specified Kushka and Termez as the ports of entry for Afghan exports, with transportation across the Amu Darya to the latter being provided by the Soviets. Goods were to be shipped from these cities by rail to appropriate ports – "Klaypeda, Batumy, Baku, etc." – and the Soviets agreed to perform numerous services in connection with the shipments. Similar treatment was to be accorded Afghan imports. Payments for services rendered were to be made in American dollars. Complete texts of these agreements may be found in Appendix III.

The 1955 treaty was extended in October 1960. The new treaty also

[29] ECAFE/I&T/Sub.4/2, p. 13.

included Soviet commitments to develop the port of Sher Khan Bandar and otherwise facilitate transport on the Amu Darya. In general, these and subsequent lesser agreements have been quite favorable to Afghanistan, and Afghan goods in transit through the USSR increased 77% between 1959 and 1961.[30] The most recent renewal and amplification of the 1955 treaty was signed in 1964. A number of trade agreements between the two countries have also been favorable to Afghanistan, offering that country assured markets and short-term credits.

Louis Dupree, however, points out that the Soviets manage to make a little something besides political gains on these arrangements:

> When an item crosses the Afghan frontier from the USSR, the Soviets immediately telegraph Kabul and order the Afghans to debit the proper account. Accounting for goods moving in the opposite direction is more casual. Weeks and even months may pass between the time an Afghan export item crosses the Amu Darya and the Soviets acknowledge receipt. Afghan merchants have told me the Russians sometimes offer one price in Kabul but actually pay another, lower one, after receipt of the goods . . .[31]

There are other problems connected with the physical movement of goods to or from Afghanistan through the USSR. The Amu Darya is not yet crossed by a bridge and the use of ferries across the river entails at least three transshipments between Soviet trains and Afghan trucks and vice-versa. Within Soviet Central Asia, the railway system is overburdened, partly because the physical geography of the region offers few feasible exit routes (through Krasnovodsk, Tashkent-Orenburg and the Turksib Railway) and the rail system handles 80%–85% of the long-distance traffic. Some new railroads have been built in the region in recent years but they have not yet solved the problem. Even the waterways between the Aral Sea and the Black Sea are underutilized.[32]

The second reason for the inadequacy of the transport system in Soviet Central Asia is the rapid economic development taking place there in recent years. Irrigated agriculture has become very important, especially cotton culture.

[30] V. G. Kukhtin, "Problema tranzita v ekonomike i politike Afganistana", in Akademiia Nauk SSSR, Institut Narodov Azii, *Voprosy ekonomiki Afganistana* (Moscow: Izadelstvo vostochnoi literatury, 1963), p. 54.

[31] Louis Dupree, " 'Pushtunistan,' " Part III, *AUFS Report,* December, 1961, pp. 3–4.

[32] V. F. Pavlenko, "The Transport-Geography Situation and Inter-Regional Links of Central Asia," *Geografiya i Khozyaystvo,* no. 12 (1963), in *Soviet Geography: Review and Translation,* IV (November 1963).

> The policy of regional specialization on cotton has put considerable strain on the existing railway links with the rest of Russia, which traverse long stretches of commercially unresponsive country and have occasioned considerable problems of excessive coal use and of water deficiency ... Middle Asia is probably more dependent on its railways than any other Soviet region, in a country where the railway is still dominant. [33]

Some hope for relieving the burden on the rail system is focused on the Kara Kum Canal which will connect Kerki on the Amu Darya with Krasnovodsk on the Caspian Sea. In theory, both Soviet and Afghan goods could then travel the entire distance between the Amu Darya and the Black Sea by water. This may not prove feasible, however, not only because of the distance, and hence time, involved, but also because the third and final stage of the canal project is not due for completion until about 1980 and by that time better routes should be available. [34] In addition, the Amu Darya itself is barely navigable because so much water is being removed from it by evaporation and by Afghan and especially Soviet irrigation projects. Irrigation is likely to increase and any projects to improve navigation on the river will be very expensive and probably uneconomic.

Increasing trade with and transit through the Soviet Union has also wrought changes on the Afghan side of the border. Mazar-i-Sharif since the 1930's has been the principal link between Kabul and the Soviet Union and the transit trade since the early 1950's has become very important in the city's economy. Since the Salang Pass route was opened, however, Sher Khan Bandar is becoming the main Afghan river port and Mazar is being increasingly bypassed. The nearby natural gas fields, though, are proving a new boon to the ancient Karakul-trading town. Large gas pipelines lead into the Soviet Union and to the thermal power and chemical fertilizer plants in Mazar. Ak Chah, another ancient town and terminus of a caravan route to Kelif on the Soviet bank of the Amu, has been languishing in recent years with declining traffic on that route. It may be due for a revival, however, as new highways open up nearby mineral deposits for Afghan exploitation. The Soviet Union would seem the most logical market for some of the production, at least, and Kelif may again become an important transit outlet for Afghanistan.

[33] David J. M. Hooson, *The Soviet Union* (London: University of London Press Ltd., 1966), p. 285.

[34] A good article by I. A. Kuznetsov, with map, on this canal scheme may be found in Akademiia Nauk SSSR, Sovet po Problemam Vodnogo Khoziaistva, *Upravlenie Poverkhnostnymi i Podzemnymi Vodnymi Resursami i ikh Ispolzovanie* (Moskva: Izdatelstvo Akademii Nauk SSSR, 1961).

Afghanistan's principal outlet to the sea has always been, continues to be, and shall for a long time to come be the port of Karachi in West Pakistan. Though this is Afghanistan's traditional and natural route to the sea, it has not, as we have seen, been a very free or secure one. It is vulnerable to both physical limitations and political impediments. The acutely hazardous nature of Afghanistan's land-locked status became evident as early as 1949 when Peter Franck observed,

> Afghanistan's most immediate and acute trade difficulty is its lack of direct access to the sea. All external trade has to go across Pakistan and sometimes India. Karachi's inadequate harbor facilities must often be supplemented by those of Bombay, 500 miles further away from the Peshawar railroad. Overland transportation facilities between the Afghan border and Karachi are badly overtaxed; roads are narrow and long, and the railroads slow and continuously in need of repair. Traffic on both is handicapped by shortages of cars, gasoline and spare parts. [35]

The subsequent closures of the border in 1950 and 1955 only illustrated Franck's point, for the physical problems were compounded by political ones. He was able to observe the situation shortly thereafter and described it this way:

> The growing political difficulties with Pakistan resulting from the latter's administrative incorporation of the North West Frontier Province into a unified West Pakistan State early in 1955, led to a new interruption of transit trade which not only cut off the vital imports of petroleum products and machinery for the various development projects but also interfered seriously with export shipments of fruit and furs . . . [36]
>
> As a result of the recurrent political strife with Pakistan, Afghanistan's age-old dreams of a free zone in the port of Karachi have collapsed. Moreover, the Afghanistan government has come to realize that little support can be expected from the United States in relation to Pakistan. [37]

The Afghans, while sorely distressed at this disruption in their normal trade, look back on it now in a rather different light. A high Afghan official considers, for example, that the 1955 closure was "a blessing in disguise" because it led to closer relations with both the Soviet Union and other "nonaligned" states, thus lessening Afghanistan's dependence upon Pakistan and her ally, the United States. The Soviets, he feels, saved his

[35] Franck, *op. cit.*, p. 305.

[36] Peter G. Franck, "Economic Progress in an Encircled Land," *The Middle East Journal*, X, Winter 1956, p. 54.

[37] *Ibid.*, p. 58.

country from "a Pakistani plot to isolate Afghanistan." [38] Be that as it may, Pakistan was still vital to Afghanistan. The United States, moreover, was concerned about Afghanistan's gravitation toward the Soviets and pressured the two sides into signing a transit agreement in May 1958. The Americans turned the trick by promising funds for improvements in the port facilities of Karachi, the Pakistani railways, border transfer points and Afghan roads. [39] This was the first step also, as mentioned before, in implementation of the recommendations of the 1957 Koebig and Koebig report. It also followed soon after ECAFE's first consideration of the problems of Asian land-locked states, on Afghanistan's initiative.

The 1958 Afghan-Pakistani transit agreement provided for free transit through Pakistan; exemption from customs duties, taxes and charges of all kinds except for administrative and transportation charges; simplified, priority shipment arrangements; and improved rail facilities. It was not long, however, before this agreement lost its value, at least temporarily, as the border between the two neighbors was closed between September 1961 and July 1963.

This most serious interruption in Afghanistan's transit trade was very damaging to all parties.

Louis Dupree reported after the 1961 border closure, describing the large quantities of United States aid goods piled up in Pakistan. "In addition," he said,

> the Peshawar Chamber of Commerce recently complained to the Pakistan government about the adverse local economic effects of the border closing, and the Pakistan Minister of Commerce in Rawalpindi, now generally concerned, plans to issue statistics soon to indicate how much each country has suffered . . .
>
> Several UN efforts, especially the malaria eradication program of WHO, were initially endangered, but the UN recently agreed to ship its future project supplies through the Soviet Union. [40]
>
> Obviously United States aid programs in Afghanistan must be carefully re-examined in the light of the border situation, and the fate of each project determined by the feasibility of completion without excessive extra expense. When United States officials confront Afghan officials with this problem, the Afghans, sometimes, accuse the Americans of trying to exert pressure on them to re-open the border by threatening to terminate Agency for International Development (AID) programs. This Afghan attitude tends to anger

[38] Interview with Dr. A. G. Ravan Fahardi, Director General for Political Affairs, Royal Afghan Foreign Ministry, July 5, 1967. The Afghans were greatly impressed by the Soviet airlift of their grape crop, discussed earlier in this chapter.

[39] Michel, *op. cit.*, p. 9.

[40] Dupree, " 'Pushtunistan,' " Part II, p. 3.

the Americans who are genuinely trying to find ways to help Afghanistan continue its development in spite of the difficulties posed by the Afghans' unilateral closure of the border. [41]

In addition to this, the Indian airlift, discussed above, added to the airlift of Karakul skins to Beirut for transshipment to New York and London, increased Afghanistan's costs considerably. Another embarrassment was some 500,000 Afghan Powindahs (nomads) who, for the first time in history, were prevented from crossing into Pakistan for winter pastures. Thousands of animals, deprived of pasture, had to be slaughtered, and during the early months of the border closure there were armed clashes between Afghan and Pakistani herdsmen. Also, many Afghan migrant workers could no longer provide their labor when it was needed in Pakistan, nor send home the money they would have earned there.

After the border was reopened, relations between Afghanistan and Pakistan began to improve. This was undoubtedly due largely to the retirement of Mohammed Daoud from active Afghan political life and the consequent muting of the Pushtunistan claim, but partly also to Afghanistan's better bargaining position as a result of her stronger ties with Iran and the Soviet Union. Undoubtedly other factors were the realization even in Pakistan that when transit trade through Pakistan ceases, everyone suffers (except the Soviets, not yet friends of the Pakistanis), and also the growing concern of the world community as evidenced at the Law of the Sea Conference in 1958 and subsequent ECAFE meetings. At any rate, the 1958 transit agreement was extended for one year in 1964. In the same year Pakistan undertook to build the long-projected Chaman-Spin Baldak rail extension. Also, Kabul-Peshawar air service and direct Afghanistan-Pakistan telephone service were inaugurated.

In March 1965 the two countries signed a new five-year transit agreement. It provided for some additional transit facilities, consideration of an extension of the railroad from the Pakistani railhead at Landi Khana through the Khyber Pass to Tor Kham, and commitments to meet and consult once a year to review the working of the agreement and to submit disputes over its interpretation to arbitration. An annex and a protocol to the Agreement spelled out in considerable detail the actual procedures for handling transit goods. The entire arrangement was, of course, reciprocal. (See Appendix IV for complete texts of these agreements.) Afghanistan had wanted at least a ten-year agreement and still other concessions, but Pakistan was awaiting the results of the United Nations

[41] *Ibid.*, p. 10.

Conference on Transit Trade of Land-locked Countries which was to open in June.

At that Conference, Afghanistan avoided lodging any complaints against Pakistan and the Afghan delegate at one point even said that

> [h]e sincerely hoped that that process of consultation between the two countries, which historically had much in common, would exemplify the way in which the problems of land-locked and transit States could be resolved to the satisfaction of both parties. [42]

Dr. Fahardi says now that Afghanistan is satisfied with the Convention produced by the Conference except for one article. For that reason, she signed the Convention but may not ratify it. Pakistan has as yet neither signed nor acceded to it. Afghanistan has no serious complaints about her access to the sea at present, except for some railroad bottlenecks. As a matter of fact, according to Dr. Fahardi, if there continues to be good co-operation between Afghanistan and Pakistan there will be no more need for the long-sought free port for Afghanistan in Karachi. It is better for Afghan traffic to receive "national treatment." He feels that free ports have lost their meaning in today's world.

There are some problems, however. There are insufficient railway wagons in Pakistan and, since Pakistani defense and food transport have prior claim on existing facilities, Afghan goods pile up in warehouses in Karachi. Also, Afghanistan still wants the railroad extended through the Khyber Pass, but both Pakistan and the United States, which would probably pay for such a project, feel it would not be economic. Another factor is that truck haulage through the pass is a monopoly of Pathan tribesmen, whom both Pakistan and Afghanistan want to keep happy.

Rail facilities within West Pakistan are, without doubt, still inadequate. During the Second World War the Indian rail system deteriorated badly onder the impact of extraordinary demands and only the skimpiest maintenance and repair. Before it could recuperate, the network was divided, with only two of the seven railway groups, the North Western Railway and the East Bengal Railway, going to the new state of Pakistan. Increasing traffic, inadequate capital and a truncated system have combined to cause further deterioration. In addition to all this, both the rail and road systems in West Pakistan were designed for military and strategic purposes and ill serve commercial needs. Pakistan has been trying hard to improve the situation, but it is still not good.

Pakistan has found Afghan transit trade to be profitable and is trying

[42] TD/TRANSIT/SR.13, p. 9.

to encourage it. This transit trade has helped make the reorganized Pakistan Western Railway, operated by the provincial government, a profitable enterprise. She has provided for this traffic two sheds in the port of Karachi and another for storage in Peshawar. One persistent problem is smuggling of goods bound for Afghanistan into Pakistan, particularly from Landi Kotal, near the Khyber Pass. The Pakistani government does not enforce the smuggling laws in this tribal area and the smugglers have developed a very efficient and reliable delivery system for all kinds of foreign goods. This not only injures both the Afghan and Pakistani economies, but diminishes the value of trade statistics. Smuggling is estimated to amount to some $ 6 to $ 10 million annually. [43]

While Afghan transit trade is moving through Pakistan without serious interruption, it must be noted that it continues to be based on short-term bilateral agreements which must be renegotiated frequently. It depends also on good relations between the two countries. These obtain at present but there is no assurance that they will indefinitely, for the Pushtunistan issue, while quiescent, is not yet dead.

Afghanistan, Pakistan and Pushtunistan

Of all the colorful and romantic regions of the old European empires, few were more so in the popular mind than the North-West Frontier Province of India. But this remote marchland was not very romantic to those living there. To the British it was their first line of defense against the wild nomadic peoples who had many times before swept out of the deserts and mountains of Central Asia through the Gumal, Boland, Khyber and other passes into the fertile Indus Valley below. To the scores of tribes living there, most of them Pushtus, it was home, and "home" meant the whole region from the Hindu Kush to the Indus and beyond into Kashmir. Their homeland had been artificially divided by the Durand Line, but they paid little attention to lines drawn on paper by foreigners. They roamed more or less freely back and forth across the line, visiting, trading, raiding or, most commonly, practicing transhumance. The British, ever conscious of strategic considerations yet devoted to the principle of indirect rule where feasible, maintained strong garrisons at Peshawar and smaller ones in other towns and attempted to police the region in a general way while granting the local people a large measure of local autonomy

[43] Interview with Mr. Muhajid Husain, Vice Consul at the Pakistani Consulate General in New York, July 6, 1967. Additional details on smuggling in this area may be found in *The New York Times* for March 3, 1968.

and administering them rather loosely. They distinguished between the "tribal areas" in the mountains, the true frontier region, and the "settled districts" in the valleys and lower hills, occupied by closely related peoples who had settled down to agriculture and village life.

The Durand Line was unquestionably an arbitrary one, making no sense geographically, economically or ethnically. It was a strategic and administrative line and no more. Significantly,

> [t]he ethnic boundary of the Southwest Asian realm, as contrasted to the distinctively South Asian (or Indian) realm, lies between the Indus River and the foot of the mountains rather than at the mountain crests. Indeed, the North-west Frontier and Baluchistan could as well be part of Afghanistan or some southwest Asian state, were it not for the extension of British political power here in the nineteenth century. [44]

When this British power was about to be removed in 1947, a Pushtu leader from the North-West Frontier, Abdul Ghaffar Khan, began agitating for accession neither to India nor to Pakistan, but for the independence of the frontier as Pushtunistan. A referendum was held in the area and the voters chose to accede to Pakistan. Afghans and Pushtu nationalists denounce the referendum as having offered "no more than a Hobson's Choice," being held "on religious preferences," and "that even this limited and misled referendum was held in a state of hurried secrecy and public coercion." [45] Afghanistan in 1947 cast the only vote in the United Nations against Pakistan's admission, solely because of the Pushtunistan issue.

Ghaffar Khan and others continued their agitation and in 1949 Afghanistan joined the fray officially and strongly, backing the demand for an independent Pushtunistan – one which would be carved only out of Pakistani and not Afghan territory. Relations deteriorated rapidly with Pakistan, which had no intention of giving up any portion of her national territory, and certainly not such a strategic part. Worsening relations led to the border closing in 1950, after which the campaign, which had become almost exclusively an Afghan one, intensified rather than subsided. It continued with varying degrees of intensity through the 1950's, punctuated by another border closing in 1955, an Afghan raid on the Pakistani Embassy in Kabul in 1956, and armed clashes in the Bajaur area of the Frontier in September 1960 and March 1961. It was capped by the 1961–63 border closure and the retirement of Prime Minister Sardar

[44] Norton Ginsburg, ed. *The Pattern of Asia* (Englewood Cliffs, New Jersey: Prentice-Hall, Inc., 1958), p. 643.

[45] Rahman Pazhwak, *An Article on Pakhtunistan; A New State in Central Asia* (London: Royal Afghan Embassy, 1960), p. 24.

Mohammed Daoud in Kabul. Antagonism over the Pushtunistan issue and the intertwined matter of Afghan access to the port of Karachi grew so bitter that both the Shah of Iran personally and President Kennedy of the United States through Ambassador Livingston Merchant tried to mediate.

After the border was reopened and diplomatic relations were resumed in 1963, the Afghans decided to separate the two questions – Pushtunistan and their access to the sea – and they have remained separate ever since. This has pleased the Pakistanis, who are quite willing to discuss the one but completely reject the other. The Afghan propaganda campaign subsided, but did not expire. The demand for an independent Pushtunistan, whatever its borders, was downgraded to a demand for autonomy for the Pakistani Pushtus. Some extremists on both sides of the Durand Line continued to agitate for independence, but little has been heard of this in recent years. "In the concluding session of the Loya Jirga of 1964," for example,

> the government's policy regarding Pashtunistan received endorsement. The mild statement of continued (and "unchangeable") support for the people of Pashtunistan revealed its true significance in the phrase "we await the day" when the issue will be settled according to the wishes of the people of Pashtunistan. [46]

By the summer of 1966 even that battle-scarred agitator Abdul Ghaffar Khan was reduced to saying in an interview in Kabul only that "he would urge [President Mohammed] Ayub [of Pakistan] to take action to give Pakhtoons autonomy within Pakistan 'without further delay.' " [47] On August 24, 1966 Afghan Prime Minister Mohammad Hashim Maiwandwal delivered a major policy speech over Radio Afghanistan. His only reference to the Pushtunistan question was,

> Afghanistan's peaceful efforts for attaining the right of self-determination of our Pakhtunistani brethren must firmly be continued and efforts be made to create an atmosphere of understanding, confidence and realism in order to pave the way for the solution of this problem, itself a remnant of colonialism, and thereby fulfill the sincere wishes of the leaders and progressive elements of Pakhtunistan. [48]

It is evident that the fiery demands for an independent Pushtunistan and bitter denunciations of the British and Pakistanis, so prevalent in the

[46] Theodore S. Gochenour, "A New Try for Afghanistan," *The Middle East Journal*, XIX (Winter 1965), p. 18.

[47] *The Times of India*, reported in *The Asian Recorder* for 20–26 August 1966.

[48] *The Kabul Times Annual 1967*, p. XXVI.

1950's, have been replaced by mild expressions of concern and suggestions for self-determination. But two questions remain: Why did Afghanistan pursue the issue so vigorously in the first place and why has Pakistan resisted even another referendum so firmly? No answer to the first question is readily available, but a few varying views might be helpful.

One of Afghanistan's most diligent propagandists on the Pushtunistan issue has been Abdul Rahman Pazhwak, leader of the Afghan delegation in the UNCTAD Committee on Preparation of a Draft Convention Relating to Transit Trade of Land-locked Countries in 1964, and President of the United Nations General Assembly 1966–67. While serving in the Afghan Embassy in London during the 1950's and early '60's, he turned out numerous pamphlets, books, press releases, etc. Here is a sample written in 1960, during one of the more intense periods of agitation:

> The present struggle of the people of Pakhtunistan is but a continuation of their fight against the British, with the same purpose and the same logic . . . [T]hey have always struggled for their independence against each and every invader who has encroached upon their liberty . . . [49]

He denies the validity of the concept of state succession (e.g. Pakistan succeding Britain in a legal sense), labels the status of "Pakhtunistan" during the British period as "that of a Protectorate," and insists that the artificial Durand Line "did not in any way alter the national integrity of the people of Pakhtunistan, nor did it make Pakhtunistan an integral part of the British Indian Empire." [50]

A Pakistani scholar, in discussing "Afghanistan's Frontier Policy," speculates that "a friendly or subservient Pakhtoonistan would enable Afghanistan to use the Indus river, but even then the river would be useless as long as Peshawar in the north and Karachi in the south remain in Pakistan, and can block Afghanistan's foreign trade." [51] Some support for this thesis is lent by early Afghan claims for a Pushtunistan that would include all of Baluchistan as well as the North-West Frontier; i.e., all of Pakistan west of Kashmir and the Indus. (See Map 3.) Since this claim was very weak on ethnic grounds and outrageous in even suggesting that Pakistan would surrender half of her national territory and population and such major cities as Peshawar and the then capital, Karachi, it did not long survive the political wars. It was simply too transparent an attempt

[49] Pazhwak, *op. cit.*, pp. 19–20.

[50] *Ibid.*, p. 26.

[51] Ali Tayyeb, *Pakistan: A Political Geography* (London: Oxford University Press, 1966), p. 196.

to obtain "a free and sceure access to the sea" at the expense of another state's territorial integrity (and probably existence). Moreover, as Pakistan survived her first few years, to the astonishment of many, it became clear that she simply would not permit herself to be partitioned between India and Afghanistan.

Suspicion of Afghan motives remained strong, however. The same Pakistani scholar reviews examples of Afghan expansionism, including "repeated attempts to rule the Indian plains," and asserts that in the nineteenth century she was squeezed between "the overwhelming power of Russia and Britain." She tried again when Pakistan (weak) succeeded Britain (strong) as ruler of the Indus Valley.

> The absence of a definite natural boundary and the unwillingness to accept the legality of the transfer of the Durand Line to Pakistan, provides the necessary excuse and the opportunity [to descend again upon the plain] which Afghanistan finds it difficult to relinquish. [52]

This view is widely at variance with the popular notion of Afghanistan as a weak buffer state owing its existence solely to an understanding between Russia and Britain. It does have some substance, however, and is shared by Fraser-Tytler, whose opinion of the Afghans opened this chapter. He strongly opposes the whole idea of a Pushtunistan and feels instead that the tribes of the Frontier are

> an anachronism and a danger to the stability of northern India and the peace of Central Asia. The remedy is the fusion of the two states of Afghanistan and Pakistan in some way or other . . . history suggests that fusion *will* take place, if not peaceably, then by force. [53]

An American view of the Pushtunistan issue was expressed in 1959 by the present desk officer for Afghanistan in the United States Department of State:

> Afghan interest in the Frontier area flows from two factors. From the standpoint of the men who rule in Kabul, both are pertinent and legitimate. First, the Frontier is in a sense "Afghanistan irredenta." Second, the Pukhtun tribes constitute a source of power which can and has made and unmade Afghan governments. The two elements are closely interrelated in the minds of many Afghans and have in recent years been combined and elaborated in the "Pukhtunistan" movement. "Pukhtunistan," however, is less an end than an instrument. [54]

[52] *Ibid.*, p. 197.

[53] Fraser-Tytler, *op. cit.*, p. 300.

[54] James W. Spain, *Pakistan's North-West Frontier: Political Problems of a Borderland,* (unpublished Ph. D. dissertation, Columbia University, 1959), p. 355.

> While the break-up [of Pakistan] has not occurred, Afghan enthusiasm for Pukhtunistan has to a considerable degree waxed and waned as Pakistan's stability has deteriorated or improved. Even now, "Pukhtunistan" remains as the most useful and practical depository for Afghan irredentist feelings. In addition, of course, it serves as an effective instrument for countering Pakistani pressure on Kabul over the whole gamut of mutual relations. Above all, it has to some degree diverted the attention of the border tribes from objectives within Afghanistan.[55]

This reference to the Pushtunistan issue being due to domestic politics is by no means unique. Indeed,

> some observers believe that the Afghan claim to Pakhtunistan is for purely internal factors. The present rulers belong to the Yahya Khel family of the Durranis which ruled over Peshawar during the Sikh period . . . Furthermore, by bringing more Pathans under their sway the Afghan rulers may hope to strenghthen the Pashto speaking element . . .[56]

Whatever the reasons for the Afghan drive for a Pushtunistan, it has been checked by Pakistan's determined resistance. The reasons for this resistance are clear. The strategic value of the Frontier region has already been discussed, and that alone would make it worth retaining. But there is also reason to believe that, while development has barely begun, the region has considerable economic potential. The Vale of Peshawar is a prosperous agricultural area, "the most intensively cultivated tract in all of West Pakistan."[57] Other areas are also under irrigation agriculture and the Pakistani government has undertaken irrigation and power projects on the Kurrum, Warsak and Gomal Rivers to enrich the land still further. West Pakistan is very poor in minerals and those that do exist are generally remote and difficult to exploit. Still, iron near Chitral and coal north of Quetta have been commercially mined and other minerals may be discovered with more intensive exploration.

More important than economics, however, is the fact that Pathans play an important role in the life of Pakistan. They have long been a dynamic people and diffused far and wide among the other peoples of West Pakistan, Kashmir and northern India. Ali Tayyeb calls the North-West Frontier Province "the most prominent rival of the Punjab!" He says that it resisted partition of India, but

> once the decision was taken, the Frontier Province showed a greater enthusiasm for Pakistan, and has made more rapid economic progress and main-

[55] *Ibid.*, pp. 363–364.

[56] Zubeida Hasan, "The Foreign Policy of Afghanistan," *Pakistan Horizon*, XVII (First Quarter, 1964), p. 56.

[57] Ginsburg, *op. cit.*, p. 647.

tained a more stable government than any other province of the country, thus producing a feeling of envy, especially in the Punjab. [58]

This progress has been the result not only of the Pathans' own ambitions and abilities, but of a deliberate policy of the Pakistani government. After achieving independence, Pakistan did not follow the British practice of stationing regular army troops in the Frontier area. Instead, she relied on local militia, police and scouts to provide security and internal order. She also encouraged Pathans to join the army of Pakistan. This display of confidence in the people helped to win their confidence in the government. Not only was an effort made to improve the economy of the region, thus enabling the Pathans to settle down and improve their living standards without resorting to brigandage, but a drive was undertaken to integrate both the region and the people into the country as a whole. In 1955, for example, as part of a move to improve administration and more nearly match the weight of East Pakistan, all of the provinces, states, districts and agencies in western Pakistan, including the Frontier, were merged into one province of West Pakistan. This provoked the Afghans, but helped the Pathans. Shortly after assuming power in 1958, Marshal Mohammed Ayub Khan transferred the capital from Karachi provisionally to Rawalpindi pending completion of a new capital nearby to be called Islamabad. This was done for a variety of reasons unrelated to Pushtunistan, but it did bring the center of power closer to the Pathans and heighten their sense of identification with Pakistan. Today, not only is much of the trade and industry of West Pakistan in the hands of Pathans, but the Commander-in-Chief of the army and many other commanders, the Governor of West Pakistan, the Minister for Railways and Communications and President Ayub Khan himself are Pathans, and even most of the pilots in the harbor of Karachi!

Finally, it must be noted that Pakistan, like India, is trying to weld a nation-state out of a widely varied group of peoples who have nothing more in common than religion and even here there are minority groups. To surrender the Pathans of the Frontier, or even to give them a large degree of autonomy, would be an admission of failure to assimilate them into the Pakistani society. More than that, it would set an example for many tribal groups in Baluchistan and in the East Wing of Pakistan, where there is already a strong separatist feeling, and could lead to the disintegration of Pakistan. For all these reasons, then, Pakistan is not likely to concede any kind of Pushtunistan, regardless of continued Afghan support for it.

[58] Tayyeb, *op. cit.*, p. 177.

A new situation is developing, however, which might induce Pakistan to make other concessions to Afghanistan, particularly in regard to her access to the sea. The growth of the Afghan economy is unquestionably dependent on free transit through Pakistan. As Johannes Humlum puts it,

> The future of the Helmand Valley project... depends absolutely on the free export and import of merchandise through Pakistan. Afghanistan, in the long run, will not be able to exist without maintaining good relations with Pakistan, master of the maritime exits of the country. Karachi is the natural port of Afghanistan and will remain so, even if new railroads in years to come make import and export possible through Persian Gulf ports. [59]

At the same time, however, this very growth of the Afghan economy is of great present and potential value to Pakistan. The Koebig and Koebig report of 1957 included this comment:

> Although the geographic location of Afghanistan obviously demands the willing cooperation of Pakistan in order to attain complete freedom of trade and communication, it should be noted that Afghanistan prosperity most certainly will stimulate the economy of Pakistan. A ready market for quality agricultural products of Afghanistan is available now in Pakistan. It is expected that future mineral exploration and development in Afghanistan will provide much needed raw materials for the growing heavy and light industry of Pakistan. In turn, Pakistan manufactures of all types, including construction materials, may be distributed in Afghanistan, to the mutual benefit of both countries. Transit shipment to and from Afghanistan, if completed promptly, will earn additional hauling revenues for the Pakistan railways as well as service and handling charges for Karachi port. [60]

The validity of both of these statements was amply demonstrated during the unfortunate border closure of 1961–63; they are certainly no less true today. Pakistan is now Afghanistan's fourth best customer for all exports and her principal market for fresh fruits and oilseeds, while Afghanistan is an important purchaser of a wide variety of Pakistani products, particularly cotton textiles and manufactured consumer goods.

The growing interdependence of Pakistan and Afghanistan is illustrated by another new factor: Afghanistan is once again becoming a crossroads of commerce, a transit state herself. Fraser-Tytler predicted that with the development of Soviet Central Asia, the USSR would demand access to the Arabian Sea. He suggested a railroad from the Soviet railhead at Kushka through Herat and Kandahar to Chaman, a geographically easy

[59] Johannes Humlum, *La Géographie de l'Afghanistan* (Copenhagen: Gyldendal, 1959), p. 357. This is the best geography of Afghanistan in any language, a very fine and useful work.

[60] Koebig and Koebig Report, pp. 1–2.

route. The railroad idea, as we have seen, has been rejected, but the Soviets are, indeed, interested in access to the Arabian Sea. As early as 1964 they and Pakistanis began discussing reopening of the ancient Silk Road through Afghanistan. In February 1966 they reached agreement on it and in one test run, trucks carrying fresh and dried fruit from West Pakistan reached Tashkent in ten days.

Apparently final arrangements are being held up by an argument over whose trucks should be used. Both the Pakistanis and Afghans are insisting on using their own.[61] Thus, Afghanistan is able to exercise some leverage of her own in transit matters. If this route does develop, and it should, spurred as it is by the closure of the Suez Canal, Pakistan's dependence on Afghanistan will be increased. The two countries will have even more reason to forget Pushtunistan and live together in peace. Afghanistan should have no concern about her access to the sea.

[61] *The Christian Science Monitor,* November 9, 1967. The same article also carried further details of a story reported in *The Times* of London on May 13, 1966 about Pakistan and China reopening another portion of the Silk Road between Gilgit and Sinkiang through Hunza, near what was to have been part of Pushtunistan.

CHAPTER IV

BOLIVIA

> Bolivia is a weak state. Of all the countries in Latin America, Bolivia has the smallest proportion of agricultural land to total area (0.3 per cent), and the largest proportion of the total national territory outside of the effective territory. It has only 0.2 of an acre of crop land per person. A larger proportion of its population is illiterate (69 per cent) than of any other Latin American country except Haiti. Furthermore, the Bolivian population is arranged in scattered small units of settlement, isolated from one another and from the outside world by physical barriers . . .
>
> The internal force by which a state might be enabled to expand across such physical barriers is lacking in Bolivia. Like Ecuador and Peru, this state is burdened by the problems arising from the presence of incompatible racial and cultural groups, the Spaniards and the Indians . . . Among all these diverse elements the Bolivian state has never been able to develop any strong sense of political coherence . . . [1]

These and other fundamental geographic factors have directly influenced the history of Bolivia, from pre-Inca times to the present. They are still of paramount importance to a Bolivia which is striving, for the first time in its history, to strengthen its internal bonds and develop a "strong sense of political coherence." Bolivia is still a weak state, and this weakness has caused her to strike out in bitterness and frustration at her neighbors. She struck militarily at Paraguay in the Chaco War (1932–35) in an effort to acquire frontage on the navigable Paraguay and Paraná Rivers. Since 1910 she has been striking politically at Chile. Her primary goal has been to obtain an outlet to the sea, though she has never defined what she means by this term.

The Geographic Setting

Bolivia has an area of over 400,000 square miles located in the heart of

[1] Preston E. James, *Latin America* (3rd ed. rev.; New York: The Odyssey Press, 1959), p. 205–206.

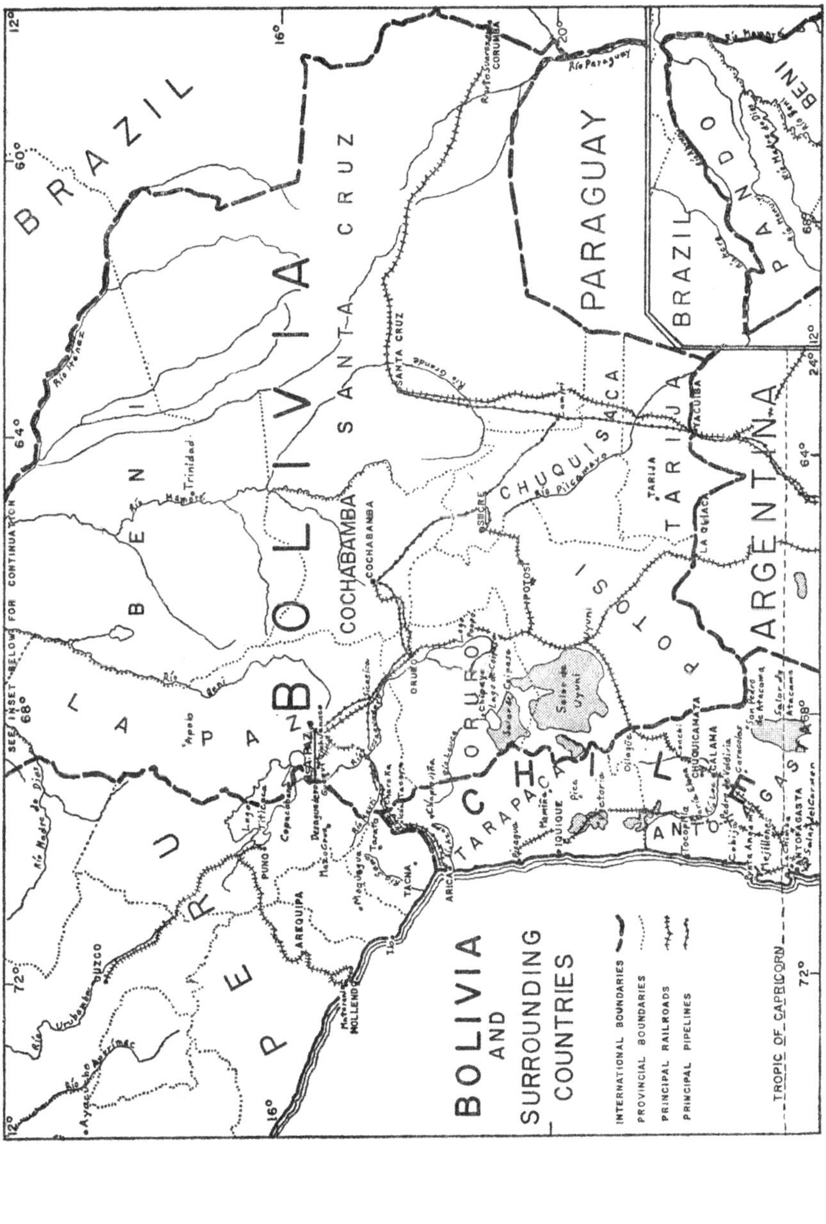
BOLIVIA
AND
SURROUNDING
COUNTRIES
INTERNATIONAL BOUNDARIES
PROVINCIAL BOUNDARIES
PRINCIPAL RAILROADS
PRINCIPAL PIPELINES
TROPIC OF CAPRICORN
BRAZIL
PARAGUAY
ARGENTINA
PERU
CHILE
BOLIVIA
PANDO
BENI
LA PAZ
SANTA CRUZ
COCHABAMBA
ORURO
POTOSI
CHUQUISACA
TARIJA
TARAPACA
ANTOFAGASTA
SEE INSET BELOW FOR CONTINUATION
COCHABAMBA
SANTA CRUZ
SUCRE
POTOSI
ORURO
TARIJA
LA QUIACA
YACUIBA
CORUMBA
ARICA
TACNA
IQUIQUE
ANTOFAGASTA
AREQUIPA
PUNO
MOLLENDO
CUZCO
CHUQUICAMATA
CALAMA
Río Paraguay
Río Grande
Río Pilcomayo
Río Mamoré
Río Beni
Trinidad

MAP 5

South America astride the Eastern Cordillera of the Andes Mountains. [2] Because of her perennial weakness and inability to colonize and defend her frontiers, Bolivia has lost more than one half of her original territory to her neighbors. [3] A large part of the remaining area is "outside the effective national territory," or ecumene, of Bolivia because it does not "actually contribute to the economic support of the citizens of the country." [4] This includes much of the Departments of Beni, Pando and La Paz, large portions of Santa Cruz and the entire Western Cordillera of the Andes. If we were to include in this category areas in which the people have little or no political awareness and are only nominally subject to the authority of the state, it would probably cover a considerably larger area. This political fragmentation of Bolivia is largely the result of history and geography.

The great Andes mountain range splits in southern Peru into two cordilleras. The Cordillera Oriental (Eastern) comprises a number of smaller ranges trending generally northwest-southeast until about latitude 17° south, where they assume a north-south orientation. The Cordillera Occidental (Western), shared by Bolivia and Chile, consists mostly of a broken chain of volcanoes, some rising over 20,000 feet above sea level, and small groups and ranges of mountains with many high passes between them, some of them quite broad. Between these two cordilleras is a steppelike plateau with an average elevation of over 12,000 feet, commonly called the Altiplano. The Altiplano is actually a series of intermont basins separated by eastward extending spurs of the Western Cordillera. Some of these basins contain Lakes Titicaca and Poopó and the *salares,* or salt flats, of Coipasa and Uyuni. Together, these three regions are called the Highlands and in this area, which comprises about one third of Bolivia, live more than three million of the estimated total of 3,751,000 Bolivians. [5] All of the important cities, with the exception of Santa Cruz, are located in the Highlands and here most of the economic, political and

[2] Most statistics concerning Bolivia are at best only educated guesses and are often misleading. They should be treated with caution. The exact area of Bolivia, for example, is still unknown since the boundary with Brazil is still not delimited. Estimates vary with the method of measurement used.

[3] Harold Osborne, in his *Bolivia; A Land Divided* (2nd ed.; London: Royal Institute of International Affairs, 1954), p. 2, gives the area of Bolivia in 1825 as approximately 904,952 square miles, of which 189,353 were lost to Brazil, 96,527 to Peru, 94,010 to Paraguay, 65,924 to Argentina and 46,333 to Chile. Other writers cite different figures which do not vary greatly from these.

[4] James, *op. cit.*, pp. 6 and 11.

[5] 1966 official estimate, cited by J. Valerie Fifer in "Bolivia's Pioneer Fringe", *The Geographical Review,* LVII (January, 1967), p. 1.

cultural activities of the country occur.

The remainder of Bolivia is generally divided into two parts – the lowland plains, or Llanos, covered for the most part with tropical rainforest (*selva*), tropical savanna, and semideciduous forest, which comprise more than half of the national territory in the north and east; and the Yungas, or deep valleys, on the northeastern margin of the Cordillera Real, northeast of La Paz and north of Cochabamba. The Llanos are sparsely populated, mostly by very primitive Indians who live largely by hunting and subsistence agriculture. The Yungas are a rich agricultural area and densely populated, largely with people of European origin or mestizos with little Indian blood.

Between the Cordillera Occidental and the Pacific Ocean is the inhospitable desert of Atacama, now Chilean territory but formerly held by Peru and Bolivia. The Atacama consists largely of a longitudinal series of *bolsones,* or dry basins. This area is called the pampa. The pampa is almost completely devoid of vegetation but is underlain with enormous mineral wealth. There is a coastal range of steep hills and escarpments, generally between 3,000 feet and 6,000 feet high, which in places abut the sea. In other places there are narrow shelves between the hills and the sea and it is on these shelves that the coastal towns are situated. Along the coast there are no natural harbors and little or no protection from the storms of the Pacific Ocean. There are, in fact, no good natural harbors in the 2,000 miles of Peruvian and Chilean coastline between Callao and Valparaíso, and even these major world seaports do not have truly good harbors and must be protected by breakwaters.

The pattern of climate which would be normal for this area, considering its latitude and location in relation to the oceans, is disrupted by two principal factors – the Andes Mountains and the cold Humboldt, or Peru, Current.[6] The Andes form a barrier to the exchange of winds and air masses across the continent. Thus, the east and northeast of Bolivia receive heavy rainfall borne by winds blowing off the Atlantic Ocean and over the Amazon basin. The Yungas are also quite humid, but the precipitation decreases on the higher slopes of the cordilleras in the east. The Altiplano, in the rain shadow of the Eastern Cordillera, receives very little precipitation from these easterly winds. Rain-bearing clouds carried on westerlies across the Peru Current bring some summer rains to the high, relatively cold Altiplano, but deposit virtually no rain on the lower Atacama. Thus, the Altiplano is semiarid while the Atacama is one of

[6] While geographers in recent years have generally agreed to call this current the Peru Current, Chileans, perhaps understandably, still call it the Humboldt Current.

the driest regions in the world. In some parts of the Atacama Desert no precipitation has ever been recorded. The Altiplano is continually swept by strong winds. On both the Altiplano and the Atacama there are great ranges of temperature between day and night and the landscapes are bleak. The climate is altogether harsh and dreary.

Most of the Altiplano and the Atacama are regions of interior drainage. Only the Río Loa among the exotic rivers flowing westward out of the cordillera reaches the Pacific Ocean. All the others which rise in the high springs and snowfields flow into lakes which have no outlets or simply disappear into the ground. Even those rivers which have been sources of so much contention among Peru, Bolivia and Chile, such as the Mauri, the Uchusuma and the Lauca, essentially begin nowhere and end nowhere. Only the Desaguadero, which flows out of Lake Titicaca and into Lake Poopó, is navigable, but only for small boats for a short distance. It is most difficult in this area to determine watersheds, for the rivers frequently cut across the ridges, backtrack, disappear into sinks or flow only seasonally through a maze of tributary canyons. Among the intermittent streams which traverse the desert, only the Lluta and the Azapa, both of which at times reach the sea near Arica, are reliable enough to provide water for fairly extensive areas of irrigated agriculture. On the southern margin of the Atacama, the Rivers Salado, Copiapó and Huasco, particularly the latter two, also support rather intensive irrigated agriculture.

One of the conditions which has exacerbated many of the disagreements between Bolivia and Chile has been the great disparity in the wealth and levels of economic development of the two countries. Measured by any standard, the people of Chile have generally lived better than the Bolivians through their history and have had greater opportunities to develop sophisticated political and cultural institutions. Bolivia, however, has been described a "a beggar sitting on a throne of gold" because of her great undeveloped natural resources. These resources are now being developed to a greater extent than ever before for the benefit of the Bolivian people.

Both the Altiplano of Bolivia and the Atacama Desert of Chile and the mountains which enclose them are rich in a variety of minerals. Mining, in fact, is the only economic activity of any national importance in the region. Some of the richest copper mines in the world are in the Atacama Desert and its extensive nitrate deposits were the cause of the bitter War of the Pacific which began in 1879. Other minerals, such as iodine, molybdenum and gold, are important by-products of these major exports. Silver was important in the 1870's. In the volcanic areas of the Andes are scores of small sulphur mines and there are smaller deposits of iron ore, marble and other minerals in the desert, possibly even uranium. Bolivia was built on the silver of Potosí and now rests precariously on the export of tin and tungsten from this same area. Petroleum, lead, antimony, gold and other minerals are also important to Bolivia. This overwhelming dependence on mining has made the entire northern third of Chile and western quarter of Bolivia a most unstable area politically and economically. With every fluctuation in the supply or quality of an ore or the market price for it, the economy has boomed or crashed, with almost equally disastrous effects on the communities of the area.

The principal agricultural region of Bolivia is the Yungas and of Chile the Central Valley, both far from the area under consideration. On the Altiplano grazing and subsistence agriculture occupy the great majority of the people, but not in the Atacama Desert. The most important river oases, because they are also administrative and communications centers, are Calama on the Loa, Copiapó on the Copiapó, and Vallenar on the Huasco. There is also a string of smaller oases located at the heads of alluvial fans at the very margin of the Altiplano well within Chilean territory. [7]

These oases are able to supply only about 10% of the staple foods of the some 500,000 people of northern Chile. A Chilean Government report reveals that the city of Antofagasta, which contains about one fifth of the people in the North, must import 98% of its meat, 95% of its butter, and smaller percentages of other staples from abroad or from the Central Valley of Chile, and this food is carried largely by sea. [8]

After mining, the most important occupation in the Norte Grande of Chile is commerce and the transportation associated with it. [9] A number of people are employed solely or largely in handling transit trade for Bolivia. Others deal in imports and exports for the Northern Zone itself. As the copper mines and seaports grow, the business of supplying them with their needs grows also. Until recently, Arica was a free port through which flowed imported luxury goods not available elsewhere in Chile.

The contrasts between the Altiplano and the Atacama are numerous

[7] The boundary between Chile and Bolivia does not, in fact, consistently follow any "natural" line; neither the edge of the Altiplano, the continental divide, nor a line connecting the highest peaks of the Andes. In the far north of Chile, especially, the terrain is very similar to that of the adjacent portion of Bolivia.

[8] Chile, Corporación de Fomento de Industria y Comercio (CORFO), untitled. Unpublished mimeographed report. Santiago, September 29, 1961.

[9] "El Norte Grande" is a term Chileans often apply to the three northernmost provinces; the provinces of Coquimbo and Aconcagua just to the south are sometimes called "El Norte Chico." The North is frequently called "La Zona Norte," even in official documents.

and important, but one of the most striking is the character and distribution of the people in the respective areas. The density of population in Bolivia is highest in the basin of Lake Titicaca, where the lake moderates the rigorous climate sufficiently so that maize and wheat will ripen. There is also adequate rainfall for a variety of crops. Because of the relative ease of travel through the Lake Titicaca basin, most traffic in western Bolivia is channeled in a north-south direction. This was the center of a flourishing civilization long before the Incas created their empire, and the population is still virtually all Indian. Further south, the population density decreases, but a traveller is rarely out of sight of some sign of human habitation – a hut, a stone corral, llamas grazing, cultivated fields. The majority of these people are Aymarás, a notably conservative group. Intermingled with them are many Quechua-speaking people and some Europeans, particularly in the towns.

In Bolivia as a whole, some 53% of the people are Indian, 32% mestizo (In Bolivia they are called Cholos.), and 15% are European. [10]

In Chile the desert is sparsely settled and few people live outside the cities, mines and oases. In the smaller oases, particularly those strung along the foothills of the Cordillera and in the upper reaches of the river valleys, most of the people are mestizos with very little European blood. They look, dress and act very much like the Indians of Peru and Bolivia and they may be considered as Indians. [11] These oasis dwellers have been on their land since long before the Incas came and have remained through all the political, economic, military and social upheavals that have characterized the area since the fifteenth century. They will probably remain after the last mine has been worked out and the last railroad rusts into the desert. They are the only element of stability, of permanence, in a notably unstable area.

Most of the people in northern Chile, however, are urban, concentrated in cities and mining camps. The world's largest open pit copper mine is at Chuquicamata, near Calama. It supports a population of over 25,000, all of whom are connected with the mine. The nitrate mines at María Elena and Pedro de Valdivia, the only important producers of natural nitrates in the world, sustain other sizable towns.

Every important city in northern Chile, other than the oases and mining

[10] James, *op. cit.*, p. 206.

[11] Chile is known as a mestizo country, but the word is rarely used there, nor is the word "Indian". The Indians are generally referred to as "indígenas," or indigenous people, while the rest of the more than 7,700,000 Chileans, many of whom are technically mestizos but have very little Indian blood, are called simply "Chilenos."

camps, is a seaport. Arica, Pisagua, Iquique, Tocopilla, Mejillones, Antofagasta, Taltal, Chañaral and Caldera all exist principally to handle exports of minerals from both Bolivia and Chile and imports of nearly everything else destined for the Atacama and the Altiplano. All of them have some importance as fishing ports and some have or have had other functions; nonetheless, it is quite likely that were it not for mining in the interior there would be no need for these ports and they would not exist, except, perhaps, as very small communities.

Bolivia has been handicapped by serious transportation and communication problems since the days of the early Spanish settlements. The handicap was only a nuisance while the area was but a remote province of Peru or Argentina, but became so serious upon the attainment of independence in 1825 that Bolivia has steadily lost outlying portions of her territory to her neighbors. As the country quickens the pace of economic development, the poor internal transportation system acts as a persistent drag. As foreign trade becomes ever more important to this economic development, Bolivia's remoteness from the Atlantic and Pacific Oceans further impedes healthy growth of the economy. Bolivians consider this a justification for a port of their own on the Pacific. The real problem, however, seems to be not lack of a port, but inadequate communications within the country and with the world.

The only paved roads in the country connect Cochabamba and Santa Cruz, two cities which are still not connected by rail, and La Paz and Oruro. Paving is now in progress on the Oruro-Cochabamba road. Many of the remaining roads are incredibly bad and there are in Bolivia relatively few motor vehicles to use even these roads. The railroads, with some important exceptions, serve the cities and mines of the Highlands. The line from Santa Cruz to Corumbá, Brazil, opened in 1955, and the line from Santa Cruz to Yacuiba, Argentina, completed in 1965, connect with those countries' rail networks and provide Bolivia with access to the Atlantic Ocean at Santos and Rosario respectively. Another line runs from Uyuni to La Quiaca, Argentina, where it also ties in with the Argentine rail net. Other railroads connect the Altiplano with the Pacific Ocean at Arica and Antofagasta, Chile, and Mollendo and Matarani, Peru. The vast northeast has not even been penetrated by a railroad and only a few short motor roads exist in the Departments of Pando and Beni. All surface transportation in the country is subject to frequent and serious interruptions by floods, landslides and other natural forces. Furthermore, the lack of sufficient railroads is complicated by the poor maintenance and poor management of those which do exist. Osborne makes an interesting observation on this point in view of Bolivia's claim for a port of her own on the Pacific coast:

> There is a deficiency of modern equipment, particularly locomotives, and maintenance has suffered from lack of funds. Rationalization is made difficult by the fact that the lines are operated by four different private companies and five state agencies. Their combined capacity is inadequate to the normal volume of Bolivia's traffic and heavy congestion, particularly at the port of Arica, is a usual occurrence... Without transport a port serves no useful purpose and an even more urgent requirement would seem to be the amplification of railroad capacity to the existing ports. [12]

The Bolivian Government has recognized this severe deficiency in internal circulation, however, and is taking steps to rectify it. At the end of 1964 six Bolivian railroads were merged into a 2,064 kilometer system operated by a new Government entity. Many surplus employees were discharged, some short lines were closed down and costs were reduced. Though Brazil donated fifteen locomotives, however, the Bolivians were not purchasing either locomotives or rolling stock. Osborne's comment of fourteen years ago remains essentially valid.

Because of the immense problems of surface travel in Bolivia, air transport has become very important. The principal civil air carrier is Lloyd Aereo Boliviano (LAB), in which the Government has a large financial interest. LAB connects most of the major and many smaller cities with scheduled and charter flights. It is not, however, a reliable airline. Its equipment is old and poorly maintained, its pilots skilled but inclined to take unnecessary risks. LAB maintains the only regularly scheduled air service between Chile and Bolivia, flying two round trips a week between Arica and La Paz. Several foreign airlines serve La Paz from Peru, Brazil and Argentina, but jet planes cannot as yet operate from La Paz's airport. It is located at El Alto on the Altiplano at an altitude of over 14,000 feet. The airports at La Paz and Cochabamba are the only ones in the country with paved runways, and at all airports safety and navigation equipment leave much to be desired. Even if air transport within Bolivia were improved and greatly expanded, it still could not substitute for efficient surface transport, but only supplement it. At present the United Nations Development Programme is sponsoring a survey of Bolivia's transportation, including pipelines and her access to the sea.

Communications as well as transportation are inadequate in Bolivia for the development of a modern economy. Bolivia has less than one telephone per 100 persons and only 8,000 miles of telegraph lines and

[12] Osborne, *op. cit.*, p. 38.

forty radio stations including relay stations.[13] Most of these are concentrated in and between the chief cities of the Highlands, with extensions to Santa Cruz. Even the existing facilities are not always adequate to surmount the natural obstacles separating the major cities.[14]

Historical and Political Background

Ever since the Atacama Desert assumed major importance in the middle of the nineteenth century, writers have been reaching back into history, culling phrases from ancient manuscripts and fragments from crude maps to back up their claims that it belonged to Peru or Bolivia or Chile. As recently as January 1964, responsible Bolivian public figures have written their versions of the history of the dispute over the Atacama, reaching as far back as the pre-Inca occupation of the desert. Far from being dead then, the remote history of this area is still a lively and controversial topic.

The oldest known groups in the area were the Urus and Chipayas. The Atacameños lived in scattered oases throughout the desert. "Their culture showed strong influence from the Central Andes in many specific features, but owing to their sparse population, they could not support Central Andean social, political and religious patterns."[15] Along the coast, in small sheltered coves where springs provided fresh water, lived groups of people called Changos. These peoples probably lived about 300 A.D.[16] The great civilization based on Tiahuanaco was created by unknown people, but was probably destroyed about 825 A.D., possibly by the Aymará, a people of unknown origin who conquered the primitive Urus and Chipayas. Of all these people, only the Aymará survive in any num-

[13] United States Bureau of International Commerce, *Basic Data on the Economy of Bolivia* (OBR-63-126) (October 1963), p. 5.

[14] During an emergency rescue operation following the crash of a LAB DC-6 in March 1963 near the point where Chile, Peru and Bolivia meet, the United States Air Force radio located at the airport in Tacna, Peru was sometimes unable to reach La Paz, less than 200 miles away. Messages had to be relayed between the two cities by more powerful transmitters in Panama. We would seem to have progressed very little since the early Spanish colonial times in South America when messages between cities fairly close together were sometimes sent by ship through Panama rather than directly overland.

[15] Julian H. Steward and Louis C. Faron, *Native Peoples of South America* (New York: McGraw-Hill Book Co., Inc., 1959, p. 262. This book is a general summary of the *Handbook of South American Indians,* published in six volumes between 1946 and 1950 by the Bureau of American Ethnology, Smithsonian Institution, with theory, interpretations and comments added by the authors. It is a most useful reference.

[16] Harold Osborne, *Indians of the Andes: Aymaras and Quechuas* (Cambridge: Harvard University Press, 1952), p. 53.

bers and they have played a vital role in shaping the character of Bolivia.

The origins of the people called Incas by the Spaniards, like those of their predecessors and contemporaries, are unknown, but they probably founded Cuzco about 1100 A.D. and began expanding outward. Between about 1438 and 1525 they conquered or otherwise subjected to their rule all the people living between the River Ancasmayu in Ecuador and the River Maule in Chile, just south of the modern city of Talca, where they were stopped by the fierce Mapuche, whom the Spaniards later called Araucanians. The Mapuche were to continue their resistance to invaders for over 400 years. While the Incas were able to march through the Atacama, they never fully integrated the area into their empire and it was only very tenuously held. Nonetheless, at the time of the Conquest, the entire Andes chain, including the Altiplano of Bolivia, and all the intervening territory to the Pacific Ocean from Ecuador to the Maule was united in one empire administered from Cuzco.

After the Spanish Conquest of Mexico and Central America in the 1520's, the conquerors turned toward the Pacific Coast of South America. In 1532 Francisco Pizarro and Diego de Almagro began the conquest of Peru. Pizarro entered Cuzco on November 15, 1533 and shortly placed upon the Throne of the Sun the Inca Manco II as successor to the murdered Atahuallpa, victor in the recently concluded civil war against his brother Huascar.

The Spanish king, as was customary in those days, generously bestowed enormous grants of territory which had been occupied for centuries by other people upon soldiers, adventurers and other favorites, often without the slightest knowledge of the geography of the continent. The boundaries of Almagro's and Pizarro's grants, for example, were vaguely defined and they disputed the possession of Cuzco, whose precise location was unknown to the king's geographer. In order to get Almagro out of Cuzco, Pizarro suggested that he go south to explore his domain. Taking a route across the Altiplano, Almagro crossed the Cordillera into what is now Chile somewhere north of Santiago, probably into the Vale of Chile, the valley of the Río Aconcagua.

Almagro penetrated to what had been the farthest reaches of the Inca Empire but encountered only rather unpromising country and hostile Indians. While fighting hunger, cold, disease and Mapuche, he heard rumors from the north of an Inca rebellion under Manco II and the occupation of Cuzco by his bitter rival, Hernando Pizarro, older brother of Francisco. He thereupon left for Cuzco to protect his more valuable interests there and abandoned Chile, marching this time through the

Atacama along the string of foothill oases. On the way he reshod his horses with copper horseshoes made in Inca furnaces with copper from a place called Chuquicamata. The Incas also used other objects made of copper, including some weapons. The Spaniards, however, were not looking for copper.

Almagro with his "men of Chile" reached Cuzco early in 1537, broke the Inca siege and took Cuzco for himself, capturing Hernando Pizarro and other leaders of his faction and beginning the long series of bloody civil wars among the Spaniards which has continued, in one form or another, well into our own century. Gonzalo Pizarro, younger brother of Francisco, survived the civil wars by leaving Peru for his own estates – Charcas, in what is now Bolivia. The Indians were not finally defeated until 1572, when the new Viceroy of Peru, Francisco de Toledano, executed Tupac Amaru, successor to Manco II and the last of the Incas, in the principal square of Cuzco.

Shortly after the Conquest was completed, Spain divided her holdings in the New World into two huge administrative areas, the Viceroyalties of New Spain, embracing all Spanish territory in North America as far south as Panama; and Peru, which included all territory held by Spain in South America. As settlers entered the New World and the colonies grew in size and economic activity, these administrative units were divided into two additional viceroyalties and subdivided into captaincies-general and *audiencias,* or presidencies. Each of these, in turn, was divided into provinces, *intendencias,* and eventually into smaller units. At no time, however, were these administrative units considered as separate colonies, as were the English settlements in North America. And at no time were the Spaniards particularly concerned with fixing boundaries between these units with any precision, except, at times, between the viceroyalties.

The Viceroyalty of Peru was administered from Lima, The City of Kings. Within the Viceroyalty of Peru, the Audiencia of Charcas was created in 1559 and the Captaincy-General of Chile about the same time. Thenceforth, a steady stream of royal *cédulas,* or decrees, flowed out from Spain, granting fiefs and creating administrative, judicial and military districts of various types, all overlapping and duplicating in a manner that would have created unbounded chaos in a society more accustomed to precision and order.

The Viceroyalty of Río de la Plata was created by royal *cédula* on August 12, 1776, with its capital at Buenos Aires. It consisted of all of what had been Peru east of the Western Cordillera, including Charcas, though it is far from clear whether at that time Charcas extended to the

Pacific Ocean. The inclusion of Charcas in Río de la Plata was, in a sense, natural, for the southern part of the audiencia was settled from Buenos Aires and ties with the new viceroyalty were still strong. Chile, though nominally still part of Peru, was growing in power and in 1798 was separated almost completely from the viceroyalty.

When the Spanish Empire in America began to fall apart, beginning with the successful rebellion of Buenos Aires in 1810, the revolutionary leaders agreed among themselves that there should be no squabbling over boundaries. They decided to invoke the ancient principle of *uti possidetis juris,* which meant that the boundaries of the new states would conform to the boundaries of the former administrative districts, at least for the present. Though it is certainly obsolete in Latin America now, it is still invoked upon occasion in border disputes and cited by Bolivian writers to support their condemnation of Chile's actions in the Atacama.

By now, interpretations of many fragmentary, vague, inaccurate and frequently conflicting documents and maps have proliferated so greatly and have themselves been reinterpreted so often, that Bolivia, Peru and Chile have all been able to build up substantial cases for their ownership of the Atacama Desert in 1810. After attaining independence in 1825, however, Bolivia managed to assert jurisdiction over a portion of the desert and built up the port of Cobija.

President Santa Cruz of Bolivia still harbored in the 1830's the old idea of uniting Bolivia and Peru. By 1835, Peru was so weakened by repeated civil strife and economic misfortunes that he was able to induce Peruvian President Orbegozo to sign a treaty of confederation with him. Santa Cruz was named Protector of the Peru-Bolivia Confederation, consisting of the three states of North Peru, South Peru and Bolivia. Chile felt herself threatened by the Confederation and attacked Arica, which had been declared a "common port" of Bolivia and South Peru, and also Callao in 1837. After a series of defeats, Chile won the final battle at Yungay in January 1839 and the Confederation was dissolved. This affair sowed the seeds of enduring bitterness between Chile and Bolivia and, to a lesser extent, Peru. At the same time, the seeds of an even greater conflict were being sown further south, in the Desert of Atacama, a conflict which was to result in full-scale war.

Since prehistoric times the Indians of Peru had used guano from the islands and coastal cliffs near the Humboldt Current as fertilizer, though on a very small scale. The Spaniards knew of it, but had little interest in it. Alexander von Humboldt introduced it into Europe about 1830, but its value was not fully appreciated until about ten years later. As the demand increased Peru began exploiting its deposits on a large scale. Chile was also becoming interested in the desert and in 1842 President Bulnes, in a report to the Congress, declared rather matter-of-factly that Chile extended northward to 23° S., including the small landing place at Mejillones. This was the first definite, official claim by Chile to a portion of the Atacama Desert and, since it overlapped the Bolivian claim by some two degrees of latitude, was the first direct confrontation of the two countries over their common boundary. For the next thirty years Bolivia and Chile contested for control of the southern Atacama, with Peru exploiting some nitrate deposits in the Province of Tarapacá. In 1866, Bolivia and Chile signed a treaty which fixed their boundary at 24° S. and arranged for joint exploitation of part of the desert.

The history of the economic development of the Atacama Desert between 1866 and 1879 is extraordinarily complex, involving a number of governments, companies and individuals in Chile, Bolivia, Peru, North America and Europe. Briefly, Peru was developing the guano and nitrate deposits of Tarapacá with little or no political difficulty. Bolivia attempted to reap profits from the exploitation of the guano, nitrates, copper and silver in her "Littoral Province," but "the economic and social conditions of Bolivia had made impossible a colonization of the littoral with Bolivian population and almost no Bolivian capital had been invested." [17]

Chile was expanding from her compact and relatively homogeneous base in the Central Valley. She was pushing against the Mapuche Indians, who still remained unconquered south of the Río Bío-Bío; pushing against the Argentines in Patagonia and at the Strait of Magellan; and pushing against the Bolivians in the north. In all cases, the expansion was accomplished at least as much by infiltration as by direct confrontation, but nowhere more so than in the Atacama Desert. Chile needed outlets for her surplus labor and capital and both were extensively employed in the north. Chilean capital and workers were instrumental in the initial development of the nitrate mines of Tarapacá, building of the port of Arica, and construction of public works and railroads as far north as Tacna. The population of the Bolivian littoral was overwhelmingly Chilean. [18] This intense commercial activity of Chile in the desert and the inevitable conflicts between Chilean workers and the local inhabitants

[17] Luis Peñaloza, *Historia Económica de Bolivia*, Vol. II (La Paz: n.p., 1954), p. 168.

[18] "It is calculated that from 93% to 95% of the population of the ... coast was Chilean ... The small Bolivian coefficient was made up of public employees, the police and the garrison." Gonzalo Bulnes, *Chile and Peru: The Causes of the War of 1879* (Santiago: Imprenta Universitaria, 1920), p. 42.

were complicated in the 1870's by the large-scale manipulations of the "nitrate kings" in New York and the British and continental European investors.[19]

The political events during this period were equally complex. Chile had a generally stable government, with three successive presidents who served out their full ten-year terms, though not without an occasional attempted revolt. Peru and Bolivia, on the other hand, had most unstable governments. Peru actually had a civil war, while Bolivia suffered a dreary succession of rebellions, coups, intrigues and assassinations. In the Latin American tradition, the losers in all of these political upheavals sought and were granted asylum in neighboring countries. They frequently engaged in political activities and sometimes in military expeditions against their own countries using their host countries as bases. These economic and political rivalries led to a secret treaty of mutual protection between Peru and Bolivia in 1873 and war between them and Chile in 1879.

In order, as she claimed, to protect the interests of her nationals and their economic activities, Chile sent a military force north by sea, and on February 14, 1879, occupied the city of Antofagasta. The Chilean troops were welcomed with cheers and Chilean flags by the predominantly Chilean population. The Chileans went on to occupy Cobija and Tocopilla and on the 16th took the silver mines of Caracoles, all without any resistance whatever. Bolivia declared war on Chile on March 1, but Peru tried to arbitrate between the two countries, probably to stall for time until she could mobilize her troops and refurbish her deteriorating navy.

Chile occupied Calama on March 23rd after a brief skirmish and shortly thereafter took the rest of the Bolivian territory west of the Andes. She then used the Secret Treaty, which was no longer a secret, as an excuse to declare war on both Bolivia and Peru on April 5. Despite attempts at mediation by other interested countries, the War of the Pacific continued until October 20, 1883, when Chile and Peru signed the Treaty of Ancón. By this time Chilean troops had occupied Lima and nearly all of southern Peru. In the treaty Peru ceded to Chile the province of Tarapacá and left the future of her occupied provinces of Tacna and Arica to be decided by plebiscite.

Bolivia finally saw the hopelessness of her position and on April 4,

[19] William J. Dennis, in his *Tacna and Arica: An Account of the Chile-Peru Boundary Dispute and of the Arbitration by the United States* (New Haven: Yale University Press, 1931), p. 67, describes in great detail the titanic struggle over nitrates, which he considers the principal cause of the War of the Pacific. "Both Chile and Peru were racing towards national bankruptcy. By the time the war began each had a large annual deficit and neither was paying interest on its debt."

1884, signed a Pact of Truce with Chile. This was to be only a provisional arrangement, pending a final settlmeent. It provided for cessation of hostilities, resumption of commercial relations between the two countries, continued occupation of the Bolivian littoral by Chile, and free transit of Bolivian goods through the port of Antofagasta. [20] Thus ended the War of the Pacific, with Bolivia deprived of her seacoast, Peru stripped of her three southern provinces and Chile in actual possession of all the territory between the rainforest of the south and the Río Sama in the north and between the Andes and the Pacific Ocean. She took prompt action to integrate these newly won territories into the state. She organized the Province of Tarapacá in 1884 and the Province of Antofagasta in 1888 and began the "Chilenization" of Tacna and Arica. [21]

On October 20, 1904, Chile and Bolivia signed a Treaty of Peace, Friendship and Commerce. This treaty gave Chile permanent possession of the Bolivian littoral; delimited the new boundary between the two countries; required Chile to build, at her own expense, a railroad from Arica to Alto La Paz within one year of the date of ratification and within fifteen years turn over the Bolivian portion of the railroad to that country; and made certain financial settlements. It also bound Chile to grant Bolivia in perpetuity "the broadest and freest right of commercial transit through her territory and ports of the Pacific" and gave Bolivia the right to maintain customs agencies in Arica, Antofagasta and such other ports as might be agreed upon later. It granted each party most-favored-nation treatment, arranged certain technical details and ended by requiring that all questions arising out of the meaning or execution of the treaty should be submitted for arbitration to His Majesty, the Emperor of Germany. [22] This treaty, with subsequent modifications, has served for nearly sixty-four years as the basis for relations between Bolivia and Chile. [23]

Bolivia was dissatisfied with the Treaty of 1904 and in April 1910

[20] The complete text of the Pact of Truce may be found in Jorge Escobari Cusicanqui, *El Derecho al Mar* (La Paz: Editorial Juventud, 1964), p. 218. Escobari is former Undersecretary of the Bolivian Foreign Ministry and editor of "The Red Book." He has been Ambassador to Colombia and is considered to be among Bolivia's ablest diplomats.

[21] For a most detailed description of the exploration, settlement, surveying, place names, and political organization of the Atacama Desert, see Ernesto Greve, *Informe Sobre la Demarcación de los Paralelos de los Grados 23 y 24 de Latitud Meridional, Elevado a la Superintendencia del Salitre* (Santiago: La Ilustración, 1932).

[22] The full text of the Treaty of 1904 appears in Escobari, *op. cit.*, p. 228.

[23] All of these modifications had the intention and the effect of clarifying and amplifying the free transit rights accorded Bolivia.

MAP 6

TACNA-ARICA AREA

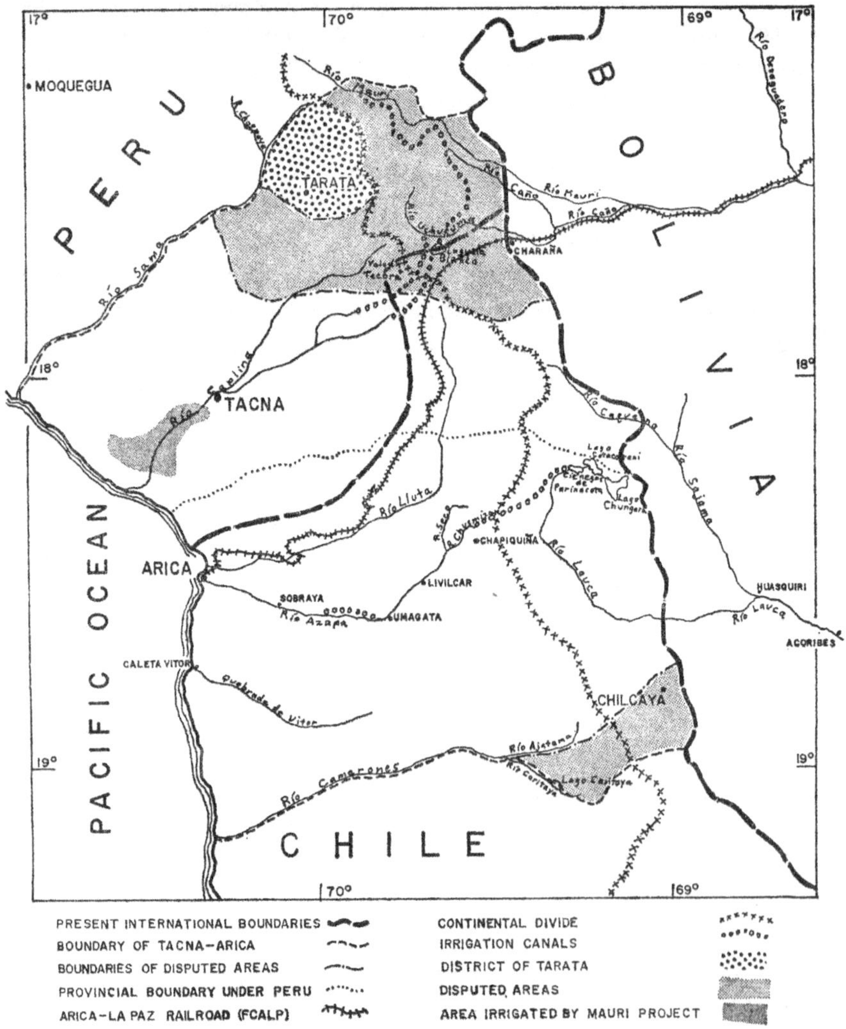

began a campaign for its revision. In a note to his counterparts in Santiago and Lima, the Bolivian Foreign Minister expressed the hope that Bolivia might obtain all or part of Tacna-Arica. It achieved nothing. The same tactic was tried again in 1919 and was similarly unsuccessful. Both Bolivia and Peru were inspired by the ideals of Woodrow Wilson and saw in them hope for retrieving what they had lost in the War of the Pacific; the League of Nations appeared to be the vehicle by means of which they could accomplish this objective. They acted independently, each trying her own approach. Bolivia appealed to the First Assembly of the League which met in 1921. She formally requested revision of all treaties which resulted from the War of the Pacific and in particular the Treaty of 1904. The matter was referred by the Assembly to a commission of jurists for an advisory opinion. The commission reported on September 21, 1921 that Bolivia's demand was inadmissable since the League Assembly had no power to modify a treaty; only the signatory states could do so. Both Chile and Bolivia agreed in floor speeches to discuss the matter privately. Bolivia withdrew her demand for League action, reserving her right to bring up the matter in the future. [24]

Bolivia followed up by initiating an exchange of notes with Chile in January 1923 in which she proposed revision of the Treaty of 1904. Chile flatly refused to consider revision, but expressed willingness to negotiate a new treaty based on Chile's permanent retention of Antofagasta. Bolivia thereupon decided that in view of Chile's rejection of revision, it would be discourteous of her to bring the matter up at the imminent fifth Pan American Conference to be held in Santiago, so she did not attend. Bolivia then tried to win support for her cause at the International Law Congress in Buenos Aires in 1925 and failed once again. After this defeat she gradually abandoned efforts to secure revision of the Treaty of 1904 in favor of other methods of obtaining an outlet to the sea.

After the signing and ratification of the Treaty of 1904, the only unfinished business remaining from the War of the Pacific was the final disposition of the Peruvian provinces of Tacna and Arica. According to Article 3 of the Treaty of Ancón, a plebiscite should have been held in the provinces in 1894, but neither Peru nor Chile seemed particularly

[24] José Carrasco, in *Bolivia's Case for the League of Nations* (London: Selwyn and Blount, 1920), p. 143, made a strong plea at the time for the return of Antofagasta to Bolivia, since it was then, after completion of the railroad to Oruro, the port for all of southern Bolivia. He even proposed moving the Bolivian Government to Antofagasta and making it a model city. "In the matter of the population, its people are mobile and cosmopolitan, but it would only take ten years to make it Bolivian [sic!]."

anxious to press the point. As time passed, however, Chile intensified her efforts to "Chileanize" the population of the provinces and Peru began to pressure Chile for a plebiscite. The importance of the area, while it was not rich in natural resources as was Tarapacá, was still considerable. Finally, an attempt was made in 1925 to hold the plebiscite with the United States rendering her good offices. So many difficulties were encountered, however, that the attempt was given up and the dispute was finally settled through bilateral negotiations, still using the good offices of the United States, with the Treaty of Santiago of 1929.

Among the many terms of the Treaty were these: The territory was to be divided between the two countries, with Tacna being returned to Peru and Arica to be retained by Chile. The boundary was to run parallel to the Arica-La Paz Railroad and about ten kilometers north of it as far as the boundary between Bolivia and Chile, except that the important sulphur deposits of Tacora Volcano were to remain within Chile. Chile was to grant Peru on Arica Bay a wharf, customs house and railroad station. Chile was to pay Peru an indemnity of six million pesos. A monument was to be erected at Chilean expense on the demilitarized Morro of Arica to symbolize the friendship between the two countries. It was generally considered at the time to be a sound and honorable settlement and all parties were pleased with it except Bolivia, which got nothing out of all the negotiations.

In a Complementary Protocol to the Treaty, signed the same day and to be considered an integral part of it, it was stipulated that the port facilities which Chile must give to Peru at Arica were to be for absolutely free transit. Furthermore, and this point is of supreme importance, both parties were prohibited from ceding to a third power the whole or any part of the territories they received under the Treaty, and from constructing new international railroad lines across them without the consent of the other. The transfer of Tacna to Peru took place on August 28, 1929 and the Tacna-Arica dispute was finally resolved. [25]

During the 1930's, Bolivia was engaged in other matters, notably the Chaco War, and the question of an outlet to the Pacific was not seriously raised again on an international level until 1943. In that year the President of Bolivia, General Enrique Peñaranda, toured the Americas and used the occasion to raise the issue, most forcefully in Mexico and the United States. His Mexican speech, in which he asserted Bolivia's "permanent and inalienable right to aspire to her own port on the Pacific," sparked a

[25] The text of the Treaty of Santiago, in English, may be found in Dennis, *op. cit.*, p. 315.

new propaganda battle between Bolivia and Chile.[26] He pressed the matter with President Roosevelt and Secretary of State Hull, and received courteous but noncommittal replies, which, of course, have been interpreted by Bolivians as favoring their cause.

During the next few years, Chile repeatedly and vigorously reiterated her stand that the Treaty of 1904 was an irrevocable historic fact, but that she was willing to negotiate new concessions to Bolivia. Bolivia, however, revived her thesis that treaties could be revised without the consent of all parties thereto and presented it at both the San Francisco Conference which established the United Nations in 1945 and the Ninth Inter-American Conference in Bogotá which drafted the Charter of the Organization of American States (OAS) in 1948. Finally, in June 1950, the two contending governments exchanged notes agreeing to a conference "to seek the formula which could make it possible to give to Bolivia her own sovereign outlet to the Pacific Ocean, and to obtain for Chile compensations that would not have territorial character and which effectively take into account her interests." Bolivians have since referred to this phrase as "The Promise of 1950."[27] By the middle of 1951, however, this opening had been lost because public discussion focused on a suggestion of President Gonzales Videla of Chile to President Truman of the United States that the "compensation" could consist of the use of the waters of Lakes Titicaca and Poopó to irrigate the entire littoral, benefitting Chile, Peru and Bolivia.[28] Peru ended the discussion by invoking

[26] One of the tracts to appear at this time was by Rómulo Meneses, *El Imperativo Geográfico en la Mediterraneidad de Bolivia* (La Paz: Editorial Renacimiento, 1943). Meneses was the leader of the Bolivian branch of Victor Raúl Haya de la Torre's APRA party. His book was an attempt to present Bolivia's case in "geographic" terms; i.e., the "natural gravitation" of the Altiplano toward the nearest ocean, the Pacific. He quoted Friedrich Ratzel and Ellen Semple to support his deterministic view. He proposed that Bolivia receive all the territory from the Río Desaguadero to the middle of the Province of Antofagasta, asserting that Arica is the natural outlet for the Altiplano and should belong to Bolivia.

[27] Note from the Chilean Foreign Minister to the Bolivian ambassador in Santiago dated June 20, 1950. The complete text appears in Escobari, *op. cit.*, p. 262. This quotation is frequently cited by Bolivians as evidence of a promise which Chile has failed to keep, neglecting, however, to cite an earlier passage in the same note in which Sr. Walker, the Foreign Minister, states that Chile has been disposed to study such a possibility "together with defending the legal situation established in the Treaty of Peace of 1904."

[28] In his address to the foreign ministers of the Americas in Washington on March 26, 1951, President Truman said, in part, "The American Republics are full of breathtaking possibilities for future economic development . . . I like to think of a project about which I talked to the President of Chile, which contemplates the diversion of water from those high lakes between Bolivia and Peru, for making a

the protocol to the Treaty of Santiago concerning cession of territory and by refusing to consider use of the lake she shares with Bolivia for such a purpose.

Early in April 1952, Bolivia, for the first time in her history, underwent a profound revolution, social and economic as well as political. It was the second of only three experienced thus far in Latin America, the others being those of Mexico and Cuba. On April 9 the Government of the Movimiento Nacionalista Revolucionario (MNR) under Victor Paz Estenssoro took office and decided to sublimate the dispute with Chile temporarily in favor of radically upgrading the Bolivian economy. Accordingly, after some preliminary sparring, the Bolivian and Chilean foreign ministers met in Arica in January 1953 and settled some technical matters relative to movement of cargoes through that port. Two years later, another treaty on economic matters was signed and Bolivia temporarily suspended her campaign for an outlet to the sea. Another disagreement between the two countries, however, was beginning to reach the stage of a serious dispute. This concerned the diversion by Chile of water from the Río Lauca into the valley of the Río Azapa for an irrigation project (see Map 6), and for another decade Bolivia's objection to this diversion and her campaign for a "*salida al mar*" were intimately bound up and led to Bolivia's withdrawal from the OAS in 1962.

From its beginning in 1939 until the matter was fully aired in an emergency meeting of the OAS requested by Bolivia in April 1962, the Río Lauca dispute grew steadily more acrimonious, with nearly all the acrimony coming from the Bolivian side. During the third session of this emergency meeting, Ambassador Sarmiento of Bolivia included in his long speech on the Lauca, these comments:

> In this struggle of rights or recoveries, Bolivia has another greater; her enclosure, which places her in cases like the Lauca at a notorious disadvantage in remedying the aggression of which she has been the victim, which would justify legitimate defense.
>
> Geographic enclosure is the great problem of Bolivia; from that is derived the gravity that the aggression committed by the Government of Chile has. The system of free transit in situations such as the present is extremely fragile.

garden on the coast of South America to the west of Chile and Peru and in return giving Bolivia a seaport on the Pacific. I had a very pleasant conversation with the President of Chile on that subject . . ." *Pan American Union, Proceedings of Fourth Meeting of Consultation of the Ministers of Foreign Affairs* ("Conferences and Organizations Series," No. 12, Washington, 1951), p. 132. The controversy aroused by this "very pleasant conversation" soon died out, but was revived some eleven years later when another American official publicly made a similar suggestion.

With a simple administrative arrangement, without the necessity of force, Bolivia could be blockaded. [29]

Similar comments were interspersed throughout the Bolivian literature generated by the dispute and the connection between the Lauca and *salida* issues became more and more evident after the OAS on May 24 refused Bolivia's request for urgent punitive measures under the Rio Treaty and referred the dispute back to the two parties. On September 3, 1962 Ambassador Sarmiento sent the Chairman of the Council of the OAS a message in which he announced that Bolivia would suspend attendance at all meetings of the Council and specialized agencies of the OAS until that body took firm steps to bring about a "just solution" of the Lauca dispute. [30]

Later in the same month, Bolivia raised the *salida* question at the 17th session of the United Nations General Assembly. During the general debate on September 28, Foreign Minister Fellman summed up the core of the Bolivian position:

Finally, Bolivia is the only country in the world that was deprived of its coastline – that is, more than 150,000 square kilometers – because of an unjust war. In each Bolivian, without exception, there is an unshakable desire to return to the sea. At this time in history, when new concepts of international solidarity obtain, there is no reason that might justify the holding of an entire nation in imprisonment. In due course, Bolivia will invoke the spirit of solidarity of all peoples, to which it has so much contributed, so that a just solution will be found for its tragedy of imprisonment. [31]

Foreign Minister Martínez replied for Chile: "In view of the statement just made by the Foreign Minister of Bolivia I am happy to be able to say that no country has granted more extensive facilities to a land-locked country than Chile has granted to Bolivia." He went on to discuss these facilities, Chile's offer to build two more highways from Chilean ports to Bolivia, and Chile's granting of facilities to Bolivia for construction of a petroleum pipeline to Arica. He continued,

Bolivian cargoes crossing Chilean territory are subject to no administrative formalities of any sort, not even those that normally might be required for statistical purposes. The transit of passengers is subject to no regulations other than those required for the identification of persons. In these, and in other

[29] Organization of American States (OEA), Pan American Union ("Council Series," OEA/Ser. G/II C-a-444) (3 May 1962).

[30] OEA/Ser. G/V C-d-1018, 4 September 1962.

[31] United Nations, General Assembly, *Provisional Verbatim Record of the 1137th Plenary Meeting* (A/PV. 1137, 28 September 1962).

ways . . . Chile has been concerned with granting all possible facilities to Bolivia so that its foreign trade can develop without let or hindrance.

He concluded by saying that Bolivia's trade is subject not to the laws or will of a foreign country, as Bolivia had charged, but rather to the "sacred law of the treaties in force between the two countries . . ." [32]

These brief presentations of the Bolivian and Chilean cases on the *salida* question may be considered as early contributions to a debate at the highest international level, since it was at this same Assembly that machinery was set in motion to have the United Nations consider the transit rights of land-locked states in general. Bolivia's conditional and partial withdrawal from the OAS also led to anxiety that the Organization might be weakened in its attempts to deal with the Cuban threat. This concern became acute in October 1962 with the unfolding of the Cuban missile crisis, and Bolivia was prevailed upon to return to demonstrate inter-American solidarity. She did so on October 26.

After the missile crisis quieted down, Bolivia remained in the OAS. In November, Sarmiento met with the United States, Mexican and Brazilian delegates who constituted the inter-American committee studying the Lauca problem. Through him, Fellman threatened not only to withdraw from the OAS, but to take the matter to the United Nations if it were not resolved before Chile began making full use of the Lauca waters.

It was at this point of rising tension that Ambassador Teodoro Moscoso, United States Coordinator of the Alliance for Progress, attempted to place the Lauca problem within the context of Latin American cooperation. In discussing the Latin American Free Trade Association (LAFTA), he said,

This concept of an integrated economy for all of Latin America also opens up new vistas and approaches for the solution of old disputes. The Bolivian-Chilean dispute over the waters of the Lauca River might well find an equitable and constructive solution if, in the framework of a common market, these two countries were joined by Peru in developing an area-wide authority under which the waters of the entire Lake Titicaca system would be harnessed for the production of an abundance of electric power for irrigation, and for a variety of other purposes. [33]

This suggestion was not really new. It had been presented, in one form or another, many times in the past, notably by President Truman in 1951. This time, however, both Bolivia and Peru objected, claiming that they

[32] *Ibid.*

[33] Address of Mr. Moscoso before the Coordinating Committee of International Activities of Private Enterprise, Mexico City, October 26, 1962, unpublished text.

had "exclusive sovereignty" over the lake under a 1957 treaty. (This treaty will be discussed in more detail in Chapter VII.) Moscoso's suggestion, of course, was perfectly reasonable but rather poorly timed and perhaps indelicately phrased. As a result, his effectiveness in dealing with Latin American nations in connection with the Alliance for Progress was considerably reduced.

Through the end of 1962 and into 1963 Bolivia continued to belabor Chile over the Río Lauca issue, while the OAS continued to mediate the dispute informally. At this point, Chile expressed in public what had been known privately for some time, her strong distaste for Bolivian Foreign Minister José Fellman Velarde as an individual. His past record of meddling in domestic politics while in exile in Chile and Peru, his unyielding position, his aggressiveness and his intemperate, even venomous, speeches and public statements combined to make him, personally, a major stumbling block in the path of progress toward renewal of relations between the two countries. Chile demanded his resignation as a precondition to renewal of relations. Fellman refused to resign until Chile made important concessions on an outlet to the sea. Fellman apparently felt he needed some success, however small, in order to maintain his power within the party and the Government in some other capacity when he did resign.

Tension rose again in March 1963 with more demonstrations in La Paz and a sharp increase in the intensity of the anti-Chilean propaganda campaign in the press and radio. Some of the radio broadcasts hurdled the mountain barrier and were heard in northern Chile. Many boxcars being returned from Bolivia to Antofagasta on the Antofagasta-Bolivia Railway (FCAB) had anti-Chilean slogans chalked on them. Bolivia protested the considerable backlog of Bolivian imports piled up on the wharves of Antofagasta, alleging that the delays in shipments were due to a calculated policy of the Chilean government. Investigation, however, revealed that the primary cause of the delays seemed to be the tendency of Bolivian importers to use the boxcars for storage of their goods – at little or no cost to them – instead of unloading them and permitting them to return to Antofagasta to be reloaded.[34] Bolivia also initiated a new propaganda technique, adding "*Salida al Mar*" slogans to postmarks on mail destined abroad. When some of this mail reached Chile, the Govern-

[34] This investigation was conducted informally by both the Railroad itself and official organs. The findings confirmed the result of a similar investigation conducted by a team of United States, United Nations, and Bolivian officials in 1956. The local press gave extensive coverage to this incident over a period of about two months, but in a restrained and objective manner.

ment momentarily lost its composure and ordered all mail with these offensive cancellations returned to Bolivia. When the authorities were reminded that such action would violate regulations of the Universal Postal Union, they contented themselves with just blotting out the slogans. Bolivia soon discontinued this tactic.

The anti-Chilean campaign reached a climax during the "*Semana del Mar*," or "Week of the Sea," ending on March 23, a Bolivian national holiday called "*Día del Mar*," or "Day of the Sea." Its ostensible purpose is to honor Eduardo Abaroa, leader of the "heroic" defense of Calama against the Chileans in 1879. In recent years, however, it has come to be used as the annual culmination of Bolivia's campaign for an outlet to the sea. It was characterized in 1963 by an exceptionally large and vigorously anti-Chilean parade, featuring workers' groups and schoolchildren singing anti-Chilean songs and chanting anti-Chilean slogans. There were many inflammatory speeches, newspaper editorials and radio programs. Within the next two days two more events occurred which added fuel to the fire. Bolivia was nominated to replace Venezuela as the "Latin American representative" on the United Nations Security Council and Chile published her long-awaited White Book on the Río Lauca controversy.

The situation had deteriorated so badly that Foreign Minister Martínez on March 28 broadcast a radio report to the Chilean people on the Lauca and *salida* issues. Such a broadcast is a most unusual event, for in Chile the Foreign Minister is considered to be a diplomat, a public servant who performs his delicate functions quietly and in private, and not a politician who frequently exhorts the masses, as in some countries. Martínez, moreover, was generally considered an exceptionally able diplomat, highly respected in Chile and abroad. His broadcast made a deep impression on the Chilean people, many of whom, perhaps, learned for the first time how serious the Bolivian campaign had become. After the broadcast, the Chilean press began to treat the whole affair rather more seriously, instead of tossing it off as merely more domestic political talk by those "irresponsible politicians" on the Altiplano.

Since 1961, according to Martínez, Chile had invited Bolivia to study (1) installation of customs warehouses and a customs agency for Bolivia in Arica, (2) construction of highways from Iquique and Arica to Oruro, (3) elimination of intermediaries in the dispatch of merchandise bound to or from Bolivia, (4) establishment of port charges favorable to Bolivia, (5) facilities for the functioning of air navigation enterprises in both countries, and (6) other measures for expediting Bolivian transit trade.

Bolivia rejected these invitations. Regardless of Bolivia's actions, Chile would defend her territorial integrity. [35]

Fellman replied to this speech with a radio address of his own on April 3, 1963 which he also directed to the Chilean people, revealing to them, as he put it, things their government had never told them. He pointed out that in spite of the great provocation of the Lauca diversion, Bolivia had magnanimously refrained from cutting off the water supply of the city of Antofagasta at the Río Silala in retaliation. [36] He asserted that all of the wealth drawn from the desert which had been Bolivian has gone to "four or five fabulously powerful and fabulously rich companies" and that the irrigated land in the Azapa Valley belongs to "a few privileged ones" who do not work the land themselves. He stated several times that Bolivia had no quarrel with the Chilean People, but only with their government. He denied that the Lauca Affair was created because of Bolivian internal politics, but rather it was due to Chilean internal politics: the necessity to pacify the *Ariqueños* [37] who were disturbed about the withdrawal of many of Arica's free port privileges "one month" before the opening of the Lauca project on the 14th of April, 1962. [38] There were also Chilean municipal elections approaching.

> The Government of Bolivia is not confronted, as is the Government of Chile, with a growing popular discontent caused by economic difficulties, monetary instability or lack of popular support . . . The resentment over the diversion of the Río Lauca and, above all, the inflexible will to return to the sea are in each Bolivian without any distinction, whatever his political position may be. [39]

Fellman continually switched from the Lauca theme to the *salida* and back again, tying them together. He called Bolivia a "prisoner nation" and said the Lauca diversion only makes her "enclosure" worse. He denied

[35] Chile, Ministerio de Relaciones Exteriores, *Discursos y Documentos, Relaciones entre Chile y Bolivia; No. 1,* (Santiago, March 28, 1963).

[36] The cities of Antofagasta and Calama receive most of their water through two pipelines built and still operated by the FCAB basically to supply the railroad. Their dam is located on the Río Siloli (as it is known in Chile) just inside the border east of San Pedro de Conchi. The river rises, however, from springs about two or three kilometers over the border in Bolivia. This same point was made by a Bolivian delegate during the OAS debates and prompted the retort by the Chilean delegate that there are also several Bolivian towns whose water supplies originate in Chile.

[37] Residents of Arica.

[38] Actually, this action was taken in December 1961.

[39] Fellman's entire speech may be found in Bolivia, Ministerio de Relaciones Exteriores y Culto, *Rumbo al Mar: Documentos Trascendentales* (La Paz: 1963), pp. 45–76.

that Bolivia had *ever* asked for or insinuated the revision of the Treaty of 1904!

These two speeches are quite significant, for they represent the first reasonably frank public debate by the two foreign ministers. Furthermore, they removed whatever doubt anyone might still have had that the entire controversy over the Río Lauca was, or at least had become, simply one aspect of the main problem: Bolivia's campaign for an outlet to the sea. They also revealed certain facts and opinions which had not been aired in public before and, indeed, provided much food for thought for the impartial observer. They did nothing, however, to clear the air or lessen tension.

On June 11, 1963 Fellman sent Chairman Gonzalo Facio of the OAS Council a long note in which he claimed that the situation was getting worse. Then, "I regret to inform you that the Government of Bolivia has decided to permanently withdraw its Delegate to the Council of the OAS." [40] So once again, Bolivia resorted to drastic action, justified by her own unique interpretation of the meaning and import of a document, in this case the OAS resolution of May 24, 1962.

On August 6, Bolivia received what appeared to be a magnificent gift in the form of an offer from Argentina for free use of the port of Barranqueras in the city of Resistencia on the Paraná River and the use of the railroads from La Quiaca and Yacuiba which lead to the port. Bolivian ships under 2,000 tons flying the Bolivian flag could maneuver freely in the harbor and control their own loading and unloading. This "gift", however, which looked like a bonanza at the time, has turned out to have very little real economic value, as will be explained in some detail in the next section.

The debate between the two countries continued during the summer of 1963, with *The New York Times,* through its news and Letters to the Editor columns, unofficially replacing the OAS as intermediary.

In an interview with *The New York Times* on October 4, Fellman said that "the cession of Mejillones and the creation of a Bolivian enclave around the port would satisfy his Government *at this time* [italics added] in its dispute with Chile." Bolivia would not ask for a corridor, but would be content to use the Antofagasta-Bolivia Railroad (FCAB) for access to this port. In return, "Bolivia would be willing to divert water from five small rivers high in the Andes to help irrigate northern Chile's vast desert." Fellman then reviewed the Río Lauca issue and accused Chile of

[40] OEA/Ser. G/V C-d-1107 18 June 1963.

violating the Declaration of Montevideo of 1933 on international rivers and lakes. He said there was a great pressure within Bolivia for an actual corridor to the sea and even for the recovery of "considerable territory lost to Chile." He said that the refusal of Chile to cede Mejillones could only lead to a more intensive campaign by Bolivia. "He declared, however, that Bolivia is only demanding that Chile carry out her promises of 1950 and 1961. He alleged that the Arica-La Paz Railroad (FCALP) and the FCAB "have the most expensive freight charges in the world." He also charged that Bolivian traffic through Chile had been interfered with and that Bolivian goods had been inspected by Chilean customs in violation of international agreements. [41]

This interview is significant for a number of reasons. It contains the final official public statement by either side on the Lauca question to date and it contains the first official public statement on precisely what Bolivia might be willing to consider a suitable "outlet to the sea." Finally, it marked the end of the unofficial role of intermediary played by *The New York Times*. From this point on, Bolivia pressed her case for an outlet to the sea through other channels, and rather more intensively than at any time since the Lauca issue became prominent.

On October 25, 1963, President Victor Paz Estenssoro of Bolivia addressed the General Assembly of the United Nations. In his speech, his only reference to Bolivian-Chilean relations was his linking of an outlet to the sea with stabilized prices for raw materials as being essential for the development of Bolivia. After the session, Paz said that Bolivia was not planning to submit the *salida* issue to the United Nations "at this time." He did say, however, that "we have experienced war and we are still suffering its consequences because an unjust war imprisoned us in our high mountains." [42]

On December 20 Fellman announced that Bolivia would not attend the 11th Inter-American Conference to be held in Quito in April because "Bolivia cannot attend an Inter-American Conference that will not consider our claims to a port on the Pacific." He hoped for another postponement of the conference, which was originally scheduled for 1960. [43] At that time, Bolivia had announced she would not attend the Conference because of the Río Lauca affair. An impartial observer can only be led to inquire why these issues are not to be considered at inter-American

[41] *The New York Times,* October 13, 1963.
[42] *The New York Times,* October 26, 1963.
[43] *The New York Times,* December 22, 1963.

conferences if Bolivia actually has, as she claims, the support of all the peoples of Latin America.

Within a few weeks of each other, by sheer coincidence, the Foreign Ministers of both Bolivia and Chile were replaced. On December 17, 1963 Carlos Martínez Sotomayor was appointed Chile's Ambassador to the United Nations and was replaced by Julio Philippi Izquierdo. This move was apparently part of the pre-election maneuvering within the Chilean cabinet and had no connection with Bolivian-Chilean relations. Then on January 25, 1964 José Fellman Velarde was replaced by Fernando Iturralde Chinel. Fellman was appointed Minister of Government on March 31. While this change was also a matter of internal politics, one direct result was a less belligerent atmosphere in La Paz and a greater likelihood of early resumption of relations and discussion between the two countries of their outstanding differences.

Elections were held as scheduled in Bolivia on May 31, 1964, though there had been speculation that they would be postponed under pressure from Vice President Lechín and former President Hernán Siles Suazo, who had broken with President Paz. There was also a possibility of mass violence. This did not materialize, however, and President Paz was re-elected without opposition for another four-year term with Air Force General René Barrientos Ortuño as his Vice President.

On June 15, 1964, former President Siles held a press conference at which he read a lengthy statement in reply to his recent expulsion from the MNR. He then displayed a sealed envelope which he claimed contained documents which revealed "acts committed against the interests of the nation."

The first of the documents was a transmittal letter from Siles explaining why he was turning the other two documents over to the Armed Forces. (His reasons were primarily political, dressed up in the guise of "national interest.") The second was a letter from four MNR exile leaders in Lima, including Siles, dated August 12, 1950 to Victor Paz, who was then in Montevideo. In the letter, Paz was informed of a statement the exiles had drafted concerning the negotiations then in progress between the Bolivian and Chilean governments. They understood, from a story which had appeared in the Chilean magazine *Ercilla,* that the negotiations were based on a trade of a strip of land north of Arica for the use of Lake Titicaca waters for irrigation and hydroelectric projects in northern Chile. These negotiations were presumably an outgrowth of the Chilean "Promise of 1950" made two months earlier and were the origin of the suggestion President Truman made before the OAS in Washington the following year. The draft statement of the MNR exiles cited the importance to Bolivia of access to the sea but did not comment on the supposed terms of the negotiations.

The third and last of the documents was Paz' reply to this letter, dated September 25, 1950. Paz objected to negotiating with Chile at all at that time, saying,

> For us, the problem of a seaport does not figure among the front rank of problems facing Bolivia. The affirmation which is often made that our underdevelopment is due mainly to the lack of an outlet to the sea is both sterile and misleading since it seeks to divert public attention from the true causes of Bolivia's stagnation. It would be more useful and more constructive from the point of view of national interest to place all of our talent, energies and resources in developing the great potential economic and human elements which are found in Bolivia... We could then enter into a peaceful and cordial negotiation with Chile on the basis of equality which could really be a negotiation for mutual benefit. [44]

Chief of Staff General Ovando and most La Paz newspapers felt that the documents were really very insignificant and there was a general feeling of having been let down after the dramatic buildup by Siles. This would seem to be another indication of reduced concern over the *salida* issue since the departure of Fellman from the Foreign Ministry. Most of the opposition parties, including those headed by Lechín and Walter Guevara Arze, co-founders of the MNR, took a position similar to that taken by Paz in 1950, charging that he, Paz, had changed his policy after coming to power for the second time (in 1960) and used the *salida* and Lauca issues to distract the attention of the people from the problems that confronted them. The Bolivian opposition parties thus placed themselves in the position of lending credence to the perennial Chilean charge that the whole *salida* issue, including the Río Lauca affair, is largely a matter of Bolivian internal politics and not an urgent concern at all. They continued to support the *salida* demand, but felt that Paz had used it for his own ends. [45]

President Paz refused to comment on the documents, as did all other Government officials – except Minister of Government José Fellman Velarde. After an interview with Paz on June 18, he issued this statement:

[44] The complete texts of all three documents were published in *El Diario,* La Paz, June 19, 1964.

[45] *El Diario,* La Paz, an independent daily, on June 20, 1964 carried the statements of three opposition parties. Other statements appeared in the organs of the various parties.

> It is evident that the policy approved by the past leadership in regard to Chile consisted of developing the country and strengthening ourselves as a step prior to any negotiations. It has been the Chilean Government, by unilaterally and arbitrarily diverting the waters of the Río Lauca, which has made the problem of our land-locked status the order of the day since the only item which we can offer Chile in return for our own sovereign outlet to the Pacific is part of the waters of a few small rivers which, like the Lauca, cross our border with Chile. With the consumation of the Río Lauca incident by Chile, our patriotic obligation, naturally, is to defend the Lauca since it is an instrument of negotiation for the seaport question and to insist continually in all forms upon a solution for our port problem. [46]

Fellman, if nothing else, was being consistent, using almost the same words he had used in his press release of December 30, 1962 and in his interview with *The New York Times* on October 4, 1963. His position also bears a strong resemblance to that taken by Mario Gutiérrez and his Falange Socialista Boliviana, except that Gutiérrez wished to use Lake Titicaca water as "an instrument of negotiations" with Chile for a port. Fellman was known, however, to oppose giving any Lake Titicaca water to Chile under any circumstances.

Siles' "revelations" generated the uncovering of more documents on the *salida* issue, some of doubtful validity and most used primarily by the opposition to belabor the government, but this was soon overshadowed by more antigovernment strikes, rioting and other activities directed by Juan Lechín. President Paz imposed press censorship in August and exiled Siles in September. Vice President Barrientos began making his presidential aspirations known and the situation continued deteriorating. By November 3, heavy fighting was taking place and Paz, on the following day, fled into exile in Lima. On November 5, 1964, Barrientos, supported by the United States, took over as acting President. Like his predecessors, he was committed to pressing Chile for a *salida al mar*.

There is reason to believe that just before his overthrow Paz was becoming willing to talk with the Chileans about their outstanding problems, and shortly after his fall, the provisional military government sent up quiet and confidential trial balloons. They soon withdrew them, however, and gradually fell into the old pattern of hostility toward Chile. The *Día del Mar* celebrations in 1965 were orderly, but Chile was again vigorously condemned by the crowds, despite Chilean President Frei's overtures to the Bolivian Minister of Agriculture at an FAO conference in Chile the day before for a resumption of diplomatic relations. The harder line was evident at the United Nations Conference on Transit Trade of Land-

[46] *Presencia* (Catholic daily), La Paz, June 19, 1964.

locked Countries during the summer of 1965, and propaganda continued pouring from the military government in La Paz against the Christian Democratic government in Santiago through 1966. The line became even harder after the election of Barrientos as constitutional President in July 1966. When a hemispheric heads-of-state meeting was called for April 1967 at Punta del Este, Uruguay, Barrientos announced he would not attend.

He sent a long letter on April 8, 1967 to President General Oscar Gestido of Uruguay reviewing Bolivia's whole case for an outlet to the sea. He said that at the preparatory meeting of foreign ministers in Buenos Aires, in February 1967, Bolivia had requested inclusion of this matter on the agenda of the Punta del Este meeting as one of "the problems which impede an effective American cooperation." Barrientos claimed that the conference should not consider economic integration of Latin America without first considering the "existing deficiencies and injustices," and that such discussion would be ineffective without including "the free access to the routes of world commerce." Bolivia, therefore, as she had on several similar occasions in the past, felt it inappropriate to attend the Conference. [47]

Chile replied with an even longer letter dated May 29, 1967 from the Foreign Minister, Gabriel Valdés S., sent to each of the American foreign ministers. In it he reviewed the entire Chilean case and emphasized Chile's desire to renew relations and cooperate with Bolivia and work toward economic cooperation and development. [48] But there is no evidence that Bolivia is yet ready for such cooperation and, despite all of the intensive work in and outside the United Nations on securing transit rights for land-locked countries, Bolivia's campaign for a "*salida al mar*" continues.

Bolivia's Developing Economy

Since the Revolution of 1952, the Bolivian Government has been engaged in a race between economic development and complete national collapse. The MNR almost immediately began a series of drastic moves which have largely transformed Bolivian political, social and economic life.

[47] The texts of this letter and several earlier documents are contained in the pamphlet *¿Por Qué Bolivia no está Presente en Punta del Este?*, La Paz: Ministerio de Relaciones Exteriores, 1967.

[48] The text of the letter may be found in the pamphlet *Chile Responde al Presidente de Bolivia*, Santiago: Ministerio de Relaciones Exteriores, 1967.

Agrarian reform was initiated; the tin mines of the three great "tin barons," Hochschild, Aramayo and Patiño, were nationalized; suffrage was extended to women, the landless and illiterates; a massive attack was begun on ignorance and illiteracy; the labor unions were strengthened and brought actively into politics; the army was virtually destroyed and replaced by an armed militia composed of workers and miners; plans were made for the diversification of the economy. Attempts of various kinds were made to integrate the many fragments of Bolivia into a unified state, in effect to make the ecumene coextensive with the political boundaries of the state. Development of the lowlands of the Oriente began on a large scale, elaborate social welfare programs were introduced, some transportation improvements were initiated, and, perhaps most important, the Indians and Cholos were brought into the national life. All forms of racial discrimination were forbidden. Even the term "Indian" is rarely used today; the preferred term is "*campesino.*"

At first this upheaval created far more problems than it solved. Liberated peasants seized land on their own or streamed into the cities; agricultural production declined disastrously; skyrocketing labor costs, outmoded equipment, exhaustion of the richest veins and inefficient management turned the mining industry from the mainstay of the economy into a severe drain on its resources; the jails were filled with political prisoners and many capable people were forced into exile; the militia began getting out of hand, often terrorizing the countryside for its own aggrandizement; the labor unions, testing their newfound strength, made unreasonable demands which were often granted; foreign investment was frightened away; inflation was rampant.

Some indication of the enormity of the task facing the MNR is given in this passage from a 1958 United Nations report on Bolivia:

> In geographic, historic and economic aspects, Bolivia constitutes in Latin America a peculiar case and one of great interest. In general, this country reproduces many of the characteristics common to the rest of the continent. Nevertheless, in its geographic position, in its physical environment, in its demographic composition and in its social hierarchization, the Bolivian history and economy show unique characteristics. It could even be asserted that in this republic have been shown in their most acute and dramatic form many of the problems which, with less intensity, have affected the economic and political evolution of the rest of the countries which make up this region of the globe. [49]

[49] United Nations, Economic and Social Council, Economic Commission for Latin America (CEPAL), *Análysis y Proyecciones del Desarrollo Económico.* Vol. IV: *El Desarrollo Económico de Bolivia* (E/CN. 12/430 y Add. 1/Rev. 1, February

One aspect of the Government's attack on these problems was the consolidation of the nationalized tin mines under the Corporación Minera de Bolivia (Comibol). Rehabilitation of Comibol began after 1959 under the "Triangular Plan" and has involved almost complete reorganization of this government entity, large investments in modern machinery, the opening of new bodies of tin and other metallic ores, and other measures. These have had the effect of increasing production and eliminating the chronic annual deficit of Comibol. [50] The program also calls for strengthening the private mining industry, but progress in this sector has been slow.

Bolivia has been active in promoting price stabilization agreements for tin among the major producers and consumers of the world. She has also been seeking financing for the construction of tin smelters within the country. (At present, all tin ore is exported to the United Kingdom and the United States for smelting and refining.) This desire for smelters is as deeply felt a national aspiration as is the desire for an outlet to the sea, though it has not produced the same intense, emotional campaign that the latter issue has.

The Government is fully aware of the dangers of relying so heavily on one commodity for its foreign exchange receipts. It is therefore, for the first time in Bolivian history, investing heavily in diversification of the economy. Small manufacturing industries have been encouraged, petroleum production has greatly expanded and commercial crops such as rubber and coffee have shown marked gains. Probably the most dramatic and far-reaching of the attempts to diversify has been the colonization of the Llanos and the consequent spectacular rise in agricultural production there.

Colonization in this area has been tried before, but on a much smaller scale, with little planning and with a notable lack of success. The new colonies are better planned, better located and better financed and the colonists seem to be well chosen. The colonists include many European immigrants, particularly Italians; Japanese and Okinawans; demobilized soldiers; and Indians from the Altiplano. As a result of this colonization, Bolivia is now exporting sugar and rice. Important increases have also been achieved in the production of wheat, vegetables, jute, soybeans, peanuts and other crops.

This development of the Oriente is having other beneficial effects be-

1958) (México, D.F., 1958), p. 5. This document shall hereinafter be cited as CEPAL, 1958.

[50] In 1966 Comibol made a profit of $ 4 million. *The New York Times,* January 23, 1967.

sides an increase in the supply of food and industrial crops. The Bolivian army is doing important pioneer work in clearing land for settlement and building roads, thus providing additional land for many landless peasant farmers; [51] the population imbalance between the Highlands and the Lowlands is very gradually being redressed; and the growing population makes less likely the possibility that Bolivia's more powerful neighbors might try to move in to fill the vacuum.

An intensive development and colonization program cannot progress very far without a concurrent expansion and improvement of the transportation network. This is being done in Bolivia, but it is not easy.

> In few regions of the world does transport present such problems as in Bolivia, problems derived in large part from the geographic situation of the country, from the configuration of its territory and, above all, from the most unequal distribution of its population, concentrated in the mountainous region and supplied from centers situated at great distances. [52]

This problem existed, as we have seen, in Inca times and during the colonial period and still persists. Now, however, something is being done about it.

The cities of Cochabamba and Santa Cruz de la Sierra, most dramatically and importantly the latter, have served as the jumping-off places for this colonization. The roads and improved waterways running northward from Santa Cruz are part of the Government's plan to link the Andes and the Amazon Basin in a meaningful manner for the first time in history. At the same time, the Santa Cruz-Yacuiba railroad and oilfield development to the south of Santa Cruz tend to divert some attention from the ties with the Altiplano, while the Santa Cruz-Corumbá railroad, the new roads being pushed into the departments of Beni and Pando, particularly into the valley of the Río Chapare, and the even more impressive colonization and road-building efforts on the Brazilian side of the border are exerting an even stronger pull on the Oriente toward Brazil. [53]

[51] Some ten million acres have been allotted by the Government for colonization in 1967 alone. *The New York Times,* January 23, 1967.

[52] CEPAL, 1958, p. 209.

[53] J. Valerie Fifer emphasizes the links between the Llanos and the Altiplano in her articles "Bolivia's Boundary with Brazil: A Century of Evolution," *The Geographical Journal,* CXXXII (September, 1966) and "Bolivia's Pioneer Fringe". Raymond E. Crist, however, stresses "the magnet of the Brazilian continental economy" and "the flow of produce and persons ... *from* Bolivia and *to* Brazil" in his article "Politics and Geography; Some Aspects of Centrifugal and Centripetal Forces Operative in Andean America," *The American Journal of Economics and Sociology* XXV (October, 1966). Another fine recent article on this subject is Alexander T. Edelmann, "Colonization in Bolivia: Progress and Prospects," *Inter-American Economic Affairs,* XX (Spring 1967).

Much of the investment capital for the economic development of Bolivia is coming from abroad. The United States alone provided Bolivia, in the form of grants and loans, $ 198,068,000 between 1954 and 1962,[54] while aid in 1963 amounted to over $ 65 million.[55] In addition, financial assistance has come from Argentina, the United Kingdom, Japan, West Germany, the Inter-American Development Bank, the World Bank, the International Monetary Fund and the United Nations. Technical assistance is being provided by the United Kingdom, Japan and Israel in addition to the large American program. The United States Peace Corps and British volunteers are engaged in some projects in Bolivia. Bolivia is also encouraging private investments, both domestic and foreign, with Japan by far the largest investor and the United States and other countries trailing behind.

The Ten Year Development Program was submitted to the Committee of Nine under the Alliance for Progress in 1962. It was based on expansion of transportation, electric power, and better distribution of the population. It is worthy of note for the purposes of this study that this plan does not provide for any kind of development program for the basin of the Río Lauca, nor are any provisions made for revision of the plans should Bolivia somehow obtain her own sovereign outlet to the sea. Whether or not such revision might be necessary can best be determined by an examination of the patterns of Bolivia's foreign trade and the ports through which this trade passes.

It is a well-known fact that Bolivia's economy today is based almost solely on the export of minerals, chiefly tin, as it has been continuously since the earliest Spanish settlement there. In 1965, for example, minerals accounted for about 95% of Bolivian exports, while tin alone amounted to some 76% of the total exports. Other important mineral exports are (in order by value, 1965) antimony, lead, silver, zinc, copper, gold, and tungsten. Petroleum exports have been dropping since 1958 and in 1965 earned only $ 689,000 out of a total export value of $ 131,836,000.[56] Bolivia's imports are far more diversified, both in composition and origin. Her principal imports are foodstuffs, machinery, vehicles and manufactured goods. Imports totaled $ 102,721,000 in 1964.[57] This export-import ratio is changing, however, as the country develops under the Ten

[54] OBR-63-126, p. 8.

[55] *The Christian Science Monitor,* June 3, 1964.

[56] Bolivia: Instituto Promotor de Inversiones en Bolivia, *Brief Information on Bolivia 1967,* La Paz: Ministerio de Economía Nacional, 1967.

[57] *Ibid.*

Year Plan. Food imports are rising only gradually, while imports of capital goods and industrial raw materials are rising rapidly.

Bolivia's most important trading partners have for long been the United Kingdom and the United States, with other countries in Western Europe and Japan and Canada having varying degrees of importance in her import or export trade or both. Her only important trading partner in Latin America has been Argentina, while trade with Chile has never been very important except in a few minor products. This lack of trade with Latin America was the principal factor in Bolivia's decision to remain outside the Latin American Free Trade Association, but she finally joined in December 1966 in response to external pressures and an improved economy.

Bolivia's Access to the Sea

All of the factors of Bolivia's existence as a state – her location, topography, relations with her neighbors, population distribution, history, composition and direction of her foreign trade – have combined to determine which of her neighbors' ports this land-locked state will use for her own trade.

Bolivian relations with Paraguay have never been warm and since the Chaco War of the 1930's have for the most part been distinctly cool. After the Bolivian Revolution of 1952, the MNR Government managed to retain only formal and correct relations with the military dictatorship of Alfredo Stroessner. Since the military coup in Bolivia in 1964, however, relations have warmed considerably. This, combined with intensive development work in the Oriente and the continuing suspension of relations with Chile, has brought the two countries closer together. *The Christian Science Monitor* commented in 1964,

> Since Bolivia was frustrated in its drive to the Atlantic – 30 years ago in the Chaco War – its diplomacy has been centered on encouraging friendly rivalry between all the powers of the Plate to secure the best outlet advantage. Sooner or later, in or out of the Latin American Free Trade Association, Bolivia will want to move some of its surplus export production, including oil, via the Plate tributary system, with which it is linked. [58]

Bolivia has, indeed, been developing new outlets to the sea in the region of the Río de la Plata (River Plate), and has had some successes with Brazil and Argentina, as we shall see shortly, but as for Paraguay, despite

[58] *The Christian Science Monitor,* February 29, 1964.

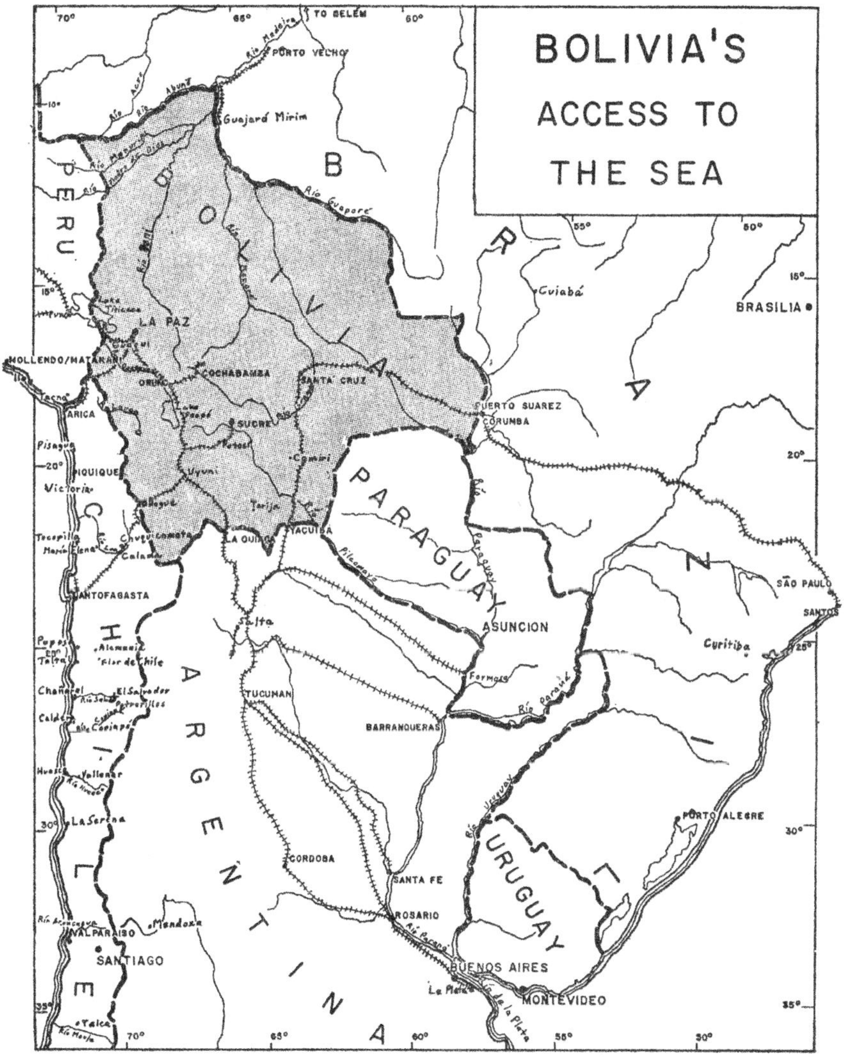
BOLIVIA'S
ACCESS TO
THE SEA
BOLIVIA
PERU
BRAZIL
PARAGUAY
CHILE
ARGENTINA
URUGUAY
LA PAZ
COCHABAMBA
SANTA CRUZ
SUCRE
ASUNCION
BUENOS AIRES
MONTEVIDEO
SANTIAGO
BRASILIA
SÃO PAULO
SANTOS
PORTO ALEGRE
ROSARIO
SANTA FE
CORDOBA
TUCUMAN
BARRANQUERAS
ANTOFAGASTA
ARICA
IQUIQUE
VALPARAISO
PUERTO SUAREZ
CORUMBA
YACUIBA
LA QUIACA
PORTO VELHO
TO BELEM

MAP 7

the glowing public statements the two countries have made about boosting traffic on the Paraguay and new free ports for Bolivia on that major tributary of the Plata, the situation remains much as J. Valerie Fifer described it in 1966:

> Despite the acquisition of the "windows" on to the Paraguay in 1903, and confirmation by Brazil in 1910 of Bolivia's right to free transit on the Paraguay river (as well as on the Amazon and Madeira rivers), the Paraguay route may at present be totally disregarded as a Bolivian outlet. The "windows" have for the most part remained remote and virtually untouched, except by army units laboriously erecting the boundary's demarcation. [59]

If, as a result of development of the Oriente and friendlier relations with Paraguay, the Paraguay-Paraná-Plata system does become more important to Bolivia, both Argentina and Uruguay would stand to gain. Uruguay has been considering offering Bolivia some kind of privileges at one or more of her ports, but so far the volume of trade does not seem to warrant it. [60]

Besides the railroads and pipelines running from southeastern Bolivia into Argentina, that country's only major concession to Bolivian pressure has been the offer of a free port at Barranqueras in August 1963. This offer has turned out to have been much more of a propaganda coup for Bolivia than an economic asset. It appears that the free port offer is foundering on two basic realities of economics: little to ship through the port and no good way to ship it. Despite rudimentary development of Bolivia's Oriente, both imports to and exports from the area are still not very large. Also, because of the weak internal transportation system in Bolivia, any thought of shipping out minerals from the highlands through Barranqueras is highly unrealistic at the present time, though the suggestion is made every so often. As for transportation between the port and the Oriente, the Santa Cruz-Yacuiba Railroad was completed only in 1965 and still carries very little traffic, and the offer of use of the La Quiaca railroad is unlikely to benefit Bolivia greatly. La Quiaca has long been one of the four principal entrepôts for Bolivia, but traffic bound to and from Bolivia has generally used the Argentine port of Rosario, further down the Río Paraná. While the rail route between Barranqueras and La

[59] Fifer, "Bolivia's Boundary with Brazil," p. 371.

[60] *The Christian Science Monitor*'s comment on December 30, 1966 that "[l]and-locked Bolivia, long oscillating between Pacific and Atlantic, has turned definitely eastward and thrown in its lot with Argentina via the tributary outlets of the River Plate" seems still to be a bit premature, despite the current comradeship between the generals ruling Bolivia and Argentina. Lofty oratory and elaborate plans are no substitute for the hard facts of economics and geography.

Quiaca is shorter, it passes through very sparsely populated country and the river between Rosario and Barranqueras is difficult to navigate. Ocean-going vessels can regularly go no farther upriver than Santa Fé. Furthermore, Bolivia has no merchant fleet of her own and acquiring one is costly. It is unlikely, therefore, that Barranqueras will be of very great importance in the near future.

Despite the gradual increase in economic activity along the Bolivian-Brazilian border in recent years and Bolivia's continuing good relations with Brazil (led by still another general!), very little Bolivian trade passes through Brazil. Bolivia has been granted free port facilities in Santos, Belêm, Corumbá and Pôrto Velho, but Bolivian trade using Brazilian ocean ports must pass through thousands of miles of sparsely populated country over difficult terrain using inadequate transportation and still face high port costs, especially in Santos. Even shipping goods down the internationalized Amazon River system to Belêm is only slightly less costly than shipping them from the Oriente to La Paz by air and then to the Pacific by rail. New roads from the Beni to La Paz should bring costs of transport over the Andes and the Altiplano to the Pacific below those of shipping to Atlantic Coast ports.[61] It is simply uneconomic to use Brazilian seaports except for high value products such as petroleum.[62] This may change in the future, however, as the Llanos of Bolivia gradually reach their full production potential. Brazil alone could absorb a fair share of the potential exports of this area. Meanwhile, only Corumbá of the Brazilian ports is active in Bolivian trade.[63]

While extensive use of the Amazon River system for Bolivian trade has long proven impractical and will probably remain so for the foreseeable

[61] Cornelius H. Zondag, *The Bolivian Economy 1952–1965; The Revolution and its Aftermath* (New York: Frederick A. Praeger, Publishers, 1966). This is an excellent, detailed study of Bolivia's economy, particularly its transportation.

[62] Sugar, for example, after long and careful study, is now being shipped from the Llanos to Cochabamba by truck, thence by train to Antofagasta for export to the United States. Interview with Michael B. Yohn, Bolivian desk officer, United States Department of State, July 20, 1967.

[63] The Madeira-Mamoré Railroad, built by Brazil primarily for Bolivian use in the latter part of the 19th century, bypasses a series of rapids between Guajará Mirim and Pôrto Velho, and was supposed to help Bolivia take advantage of the rubber boom. It took over forty years, many millions of dollars and thousands of lives to complete, but it has never been successful. The collapse of the rubber boom, the opening of the Panama Canal and the difficult environmental conditions combined to doom the railroad from its opening in 1912. The Brazilian army began building a parallel road in 1966 and at the same time took over administration of the railroad. When the road is completed, possibly by the middle of 1969, the railroad will be abandoned. The road may well serve Bolivia better than the railroad could have.

future, there is one other possibility for improving Bolivia's access to the sea through Brazil – overland. The Santa Cruz-Corumbá and Corumbá-Santos railroads are two of several links in what was originally envisioned as a trancsontinental railroad connecting the Pacific Ocean port of Arica with the Atlantic Ocean port of Santos. [64] The only missing link in this route is that between Cochabamba and Santa Cruz, Bolivia. This points up again the weakness of Bolivia's internal transportation system, particularly the railroads. While the Bolivians seem to be committed to highway rather than railroad building (with the advice and financial assistance of the United States AID mission) and have no concrete plans to complete this railroad, the Brazilians are known to be interested in its completion. Short stretches are being added continually, but no adequate financial aid is available and it is unlikely to be completed in the near future. Bolivia, moreover, still has sizable financial obligations to Brazil for construction of the Santa Cruz-Corumbá line, to Argentina for construction of the Santa Cruz-Yacuiba line, and to Chile for maintenance and service costs on the Arica-La Paz Railroad.

Bolivia has long used the port of Mollendo, Peru, as one of her principal entrepôts, and Bolivia and Peru, as we have noted, have been closely associated since Inca times. There are no serious contentions between the two countries and there has never been any serious interruption of Bolivia's transit trade through Peru. One problem with this route, however, is that while goods may be railed between Mollendo and Puno, Peru and between Guaqui and La Paz, Bolivia, they must be transshipped by steamer across Lake Titicaca between the two lake ports. The rail link between Puno and Guaqui has been under intermittent construction for several years and if ever completed should greatly improve service on the La Paz-Mollendo route. The Peruvian Corporation Limited (owned by a Canadian holding company), however, is on the verge of bankruptcy and in no position to complete such a short, but difficult, undertaking. [65]

[64] An early discussion of the progress and problems in completing this gap in the transcontinental railroad, first proposed in 1928, may be found in "Bolivia and the Arica-Santos Railway," by Captain LeRoy Bartlett, Jr. in *The Military Engineer* XXXIII (July-August 1941). Captain Bartlett concluded his article, "The economic feasibility of the Vila Vila-Santa Cruz project has been reported upon to the Export-Import Bank. The strategic value to the United States of a transcontinental line across the heart of South America is a subject to be determined by our War Department in connection with our plans for hemisphere defense. The political value of completing the line, to Bolivia primarily, but to her territorial and Pan-American neighbors as well, cannot be doubted." p. 307.

[65] For details on the railroad's financial problems, see *The Christian Science Monitor* for July 6, 1967.

Matarani was built by the Peruvian Government to supplement the existing port of Mollendo, seven miles to the south. Matarani was opened in 1941 and is now connected by rail and road with Mollendo. Unlike Mollendo, it is partially protected by a breakwater and has piers at which several ships can tie up at once. It also has facilities for handling bulk grain and has other modern facilities which Mollendo lacks. Most ordinary general cargoes use either port and they are often considered as one port.

Arica, Chile, it may be recalled, became Bolivia's principal seaport after the War of the Pacific and the completion of the FCALP, but soon the bulk of Bolivian transit trade shifted back to Antofagasta, where it remains. Arica, however, has since about 1960 been involved in a major development program, of which new port improvements are a major project. A new quay connected directly with the Tacna-Arica Railroad has been constructed for the use of Peruvian transit trade, and a larger quay with new berthing and warehousing facilities for both Chilean and Bolivian trade.

Charges for lighterage are standard, but both Bolivia and Peru receive favorable tariffs for their use of the mole. In addition, Bolivia receives free transfer of cargo from mole to warehouse and free warehousing for goods awaiting transit . . ." [66]

There are also plans for the electrification of the Chilean section of the FCALP (using electricity generated at Chapiquiña as part of the Río Lauca project) and elimination of the cog section on the edge of the Altiplano. This should reduce the total journey between Arica and La Paz from eighteen to ten hours. Despite the continuing dependence of the FCALP on Bolivian traffic, the city of Arica is no longer thus dependent. Barely one quarter of the port's business consists of Bolivian trade and even the port itself is becoming relatively less important to Arica as manufacturing, fishmeal production and tourism increase.

Antofagasta is the largest city between Arequipa and Valparaíso and by far the best equipped port used by Bolivia. Besides not having to depend on lighters, as Arica did until very recently, Antofagasta handles all of the traffic to and from Chuquicamata and is thus insulated against severe drops in Bolivian traffic. More ships find it profitable to call at Antofagasta than at either Arica or Mollendo/Matarani. The FCAB (Antofagasta-Bolivia Railway) also has a shallower gradient and lower tariffs than the FCALP, and a single administration operating the entire

[66] J. Valerie Fifer, "Arica: A Desert Frontier in Transition," *The Geographical Journal*, CXXX (December, 1964), p. 514.

line, though the Bolivian Government is negotiating to buy out the Bolivian section from its British owners. As an indication of their relative importance, Arica handled 46,578 metric tons of Bolivian cargo in 1962, while in the same year Antofagasta handled 191,735 metric tons. [67]

Not one of the three major west coast ports (Mollendo/Matarani, Arica and Antofagasta) has a good natural harbor, first class port facilities or completely adequate rail and road connections with Bolivia. All are subject to serious backlogs of cargoes, severe pilferage, storms, strikes and other problems. Bolivia's rights to unrestricted use of these ports gives her a degree of flexibility, however; imports, at least, can often be shifted to the other ports if one is not rendering satisfactory service. United States aid shipments are a fairly reliable indication of the conditions in these ports. In 1956, for example, when Mollendo/Matarani had an unexpected surge of incoming traffic, aid shipments were diverted to Arica and Antofagasta. In 1958, when inefficiency and pilferage in Arica created unbearable problems, cargoes were diverted to the other two ports. In 1962, when dock workers in Antofagasta went on strike, Arica and Mollendo/Matarani were used. Shipping lines also have flexibility in arranging their ports of call with Bolivian cargoes according to their schedules, weather conditions, port conditions, etc. Bolivian Government shipments generally use Mollendo or Arica. Bolivian exports, as already noted, move out primarily through Antofagasta.

The long-discussed project of a highway between Ilo and La Paz, agreed upon formally in 1957, received another boost in October 1965 when the Presidents of Peru and Bolivia agreed in Lima "to initiate concurrent requests for international financing" for the project. [68] Bolivia, as we have seen, has rejected Chilean offers of highways between her smaller ports and the Altiplano.

Another foreign trade facility should be mentioned besides railroads, roads, and ports. One of Bolivia's great hopes for the future is the export of petroleum from her large reserves in the Departments of Santa Cruz, Chuquisaca and Tarija. They are owned by the Government and operated by the Government agency Yacimientos Petrolíferos Fiscales Bolivianos (YPFB). There are refineries in Cochabamba and Sucre. Several foreign oil companies, notably Gulf Oil Corporation, are also operating in Bolivia. From the major fields at Santa Cruz and Camiri, pipelines extend into Argentina and to La Paz. In 1958, under terms of a 1957 Accord with Chile, Bolivia built a branch of the Camiri-La Paz pipeline from

[67] *Ibid.*, p. 509.
[68] *The New York Times*, October 19, 1965.

Sicasica on the Altiplano down to Arica through the same pass utilized by the FCALP and the Río Mauri canal. This pipeline cost $ 12,000,000 and has a theoretical capacity of 50,000 barrels a day. [69] It carries crude oil to Arica for export. It never had carried very much, however, until October 1966, when Gulf began pumping an average of 18,000 barrels a day from the new Caranda oil fields near Santa Cruz through a new pipeline. Despite recent drops in Bolivian petroleum exports, Gulf, apparently, is very optimistic about both the supply of and demand for Bolivian petroleum. [70] This confidence is being justified both by rising Bolivian domestic consumption and by increasing demand for petroleum that does not have to travel around the Cape of Good Hope to avoid the blocked Suez Canal. Studies are also under way for the laying of natural gas pipelines which would essentially parallel the major oil pipelines.

Bolivia's Campaign Against Chile

Bolivia was described at the beginning of this chapter as a weak state. It is more than that, it is an historical accident, a state created out of the unorganized territory left over after all the surrounding Spanish colonies had become independent. Bolivia was permitted by her neighbors to come into national existence only as a buffer separating them. From this inauspicious beginning, Bolivia has gone steadily down hill, weakened further by her tumultuous politics.

Bolivia has never made any important contribution to world civilization, not even in art, music or literature as have many other Latin American nations. Even the famous university of colonial Chuquisaca (now Sucre) has dwindled in stature and has not been replaced in prestige by the new one in La Paz. She has managed to retain less than half of her original territory. In her long history she has never won a war and has lost every battle but one. Her drive toward the sea in the Chaco War was checkmated by Paraguay's counterdrive toward her oilfields, and Paraguay is not a notably powerful state. All the concessions she has received from Chile since the War of the Pacific have been granted by Chile, not won by Bolivia. In 143 years of national independence, she has not been able, until very recently, even to begin utilizing her considerable natural resources for the benefit of her people. Bolivia has never been very important in the world and is not today. The contrasts with her antagonist,

[69] *The New York Times,* September 20, 1958.

[70] Compiled from *The Wall Street Journal,* September 27, 1966 and *The New York Times,* January 23, 1967.

Chile, could not be sharper. Bolivia is a study in futility. This futility and frustration underlie all of her international actions and help explain her emotional approach to her problems. Rioting in the streets, propaganda slogans on postmarks, appeals to "international solidarity" and "natural justice" rather than to law, repeated petulant refusals to attend inter-American conferences, are not signs of a confident, mature state.

This background can also help to explain the very different ways in which Bolivians and Chileans look at one another. Chileans are generally contemptuous of Bolivians, considering them ignorant and uncouth, militarily weak, irrational and highly volatile, unable to maintain strong cultural institutions and stable democratic government, as they themselves have done. Frequently, they simply refuse to take Bolivians seriously. They consider themselves infinitely superior to the Bolivians. (The importance of the difference in racial composition of the two populations in shaping this attitude cannot be overlooked.) These are the reasons they were so unconcerned about the Río Lauca fracas and why the calm, rational Chileans find it difficult to negotiate with Bolivians about irrigation or access to the sea.

Bolivians, on the other hand, point to Chile's long history of expansion at the expense of her neighbors and her interference in their internal affairs. Chileans encroached upon Bolivia's littoral, broke up the Peru-Bolivia Confederation by armed force, seized Mejillones from Bolivia and held it for several years, plundered and massacred Peruvians and Bolivians during the War of the Pacific, forced upon the vanquished harsh peace treaties which stripped them of valuable territory, shut up Bolivia in her mountain prison, manipulated governments in Peru and Bolivia and used their exiles for her own purposes, repeatedly violated the Treaty of 1904, stole part of her patrimony (the Río Lauca waters), and perpetrated many other acts of aggression. Bolivians consider Chileans arrogant and militaristic. They continually quote Chilean emissary to Bolivia Abraham König's infamous note written in 1900, condemn the oligarchy which still rules Chilean society, and conjure up visions of mighty Chilean military forces probing her border. They are jealous of Chile's comparatively high standard of living, military strength, high standing among the nations of the world, and – her seacoast.

These psychological and historical factors, added to geography and economics and to Bolivia's relatively good relations with Peru, explain why Bolivia's campaign for a *salida al mar* has been directed almost exclusively at Chile.

But Chile has sound reasons for not granting to Bolivia many more concessions than she already has without receiving something of real value in return. Since the War of the Pacific, the far north has been of enormous importance to Chile and the most sensitive area of her national territory. Chile is now the third largest copper producer in the world and expansion of the industry is continuing. Copper provides Chile with more than half of her foreign exchange and most of her copper comes from the territory won in the War of the Pacific. The war, however, was fought over nitrates, not copper. While the nitrate industry today is only a vestige of its former size and importance, it still produces Chile's third largest export and is very important to her economy. Fishing is the most rapidly growing industry in Chile and is being strongly encouraged by the Government. The earnings of fishmeal alone approximated $ 40,000,000 in 1966 and virtually all exported fisheries products come from off the coast of the Atacama Desert. Most of the valuable sulphur deposits of the Andean volcanoes remained on the Chilean side after the border settlements, including the two largest ones at Tacora and Ollagüe. These deposits are so pure that it is profitable to mine them even above 20,000 feet and the lower grade ores are ignored.

It is not only for its wealth that the Zona Norte is of concern to the Government of Chile. The North is so different and so remote from the center of everything Chilean that there exists in the region a strong separatist feeling. This feeling does not necessarily involve a desire for attachment to any other country, as Bolivia has implied upon occasion, but the North has long felt like a stepchild of Santiago. Vast wealth has been extracted from the desert by *Santiaguinos* and foreigners and very little has been returned in the form of benefits for those who live and work there.

To counteract these sentiments, the Government has continued the Chilenization campaign begun shortly after the War of the Pacific. One step in this program was the *Ley de la Frontera Libre Alimenticia* of 1958, which permits the importation into the Norte Grande of foodstuffs prohibited in most of the rest of the country because of competition with domestic supplies. Another was the granting of free port status to Arica in 1958, which resulted in a great economic boom and the tripling of the population of the town. Smuggling into Bolivia and central Chile got out of hand, however, and this free port status was greatly restricted in 1961. The new duties do not apply to capital goods, though, and Arica has become an important assembling and manufacturing center. Factories there now turn out automobiles, radios, toys, electronic equipment, motorcycles and many other products for distribution throughout the country.

This concession was quite frankly "an effort to create a showcase on the Peruvian frontier and to 'Chilenize' this desert region." [71]

Other recent government development projects in the North include highway construction and paving, housing projects, fishing piers and markets, tourist hotels and hostels, airport improvement, etc. Even the Río Lauca project was probably as much politically motivated as humanitarian. Few of these projects, however, are really well planned and efficiently carried out. Other projects in the south apparently have a higher priority, but for political reasons, if not for economic or humanitarian reasons, Chile is likely to make greater investments in the North than heretofore.

Considering all of these factors, it is not difficult to understand why Chile reacts so strongly to a foreign power casting eyes on any part of El Norte Grande. Still, her position is not rigid and it is possible, as suggested below, that under certain circumstances Chile might be willing to make some territorial concession to Bolivia.

Throughout her long campaign for a "*salida al mar*," Bolivia has never defined precisely what she means by that phrase. She has never formally and officially stated, so far as is known, just what it is she wants of Chile. Jorge Escobari, who may be considered well qualified to express the Government's point of view, discusses in his book a long list of suggestions which have been made in Bolivia. They range from tripartite (Peru, Chile, Bolivia) administration of Arica to unconditional retrocession to Bolivia of all the territory she lost in the War of the Pacific. He discusses the good and bad features of each one in turn and fails to recommend any solution himself. Fellman suggested in October 1963 that an enclave around Mejillones would satisfy Bolivia "at this time," but did not elaborate or press the matter further. Mario Gutiérrez, leader of the FSB, says, "Arica, then, Which Has Been, Which Wants To Be, Will Be Some Day Bolivian," and threatens war if Arica is not given to Bolivia! [72] José Carrasco in 1920 urged the return of the city of Antofagasta.

Pisagua, Iquique and Caleta Vitor have been mentioned at times as possible ports for Bolivia. The present government is considering requesting an enclave around a small cove north of Arica along the Peruvian border, without a sovereign corridor connecting it with the Altiplano, but thus far has not made the plan public.

[71] *The New York Times*, May 12, 1963.

[72] Mario R. Gutiérrez B., *Alegato Histórico de los Derechos de Bolivia al Pacífico* (La Paz: n.p., 1962), p. 260. This phrase was capitalized in the same manner in the book.

Bolivia, it seems, has based her case for her own outlet to the sea on three assertions. First, she is the only state in the world which had a seacoast and lost it by aggression and is therefore entitled to some special consideration. This assertion has very little merit, for, as we have seen, Bolivia exercised effective control over only a very small strip of coast with two tiny ports for only a little over half a century. She never developed her littoral in any way, never had a navy, a merchant fleet, a fishing fleet or a maritime tradition of any kind. Maps showed Bolivia extending to the sea, but the Altiplano never had really close ties with the sea.

Secondly, Bolivia claims that she signed the Treaty of 1904 under duress and that the Treaty is therefore invalid. This reasoning does not seem to conform with international law in regard to treaties. All peace treaties are signed by the vanquished state under some degree of duress, but they are nonetheless valid. Bolivia's peace treaty was signed twenty years after the end of the War of the Pacific and far less duress than usual was involved. In addition, Bolivia received far more in the Treaty than she had a right to expect. She obtained free use of Arica, for example, something she had never been able to obtain from her ally, Peru; and a railroad from Arica to La Paz, which neither she nor Peru had the capacity to build at the time. It is worthy of note also that Bolivia has never hesitated to claim benefits, even within the past few years, granted her under the "invalid" treaty.

Thirdly, Bolivia asserts that Chile has repeatedly violated certain provisions of the Treaty of 1904 and these violations either (a) invalidate the Treaty entirely, or (b) justify her claim for an *outlet* on the grounds that the mere *access* she has obtained under the Treaty has proved inadequate for her needs and subject to the pleasure of Chile. If this assertion has merit, there may be some justification for Bolivia's claim for an outlet to the sea, though it would probably not, under international law, invalidate the Treaty. It is consequently worth examining in some detail.

Bolivia's free transit privileges rest on Article 6 of the Treaty of 1904, in which Chile granted Bolivia "the widest and freest right of *commercial* transit through her territory and ports of the Pacific." (Italics added.) Under the Convention for the Construction and Operation of the FCALP of 1905, Chile agreed to carry all Bolivian mail free on the railroad. All railroad equipment, including rolling stock, needed by the Bolivian Government for its railroads *in the interior* of Bolivia would be carried at cost. Under the Commercial Traffic Convention of 1912, Bolivia's free transit rights were amplified, traffic was regulated and more authority was given to Bolivian customs agents in Chilean ports. Although Bolivia continued to press for revision of the Treaty of 1904, for the next twenty-five years she evidently did not register with Chile any important complaint about a specific violation of these undertakings.

One of Bolivia's most serious charges has been that during the Chaco War, Chile prohibited the transit of arms destined for Bolivia across her territory. According to one disinterested observer, Chile wanted Bolivia to win the Chaco War and block Argentine expansion, thus relieving Argentine pressure on Chile. She therefore *helped* Bolivia by supplying her with arms. [73] But even if Chile did prohibit the transit of arms, she probably did so at the request of the League of Nations, which was trying to stop the war. She was able to do so because the Treaty of 1904 stipulated only the free transit of *commercial* traffic. This oversight (from the Bolivian viewpoint) was rectified by the Convention on Free Transit of 1937. This Convention stipulated that "... the free transit includes all classes of cargo and in all times without any exception." It also included free transit for passengers, added to the rights and privileges of Bolivian customs agents and contained many technical provisions. Thus it would seem inappropriate for Bolivia to resurrect the Chaco War incident since it was not a violation of the Treaty of 1904 and under the 1937 Convention it could not happen again.

The second major alleged Chilean violation of the Treaty of 1904 was her embargo in 1952 of tools, equipment and food destined for the Bolivian tin mines which had recently been nationalized. This was apparently done under a Chilean court decision which authorized private persons to seize goods consigned to the mines in compensation for assets lost through the nationalization process. Once again, this was not precisely a violation of the Treaty. To close that loophole, the two countries, in the 1953 Declaration of Arica, agreed that cargo in transit to Bolivia was not subject to the jurisdiction of Chilean authorities. An incident of this type is similarly unlikely to happen again.

The Treaty of Chilean-Bolivian Economic Co-ordination of 1955 reiterated the free transit principle and expanded it to include third countries. It also included technical arrangements for financing the FCALP, further strengthened the position of Bolivian customs agents, provided for a commission to study a route for an Iquique-Oruro highway, and contained an agreement to prepare for construction and operation of an Oruro-Arica oil pipeline. The Accord actually granting Bolivia the right to build this pipeline from Sicasica to Arica was signed in 1957.

[73] Ronald Stuart Kain, "Bolivia's Claustrophobia," *Foreign Affairs,* XVI (July, 1938).

Besides concluding all of these agreements, Chile has repeatedly offered to discuss additional concessions with Bolivia. A conference on this subject was in progress in November 1961 when it was suspended by Fellman in the midst of the Río Lauca crisis. Chilean Foreign Minister Martínez' speech at the United Nations General Assembly meeting in September 1962 summarized the facilities granted to Bolivia. The Chilean Foreign Ministry has issued a most detailed account of them, replete with statistics, tariff schedules, etc., demonstrating that these facilities, particularly the port of Arica and the FCALP, are primarily for the benefit of Bolivia and that they are "equal to or superior to those of any other mediterranean country." [74]

Bolivia has indirectly admitted the validity of this claim by making no charges more serious than the two discussed above. The other violations alleged by Bolivia, mostly during the period of tension over the Río Lauca, include such things as "illegal restrictions" of Bolivian mineral exports in Antofagasta in July 1962; violations of the seals placed on warehouses by the Bolivian Customs Agents in Arica during October 1962; mishandling resulting in spoilage of a cargo of flour destined for Bolivian miners in Antofagasta in November 1962; [75] high tariffs charged for Bolivian tin moving from Catavi to Antofagasta (over a railroad which in Chile is privately owned); and delays of the nature referred to previously.

Bolivia also assumed a very different attitude in the first two United Nations conferences which dealt with the question of access to the sea. The contrast with her intense propaganda campaign is clear. In 1958, for example, the Bolivian delegation to the Conference on the Law of the Sea was headed by Walter Guevara Arze and included Jorge Escobari. [76] During both the Preliminary Conference and the deliberations of the Fifth Committee of the main Conference, they were most cooperative and reasonable and made sound, constructive contributions to the work of the Conferences. In the Preliminary Conference, Sr. Guevara called attention to some of the bilateral agreements with Chile discussed above. He suggested, on the basis of Bolivia's experience, that the main Conference

[74] Chile, Ministerio de Relaciones Exteriores, *Facilidades de Libre Tránsito Que Chile Otorga a Bolivia* (Santiago, 1963) p. 3.

[75] Note from Fellman to the Brazilian Ambassador in Santiago dated May 10, 1963, quoted in *La Nación* (La Paz), May 12, 1963.

[76] Nowhere in his book does Escobari mention this Conference. Guevara was one of the founders of the MNR and former Foreign Minister. He was expelled from the party by Paz in 1960, became leader of an opposition party, and is once again Foreign Minister.

discuss pipelines as a means of transport and also the possibility of free transit being interrupted by legal action of private persons. "He suggested that some of the principles governing the Bolivian agreements with its neighbors could be included in the codification." [77]

During the Fifth Committee meetings, Bolivia consistently worked for a firm guarantee of the rights of land-locked states to access to the sea embodied in a United Nations convention because bilateral treaties may be disregarded or denounced. She further wanted to be certain that under any codification which might result from the Conference, the advantages which she enjoys by virtue of agreements with her neighbors would not be reduced nor her contractual obligations increased. Bolivia took the position that

> [b]esides the Barcelona and Geneva declarations [1921 and 1923 respectively], relations between the land-locked States and their neighbors had given rise to a series of bilateral treaties which could not be revoked. It would be inadvisable to overlook the juridical system which had been built up between the land-locked States of Latin America and their neighbors over thirty years of cooperation. [78]

After describing in some detail the relevant treaties with Chile, Guevara commented that "[t]he system set up under the agreements he [Guevara] had mentioned was functioning normally. Nevertheless, the Bolivian people would continue to yearn to possess a part of the Pacific Coast [Sic!]." [79]

Bolivia was one of the sponsors of the nineteen-power proposal which was one of the basic documents of the Conference. In its Article VII, this proposal defined the rights of the state of transit to maintain full sovereignty over its territory, communications and facilities and that the rights of the land-locked state should not infringe any of its interests. To this draft Article was appended this Note:

> The delegation of Bolivia stated that its arrangements for transit through the territory of the coastal States towards the Pacific were broad and liberal and that they remained in force at all times and in all circumstances, and that consequently the clause included in Article VII was not applicable to those arrangements. [80]

It would appear from the foregoing quotations that Bolivia in 1958 was not displeased with her facilities for access to the sea, though since

[77] United Nations, General Assembly, *United Nations Conference on the Law of the Sea, Official Records, (Preliminary Conference of Land-locked States)* (A/CONF. 13/C.5/L.1) (28 February 1958).

[78] A/CONF.13/43, p. 49.

[79] *Ibid.*, p. 19.

[80] *Ibid.*, p. 80.

1910 she has been saying just the opposite for public consumption. It should be noted that at this Conference, Chile was also most cooperative, served in a working group with Bolivia and supported the Principles of the Preliminary Conference.

During the 1964 United Nations Conference on Trade and Development, Bolivia likewise played a constructive role. She did not take this perfect opportunity to document her claims of economic "strangulation" or "asphyxiation." On the contrary, she worked closely with Chile and used their treaty relations as a good, not a horrible, example for other land-locked states.

By the summer of 1965, however, the unstable Bolivian military government had reverted to a hard line, even in the councils of the United Nations, where she had hitherto been quite cooperative. Throughout the U. N. Conference on Transit Trade of Land-locked Countries, Bolivia was among the leaders of those land-locked states which were demanding unlimited access to the sea and firm guarantees of this right. The Bolivian representatives also appeared to be more belligerent and less capable than those at earlier conferences. Once again they reverted to such phrases as "the recovery of its coastline was an inalienable right based on incontrovertible historical and legal titles" [81] and "the international conscience recognized that Bolivia was not a land-locked country, but a State which, owing to transitory circumstances, was temporarily deprived of access to the sea through its own coast." [82]

The Bolivian delegate even declared at the 8th session on June 11, 1965

> that he wished to make two important facts perfectly clear in connexion with Bolivia's attitude to the conference: Bolivia considered its right to the restoration of its Pacific coastline to be inalienable, and the fact that it had entered into bilateral agreements in order to reduce the disadvantages caused by its temporary lack of that coastline must not be taken as indicating any intention on its part of relinquishing its claim to territory on the Pacific.
> ... Bolivia was happy to acknowledge that it had always received helpful and considerate treatment from Argentina, Brazil, Paraguay and Peru in connexion with its transit problems. [83]

Chile is much closer, in many ways, to the great majority of Bolivians than any of their other neighbors and despite the new international convention and agreements on transit for land-locked states, despite Bolivia's

[81] TD/TRANSIT/SR.26, p. 5.
[82] TD/TRANSIT/SR.36, p. 5.
[83] TD/TRANSIT/SR.8, p. 10.

gradual shift toward an Atlantic orientation, despite the fact that Chile has provided by far the best transit facilities Bolivia (and perhaps any other land-locked state) has, it appears that as long as Bolivia is a weak state with only a rudimentary national consciousness and an unstable government lacking true popular support, that government will continue to use anti-Chileanism and the *salida al mar* campaign to weld some degree of national unity and maintain itself in office, though under the new Foreign Minister, Walter Guevara Arze, it might moderate its tone somewhat.

CHAPTER V

UGANDA

Although tribal pressures doubtless played a significant part in causing Ugandans to include elements of federalism in the constitution, it is difficult to determine the extent to which federalism exacerbated existing tribal tensions. Certainly the knowledge that political action won federal status for five states had an impact on less successful peoples. Similarly the tendency to base statehood on a tribal foundation caused the emergence of movements aimed at border rectification. Federalism with a tribal basis seems to possess inherently unstable features, for it cannot possibly be adapted to fit the overlapping patterns of Uganda's ethnic structure. Efforts to build a sense of national unity are especially vital in preventing bitterness, fear and separatist tendencies from hindering the growth of a strong and viable state. [1]

This problem of national unity is the most serious challenging the new state of Uganda, more serious even than her access to the sea, for though landlocked, Uganda's goods transit Kenya to and from the Indian Ocean with no interference by means of a unified East African transportation authority. East African unity has been a somewhat ephemeral thing, waxing and waning in response to political and economic developments in one territory or another – or outside the region altogether. It is one of the paradoxes of African politics that some form of federal state embracing at least Kenya, Tanzania and Uganda, the dream of many in all three countries for decades, would assure Uganda her unquestioned access to the sea, but it is precisely this question of federalism in Uganda which has been the major obstacle in the path of a larger East African federation.

The Geographic Setting

Uganda is a small country astride the equator in the heart of what was

[1] Donald Rothchild and Michael Rogin, "Uganda," in Gwendolen M. Carter, ed., *National Unity and Regionalism in Eight African States* (Ithaca, New York: Cornell University Press, 1966), p. 418.

MAP 8

UGANDA

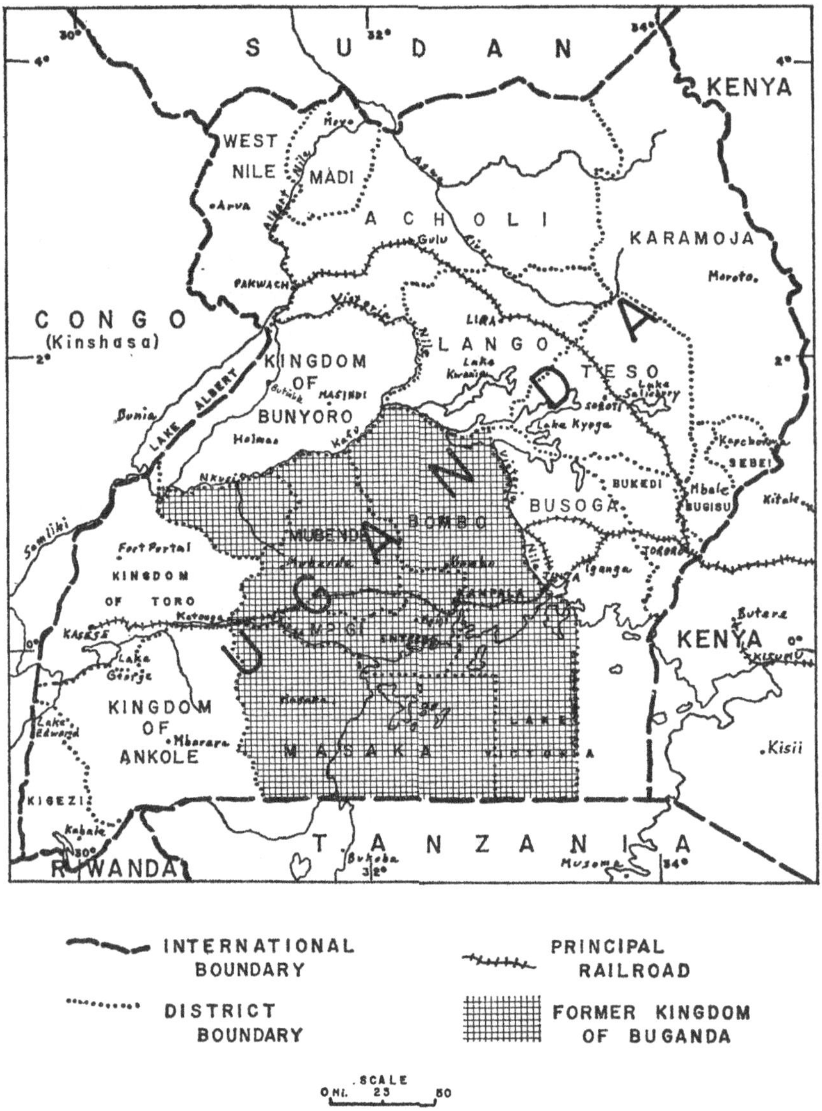
SUDAN
KENYA
WEST NILE
MADI
ACHOLI
Gulu
KARAMOJA
Moroto
PAKWACH
CONGO
(Kinshasa)
LIRA
LANGO
KINGDOM OF BUNYORO
MASINDI
TESO
Lake Kyoga
BUKEDI
SEBEI
Mbale
BUGISU
BUSOGA
MUBENDE
BOMBO
Fort Portal
KINGDOM OF TORO
Katonga
KASESE
Lake George
MPIGI
KAMPALA
ENTEBBE
Iganga
TORORO
KENYA
KINGDOM OF ANKOLE
Mbarara
MASAKA
LAKE VICTORIA
Kisii
KIGEZI
Kabale
RWANDA
TANZANIA
Bukoba
Musoma
UGANDA
INTERNATIONAL BOUNDARY
DISTRICT BOUNDARY
PRINCIPAL RAILROAD
FORMER KINGDOM OF BUGANDA
SCALE
0 MI. 25 50

for half a century known as British East Africa.[2] Most of the country is located on the great East African plateau. The most prominent topographical features are Lake Victoria, of which Uganda owns most of the northern half; the Western branch of the Great Rift Valley, which extends from the Adriatic Sea and the Jordan Valley through eastern Africa to branch out and reach well into Mozambique and containing several of the Great Lakes of Africa; and the high mountain massifs of Ruwenzori on the Congo border (16,763') and Elgon (14,178') on the Kenya border. Much of the south and central portion of the country is swampy, but the northern portion, part of the Sudan Basin, is drier.

Writers repeatedly refer to Uganda's location as being a handicap, using such phrases as "Uganda has always suffered from her land-locked location,"[3] and "entirely land-locked and dependent for its contacts with the outside world on facilities offered by its neighbors."[4] There are, however, some advantages inherent in her location which strengthen her position vis-a-vis her neighbors to the north, if not those to the east and south.

> The geographic location of Uganda, far inland in the Lake Plateau of Eastern Africa, at an elevation of 3500 to 4000 feet, is both its greatest strength and its greatest weakness in its relations with the outside world. The whole of the country drains from Lake Victoria through Lake Kioga into Lake Albert and thence into the Nile. Uganda, thus, covers the gathering grounds of the White Nile. It becomes all the more important because in the early part of the year more than half the supply of water to the Lower Nile comes from the Lake Plateau. This control of the head-waters of the Nile, the life-giving stream of Sudan and Egypt, gives great bargaining strength to Uganda, because in international law, an upper riparian state is entitled to divert the flow of an international river at its own discretion . . . Sudan and Egypt must, therefore, continue to have close association with Uganda and offer it certain priorities of mutual interest.[5]

The climate and vegetation of Uganda reflect her location in the transition zone between the tropical forest lands of the Congo Basin and the subtropical savannas of the east, modified by her elevation. Throughout most of the country, temperatures are moderate (in the low 70°'s F)

[2] The area of Uganda is variously given as anywhere from 80,000 to over 92,000 square miles, depending on the amount of open water included in the estimates. There are no disputed boundaries, so only variations in lake levels and computations affect estimates of area.

[3] Harm J. de Blij, *A Geography of Subsaharan Africa* (Chicago: Rand McNally and Company, 1964), p. 265.

[4] L. Dudley Stamp, *Africa: A Study in Tropical Development* (2nd ed.; New York: John Wiley and Sons, Inc., 1964), p. 392.

[5] R. Dutta, "Uganda; A Geopolitical Study," *Modern Review*, (January, 1965), p. 18.

throughout the year and rainfall is also moderate (40″ to 60″) and distributed throughout the year, though with maxima in about April to May and October to December. The north, near the Sudan border, tends to be both hotter and drier, as well as lower, but nowhere in the country, except for the swampy areas, does climate or drainage specifically discourage settlement.

The relative uniformity of the physical geography of the country, combined with the many invasions from all directions in the past, has resulted in the population of Uganda being rather evenly distributed throughout the national territory, rather than scattered in nodes of settlement in favored areas as in most of Africa. The greatest concentration of people is around the north shore of Lake Victoria and along the southern portion of the Kenya border. The region around Lake Victoria, including the Kenya and Tanganyika shores, is in fact one of the most densely settled regions in all of Africa, basically a sparsely populated continent. Uganda is also one of the most densely populated states in all of Africa, with some seven and a half million people in 1966.

Uganda's status as a British protectorate rather than a colony like most of Kenya or a trust territory like Tanganyika was of little importance in most respects, but it did affect the composition of the population. All but a relative handful are native Africans with only some 12,000 Europeans and 80,000 Indians, other Asians and other non-Africans living there. Alienation of land to non-Africans was least in Uganda and she was able to escape the complications of a "white settler" minority such as Algeria, Kenya, Rhodesia and South Africa have experienced. Neither the plantation system nor latifundia has become established here, and the dominant form of land tenure is the peasant smallholding. This has both economic advantages and disadvantages, of course, but it has been of great social value to Uganda in her nation-building efforts.

The African population, however, is far from homogeneous. The very diversity of the African population has led, in fact, to the "federalism with a tribal basis" discussed in the quotation which opened this chapter. The boundaries of Uganda were drawn by European powers for their own political purposes and bear no relation to the distribution of ethnic groups in the region. This is true of most African states, of course, but in the case of Uganda the problem is compounded by her location on one of the primary migration routes of Africa. While the southern portion of the country is inhabited largely by Bantu-speaking groups, of whom the most prominent are the Baganda, Kiga, Ankole, and Toro, the north central part contains largely Nilotic peoples, particularly the Acholi and Longo, in the east are mostly Nilo-Hamitic tribes, including the Teso, Karamojong, Gisu and Soga, and the far northwest contains Sudanic groups, among them the Lugbara. The borders cut through the territories of all of these peoples. Fortunately, this has not proven as much of a problem as it has, for example, in West Africa, but it is a latent issue and may become important in the future. What is more important is the fact that the differences among these peoples *within* Uganda, particularly of political, social and economic development, have led to frictions and must be counted as the most important centrifugal force operating in the country. Much has been done by the present government to resolve this problem, but it is still doubtful how close to resolution it is.

Complicating the ethnic situation (and the economic one) still further are two modern types of in-migration. The first is a steady and peaceful infiltration of workers from all over East Africa into the most favored areas of the basin of Lake Victoria in Tanzania and Uganda, particularly the latter. Most of these are from Kenya and have been able to cross the borders freely because of the close relationships among the units of East Africa. This is beginning to pose both social and economic problems, however, and barriers are now being erected to migration among the three countries. More immediately serious is the presence in Uganda of some 140,000 refugees from political and tribal turbulence in her northern, western and southwestern neighbors. They include about 70,000 from Rwanda, 40,000 from the Sudan, and 25,000 from the Congo. [6] They impose an economic burden on a small, underdeveloped state, to be sure, but what is more alarming is their presence so close to the borders of their homelands, with which Uganda wishes to remain on good terms. Consequently the government has undertaken to resettle many thousands of them away from the borders, particularly those from Sudan, Rwanda and Burundi. Dominating all population problems, however, has been the inability of the largest group in the country, the Baganda, who constitute about one-sixth of the population, to identify themselves with the state to which they gave their name. This will be discussed at greater length below.

The economic geography of Uganda is not very different from that of most of East Africa, within which it is closely bound. Uganda is preeminently an agricultural country, with some 90% of the population growing and processing both cash and subsistence crops. About 75% of the national income is derived from agricultural or pastoral activities. [7] The

[6] All figures from the 16th Annual Report of the United Nations High Commissioner for Refugees dated August 1966. Reported in *Keesing's Contemporary Archives* for 11–18 March 1967, p. 2117.

dominant subsistence crops are cereals, particularly millets and sorghums; starches, especially cassava and bananas; a variety of fruits and vegetables and some sugar. The lakes and rivers produce some $ 2.8 million worth of fish annually, much of which is sold commercially. [8]

We are interested primarily in the cash crops, however, which are grown on somewhat less than one-third of the cultivated acreage. A relatively minor one, but important in interterritorial (within East Africa) trade, is tobacco. Some of it is consumed domestically and some is exported, but an increasing proportion of it is being made into cigarettes in Jinja and Kampala which are then sold in Kenya and Tanzania. The most important cash crops by far are cotton and coffee. Native varieties of cotton had long been used domestically, but were largely replaced after American and Egyptian types were introduced in 1903. Since then cotton, mostly American Upland, has spread throughout most of the country, nearly everywhere but the northeast and far south-west. Well over two million acres are now under cotton cultivation, the best area for production being Busoga in the east. Cotton accounted for 35.9% of Uganda's total exports to foreign (non-East African) customers in 1960 and 24.6% in 1964. Cotton sales to India alone earned in 1964 $ 13,210,000 of the total export income of $ 180,409,000. [9] The drop in the importance of cotton as an export does not reflect an absolute drop, only the rapidly growing proportion of coffee exports in Uganda's economy.

Coffee is not only the dominant product among Uganda's exports, and hence in her economy, but Uganda is also the largest producer of coffee in the Commonwealth. It was first exported in 1902 and was originally grown almost exclusively by the few white plantation owners and Asians. Africans have adopted the crop readily, however, and now all but a very small amount is grown on peasant smallholdings. Coffee production has grown spectacularly since World War II and now amounts to well over half of Uganda's exports (40.9% in 1960, 54.9% in 1964). Her best coffee customer is the United States, who purchased $ 45,743,000 worth in 1964. [10] The principal varieties are the Robusta, used largely now in instant coffee and a specialty of the Baganda, and the Arabica, a higher quality type grown in much smaller quantities, mostly on the slopes of Mount Elgon.

[7] *Encyclopaedia Britannica,* 1965 ed., Vol. XXII, p. 663.

[8] J. W. King, "Nile Transport in Uganda," *The East African Geographical Review,* (April, 1966), p. 35.

[9] Uganda, Statistics Division, Ministry of Planning and Community Development, *1965 Statistical Abstract* (Entebbe: Government Printer, 1965), pp. 19, 20, and 22.

[10] *Ibid.*

With cotton and coffee alone accounting for some 80% of Uganda's exports, she is typical of many developing countries which are dependent for the bulk of their foreign exchange, if not, indeed, of their total income, on the export of one or two products. Other significant export crops are tea, which accounts for only 3.4% of the exports and goes mainly to Britain; animal feed; hides and skins; and oil seeds, nuts and kernels. The only important non-agricultural export is copper, mined at Kilembe, near the railhead at Kasese in the southwest, and shipped mainly to the United States. This amounted to 9.6% of Uganda's total exports in 1964, of which the United States took $ 3,329,000 worth.[11]

If mining of copper, tin, wolfram, gold and other minerals is of little importance in Uganda, manufacturing is even less important. Most of the country's industries are of the food processing and consumer goods type so common in developing countries. There are, however, a copper smelter and Africa's first steel rolling mill at Jinja, using power from the large Owen Falls hydroelectric project. This dam on the Victoria Nile just north of Lake Victoria was opened in 1954. It is also designed to store water for the Sudan and Egypt. Other industries are located in Kampala, Jinja and Tororo and most of those that are planned will also be located in Buganda (home of the Baganda people) or elsewhere in the south. This concentration of the most profitable agriculture, most of the industry, the largest towns and the best transportation in the region south of Lake Kioga has led to some frictions within the country, particularly since this economic power is held by the region which has also been politically and socially dominant in the country. The only economic asset of any importance north of Lake Kioga is livestock, limited to this region by the tsetse fly further south. In 1964 there were some 3,431,000 head of cattle and 2,781,000 sheep and goats in Uganda which were worth an estimated $ 33,600,000 to the economy, but only a very small proportion of this value is derived from the export of hides and skins.[12]

One impediment to the diversification of the economy sought by the government is the lack of any fuel in the country except wood, for which conservation restrictions have now been adopted. All petroleum and petroleum products must be imported. Nearly all of the country's electricity is generated at the Owen Falls station, and transmission lines are being extended out from there to much of the country. They have so far reached as far west as Kilembe, Fort Portal and Masindi and as far north

[11] *Ibid.*

[12] Figures from *Uganda; An Economic Survey* (London: Barclays Bank D.C.O., 1967), p. 13.

as Gulu and Lira. Meanwhile, industrialization is proceeding slowly, agricultural diversification even more slowly, and only fishing and tourism are showing any real signs of lessening the country's dependence upon the export of coffee and cotton.

Both of these crops are subject to wild fluctuations in price, and cotton particularly has had a history of boom and bust. With all their problems, natural and commercial, however, these crops have been most profitable and Uganda generally enjoys a favorable balance of trade, a rare thing in developing countries. If the revenue is invested wisely in improving the quality of her products and in diversifying her economy and her markets, Uganda should be able to raise her standard of living significantly without going deeply into debt or seeing her economy collapse with a sudden change in her export markets.

Uganda's imports, as expected, are much more diversified than her exports and come from many more places than her exports are sold in. A great variety of manufactured goods, machinery and transportation equipment, fuels and other petroleum products, chemicals, and small amounts of raw materials and foodstuffs are imported. Uganda's best market for her products is the United States (over $ 50.4 million in 1964, up from over $ 44.8 million in 1960), with the total sterling area a close second (almost $ 50 million in 1964, of which $ 22.4 million was earned in the United Kingdom in 1964, up $ 2.8 million since 1960).[13] In 1965, however, the United States and the United Kingdom were more nearly equal as customers, while China was a strong third (buying more than $16.8 million worth of goods), pulling ahead of both India and Germany.[14] The United Kingdom has always been and continues to be by far the most important source of Ugandan imports, supplying one-third of her total $ 92.4 million worth of imports in 1964[15] and nearly $ 44.8 million worth in 1965.[16] Japan and Germany are her second and third most important suppliers, but they trail far behind Britain.

All of these imports and exports move over one of the best transportation systems in Africa, all things considered. The most important mode of transportation in East Africa is the railroad. All of the railroads are operated by the East African Railways and Harbours (EAR and H), a service of the East African Common Services Organization, which was incorporated in December 1967 into the new East African Community.

[13] Uganda, *1965 Statistical Abstract,* p. 21.
[14] Barclays Bank, *Uganda,* p. 20.
[15] Uganda, *1965 Statistical Abstract,* p. 24.
[16] Barclays Bank, *Uganda,* p. 19.

The main railway lines are the Central and Tanga lines in Tanganyika and the Kenya-Uganda Line (originally The Uganda Railway) which connects the principal seaport of Mombasa with Pakwatch and Kasese in western Uganda.

It was the railroad, in fact, which quite literally "opened up" East Africa and particularly Uganda. But the early railway developments

> were actuated by the political and strategic requirements of the policies of imperialism which were pursued by both Britain and Germany in the latter half of the nineteenth century. The economic resources of East Africa were not known at that time. The early railways were built partly in the hope that economic benefits would accrue, but they were not designed primarily to promote economic development. [17]

This was quite true, and more shall be said about it later, but the important point is that since the turn of the century and particularly since World War II the railroads have been immensely important in the economic development of Uganda and all of East Africa and have helped to unify the region. In 1966 the Kenya-Uganda Line alone carried 1,688,000 tons of goods from Mombasa inland and 870,000 tons down to Mombasa, both new records. [18] While most of this has always been Kenyan traffic, the proportion of Ugandan traffic has been growing in recent years.

EAR and H also operates road services, but they are distinctly secondary to railway and port operation and most of the highways are built and maintained by the individual governments. In Uganda there are 3,343 miles of all-weather roads maintained by the Ministry of Works, of which about 738 miles are hard-surfaced. In addition there are some 10,780 miles of roads maintained by local authorities, but some of these are strictly dry-weather roads. [19] Uganda has the best road system in East Africa because of local responsibility for road-building, good quality construction materials, relatively short distances, and more money available for construction. The government has been wary about building more good highways and encouraging the development of a large trucking industry because of the competition it would offer the railroad. The railroad is distinctly favored for foreign trade and very little traffic makes the long journey to or from the sea by road. The highways are adequate as alternates in case of emergency, however, and the principal problem seems to

[17] *The Economy of East Africa; A Study of Trends* (London: The Economist Intelligence Unit, October, 1955), p. 53.

[18] East African Railways and Harbours (EAR and H), *Annual Report 1966* (Nairobi, April, 1967), p. 12.

[19] Barclays Bank, *Uganda*, p. 18.

be a shortage of trucks. In 1961, Uganda had only 586 public service vehicles, 8,000 commercial vehicles and 22,807 automobiles.[20] The government is now planning a road-building program emphasizing the region to the north and south of the railhead at Kasese, with some emphasis on local plantation roads.

The "Nile System," a transport system consisting of steamers and lighters on Lakes Victoria and Kioga, a road service between Masindi Port and Butiaba, and a fleet of vessels on Lake Albert and the Albert Nile, played a most important role in the economic development of the region it served from its origin in 1912 to its discontinuance in 1962.

> [F]or many years the System provided the only means whereby bulk commodities [predominantly cotton] could be transported from northern Uganda to world markets at reasonable cost, and by which most of the consumer and other goods needed in the area could be effectively distributed.[21]

The System was finally abandoned because of competition from more economical road and rail services, overage vessels and facilities too costly to replace, and severe flooding in 1961 and 1962. While never outstandingly successful financially, it did serve to generate agricultural development and help link northern Uganda with the sea.

East Africa is well served by regional and international airlines, but air transport is less used there than in many developing regions because the other modes of transport are better developed. In fact, "No parts of the region are accessible only by air." Flying is also still quite expensive for both passengers and freight. The Entebbe airport, the major one in Uganda, handled only 8,330 movements in 1964 and 2, 576 in the first quarter of 1966.[23] Nevertheless, air transport seems likely to increase, especially for tourism and export of high-value products. One enterprising Ugandan is even shipping fresh vegetables by air to London for gourmets and health faddists, competing with Israel in this market.[24] Nevertheless, surface transport is and shall remain Uganda's principal link with the sea.

[20] *Uganda: Report for the year 1961* (London: HMSO, 1963), p. 113.

[21] King, *op.* cit., p. 25.

[22] A. M. O'Connor, *An Economic Geography of East Africa* (New York: Frederick A. Praeger, Publishers, 1966), p. 187.

[23] Uganda, Statistics Division, Ministry of Planning and Economic Development, *Uganda Quarterly Digest of Statistics 4,* September 1966.

[24] Interview with John Canning, Uganda desk officer, United States Department of State, July 20, 1967.

Historical and Political Background

The transitional nature of Uganda's climate and vegetation have already been noted; the country is transitional in other ways as well. Ethnographically, the variegated population has resulted from perhaps a thousand years of immigrations of Hamitic, Nilotic and Nilo-Hamitic peoples from the north. These peoples dominated the indigenous inhabitants and, particularly in the south and west, had become by the 16th century a governing aristocracy in the many tribes, clans and other groups of Bantu-speaking peoples. Several kingdoms developed, apparently modeled on Egyptian political ideas. Among them Toro, Ankole, Bunyoro and Buganda were most important. In Ankole the distinction between the ruling aristocracy and the people was most prominent, but it gradually faded out through intermarriage in the other kingdoms. Bunyoro became the most powerful kingdom in the 17th century and remained so for nearly two centuries. In the late 18th century Nyamwezi traders and Arabs began to arrive from the east. They found no cohesion among the various kingdoms and tribes and no contacts with the outside world such as the great empires of the West African savanna had. By the mid-19th century, when Arab traders and European explorers first arrived, Buganda had supplanted Bunyoro as the dominant kingdom and it is upon this kingdom that the subsequent history of Uganda is focused.

From the beginning, organized Arab and European contact with Uganda was from the south and around the western shore of Lake Victoria. This route was not only geographically easier than the direct route from the coast, but it also avoided the hostile intervening tribes, notably the Masai. Ahmed bin Ibrahim arrived from Zanzibar in 1844 seeking ivory and slaves. Slavers from the Sudan began raiding the northern tribes at about the same time and continued their depredations long after the slave trade was suppressed farther south. In 1862 the English explorers Speke and Grant reached Buganda in search of the source of the White Nile. They found it at the outlet of Lake Victoria near Jinja and proceeded to follow it downstream through the Sudan and Egypt. In the early 1870's Egypt, aided by Britain, invaded from the north, but was checked by the diplomacy of Mutesa, Kabaka (king) of Buganda. Egypt has not since penetrated Uganda. In 1875 the American Henry M. Stanley reached Buganda and it was his visit and published account of it which really stirred interest in the area in the outside world.

Anglican missionaries arrived in 1877 and Roman Catholics followed in 1879, all impressed by the great opportunities for conversion in Buganda. But at the same time, Islam was spreading through the more loosely organized tribes of the north and Uganda became the scene of religious conflict superimposed on the existing ethnic, political and economic contrasts. Mutesa, though, was interested first in Islam and then in Christianity only because they seemed at first to offer him support against a renewed Egyptian threat. When he failed to obtain firearms from the missionaries, he turned against them and the Catholic White Fathers withdrew in 1882. Mutesa died in 1884 and was succeeded by his son Mwanga. For the next six years the entire southern part of Uganda was wracked by power struggles, involving actual fighting, among the religious denominations, Mwanga, and various factions of Ankole and Buganda. Mwanga finally consolidated his power in 1890 with the help of a motley Christian army.

Germany immediately tried to win influence with the Kabaka, but this attempt was ended by the Anglo-German agreement of July 1, 1890, which declared Uganda to be within the British sphere of influence. By this time interest in Uganda had risen considerably in Europe and a railroad from the coast was suggested as early as 1884. After 1890, it became even more desirable, partly to suppress the slave trade, partly to develop the country economically and partly to compete with the Germans in Tanganyika. In December 1890 Captain (later Lord) F. D. Lugard, representing the Imperial British East Africa Company (Ibea), chartered by the British government to advance its interests in the region, induced Mwanga to sign a treaty authorizing Ibea to keep order in Buganda. He tried to strengthen his position by using Sudanese soldiers left in Western Uganda the year before. For the next two years more fighting took place among the factions, with Lugard supporting the Anglicans and Mwanga the Catholics. Finally peace was made in 1892, with the Catholics being allocated the southern portion and the Anglicans the remainder of Buganda.

Meanwhile, Ibea was having financial problems and was struggling to meet its commitments. Its survey of a rail route was unsuccessful, the slave trade persisted, religious strife continued, and the Belgians and French were pressing in from the west. Finally, in April 1893, Sir Gerald Portal proclaimed a provisional protectorate over Buganda; it was formally confirmed in 1894 and extended to Bunyoro in 1896. In both kingdoms, however, guerrilla warfare against the British continued until 1899. Effective British administration really began with the Uganda Agreement of 1900, which granted Buganda autonomy within the Uganda Protectorate. Similar, though less complicated, agreements were signed with Toro and

Ankole in 1900 and 1901 and the British began the process of forming a viable political unit out of four kingdoms and nearly thirty distinct peoples at all stages of organization and development. Large portions of the territory were transferred to the Sudan and Kenya and it was not until 1926 that the country assumed its present size and shape.

During the European scramble for Africa, both the United Kingdom and Germany penetrated the interior of East Africa primarily for its natural resources and the only interest they had in the coast was its value in securing the interior and its commerce.

> That part of the interior in which interest centered was Uganda. Apart from other circumstances, the position of that country on Victoria Nyanza formed a key to the Nile Valley beyond and the populous and productive provinces ruled by Emin Pasha [in the Sudan]. The power holding Uganda would exercise a paramount influence in the surrounding regions. The interest with which Uganda was regarded was, however, enhanced by other considerations. It was by far the most powerful state in Central Africa, and by far the most civilized. The arts of peace were cultivated to a remarkable degree of efficiency as well as the arts of war . . . [and] there would have been the strongest objection [by Britain] to its annexation by any other country . . .[25]

Indeed, the construction of the Uganda Railway was entirely for the purpose of "opening up" the interior, though suppression of the slave trade was often cited as justification for it. Its construction dates from December 11, 1895 when the British director of the project, Sir George Whitehouse, landed at Mombasa, and actual work began in May 1896.

> From a physical point of view the enterprise was great and the builders had to overcome immense and unforseen difficulties. From the social, the economic or the political point of view the enterprise was even greater, for the building of the railway exercised a paramount influence on the history of East Africa.[26]

The railroad not only made possible the retention of Uganda as a British protectorate, but it literally created Kenya as a British colony. Still, all of its potentials were not clearly visible at the time and it was nicknamed "the lunatic line" until it proved itself economically.

Construction was slow, dangerous and expensive. By the end of 1896 only twenty-three miles of track had been laid. It did not reach the site of

[25] R. L. McDermott, *British East Africa or Ibea* (London: Chapman and Hall, 1893) quoted in M. F. Hill, *Permanent Way; The Story of the Kenya and Uganda Railway* (Nairobi: East African Railways and Harbours, [1950]), p. 25.

[26] Hill, *op. cit.*, p. v.

what is now Nairobi until 1899, but the railroad camp established there became the economic and political focal point of East Africa. Despite the adverse effects of the Boer War and the difficulty of crossing the Eastern Rift Valley, the line reached Port Florence (now Kisumu) on Lake Victoria in December 1901. The 582 miles of track had taken five and a half years and over $ 16 million to build. With the steamship service on the lake connecting Kenya with Uganda, economic development was now possible in the newly secured Uganda Protectorate. Since no minerals had been discovered in Uganda, the only way to pay for construction and maintenance of the line and for the administration of the territory was to develop commercial agriculture. Coffee, cacao, rubber, tea, sugar, groundnuts and other crops were tried with indifferent results. The really big success was cotton, and cotton exports, which began in 1904, became the mainstay of the economy. This was due almost entirely to the reduction of transport costs to the coast.

> Before [the railway's] completion, the cost of moving goods to and from the coast was quite prohibitive for all except a very narrow range of goods; ivory of course being the classic example of a commodity that could bear the cost of transport . . . Transport costs were spectacularly reduced by the building of the railway. [27]

Concentration on cotton production was encouraged by Winston Churchill, then Under-Secretary of State for the Colonies, on a visit to Uganda in 1907. He was also largely responsible for the construction in 1911–12 of the first railroad in Uganda, the line from Jinja on the north shore of Lake Victoria to Namasagali on the Victoria Nile near Lake Kioga. [28] From then on, cotton, water and rail transport, and Uganda grew together.

Buganda was and remained the core area of the Protectorate of Uganda, but its overwhelming predominance in the affairs of the country was challenged by the building of the railway connecting Lakes Victoria and Kioga and by the construction of a network of all-weather roads begun by the Governor after responsibility for the Protectorate was transferred from the Foreign Office to the Colonial Office in 1905. European settlement was discouraged, partly as a matter of policy and partly by the slowness in surveying the kingdom of Buganda to establish the titles of

[27] David Walker, "Problems of Economic Development of East Africa" in E. A. G. Robinson, ed., *Economic Development for Africa South of the Sahara* (New York: St. Martin's Press, Inc., 1964), p. 97. This book contains the proceedings of a conference held by the International Economic Association in Addis Ababa in 1961.

[28] "Development of Uganda's Communications," *Spear,* V (October, 1962), pp. 245–46.

lands granted the chiefs under the 1900 agreement. The railroad had also opened up the Kenya highlands, sparsely populated and much more attractive to Europeans. The extension of British authority from its base in Buganda into the more remote districts was also a slow process, accomplished by the classic British device of indirect rule. To make this device effective, it was often necessary to create chiefs where there were none and to apply many of the features of the Buganda pattern of administration in the other kingdoms and districts. With all the economic development, improvements in transportation and British efforts toward creating a united nation, Buganda remained virtually a world unto itself.

The original administrative division of Uganda was into four provinces, the Western, including the Kingdoms of Toro, Ankole and Bunyoro; the Eastern, including the quasi-kingdom of Busoga; the Northern, least developed of all; and – Buganda. Later, the provinces were dissolved. The four kingdoms were given separate status and Busoga was made a territory, all of them in a federal or semi-federal relationship with the central government; and ten districts and the territory of Mbale were created. This was the administrative arrangement when Uganda became independent in 1962. Like other features of Uganda, it illustrates the heterogeneity of the country, yet the overall unity within it.

World War I affected Uganda little except to place heavy demands on her manpower and the railway to the sea, and to impose restrictions on her trade. The peasant farmers of Uganda had demonstrated that they could produce large quantities of high-quality cotton. Now, after the wartime difficulties with a one-crop economy, they were encouraged to diversify. They took readily to coffee. In 1916 a ban was placed on the sale of land to Europeans except in special circumstances and under stringent conditions. While Europeans and Asians developed some tea and sugar plantations, Uganda was confirmed as a nation of peasant smallholders.

> And it has been the growth of production for export from small peasant farms that has been the main force in the development of the economy and that has provided the wealth to support the social services on the one hand and the demand for home-produced goods and services on the other, as well as the demand for a substantial flow of goods into the country from overseas. Uganda provides a text-book example of a country whose economic development has depended, and indeed still depends, upon the grafting on to a traditional and indigenous system of subsistence agriculture the production of an export crop. [29]

[29] Walker, *op. cit.*, p. 98.

During the interwar years, progress was made in spheres other than just the economic. In 1920 a measure of self-government was granted the Protectorate as a whole. Education was encouraged, a new East African currency was introduced, the Kabaka's government in Buganda developed particularly complete social services, and in 1933 an agreement was made between the Protectorate government and the ruler of Bunyoro similar to those signed with the other kingdoms a generation earlier.

Perhaps the most portentious political development, however, was the growth in the 1920's of a movement for federation, or "closer union" of the British East and Central African territories, which now included the mandated territory of Tanganyika, formerly German East Africa. The movement was generated largely by the white settlers, who saw "closer union" as a way of attaining control over the whole region. The idea was hotly debated and became tangled in many political and racial issues, not the least of which was the projected role of the Asians (mostly East Indians). The strongest objections, however, came from Buganda, which feared for its privileged position under the 1900 agreement in any projected federation. In 1926, in response to the demands for cooperation, at least, the first Conference of Governors of the East African territories was held. In 1929 the Conference established the British East African Meteorological Service; in 1932 the Conference acquired a permanent secretariat; in 1933 the posts and telegraphs of the territories were amalgamated. African opposition and the special status of Tanganyika tended, however, to delay any concrete moves toward a political "closer union."

The territories were being brought closer together, though, by "The Permanent Way," the Kenya and Uganda Railway, which was gradually being extended to and through Uganda. It reached Kampala in 1931 and a northern extension from Tororo, just inside the Kenya border, reached Soroti in 1929. With the new railroad, the Nile System and the Lake Victoria steamers, Uganda became even more closely linked with Kenya and Tanganyika economically. This linkage alone, however, did not produce any comradely feelings, for Kenya and Uganda squabbled over the rates on gasoline railed up from Mombasa and about the distribution of profits and losses between the two governments. The Great Depression, moreover, slowed economic development in all of the territories, though rather less in Uganda than in the others.

World War II had roughly the same effects on Uganda as World War I had: a severe strain on all transportation facilities, deterioration of tracks and equipment, overworking of the remaining manpower after much had been drained away for military service and labor elsewhere, and the additional strains of rapid demobilization. On the other hand, demand for Uganda's products boomed and she was able to accumulate large surplus funds for later use in development programs. The Nile System performed yeoman service and links with the Sudan were strengthened. The three East African territories continued to develop more common services, in a sort of "functional approach" to regional unity.

The war also awakened interest in political affairs among the Africans, particularly in Buganda, where there were disturbances in 1945 and 1949. From 1945 on, Africans were gradually given a greater role in the political life of the Protectorate. Mistrust was aroused, however, by the establishment in 1947 of the East Africa High Commission, with headquarters in Nairobi. This commission was established to coordinate approaches in the territories toward common problems, but many suspected it was a move toward political federation. The Commission was composed of the three governors with their executive and advisory staffs and had a legislative branch empowered to deal with matters specifically related to the common services. By this time these included the railways and harbors, civil aviation and customs as well as those mentioned previously. In fact, a *de facto* customs union had been created and a common market was well on the way to establishment.

Economic and political development continued during the 1950's. Extensions of the railway (trackage doubled between 1952 and 1962), the beginnings of industrialization under a ten-year plan initiated in 1947, the Owen Falls Dam, development of African agricultural cooperatives, the commencement of copper mining, more constitutional reforms, all were important. But much of this progress was overshadowed by the dispute between the Protectorate government and His Highness Sir Edward Frederick Mutesa II, Kabaka of Buganda (popularly known as "King Freddie") over the Kabaka's constitutional position. The dispute reached the crisis stage in late 1953 and in November the British withdrew recognition from the Kabaka. He thereupon left for Britain to plead his case there. Negotiations continued through 1954 and finally in 1955 an agreement was signed redefining Buganda's status as a province of the Protectorate and the Kabaka's role as a constitutional ruler. King Freddie left the social whirl of London to return to his palace in Kampala in October 1955. In the same year additional political reforms introduced ministerial and somewhat more representative government in Uganda. In 1958 and 1959 additional reforms were instituted, increasing the degree of Ugandan self-government. The country was clearly heading toward independence, along with Kenya and Tanganyika. The questions which engendered much speculation and debate were when and under what conditions. In December 1960 the Lukiko (parliament) of Buganda passed a resolution demanding immediate secession from Uganda and separate independence. The resolution was rejected by the United Kingdom.

The approach of independence also necessitated a thoroughgoing reappraisal of the East Africa High Commission. The Commission by 1960 was operating several "self-contained" services (those which were financed by user charges) such as the East African Railways and Harbours and the East African Posts and Telecommunications Administration, and more than thirty "non-self-contained" services (financed or subsidized by the Commission). The latter services were grouped into categories: Revenue Collection, Civil Aviation and Meteorology, Research Services, Economic Services and Other. The "other" included the Royal East African Navy, an East African Office in London, an East African Central Legislative Assembly (CLA) and nine other administrative and information offices. East Africa had gradually developed an effective common market and the term was widely used, even though it had not been achieved by design and was not fully developed.

While there were some complaints about the operation of the common services and the details of the common market, there was no doubt about their importance to East Africa. A World Bank mission to Tanganyika reported in 1961, for example, that it considered that "this 'East African' approach to common problems is valuable and should be maintained." [30] It also remarked on a problem common to all three territories:

> The northern and southern boundaries of Tanganyika by no means conform with the economic geography of British East and Central Africa . . . To date, the frontiers have not been allowed seriously to distort the natural pattern of economic development, thanks, to a great degree, to the East African customs union. It is highly desirable that future development should follow rather than struggle against the pattern set by economic geography. [31]

The mission summed up its evaluation of the arrangements with:

> The importance of the East African common market for all parties concerned appears to lie more in its potential development than in actual results thus far, either favorable or harmful. It is in this light that an effort should be made to harmonize the interests involved. [32]

Among the problems which the mission noted were the inequitable distribution of customs revenues among the three partners, inadequate pro-

[30] International Bank for Reconstruction and Development, *The Economic Development of Tanganyika* (Baltimore: The Johns Hopkins Press, 1961), p. 33.
[31] *Ibid.*
[32] *Ibid.*, p. 240.

tection for infant industries in Tanganyika (and Uganda), the tendency of industry to gravitate to Kenya, and the disproportionate benefits accruing to Kenya under the arrangement. These matters were of such serious concern throughout East Africa that the United Kingdom appointed a Royal Commission headed by Jeremy Raisman to investigate and make recommendations. The Raisman Commission made a thorough study of the entire economic and fiscal structure and reported early in 1961 that the High Commission was performing valuable services and that the common market should be retained. It recommended a distributable pool for customs receipts, an independent income for the High Commission and other reforms. A World Bank mission to Uganda commented that "The recommendations of [the] Raisman Commission, if accepted, will meet a substantial part of Uganda's legitimate objections . . ." [33] The recommendations were implemented and the situation did improve, but the approach of independence for Tanganyika (scheduled for December 9, 1961) and the other territories shortly afterward necessitated a reconsideration of the whole question of cooperation in East Africa. Accordingly, a conference was held in London in June 1961 at which the parties agreed to replace the East Africa High Commission with an East African Common Services Organization (EACSO). This new organization came into formal existence two days after Tanganyika became independent.

Meanwhile, the Belgian Congo, most of the French African territories and several of the British ones had become independent and a strong pan-African movement was developing. Within East Africa demands for both all-African and East African political unity were voiced, though some felt that these two goals were incompatible. Uganda and Kenya put pressure on Britain to grant them independence simultaneously with Tanganyika so they could immediately form an East African Federation, but Britain refused. The Mau-Mau rebellion and the white settler problem in Kenya and the continued opposition of Buganda to federation delayed independence for these territories. Many Pan-Africanists found an outlet for their activities in the Pan-African Freedom Movement of East and Central Africa (PAFMECA), founded at Mwanza, Tanganyika in 1958. This organization was largely anticolonial in nature and lost much of its driving force after the attainment of independence by most of the territories in the region. It tried to bolster itself by including southern Africa in its sphere of interest in 1962 (becoming PAFMECSA), but it declined

[33] International Bank for Reconstruction and Development, *The Economic Development of Uganda* (Baltimore: Johns Hopkins Press, 1962), p. 83.

still further after the founding of the Organization of African Unity in Addis Ababa in 1963.

Hopes for an East African federation did not die, however; rather they began to center in the new EACSO. This successor to the East Africa High Commission was constituted differently. The three prime ministers formed a central Authority, which was supported by four committees, each composed of a minister from each territory and responsible for a particular field of subjects. These fields were communications, finance, commercial and industrial coordination, and social and research services. The Central Legislative Assembly (CLA) was continued as were the common services of the former High Commission. While it did achieve additional successes in economic integration, it failed to provide a stepping-stone for federation. The reasons are a mixture of political, economic and personal problems and will be discussed in Chapter VII. At this point it is necessary only to mention that despite the reforms made in response to the Raisman report, none of the basic economic problems was solved and the disparities among the three territories even grew wider. Moreover, the delay of Uganda's independence until October 1962 and Kenya's until 1963 increased nationalistic sentiment in each territory; each was less willing to surrender its hard-won sovereignty. In addition, according to a contemporary commentary,

> [t]he politicians' enthusiasm to play politics, supportable in richer communities however deplorable, may prove a fatal luxury in struggling communities whose situation calls for drastic self-denials on the part of all. [34]

Nevertheless, with all its inequities and shortcomings, the services provided by EACSO were so much greater than those any one of the three could have obtained individually that it continued functioning through many economic and political storms until its replacement in 1967 by an even stronger organization. Still, according to one analysis, Kenya and Tanzania want to perpetuate the present concentration of administration and economic activity along the East African coast and in the Kenya highlands, while Uganda wants to permit the natural shift of power to the center of population – around Lake Victoria. She may want to go it alone.

> It is true that Federation would guarantee her a vital outlet to the coast, but she feels this is a poor bargain in exchange for perpetuating her status as a rural province at the end of the line. [35]

[34] E. N. Gladden, "The East African Common Services Organization," *Parliamentary Affairs,* XVI (Autumn, 1963), p. 435.

[35] Dutta, *op. cit.,* p. 26.

And Buganda was still a bothersome anomoly. During the pre-independence elections in 1961, according to *The Christian Science Monitor,* the political party created by Mutesa II in Buganda to advance his interests formed a coalition with the Uganda People's Congress which "made possible a truly national government that probably would not have been possible if the people of Buganda had not been led to think that they were voting for their king when they voted Kabaka Yekka." [36] Uganda became independent on October 8, 1962, but national unity still was not a reality. Prime Minister Milton Obote continued to downgrade tribalism in favor of national consciousness and in March 1963 denounced tribalism as "an issue we must destroy." [37] But in October of the same year Uganda became an "independent sovereign state" (but not quite a republic) and Kabaka Mutesa II was elected President.

If the political picture within Uganda was confusing, that in East Africa generally was even more so. Zanzibar, long considered a kind of associate of the common market and a possible federation partner, came under strong communist influence after attaining independence in December 1963 and was finally joined with Tanganyika in April 1964, after which the republic became Tanzania. [38] Tanzania continued moving leftward politically, while Kenya, now independent under President Jomo Kenyatta, became more conservative. In April 1964 the leaders of the three countries met to discuss the deterioration in their economic community. In the "Kampala Agreement" of April 29 they detailed a plan for allocating specific industries among the three partners, much as was being done in Central America, in order to arrest the drift of industries to Kenya. They also agreed to continue the common market, the common services and the common currency. [39] Progress, however, was slight.

Uganda's initial response to the Kampala agreement was lukewarm, and more recently the Ugandans have remained outside the debate as they have become more and more pre-occupied with their own political problems. The main elements in the Kampala agreement have never been implemented and the Tanzanians suspect that the Kenyans never really meant to implement them. [40]

[36] *The Christian Science Monitor,* November 14, 1962.

[37] Quoted by Rothchild and Rogin, p. 418.

[38] Zanzibar, however, has retained an unusual degree of autonomy, even conducting some foreign relations independently of the central government. Despite its official name, the country is anything but "The *United* Republic of Tanzania."

[39] For details, see "The Rectification of East African Trade Imbalances," *International Legal Materials; Current Documents,* III (November, 1964), pp. 3–12.

[40] *The Economist,* April 30, 1966.

Early in 1965 Kenyan officials learned that a shipment of Communist Chinese arms was enroute through the country from Tanzania to Uganda by road. The arms were seized, the only known deliberate interference with Uganda's freedom of transit through Kenya, but a pointed reminder of Uganda's dependence upon Kenya's goodwill for her access to the sea.

Relations continued deteriorating, wracked by differences over Rhodesia, Tanzania's announcement of withdrawal from the East African currency arrangement, squabbles over the University of East Africa and its branches in each country, and other issues. The three leaders – Nyerere, Kenyatta and Obote – realized, however, that the separatist drift must be halted and confidence in the future of East Africa restored, so they met at Mombasa in August 1965. There they agreed, among other things, to establish a mixed commission headed by an impartial expert to examine the economic ties of East Africa and make recommendations on further cooperation. The commission was headed by Kurt Philip, a Danish economist, who submitted his report in May 1966.

But Obote was still having trouble at home. His relations with King Freddie of Buganda, President of Uganda, were deteriorating rapidly. Finally, in February 1966 the Kabaka proposed removing Uganda's capital and all federal troops from Buganda. Obote then moved against him, shelling his palace and assuming the Presidency himself. King Freddie escaped through an underground tunnel and once again fled to England, this time, apparently, for good. The Kingdom of Buganda was abolished by decree on June 10, 1966. Thus, after nearly a hundred years, the status of Buganda within Uganda was resolved by very drastic action. Whether the Buganda people will continue to acquiesce in this solution, even grudgingly, remains to be seen. Nevertheless, one more step had been taken toward Ugandan and East African unity. Once again attention could be concentrated on resolving the economic problems besetting the East African states. [41]

The Philip Commission report focused on the need to spur economic development in Uganda and Tanzania. The two key recommendations were the establishment of an East African Development Bank, two thirds of whose loans were to be divided equally among the three countries and the remaining third between Uganda and Tanzania, and a "transfer tax," essentially a preferential tariff to aid industrial growth in Tanzania and Uganda at the expense of Kenya. The three heads of state met once again

[41] For two good essays giving the background of the Buganda problem, see D. Anthony Low and R. Cranford Pratt, *Buganda and British Overrule* (London: Oxford University Press), 1960.

on June 6, 1967, this time in Kampala, to sign a Treaty for East African Cooperation. This treaty will be discussed in some detail in Chapter VII and only the main features need be mentioned here.

The East African Common Services Organization was to be converted into an East African Community and its activities decentralized. Main headquarters of the Community were to be established at Arusha, Tanzania, near Mt. Kilimanjaro. Headquarters of EAR and H were to be moved to Dar es Salaam and of the posts and telecommunications to Kampala, both from Nairobi. The new East African Development Bank was to be established in Kampala. Other services were to be located in various cities. The Community was inaugurated with great fanfare on December 1, 1967 in Arusha, with President Julius Nyerere of Tanzania as first President. Great hopes are held out for it and several other states have already expressed an interest in joining.

Great problems remain to be solved, however, both within Uganda (and the other two partner countries) and among the three of them. Hope has faded several times before, though, only to be revived as the three countries continue to move toward a truly unified East Africa, in which Uganda need no longer have concern for the security of her access to the sea.

The Economy of Uganda and East Africa

In the first section of this chapter the economic geography of Uganda was covered in a general way, with emphasis upon Uganda's internal development and trade with the outside world. In the second section the development of the East African Common Market and common services was discussed as an integral part of Uganda's history and political development. Now it is necessary to focus on the role played by Uganda in the economy of East Africa and the importance of East African cooperation to Uganda's economy and to her access to the sea.

In 1911, not long after the Uganda Railway was completed as far as Lake Victoria, Kenya and Uganda were united in a postal union; in 1917 a customs union between the two territories was created. Thus economic links in East Africa are more than half a century old, far older than similar links in most parts of the world. Like such arrangements among other colonial territories they have been subjected to severe strains since achievement of self-government and independence. Throughout the colonial period in East Africa, however, the economic ties became tighter and more numerous. In 1920 the East African Currency Board was organized. In 1923, immediately after the United Kingdom formally received her mandate over Tanganyika, the three territories synchronized their tariffs and established free trade among themselves for locally produced goods. In 1927 complete free trade was established within the region, creating a firm foundation for a full common market. Other steps toward economic integration in East Africa before 1961 have already been enumerated.

Throughout the colonial period, both the desire for and the movement toward regional unity in East Africa became stronger, with Kenya, Tanganyika and Uganda the core of all proposed economic and/or political groupings. The organization of the East Africa High Commission has already been discussed. While providing for rational operation of a variety of important common services and the supervision of an incipient common market, it had its shortcomings. Among them were limited jurisdiction, inadequate financing, dominance of Europeans, centralization in Kenya, and inequitable distribution of customs and tax revenues among the three territories. Some of these were dealt with after 1961 through implementation of the Raisman Commission recommendations and the conversion of the High Commission into the East African Common Services Organization. None of the fundamental problems was solved – or even vigorously attacked – by these devices. A full economic union of the three territories was still far away, for there was no common economic policy, each territory had its own budget and development program, and most taxation was still under the control of the individual governments. Nevertheless, the reforms were significant. The United Nations Economic Commission for Africa, for example, considered that

> [t]he importance of these new proposals [for EACSO] lies in the unanimity with which they were adopted at a conference at which more than half of the representatives were members of elected legislatures. It suggests that after the territories become independent, the structure of formal interterritorial cooperation which has been admired will at least be maintained, and could even provide a basis for political federation. The longer term economic implications of this are obvious: given internal political stability, the independence in East Africa will be followed by the continued existence of an economically integrated group of three self governing African countries. [42]

The optimism of the late 1950's waned, however, with recognition that the three territories were drifting apart. Julius Nyerere, Tanganyika's outstanding political figure, argued in 1960 for federation before independence and predicted the three would go their separate ways after inde-

[42] United Nations Economic Commission for Africa, *Economic Bulletin for Africa,* (E/CN. 14/125) Addis Ababa, January 1962, p. B-40.

pendence if not already federated. The reforms of 1961 alleviated the situation and arrested the dissolution of East African unity, but only temporarily; shortly the erosion set in again. By 1963 the leaders of the three territories – Tanganyika and Uganda independent but Kenya still not – felt it necessary to reaffirm in the strongest terms their desire and intention to federate as soon as Kenya became independent. Their Nairobi Declaration of June 5, 1963 undoubtedly hastened Kenya's independence; indeed, some observers assert that that was precisely and solely the intent of the Declaration. One, J. H. Proctor, even asserts that the whole federation effort, from the Nairobi Declaration on, was strictly a ruse to bluff Britain into giving Kenya independence and presents some evidence to support his contention. [43] Be that as it may, however, it was clear by mid-1965 that federation had lost its appeal and the best that could be hoped for was the salvage of a large measure of economic cooperation.

Growing protectionism within each territory, internal politics in each, the special role of Buganda, growing restrictions on interterritorial travel, differing roles in Pan-African affairs, outside attempts to hasten or retard federation, growing nationalism in each country, competition for investment capital and foreign markets, and many other factors, in addition to those already mentioned, tended to drive the territories apart. Disputes over provisions of a federal constitution helped to widen the gaps, especially those pertaining to organization of the federal parliament, division of powers between the federal and unit governments and location of the federal capital. Uganda wanted the capital to be in her territory, advancing a number of plausible arguments in favor of her demand. Proctor, however, says that "such a demand arose from Uganda's fear of being 'the backwater of the proposed federation'; the capital was required to offset the weakness arising from its land-locked location." [44] But, in fact, the leaders of all three countries were still devoted to the ideal of East African unity, no matter how difficult its attainment might be, and in 1966 and 1967, we have seen, they took steps to bring such unity closer.

Beginning in 1963, a number of outside observers made detailed economic studies of the East African "common market" and, as might be expected, arrived at different conclusions. All agreed, however, that whatever its handicaps, defects and failures, the common market was of value to all three partners and should be continued and strengthened. The first

[43] J. H. Proctor Jr., "The Effort to Federate East Africa: A Post Mortem," *The Political Quarterly*, XXXVII (January-March, 1966). Proctor feels that this "unfortunate episode" was premature and actually harmed the cause of federation.

[44] *Ibid.*, p. 52.

of these studies was by B. F. Massell in 1963. "The common market," he said,

has resulted in net gains to East Africa because of trade creation, factor mobility, economies of scale, and external economies. These gains have offset any losses that may have arisen as a result of trade diversion. Economies of scale have probably been of especial importance in East Africa and have undoubtedly contributed to the inflow of foreign capital and to the rise of interterritorial trade that has characterized recent East African development...

He went on to recommend specialization of production as part of a regional coordination of economic activities by a regional planning authority. He considered that a "Greater East African common market – one including, in addition to East Africa, several of the contiguous countries – would offer only marginal short-run gains, but would possibly make a great deal of sense in the long run." [45]

Massell objected to the redistribution of revenues as recommended by the Raisman report, but considered it better than allocation of industry in opposition to market forces. He recognized, however, the political need to arrest the growing concentration of industry in Kenya. Throughout his report, he urged strengthening of the economic ties among the three countries, at one point even suggesting "possibly through the formation of a political federation" [46] and then gradual integration of the economies of neighboring countries.

The second basic study was by Dharam Ghai in June 1964. It was highly theoretical in nature, but contained most detailed statistics and analyses of the actual effects of the common market on each of the territories. He concluded,

[I]t appears that Kenya has been the greatest net beneficiary, that Uganda has on balance gained rather than lost, and that Tanganyika has suffered a substantial net loss. This conclusion differs sharply from that arrived at by the Raisman Commission. [47]

He felt, however, that Tanganyika should not withdraw from the common market because the distributable pool was helping somewhat to redistribute income from Kenya to Tanganyika and Uganda, and because new in-

[45] Benton F. Massell, *East African Economic Union: An Evaluation and Some Implications for Policy* (Santa Monica: The RAND Corporation, December, 1963), pp. v–vi.

[46] *Ibid.*, p. 87.

[47] Dharam Ghai, "Territorial Distribution of Benefits and Costs of the East African Common Market," *The East African Economics Review*, XI (June, 1964), p. 39.

dustries had been started in Tanganyika which needed the whole East African market for their sales. He did not consider the common services or the common currency, whose advantages may have outweighed the disadvantages to Tanganyika of the common market.

Ghai's article set off a chain reaction in the economic journals. Walter Newlyn, for example, followed in November 1965 with a very detailed and sophisticated discussion of the Raisman reforms and the common market in general. Broadly, he agreed with Ghai's conclusions on the distribution of gains, but differed with him in urging agreement among the three governments on measures to influence industrial location within certain limits. "Such agreement is a minimum condition for the stability of a common market; it is also the first step towards supra-territorial planning." [48]

Arthur Hazelwood early in 1966 used Ghai's article as one of his "starting points" for another analysis and, in effect, disagreed with Ghai completely. In the first place, he said,

> It is widely assumed that the existence of the common market is the cause of the inter-territorial trade imbalances and of the structures of the economies of the three countries which the trade imbalances reflect. In fact, this commonly held view greatly exaggerates the importance and the effects of the common market . . .
> In reality, neither [the size of the East African market nor the amount of inter-territorial trade] is necessarily indicative of the importance of the *common market,* for strictly they are no more than facts about the East African market. It is wrong to suppose that facts about the one necessarily provide a basis for deductions about the other . . . [49]

Hazelwood did agree that "the absolute value of Kenya's inter-territorial exports which depend on the protection accorded by the customs union is greater than that of Uganda's and Tanganyika's," but felt this was countered to a large extent by Kenya's heavier reliance on inter-territorial trade than the other two. He concluded that it is "entirely invalid to judge the importance of the common market and its disequalising effects from the figures of total interterritorial trade and the nominal protection accorded by the customs tariff." [50] He did, nevertheless, favor continuation

[48] Walter T. Newlyn, "Gains and Losses in the East African Common Market," *Yorkshire Bulletin of Economic and Social Research,* XVII (November, 1965), p. 138.

[49] Arthur Hazelwood, "The East African Common Market: Importance and Effects," *Bulletin of the Oxford University Institute of Economics and Statistics,* XXVIII (February, 1966), p. 2. This journal shall hereinafter be referred to as *Oxford Bulletin.*

of the common market because, while it had not been very important so far, it was likely to become very important in the near future. Its dissolution "would set back the industrialisation of East Africa by many years." [51]

Hazelwood followed up this article a few months later with a critique of Newlyn's article and a continuation of the discussion. His argument was based on the inadequacy of the statistics in the Kenya Census of Manufacturing, used by Newlyn to determine gains and losses from the common market. He insisted there had as yet been no really valid demonstration that any country had actually lost from participation in the common market, let alone the extent of the loss, though of course it was obvious that so far Tanzania had gained least. [52]

Finally, Hazelwood was taken apart (in a most scholarly manner) by R. N. Wood toward the end of 1966. Wood felt that Tanzania was actually not doing very badly, was not suffering ill effects from participation in the common market, and might well do even better in the future. The real problem was to adjust the East African tariffs to her benefit. [53]

These studies illustrate that however much economists may disagree about the effects, the importance, or even the nature of the East African common market, all agree that it should be continued, strengthened and perhaps expanded, because manifestly it is the best possible road to economic development of the three countries involved. This is well illustrated by the comment concluding the annual economic review of Uganda in *The New York Times:*

> The recent tendency by the member countries to raise new tariff barriers against one another and introduce separate currencies has deterred private investment.
>
> Economic cooperation by the three countries, particularly in a customs or free-trade union, had been a strong attraction for private investment. Competition by the member countries for such investment, though, has become a disruptive force, and potential investors have not been enthusiastic about separate operations in each country instead of one serving all of them. [54]

That the political leaders in the region recognize this and have taken steps in this direction we have already seen. Now it remains only to

[50] *Ibid.*, p. 12.

[51] *Ibid.*, p. 13.

[52] Arthur Hazelwood, "The 'Shiftability' of Industry and the Measurement of Gains and Losses in the East African Common Market," *Oxford Bulletin,* XXVIII (May, 1966).

[53] R. N. Wood, "The East African Common Market: A Reassessment," *Oxford Bulletin,* XXVIII (November, 1966).

examine the interterritorial trade among Kenya, Uganda and Tanzania, their trade with the rest of eastern Africa, and their extra-continental trade.

A separate analysis of trade between Kenya, Uganda and Tanganyika – or interterritorial trade – is necessary because it is important to examine the political and economic relationships which have made possible its growth in recent years. It is largely because of the existence of certain regional institutions, and the absence of internal obstacles, that this trade has grown to a point where it accounts for about 14 percent of all imports and exports, and has thus come to represent an important element in their internal economies. By contrast, trade with neighbouring countries outside East Africa is extremely small and irregular, and accounts for no more than 3 per cent of total exports and well below 1 per cent of total imports. [55]

The growth of interterritorial trade in East Africa has been one of the most notable developments there in the postwar years. Not only has it grown at least as rapidly as foreign trade during this period, but its character has also changed markedly. As industrialization progresses in each country, an increasing proportion of manufactured goods is being included in this trade, largely in response to policies of import substitution. Moreover, this trade is to a large extent insulated from the great and often unpredictable fluctuations in the prices of the primary products exported from East Africa.

The development of interterritorial trade has undoubtedly brought considerable benefits to the region as a whole, but they are benefits which clearly vary widely in their incidence. Uganda and Tanganyika still remain much more dependent on world commodity markets than does Kenya, whose national income in any case is less dependent on earnings from foreign exports. For East Africa as a whole, however, the relative importance of inter-territorial trade is likely to increase as improvements in productivity take place, and as new goods come into production. [56]

This has happened, as was predicted by many analysts as long as fourteen years ago. It has had a particularly great effect on Kenya which, as we have seen, is obtaining the lion's share of new industries being established in East Africa. This has certainly brought her many advantages, but it has also made her more dependent on trade with her partners. In fact,

[54] *The New York Times,* January 27, 1967.
[55] *Economic Bulletin for Africa,* January, 1962, pp. B-33-34.
[56] *Ibid.,* p. B-34.

> these exports, for Kenya, are now almost 50 per cent of external exports, whereas five years ago they were just less than one-third. Similarly, although interterritorial imports into Kenya are relatively less important their share of total imports has been increasing at an even faster rate than that for exports. Both interterritorial imports and exports have doubled in the past five years and increased by 50 per cent in the last two. [57]

Exports to Uganda and Tanzania are clearly canceling out an increasing proportion of Kenya's chronic imbalance in her visible trade. [58]

As for Uganda, her interterritorial trade has also been growing, and quite as rapidly as Kenya's, but for her the relative positions of this and her export trade are reversed. Uganda's external imports increased from $ 72,800,000 in 1960 to $ 91,360,000 in 1964 and $ 114,436,000 in 1965, while her territorial imports doubled from $ 18,480,000 in 1960 to $ 37,240,000 in 1964 and jumped again to $ 46,718,000 in 1965. The comparable export figures were $ 116,452,000 in 1960, $ 180,400,000 in 1964 and $ 175,560,000 in 1965; exports to Kenya and Tanzania rose only from $18,732,000 in 1960 to $27,020,000 in 1964 and $27,240,000 in 1965. Uganda has consistently since 1960 had a chronic and growing deficit in her interterritorial trade; in 1964 it was almost $ 11,200,000, while in 1965 it was almost $ 19,600,000. These deficits are financed by Uganda's customary surpluses in her visible external trade accounts. In all cases, the great bulk of this interterritorial trade was between Kenya and Uganda, Tanzania playing a much lesser role. [59]

Another way of gauging the importance of customs union and interterritorial trade in East Africa is their effect on economic activities. According to A. M. O'Connor, without these links

> Kenya would perhaps be growing more sugar, and Uganda less, while Kampala might not be dependent mainly on Kenya for its milk supply. Close

[57] Kenya, Statistics Division, Ministry of Economic Planning and Development, *Economic Survey 1965*, p. 20.

[58] Detailed statistics may be found in Kenya, Statistics Division, Ministry of Economic Planning and Development, *Statistical Abstract 1965*, p. 22. Several things must be kept in mind regarding trade figures in East Africa. First, since the headquarters of most firms trading in East Africa are located in Nairobi or Mombasa, many of Kenya's imports may actually be destined for sale in Uganda or Tanzania. Secondly, these figures do not include "unrecorded movement" – informal border crossings of goods or outright smuggling. Finally, Kenya has a larger invisible export trade than either of the other two territories – largely tourism and remittances to non-Africans from abroad – and this helps to cover her visible trade deficit.

[59] All 1960 and 1964 figures rounded from Uganda, *1965 Statistical Abstract*, p. 18 and 1965 figures from Barclays Bank, *Uganda*, p. 20.

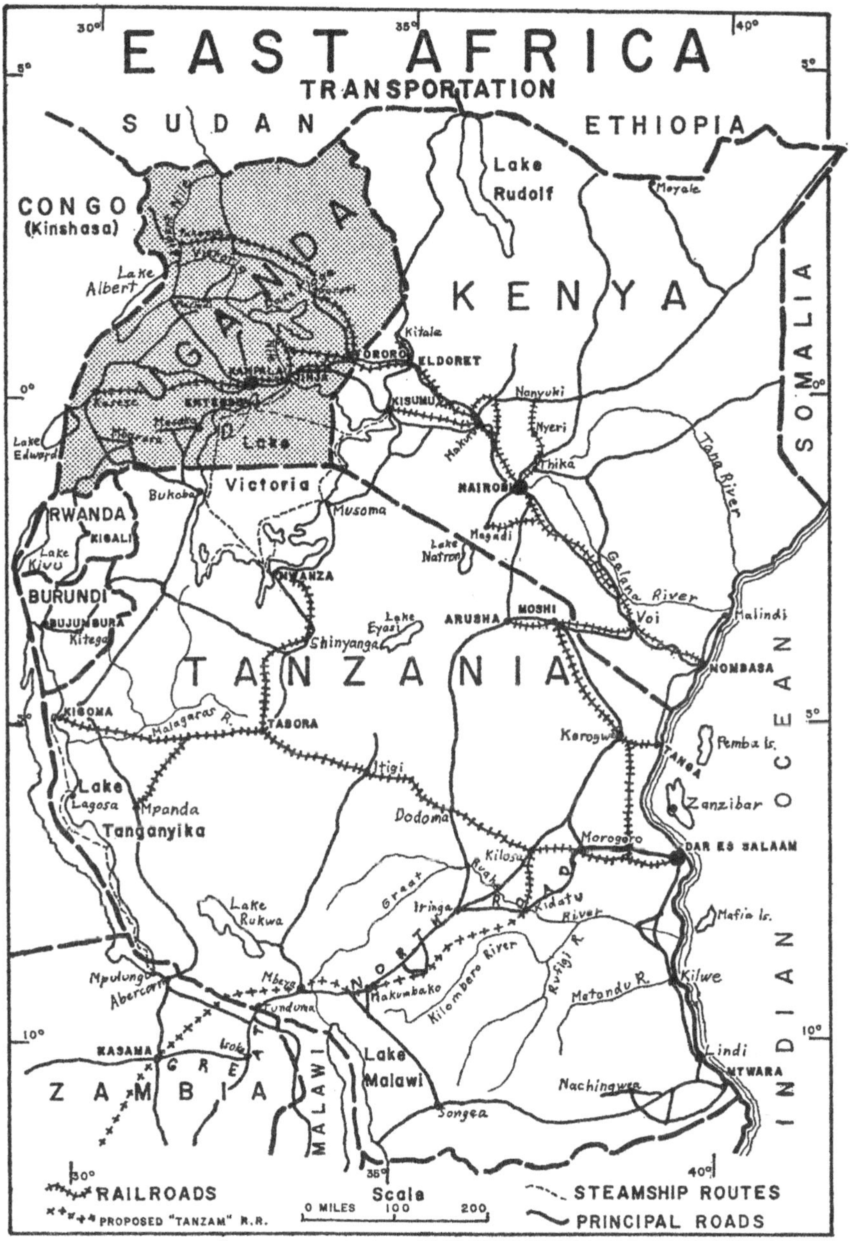
EAST AFRICA
TRANSPORTATION
SUDAN
ETHIOPIA
CONGO
(Kinshasa)
Lake Rudolf
Moyale
Lake Albert
KENYA
SOMALIA
UGANDA
Kitale
TORORO
ELDORET
KAMPALA
JINJA
KISUMU
Nanyuki
Nyeri
Thika
NAIROBI
Tana River
Lake Edward
Lake Victoria
Bukoba
RWANDA
KIGALI
Musoma
Lake Kivu
BURUNDI
BUJUMBURA
Kitega
Magadi
Lake Natron
MWANZA
Galana River
Voi
Malindi
Lake Eyasi
ARUSHA
MOSHI
Shinyanga
MOMBASA
TANZANIA
KIGOMA
Malagaras R.
TABORA
Korogwe
Pemba Is.
TANGA
Itigi
Zanzibar
Lake Lagosa
Mpanda
Lake Tanganyika
Dodoma
Morogoro
DAR ES SALAAM
Kilosa
Great Ruaha
Lake Rukwa
Iringa
Kidatu
River
Mafia Is.
NORTH ROAD
Kilombero River
Rufigi R.
Mpulungu
Abercorn
Mbeya
Makumbako
Matandu R.
Kilwa
Tunduma
KASAMA
GREAT
Lake Malawi
Lindi
MTWARA
ZAMBIA
MALAWI
Nachingwea
Songea
INDIAN OCEAN
30°
35°
40°
5°
0°
10°
RAILROADS
PROPOSED "TANZAM" R.R.
Scale
0 MILES 100 200
STEAMSHIP ROUTES
PRINCIPAL ROADS

MAP 9

political relationships are an essential factor in the production of steel in Uganda using mainly Kenya scrap and supplying mainly Kenya markets... If the customs union did not exist Uganda traders would import more goods directly from overseas and either Tanga or Dar es Salaam [both ports in Tanzania] would handle more Moshi and Arusha [cities in northern Tanzania] trade. [60]

Plainly, it is to Kenya's economic advantage to remain on good terms with Tanzania and Uganda, and especially the latter.

Trade between former British East Africa and its neighbors is regulated to a large extent by the Congo Basin Treaties,

the most important determinant of trade policies... All countries enjoy complete freedom of trade within East Africa, a principle of nondiscrimination which was established by the Berlin and Brussels Treaties of 1885 and 1890, as later amended in 1919 by the Convention of St. Germain en Laye... All the neighboring territories of East Africa lie wholly or partly within the boundaries of the conventional basin of the Congo, but not all have adhered as rigidly to its requirements as East Africa... [61]

The importance of these treaties has diminished considerably since the attainment of independence by all of the parties concerned, but the principles therein are still respected and adhered to.

Trade between Uganda, Kenya and Tanzania and their immediate neighbors has never been very large, generally under three per cent of their total trade, but "the fact that there are regular commercial channels for the exchange of goods is a favourable portent for the future..." [62] We shall be concerned here only with Uganda's trade with her neighbors, and only briefly at that.

Uganda is the principal East African trading partner of Sudan, but this trade consists almost exclusively of the flow of Uganda products, mainly coffee, northward. The trade has never been large, despite good water transport possibilities, because the core areas of both countries are far from their common border and both have tended to look eastward to the sea rather than north or south. Furthermore, whatever trade there is between the two countries is subject to considerable fluctuation, depending on political, economic and climatic conditions in the two countries. Total trade between the two countries in 1958 amounted to only $ 880,000, of which all but $ 16,800 consisted of exports of food (including coffee)

[60] O'Connor, *op. cit.*, p. 280.
[61] *Economic Bulletin for Africa*, January 1962, p. B-45.
[62] *Ibid.*, p. B-48.
[63] *Ibid.*, p. B-50.

from Uganda to Sudan.[63] Since then the trade has been negligible, not even appearing in Uganda's official trade statistics.

Most of whatever trade the former Belgian Congo has had with East Africa has tended to be with Tanganyika, largely because transportation has been easiest across Lake Tanganyika to the Central Line's railhead at Kigoma and thence, if need be, by rail as far as Dar es Salaam. One of the main reasons for building the Western Extension of the Kenya-Uganda Line (1951–56), however, was the hope of capturing more of both the Congo's normal trade and her transit trade. This hope has not yet been realized, for soon after the line was opened, political and economic problems in the Congo prevented a normal increase in trade with her eastern neighbors, and the Western Extension has so far relied mainly on the growing economy of the Kasese area, including the nearby copper mines, for its traffic. In 1958 Uganda exported $ 1,275,000 worth of goods, mainly foodstuffs and manufactured goods, to Congo, and imported $ 218,400 worth of mostly vegetable oils.[64] Since then the trade has dropped to virtually nil. There is, however, considerable local, informal trade which goes unrecorded. This consists largely of Congolese workers in Uganda purchasing goods and services and remitting part of their wages home. As conditions in Congo settle down and the western portion of Uganda develops, it is quite likely that trade between the two countries will increase.

Much of what has been said about Congo also pertains to Rwanda and Burundi, particularly the former, except on a smaller scale. There are good roads and large populations on both sides of the borders and there is every reason to believe that trade between them and East Africa will increase. Evidence of this is the deliberate reorientation, since achieving independence, of the transit trade of Rwanda, Burundi and the eastern Congo from the westerly routes to Matadi and Lobito imposed on them by the Belgians to the cheaper and more natural easterly routes to Mombasa and Dar es Salaam. An increasing orientation of Rwanda, Burundi and the eastern Congo toward East Africa is quite likely within the next few years and their eventual inclusion in a greater East Africa of some sort is entirely possible after the ties become strong enough.

Uganda's Access to the Sea

Uganda's position as a land-locked state was described succinctly by her Minister of Commerce and Industry, Jehoosh S. Mayanja-Nkangi, in his

[64] *Ibid.*, p. B-52.

address to the United Nations Conference on Trade and Development in Geneva in 1964. After discussing many problems of economic development, trade and aid for developing countries, Uganda's heavy dependence on foreign trade, etc., he concluded with:

> Finally, there is the very important issue of land-locked countries: the need for international recognition of the rights of land-locked countries to free transit through other countries for purposes of their trade. Uganda is right at the centre of Africa – it is a completely land-locked country – and this issue is therefore of interest to our delegation. Fortunately, we form part of the East African Common Services Organisation, and we have no problems of transit. However, this fact does not blind us to the necessity of supporting as strongly as we can the rights of countries such as Afghanistan to unrestricted transit through other countries for purposes of their commerce . . . [65]

Basically, Uganda does enjoy unrestricted transit across Kenya and, should she desire to use it, across Tanzania as well. She also enjoys relatively low freight rates on the Kenya-Uganda Line of the EAR and H, as well as through booking of all goods without breaking distance at the border to calculate those rates differently for passage through Uganda and Kenya. Not only was the railway originally built to serve Uganda, but Uganda transit trade is very important to the railway. Since the EAR and H is a public non-profit corporation owned by all three East African governments, it has not and is not likely to interfere with this transit trade. But transit is still subject to interference by the government of Kenya, as was illustrated so clearly only a year after the above statement was made.

On May 16, 1965 the Kenya Government seized a convoy of eleven commercial trucks carrying seventy-five tons of weapons and ammunition from Dar es Salaam around the eastern side of Lake Victoria through Kenya to Uganda. The arms, along with twenty-two Uganda soldiers and twenty-five Ugandan and Tanzanian civilians, were taken into custody near the town of Kisii, shown on Map 8. They were Chinese arms allegedly destined ultimately for leftist Kenyan Vice President Oginga Odinga, and recalled Uganda's involvement through similar arms shipments in the earlier warfare in the Congo. Uganda and Tanzania were sufficiently upset over the incident to threaten to break up the common market. The Central Legislative Assembly, which was meeting at the time, abruptly suspended its session. On May 21 President Nyerere announced that Chinese Foreign Minister Chou En-lai would visit Tanzania early in June. On May 23 the chairman of the Uganda Development Corporation said Uganda no longer

[65] UNCTAD, Annex 5 to E/CONF.46/SR.18 (E/CONF.46/STA/88) (7 April 1964), pp. 11–12.

wished to continue her arrangements with Kenya and could make such arrangements with Tanzania. Finally, on May 26, Jomo Kenyatta accepted Obote's apology and agreed to release the arms and prisoners. Patently, he wanted East Africa to be united when Chou En-lai dropped in during his grand tour of Africa.

The incident was officially ended, but certainly not forgotten. In June, the Uganda delegation at the United Nations Conference on Transit Trade of Land-locked Countries joined other land-locked states in urging that arms not be excluded from the transit goods to be granted "free and unrestricted" passage. "To allow the right of inspection of goods in transit," an Uganda representative argued, "would be to proceed on the basis of the principle that land-locked countries were criminals and transit countries guardians of law and order." The Kenya representative blandly replied that he fully appreciated the anxiety of land-locked states to "retain the means of defending themselves and preserving their security. However, that anxiety was shared by the transit countries, whose legitimate interests it would serve no purpose to ignore." He went on to suggest that the whole question of exceptions to free transit on security grounds be left to the transit and land-locked states to work out in bilateral agreements.[66] The Kenyans, as a matter of fact, took the position

> that the Conference was not the appropriate forum for the definition of principles of international law; it should concentrate on the economic aspects of the problems confronting the land-locked countries. Kenya would of course be faithful to its tradition of co-operation with its neighbours, but could not admit that any right was involved. The solution should be sought in bilateral agreements and mutual consent.[67]

Kenya's attitude is significant because Uganda's foreign trade is absolutely dependent upon transit across Kenya; she has no feasible alternative. All conceivable routes through Sudan or Congo are simply out of the question for handling all but the highest-value goods, and those could more economically be shipped by air. The route across Lake Victoria to the EAR and H Central Line railhead at Mwanza and thence by rail to Dar es Salaam would be useful only if the direct route to Mombasa were completely blocked or its use so restricted as to make it worth considering. At present it is not used at all; for Uganda it would be a tedious, time-consuming and expensive journey. The Central Line, however, is proving useful for the transit trade of Burundi and some of the transit trade of the eastern Congo and Rwanda. Combined with normal Tanganyika traffic,

[66] TD/TRANSIT/SR.19, p. 2.
[67] TD/TRANSIT/SR.26, p. 4.

this is enough to keep the port of Dar es Salaam busy. "[M]oreover, the present necessity to take a part of Zambia's transit trade through Dar es Salaam has resulted in that port working to capacity without any diversion from Uganda." [68] This is an understatement, to say the least. According to EAR and H's annual report for 1966, exports alone through Dar es Salaam increased by 101,000 tons during the year, of which 46,000 tons represented only Zambian copper. Congestion in the port is so bad that the waiting time for ships loading or discharging cargo ranged up to 119½ total days for the month of December 1966. [69]

Until recently Dar was a relatively minor port. In 1949 the East Africa High Commission concluded after a study:

> It is our view Dar es Salaam is capable of being expanded into a major port, having at least 18 deep water berths, at no greater cost than would be the provision of similar berths elsewhere, provided that certain improvements are made to the entrance channel and basin. [70]

Even in 1962 Dar was "not at present a trade port of international significance." [71] Some improvements have been made since then and the port would be adequate in normal times. In view of the political conditions prevailing in central Africa, though, it seems unlikely that Dar es Salaam will again see "normal times" in the foreseeable future. The other Tanganyikan ports, Mtwara in the south and Tanga in the north, would be useless to Uganda. Mtwara was built to serve the Overseas Food Corps groundnuts scheme beginning in 1948. It has a good harbor but has handled little traffic since the failure of the groundnuts scheme and in 1962 the railroad tracks between the port and the inland groundnuts area were torn up. Tanga is better situated geographically to handle Uganda traffic, but would be unavailable if Uganda transit trade could not cross Kenya by rail. Nevertheless,

> in a divided East Africa, Uganda, which has often chafed under the thought of dependence on Kenya for access to the world markets, could easily be tempted

[68] Letter from office of the General Manager of EAR and H in Nairobi dated August 14, 1967.

[69] EAR and H. *Annual Report 1966*, p. 27.

[70] East Africa High Commission, *Report Upon the Possibilities of Developing Dar es Salaam into a Major Port* (Nairobi, March, 1949), p. 17.

[71] Harm J. de Blij, *Dar es Salaam; A Study in Urban Geography* (Evanston: Northwestern University Press, 1963), p. 27. See pp. 11–27 for a detailed description of the harbor, with photographs.

to divert some of its trade via the new facilities at Mwanza to the central Tanganyikan route, as in pre-European times . . . [72]

Meanwhile, Uganda must rely on the direct route to and from Mombasa, Kenya.

Generally speaking, Uganda's transit facilities are adequate to handle her import and export trade. As noted previously, East Africa has one of the best transportation systems in Africa and the railway network is particularly good. EAR and H operates road and lake services, but its most important functions are the operation of the railways and ports. Throughout the years it has generally performed in accordance with the injunction laid down in the Act establishing it:

> The administration shall be administered on business principles and, so far as is not inconsistent therewith or with the principles of prudent finance, cheap services shall be provided by the Administration to assist agricultural, mining and industrial development in the territories. [73]

This has been done in a number of ways, especially by establishing special freight tariffs to favor some industries and higher rates for imports than for exports. Most of the criticisms directed at EAR and H have been for its very conservatism, its slowness in investing in new equipment or opening new routes. Particularly during the first decade after World War II, both the railroad and the port of Mombasa were seriously congested and a severe shortage of boxcars developed. The boxcar shortage persists but has been greatly relieved, while modernization, dieselization, and expansion of facilities have nearly eliminated complaints. Another project of EAR and H, dictated by political and social considerations, has been its Africanization, the substitution of native East Africans for European expatriates or Asians at all levels and in all positions. By the end of 1966 the staff was 88% African and the process is continuing. [74]

EAR and H has been adding rail lines and branches throughout East Africa since the early 1950's. The most important of these are the Western Extension to Kasese and the Northern Extension to Pakwach on the Albert Nile, both in Uganda, and the links connecting the Kenya-Uganda with the Tanga and the Tanga with the Central Line. Other routes are

[72] Irene S. Van Dongen, "Mombasa in the Land and Sea Exchanges of East Africa," *Erdkunde,* XVII, (July, 1963), pp. 37–38.

[73] Quoted in International Bank for Reconstruction and Development, *The Economic Development of Kenya* (Baltimore: The Johns Hopkins Press, 1963), p. 189.

[74] EAR and H *Annual Report 1966*, p. 3.

being considered to link Moshi and Arusha directly with Nairobi, and Dar es Salaam with Mbeya near the Zambia border. In all cases, the rail network is considered as an integrated whole, serving the entire region. Linking of the three main coast-interior routes, for example, permitted the rapid shift of locomotives and rolling stock in response to demands of harvests at different times in Uganda and Tanzania. Should any portion of the Kenya-Uganda Line be closed to traffic for any length of time, it would create havoc in the economy of the entire region. For Uganda it might mean something close to disaster since normally about 98% of Uganda's exports go by rail to Mombasa and only perhaps 2% by truck.

The Uganda government is trying to encourage traders to use the highways since the journey from Kampala to Mombasa takes less than twenty-four hours by road as compared with at least two days by rail. So far, however, only passengers have begun using the highways in great numbers. The highway between Tororo and Eldoret is not in very good condition and there are not enough trucks available to provide a feasible alternative to rail transport. Nevertheless, the highways are pressed into service when the railway is congested, as during the spring of 1966 when drought led to severe famine in Uganda and part of Kenya and to heavy imports of food for the stricken areas. Improved rail ferry services on Lake Victoria and growing use of airplanes for passengers lend some flexibility to Uganda's transport system, but basically she is still dependent on the Permanent Way for her access to the sea. [75]

Mombasa is the only important seaport in Kenya. It has two harbors: the old Arab harbor on the north side of the island on which the city is located, and the newer one at Kilindini on the west side. Kilindini ("place of deep water" in Swahili) is probably the finest harbor on the east coast of Africa. It opened in 1926 and has been steadily expanded since then. Development on the island was completed in 1958 and since then new deepwater berths, oil refineries and other facilities have been added on the mainland. The newest jetty at Port Reitz on the mainland, completed in 1965, can accomodate petroleum tankers of up to 65,000 tons and is capable of enlargement. Since the World Bank mission's study in 1962, Mombasa harbor has not only been able to handle vastly increased tonnages (21% increase from 1965 to 1966 alone), but has been able to

[75] A. M. O'Connor, in his *Railways and Development in Uganda* (Nairobi: Oxford University Press, 1965), argues forcefully against any major new railway construction in the country because it "is not the key to economic development in Uganda today . . .", p. 164.

reduce ship waiting time from about half a day to virtually zero, though there were periods when waiting time was nearly four days. [76]

Mombasa is clearly maintaining the supremacy among East African ports for which she struggled from her founding about 975 A.D. Irene Van Dongen has studied the port's success in great detail and considers one of the chief reasons for it to be "the size, population and economic progress of its hinterland as compared to the hinterlands of other East African ports." [77] She goes on to say,

> The economic strength of Mombasa's hinterland has been derived for several decades: a) from the cotton and coffee . . . grown in Uganda which were providing in recent years for as much as 80 to 87% of the Protectorate's export earnings . . . [78]

This symbiotic relationship between the port and its hinterland (of which Uganda forms a most important part) reinforces the similar relationship between Uganda and "the iron snake" which connects her with the port. Both the port and the railway, and with them the entire operation of EAR and H, a vital component of the new East African Community, would suffer severely were these relationships to be seriously disturbed.

A word remains to be said about Uganda's growing role as a transit state, serving both Rwanda and the Republic of Congo (Kinshasa). Some mention of this has already been made in connection with trade between East Africa and its neighbors, but Uganda's role in their transit trade requires some elaboration.

In 1962 an official British report included these comments:

> Uganda is a land-locked country so that there are always a number of foreign vehicles running on its roads, just as there are Uganda vehicles in the neighbouring territories. In recent years there has been some agitation about this . . .
>
> The presence of foreign vehicles is due to the close economic and social links that Uganda enjoys with her neighbours . . . Uganda is part of the route for trade to and from the Belgian Congo and the Trusteeship Territory of Ruanda Urundi . . . [79] In 1950 the value of reexports from Uganda to these

[76] IBRD, *The Economic Development of Kenya*, p. 195, and EAR and H *Annual Report 1966*, p. 26.

[77] Van Dongen, *op. cit.*, p. 18.

[78] *Ibid.*, pp. 24–25.

[79] This arrangement was detailed in a convention between Belgium and the United Kingdom dated March 15, 1921. A similar agreement of April 16, 1951 provided for Belgian piers and warehouses in Kigoma, Mtwara and Dar es Salaam. According to de Blij, however, "In spite of this 1921 Convention, Dar es Salaam captured little of the Congo's trade at any time." He cites statistics to illustrate this. *Dar es Salaam*, p. 26.

two territories amounted to £ 60,000 [$ 168,000]; by 1957 the figures had reached £ 630,000 [$ 7,764,000]. Much of this travelled by way of the railway system to Butiaba, on Lake Albert, and was then conveyed by steamer to the Belgian ports on the Lake. One of the arguments put forward for the construction of the western extension of the railway from Kampala was that it would provide a better route for this transit traffic and encourage its growth by stimulating economic development in the eastern Congo . . . [80]

Since 1956 the Western Extension has been built to Kasese and many industries have been established in East Africa with the intention of doing business in the Congo, but the optimistic hopes of the early days have not yet been realized, largely due to political problems in the Congo. Total Congo transit traffic on the Western Extension in 1958 amounted only to 18,594 tons; by 1960, however, it had grown to 28,332 tons, but following the turbulence after independence dropped to 20,703 tons in 1962 and by 1966 was only back to 22,600 tons. Until recently imports outweighed exports considerably, but in 1966 only 1,400 tons of the total consisted of imports. [81] EAR and H has granted the Congo special rates for her transit traffic and today all goods except bulk petroleum products (not included in the above figures) are carried at rates lower than those charged for domestic goods. Moreover, in Kasese there are several warehouses and four oil storage depots for the Congo. This has been important in the economy of Kasese, but, according to O'Connor, "the importance of the Congo transit traffic in the economic geography of Uganda lies mainly in its contribution to the maintenance of the new railway." [82] Some Congo transit trade will undoubtedly use the even newer Northern Extension to Pakwach, but it is unlikely to benefit more than the West Nile District for some time.

Still, the obvious geographical advantages of shipping through Mombasa (or Dar es Salaam) rather than Matadi or Lobito, combined with the long-established links between western Uganda and the eastern Congo, leave room for optimism that Congo transit traffic through Uganda will increase substantially when Congolese political conditions permit. Already highways in Uganda adjacent to the Congo are being improved, partly in anticipation of such an increase. It would clearly be of benefit to the Congo, Uganda and all of East Africa.

Rwanda has reoriented her trade almost entirely since independence

[80] E. K. Hawkins, *Roads and Road Transport in an Underdeveloped Country; A Case Study of Uganda* (London: HMSO, 1962, p. 83.

[81] 1966 figures from letter from EAR and H; others from A. M. O'Connor, *Railways and Development in Uganda*, p. 78.

[82] *Ibid.*, p. 82.

from routes through the Congo to routes through Uganda and Tanzania. The latter route, to Dar es Salaam, is little used because it entails passage through Burundi, and the two former units of Ruanda-Urundi are not on good terms at present. The route from Rwanda through Congo to the railhead at Kasese is also little used, both for political reasons (relations with Congo are also not very good) and for economic reasons. While Rwanda transit trade is given preferential rates through Uganda and the all-rail rate to and from Kasese is more favorable than that for the road-rail route through Kampala, the latter is preferred because the roads between Rwanda and Kampala are better than those between Rwanda and Kasese. The overall costs are roughly the same, so political considerations dictate the bypassing of Kasese. The EAR and H and Uganda authorities would prefer giving more business to the railroad, but that may have to wait a while. It is interesting to note in passing that all American aid shipments to Rwanda use the Mombasa-Uganda route. Again, as with Congo, there are hopes that Rwandese transit traffic through Uganda will increase. The two countries have signed a transit agreement and there seems to be every likelihood that this traffic will increase as the Rwandese economy develops.

Meanwhile, Uganda is being affected by other developments even farther south. A discussion of transit trade and access to the sea in East Africa would hardly be complete without some discussion of Zambia's problems.

East Africa, Zambia and Rhodesia

The Federation of Rhodesia and Nyasaland (Central African Federation) died on the 31st of December 1963, after ten years of a none-too-tranquil marriage. There were many reasons for its demise – varying degrees of political development, Nyasaland's economic weakness, increasing racism among the white settler minority in Southern Rhodesia, etc. – but perhaps the major reason was the desire of Nyasaland and Northern Rhodesia, and especially the latter, to change their orientation from southward to northeastward. This had been developing for a long time and the growing white settler problem in Southern Rhodesia only hastened it along. Northern Rhodesia became independent as Zambia on October 24th (United Nations Day) 1964, three months after Nyasaland became the independent state of Malawi. Relations with Southern Rhodesia steadily deteriorated as that government applied more and more of South Africa's apartheid policies in its own territory. Unable to extract an acceptable independence constitution from Britain, the new right-wing government in Salisbury declared its independence on November 11 (Armistice Day) 1965. Rhodesia, as it now calls itself, still has not been recognized as a sovereign state by any government. First Britain and then the United Nations declared an economic boycott of land-locked Rhodesia in order to compel it to surrender its new "independence" and take steps toward the rapid assumption of power by the black African majority. But the country initially hurt most by this boycott was neighboring land-locked Zambia.

Zambia has depended for her very existence as an economically viable state on the Rhodesian Railway, a common service of the old federation which still continued to function under joint ownership and control. The Railway carried Zambia's copper exports (She is the world's second largest producer.) to the sea at Beira in Portugese Mozambique and brought coal from the Wankie fields in Rhodesia to fuel the copper smelters and refineries. It also brought virtually all of Zambia's petroleum from South Africa, Rhodesia or abroad. The blockade of petroleum shipments to Rhodesia which began in December 1965 also cut off Zambia's petroleum supplies. Rationing was immediately instituted and all available surface routes from the seaports of the Congo (Kinshasa), Tanzania, Mozambique and Angola were pressed into service for an oil-lift. Most dramatic of all was the airlift of oil which began on December 19, only five weeks after Rhodesia declared its independence. British, American and Canadian planes flew oil into the Copperbelt and the Zambian capital of Lusaka from Léopoldville (now Kinshasa), Nairobi and Dar es Salaam. The airlift continued through the rainy season, carrying over seven million gallons of fuels before it ended on April 30, 1966. By that time the overland routes were able to manage the supply of petroleum and other imports, but not without difficulty.

In line with her policy of reducing her dependence upon South Africa, Rhodesia and the Portugese territories to a minimum, Zambia has increasingly relied on two routes through Tanzania for her principal connections with the sea. First is the route via the Central Line to Kigoma on Lake Tanganyika, thence by steamer to the Zambian port of Mpulungu at the southern tip of the lake, and thence by road to Abercorn and the Zambian highway system. The much more important route is the more direct (but still over 1200 miles long) Great North Road from Dar es Salaam through Morogoro, Iringa and Mbeya to Isoka in Zambia and thence into the Zambian road system. An even shorter route, but less used, is from the southern port of Mtwara in Tanzania to Mbeya and thence to Zambia. All of these routes are shown on Map 9. None of these roads is paved except for that between Morogoro and Dar, and all are being unmercifully pounded by the heavy tankers and other trucks using them. During the 1967 rainy season hundreds of trucks bogged down in mud and many bridges were washed out. The roads were simply not meant for this kind of traffic. There were not enough trucks, drivers or mechanics at the beginning, and massive efforts have been made to keep the roads open. Now about 25% of Zambia's copper exports are moving over the road to Dar and the World Bank has lent Zambia $ 17,000,000 for general road improvements. [83] In June 1966 Tanzania announced she would spend $ 1,400,000 in the coming fiscal year on developing a road link between Mtwara and Lake Malawi; Zambian traffic could then take the shortest route to the sea – across Malawi and Lake Malawi (formerly Lake Nyasa). "The Zambians envisage Mtwara as a port almost exclusively reserved for their trade." But a group of experts from the Stanford Research Institute feel that it would be much more economical to improve the existing road to Dar es Salaam. [84] As we have seen, however, that port is badly congested. It is neither highways nor airways, [85] however, which have received the most publicity in the world over the years, but the projected "Tanzam" Railway.

Since 1963 this scheme to connect Zambia with Tanzania by rail has made headlines regularly, and it has become inextricably entwined with Zambia's political differences with Rhodesia and the rest of southern Africa. It is not, however, a new proposal. Cecil Rhodes in the nineteenth century included it as part of his projected Cape-to-Cairo Railway. The proposal was revived in the 1920's. Then in 1926, in Nairobi, the first Governors' Conference, attended by Kenya, Uganda, Tanganyika, Zanzibar, Northern Rhodesia and Nyasaland (not, be it noted, Southern Rhodesia), agreed to construct such a line. Nothing was done about it, however. The scheme lay dormant through the Depression and World War II. It was revived after the war and widely discussed during the 1940's. A route between Northern Rhodesia and Mtwara was actually surveyed. The survey proved that construction over the proposed routes was feasible, but would be expensive – $ 92.4 million for the main line to Mtwara. It considered this route important, partly to relieve the line through Mozambique to Beira, but felt that "over-riding importance must be attached to" linking

[83] *The Christian Science Monitor,* October 10, 1967.

[84] *The Economist,* July 9, 1966.

[85] Zambia experimented with airlifting copper to East African ports in December 1965. While technically feasible, it is not economic and is not expected to be used on a large scale.

the Kenya-Uganda, Tanga and Central Lines, and the Rhodesian and South African systems.[86] This advice was followed and once more the "Tanzam" project lapsed into obscurity.

By 1963, however, Kenneth Kaunda and his United National Independence Party were pressing the Northern Rhodesia government to build a railway to Tunduma just over the Tanganyika border, as part of their program for reorienting the colony away from southern Africa. A survey was undertaken and estimated that such a line would cost about $ 48.7 million and take four years to build.[87] Once again, nothing was done in response to the proposal, but in Tanganyika a southern branch from the Central Line was pushed through from Kilosa to Kidatu. The immediate purpose of this line is to penetrate the agriculturally rich Kilombero Valley, and it may continue on to Makumbako. Both Zambia and Tanzania have since 1964 been trying to obtain financing for the remainder of the route to Kapiri Mposhi, on the main line of rail near Ndola in Zambia's Copperbelt. A United Nations mission studied the proposal in that year and turned it down and the World Bank did likewise.

Interest was revived again when Chou En-lai during his swing through East Africa in June 1965 offered to help build the railroad, supposedly offering to pay upwards of $ 210 million. But Kenya, Uganda, Tanzania and Zambia, acting jointly, had already approached the United States, the United Kingdom, Germany and Japan for financing and did not leap at the offer. Chou's calls for revolution in Africa had made them a bit wary. The Chinese offer, however, put the Western countries in a more difficult position. Mindful of the Aswan High Dam episode in 1956, they could not simply reject the request on economic grounds. Instead, they stalled.

In October 1965 President Kaunda of Zambia visited Tanzania and Kenya in an effort to strengthen ties with East Africa, and again the proposed railway was discussed. During 1966 Zambia and East Africa came closer together, even while the three East African partners were drawing apart.

> During the year Zambia switched from being the most northerly territory in Southern Africa to the most southerly territory in East Africa . . .
>
> Talks in Lusaka and Dar es Salaam resulted in the signing of a $ 60-million contract to build an oil pipeline from Dar es Salaam to Ndola in the Zambian copper belt, an agreement to improve both the Tanzanian ports and Mtwara airport and the setting up of a joint transport company to run a nonstop 450-

[86] *Report on an Engineering Survey of a Rail Link Between the East African and Rhodesian Railway Systems* (Nairobi: EAR and H, June, 1952), p. 7 *et passim.*

[87] Figures from United Kingdom Reference Division, Central Office of Information, *Zambia* (London: HMSO, 1964), p. 33.

truck cargo haul service along the dusty Great North Road that links the two countries.[88]

Encouraged by the prospects of large new markets for their agriculture and industries, the East African countries were instrumental in calling in mid-year a conference in Addis Ababa of twelve countries from Sudan to Mauritius to Zambia for the purpose of moving toward an Eastern African economic community.

Also about the middle of 1966, Rhodesian and Zambian officials began talks on breaking up the Rhodesian Railways. The split became effective on June 30, 1967, only a few days after President Kaunda returned from China with another "commitment" to build the Tanzam railroad. He did say, however, that a final decision would have to await replies from the other countries approached for aid and would probably be considered in July. Meanwhile, in discussing Zambia's efforts to break loose from the Rhodesian Railways and establish a new outlet to the sea, the *New York Times* commented, "Never before have the intrinsic problems of being landlocked, or of the effects of arbitrary boundary drawing of the 1890's been so amply demonstrated."[89]

Finally, in October 1967, the Zambian Foreign Minister admitted publicly what had been suspected for some time – that the Chinese had not really offered to build the railway. They had only agreed to *lend* Zambia interest-free $ 14,000,000 for another construction survey, expected to take about two years, after which a final decision on the project would be made. The Chinese had made great propaganda gains at almost no cost to them. But the railroad is still not being built and, despite loud and repeated declarations of intent to do so by the Zambians, it is not likely to be for a long time, if ever.

The political and strategic purposes of the projected railway are clear. Both the Zambians and Tanzanians, however, insist now that their motives are largely economic: to "open up" the depressed areas of northeast Zambia and southwest Tanzania. Domestic politics are involved here, but the regions apparently do have some economic potential. But neither country has yet had enough confidence in the returns to be realized to commit any of its own funds to the railroad.

Another argument for the railroad is that it would help tie together East and Central Africa and make possible the establishment of certain

[88] *The New York Times*, January 27, 1967. *The Christian Science Monitor* reported on February 1, 1967 that 6% of EAR and H's budget for the year was to be spent on improvements to harbors and equipment for Zambia's use.

[89] *The New York Times*, July 10, 1967.

large regional manufacturing industries which need the larger market. But one observer comments,

> This is, in fact, a long-term goal at best, for trade on a large and specialized scale between East and Central Africa will have to await further economic advance and development of greater purchasing power in each area.[90]

Another concludes,

> The irony of the situation is that a Tanzania-Zambia rail link would today be a means of loosening ties between eastern and southern Africa, rather than a means of welding together the countries of High Africa as was once conceived.[91]

In January 1968 American Vice President Hubert Humphrey announced while touring selected African states that the United States intended to help with reconstruction and paving of the most difficult section of the Great North Road, that between Tunduma and Iringa, Tanzania. Within the next few weeks it became quite evident that the United States was trying to upstage the Chinese by arranging modernization of the entire Great North Road, hopefully with the assistance of other interested states and the World Bank. It is hoped that the project, already under way in Zambia, can be completed before the Chinese complete their railroad survey and for a fraction of the cost of a railroad. The political and psychological motivations for the Tanzam railway are so strong that Zambia and East Africa may wish to push ahead with it, regardless of the economic consequences. The United States, however, hopes to present an acceptable alternative. In any case, it is certain that Zambia is joining East Africa.[92]

[90] Aaron Segal, "The Tanganyika-Zambia Railway Project," *Africa Report,* IX (November,1964), pp. 9–10.

[91] B. S. Hoyle, "The Proposed Tanzania-Zambia Railway," *The East African Geographical Review,* No. 3 (April, 1965), p. 52.

[92] For additional details on current and projected construction on the Great North Road, see *The Christian Science Monitor* for February 16, 1968.

CHAPTER VI

ACCESS TO THE SEA IN THE SPACE AGE

It may seem strange, in this last third of the twentieth century, when Man is reaching out to the stars and is close to harnessing the might of thermonuclear energy for his own use, to be concerned with such an old-fashioned matter as whether a merchant in the interior of a continent may be given assurances that his goods enroute to or from a merchant in another state will not be interfered with or unduly taxed merely because they must cross a line which governments have drawn between their respective territories. It is not so strange, though, for even now the overwhelming majority of mankind is earthbound and have at their disposal for commercial purposes only mechanical energy; indeed, in some places only animal energy! Moreover, notions of "sovereignty" and "nationalism", while they may seem dated and even dangerous to some political scientists, die hard and are still very much dominant in the affairs of states. These conditions are likely to prevail for many, many years, and while we may sigh and long for the day when mighty ion engines will whisk all manner of goods around the world in a twinkling without regard to lines on a map, we must still bring our eyes and thoughts back down to earth and deal with the world as it is, not as it ought to be – or might be some day. And so it is necessary to examine in some detail the need for and the problems of "a free and secure access to the sea" in the space age.

Analyses of Case Studies

As was made clear in Chapter I, land-locked states have little in common other than that they have no sea coasts and are very much aware of that fact. Even among the developing land-locked states there is no such thing as a "typical" or "average" case. Nevertheless, some of them share many similarities while differing in other respects. Rather than size or age or standard of living as measures of similarities and differences on a world-wide basis, it is more useful to compare the developing land-locked states on a continental basis. Broadly speaking, the land-locked states of each continent have more in common with one another, and with the littoral states of the continent, than with the land-locked states of other continents. The three cases studied may then be measured against the other land-locked states in their respective continents.

Afghanistan is one of four land-locked states in Asia. It is the largest by far in population, only that of Nepal even approaching it, and second largest in land area. Because of terrain and, in varying degrees because of historical ties, the natural routes to the sea for each country lie through coastal states which flank them on the south and east. Afghanistan has the largest volume of foreign trade, while that of Laos is minimal, consisting largely of opium, gold and aid goods. Laos, moreover, has overland access routes through both Saigon and Bangkok and a potential water route via the Mekong River. She is on reasonably good terms with these two neighbors and may be said to have the least pressing problem of access to the sea of the four. Mongolia has alternated between being a part of China, or at least a tributary state, and being a satellite of Russia or the U.S.S.R., and virtually all of her foreign trade has been, and still is, with these contiguous states. Only Nepal and Afghanistan make substantial use of their access to the sea at present. Nepali foreign trade, except for that with India and minor amounts with Tibet, passes almost exclusively through Calcutta. As we have seen, Afghanistan has a choice of access routes, but still relies mostly on Karachi for trade with all but her immediate neighbors.

No Asian country has yet suffered deliberate interference with its transit trade since becoming independent except Afghanistan, but none of the other three can be wholly confident that the record will remain so clean. Both Laos and Nepal have bilateral transit agreements with their transit states and it may be presumed that Mongolia has similar agreements with China and the Soviet Union. But the road to Calcutta can be cut at any time by fighting between the Indian government and East Pakistan or rebel tribesmen, the Vietnam War could spread to Cambodia and Thailand and to Laos itself, the "Great Proletarian Cultural Revolution" could disrupt road and rail transport in North China, and the land-locked states would then become helpless victims of forces over which they have no control and for which they have no responsibility. Afghanistan has been unique among Asian land-locked states in this respect, but she may not remain so.

Bolivia is the only state in the Western Hemisphere which does not have either a coastline or practicable access to the sea via an internationalized navigable river. Paraguay has had free navigation of the Paraguay-Paraná-Plata system for nearly 100 years, with only occasional threats to that free transit. But, as was pointed out in the section on Bolivia's geography, navigation on the Paraguay is limited by natural conditions and most Paraguayan foreign trade goods are railed between Asunción and Rosario or Sante Fé, Argentina. Bolivia is much larger than Paraguay in both area and population and has a much more vigorous foreign trade. At least since the War of the Triple Alliance, in which Paraguay fought Brazil, Argentina and Uruguay from 1865 to 1870, Paraguay has been on somewhat better terms with the downstream riparians than Bolivia has been with her neighbors. Still, Paraguay's security of transit depends on her maintenance of good relations with these states, especially Argentina. At present both states are ruled by authoritarian military regimes and there are few serious disputes between them.

Bolivia and Paraguay, being contiguous, are theoretically capable of providing transit for one another. In fact, however, there would be no reason for Paraguay to ship goods through Bolivia and it is unlikely she would do so except in the direst emergency. All of the geographic problems of Bolivia would be compounded for Paraguay were she to attempt to ship goods to and from the Pacific Ocean via Bolivia. Her only feasible alternative to using the Paraguay River or crossing Argentine territory would be to go through Brazil, using ports in the states of Paraná and São Paulo. Transportation is inadequate for heavy traffic, though, between Paraguay and the Serra do Mar, the range of mountains near the Atlantic coast. Practically, then, Paraguay has only one access route to the sea – through Argentina. Bolivia, in contrast, has three good routes to the Pacific Ocean, all of which are regularly used (and somewhat interchangeably at that), and several to the Atlantic Ocean capable of greater development and use. Both countries have treaties and agreements with their respective transit states regulating their transit. Bolivia, for all her public breast-beating on the subject, has never since the Treaty of Peace with Chile in 1904 suffered any interruption of consequence in her access to the sea, not even by the forces of nature.

Uganda is not unique among land-locked states in being a member of a customs union; there is also a Customs Union of West African States which includes the land-locked states of Mali, Upper Volta and Niger. The other former French African states are also heirs to transit arrangements made among them or between France and Britain on their behalf. This type of transit arrangement is known as an *Opération Hirondelle.*

Several of the former French land-locked states have experienced some difficulty with access to the sea since obtaining independence, despite these arrangements. When the Federation of Mali broke up in acrimony in 1960 after a year and a half of existence, the former French Soudan took the name of Mali and turned away from her erstwhile partner, Senegal, and the latter's big port of Dakar. Mali began developing new ties with Ghana and Guinea and redirected her transit trade from the easy all-rail route to Dakar to a new road-rail route to Conakry, capital and largest port of Guinea. Relations between Senegal and Mali were resumed in mid-1963, but are still not warm; Mali continues to use Conakry for a large proportion of her foreign trade. The transit trade of Chad and Niger has been seriously disrupted by the civil war in Nigeria. The railway in Cameroon is being extended to Fort Lamy in Chad, but meanwhile both states are innocent victims of Nigeria's internal problems. Upper Volta is fortunate in having an all-rail route to the Ivory Coast port capital of Abidjan – and good relations with the Ivory Coast. The Central African Republic, as already noted, has a river-rail route through Congo (Brazzaville).

Botswana and Lesotho are absolutely dependent upon South Africa for their access to the sea – and for many other things as well – and thus *must* remain on good terms with that republic, *apartheid* and all. This has made it virtually impossible for these two land-locked states to join the other black African states in their political and economic campaigns against South Africa. Similarly, Malawi is dependent upon both Portugal and South Africa for her fragile economic health. She has made arrangements with Portugal for the extension to Lake Malawi of the existing railroad from the Mozambique port of Nacala, which port will be almost exclusively for her use. She has also established diplomatic relations with South Africa, where many of her citizens work. When Swaziland becomes independent she will be faced with precisely the same awkward situation, except that she will be relatively richer than impoverished Malawi, Botswana and Lesotho.

The routes to the sea of Zambia, Burundi and Rwanda have been discussed in some detail in Chapter V. All are directly or indirectly linked with Uganda, but none is in quite so fortunate a position. Zambia is by far the wealthiest of the African land-locked states, but her mineral wealth can be converted into spendable cash only if it can readily reach markets in Europe and elsewhere. The same is true for the lesser wealth of Uganda, of course, but Uganda has less cause for concern about her access to the sea than any other state in Africa.

We may now also summarize the similarities and differences among Afghanistan, Bolivia and Uganda, making a cross-continental comparison.

Physically, Bolivia is the largest of the three and one of the largest of all land-locked states; Afghanistan is of "average" size and Uganda is relatively small. In population, Afghanistan is largest, Uganda, moderately large, and Bolivia the smallest, but all three are in the middle rank of the world's land-locked states in population. Uganda, however, is among the most densely populated. Afghanistan is quite mountainous, with only the southwestern and north central portions being reasonably level; Bolivia is about one-third highlands (cordilleras, Altiplano and Yungas) and two-thirds lowland; and Uganda is nearly all a moderately high plateau. The climate in all three countries varies with altitude, but Uganda has a generally moderate climate with rainfall adequate for agriculture; Bolivia has two distinct climatic regimes, cold and dry in the highlands and hot and wet in the lowlands; and Afghanistan is semi-arid throughout but with considerable ranges of temperatures.

Bolivia is well served by transportation routes to the sea, having five railroads and several roads through four of her transit states, but has a very weak internal transportation system; Afghanistan has moderately good transit facilities and an internal transportation network which has been poor and still includes no railroad, but is rapidly becoming modernized; Uganda has a very good internal transportation network, but her access to the sea, while adequate now, is limited for all practical purposes to one railroad.

Historically, Afghanistan is relatively old, one of the oldest national states in the world, though its independence was somewhat qualified until 1919; Bolivia might be considered middle-aged, but hardly mature; Uganda is young by any standards. Of the three, Afghanistan has never been a colony, Bolivia attained independence nearly a century and a half ago during the first of the great modern decolonization processes, and Uganda attained independence toward the end of the third and last of the modern breakups of empires. Bolivia claims the distinction of being the only state to have lost her seacoast by aggression; Afghanistan is the only land-locked state in modern times to have had her access to the sea deliberately and repeatedly interrupted (three times in a dozen years), and Uganda is the only one which participates as an equal partner in the operation of her own transit facilities. Afghanistan has been a battleground for centuries, repeatedly subjected to hostile invasions and being the fount of other invasions to the west and southeast; Uganda has been in the path of many peaceful migrations and has experienced little warfare except on a small scale among local tribes, factions and Christian missionaries; Bolivia has had a turbulent history, having been part of both the Inca and Spanish Empires, having fought full-scale wars with two of her neighbors and having lost territory to every one of her neighbors.

Politically, Afghanistan is a constitutional monarchy, Bolivia a unitary republic and Uganda a quasi-federal republic. Bolivia is a member of all of the inter-American organizations, including the military alliance formed under the Rio Treaty of 1947; Uganda is a member of the Commonwealth and has security arrangements with Britain; Afghanistan belongs to no regional political groupings, has no alliances with anyone, and rigidly maintains a neutralist role in the "Cold War" and other international political disputes. Bolivia is on reasonably good terms with all of her neighbors but Chile; Afghanistan with all of her neighbors, now that she has resumed relations with Pakistan; Uganda has had no serious difficulties with any of her neighbors. Bolivia had a violent and thoroughgoing social and economic revolution in 1952, but since then has made only erratic progress; Afghanistan, like Iran and Ethiopia, is adapting an ancient feudal political and social system to modern times, and successfully so far; Uganda is trying to bridge the gap between tribal and national systems. Afghanistan has pursued an activist foreign policy and has won considerable respect in the world community; Uganda has been more passive, but most constructive, concentrating mostly on domestic problems; Bolivia has huffed and puffed but has been rather ineffectual in international affairs.

Finally, Afghans have several times in history tried to reach the sea by military or political means; Bolivia alone among the three (and possibly among all contemporary mediterranean states) has developed a feeling of national claustrophobia, at least among the politically conscious elite of the country; while Uganda did not have to try to teach the sea – the sea came to her, in the form of the Imperial British East Africa Company and the Uganda Railway.

From the discussion so far, it might appear that these three countries have little in common other than their land-locked status. They have much more than that in common, however. Like all land-locked states, they are small, poor and isolated, though Bolivia is less small and Uganda rather less poor and isolated than the others. All are basically subsistence agricultural countries, though each has a specialty or two which earns valuable foreign exchange: tin for Bolivia, Karakul for Afghanistan and cotton and coffee for Uganda. Each is internally heterogeneous, with the problem of building a viable nation-state out of disparate peoples, few of whom have long been or are now imbued with "the state idea." Each has had overriding internal political problems which have tended to weaken its hand in formulating and carrying out foreign policy: chronic instability in Bolivia, rapid modernization in Afghanistan, and Buganda in Uganda. Each has been involved in, or has created, an external issue which directly or indirectly has affected its relations with transit states: the Río Lauca for Bolivia, Pushtunistan for Afghanistan, and Zambia-Rhodesia for Uganda, though clearly Uganda's role here is of a different order than the other two imbroglios. Finally, and perhaps in the long run most important, each is, or is capable of becoming in the near future, a transit state for its own transit states: Bolivia between Brazil on the Atlantic Ocean and Peru and Chile on the Pacific, Afghanistan between Pakistan and the USSR and between India and Iran, and Uganda between the Congo and Rwanda on the west and Kenya and the Indian Ocean on the east.

Most of these similarities and differences, indeed most of the real problems of land-locked states, revolve around their efforts to raise their standards of living rapidly and the role which transportation plays in this economic development. It seems worthwhile, then, to focus briefly on this relationship.

Transportation and Development

In the first of a series of studies under the Transport Research Program of the Brookings Institution, the program's director, Wilfred Owen, discusses many of the effects of poor transportation. Among his comments, those relevant to the present study include the following:

> The ability to sell in world markets is often limited by the difficulties of overland transport. Moving fifty miles to port may be costlier than moving thousands of miles by sea. And nearer home, there may be no land connections with neighboring countries, hence no way to benefit from specialization and trade. The problem is not always the complete absence of transport, but its unreliability, high cost, slow schedules, and high rates of damage and pilferage. These obstacles to movement restrict the market, increase the cost of production, and raise prices beyond the reach of consumers. [1]
>
> Transport difficulties have their political and social as well as their economic impacts. Poor transport makes it exceedingly difficult to achieve national unity. The growth process is retarded by limited opportunity for public officials to travel through their country, and by the difficulties of conducting business.

[1] Wilfred Owen, *Strategy for Mobility* (Washington: The Brookings Institution, 1964), p. 6.

Poor transport can be a major obstacle to maintaining internal security. It also limits the effectiveness of technical assistance programs. [2]

These comments, of course, can be applied to any country, land-locked or coastal, developing or developed, and transportation can be overemphasized in a development program, as Owen warns at some length, using the examples of Colombia and Turkey. Still, transportation in developing countries is today a critical factor in their economic, social and political progress. The pressures of time, the almost frenetic competition in import and export trade, rapidly rising populations, and that modern phenomenon which economists call "the international demonstration effect" and which laymen call "the revolution of rising expectations" all combine to produce an urgency and complexity in transport development unknown before.

The situation in underdeveloped areas, therefore, is not comparable to the period of primitive transport in which the developed economies previously found themselves. Transport in Asia, Africa and Latin America reflects at once a continuation of the immobility that constrained societies of earlier times, a projection into the most advanced transport technologies, and an exposure to the same frustrations of overcongestion that beset the most affluent societies. [3]

As Owen notes, other transportation factors may be even more important than its mere existence. Several of them have been pointed out in the three case studies: inefficiency leading to loss, damage and delay; overstaffing of transport facilities; natural hazards such as steep grades necessitating cogs or floods which wash out bridges and roadbeds; strikes in ports and in the transportation industry; and so on. All of these factors can be translated into cash value; that is, all of them add to the actual dollar cost of developing and operating a modern economy. But even if all modes of transport could be operated efficiently and economically in a developing country and it could freely choose which it wanted to use, the inherent costs of installation and operation would still weigh heavily in the choice and consequently in the cost of economic development.

Chart 1, modified from one included in a study by the Pan American Union, illustrates clearly that pipelines and water transport are by far the cheapest types of transport. But, as we have seen, while all land-locked states rely on ocean shipping for their foreign trade, making access to the sea vital to them, few are able to utilize effectively the other modes in this lowest-cost transport category. Bolivia uses a number of pipelines for

[2] *Ibid.*, p. 7.
[3] *Ibid.*, p. 37.

CHART I

Relation between total transportation cost and average daily cargo.

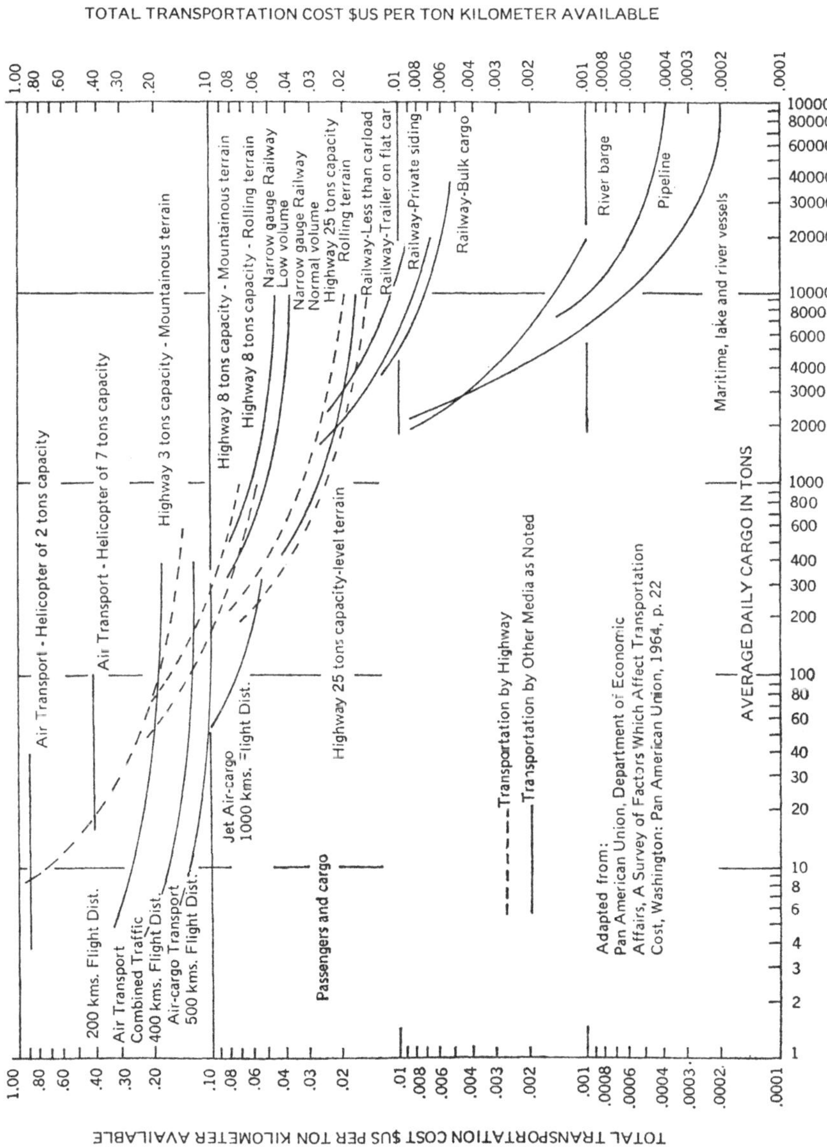

exporting small amounts of petroleum; Afghanistan is beginning to pipe natural gas to the Soviet Union; and Uganda makes some small use of steamers and railway ferries on Lake Victoria. Paraguay and several West African land-locked states make fairly extensive use of river transport. Generally, however, lake, river and pipeline transport are of limited value to the developing land-locked states – at least so far.

The most expensive mode of transport is aircraft, as shown clearly in Chart 1. Despite the romantic nature of flying, the hard facts of economics limit its use except under special topographic, political or other circumstances. "Bush lines" in such places as Alaska, Colombia or Bolivia may be locally important for carrying such things as mail, medicines, spare parts and other low bulk-high value goods, and many developing countries try to gain prestige and foreign exchange by operating aircraft on international routes. These international operations, however, carry mostly passengers and few of them as yet earn both prestige and profits. Air transport is generally not an important instrument for economic development, even in land-locked territories.

Afghanistan may be cited as a developing land-locked state which has used air transport effectively to help overcome the inherent handicaps of her enclosed location. But there are three weaknesses in this argument. First, and underlying all use of aircraft to and from land-locked states, it is dependent upon permission to overfly the transit states, permission which could be readily withheld or revoked since international law recognizes this as a sovereign right of states. Second, it is economic only for low bulk-high value goods, such as Afghanistan's Karakul and fresh, highly perishable fruits, goods which few land-locked states export in quantity. Third, it is feasible only for relatively long flights; as illustrated in the chart, it is competitive with surface transportation (except under most difficult terrain conditions) only at distances of over about 1000 kilometers. As for domestic air transport to support the international routes, Afghanistan is also cited in a study done by a RAND Corporation staff member as an example of a country which attempted to stress the dramatic and spectacular in developing internal air routes.

After the Soviet Union made her first flamboyant 100 million dollar credit offer in 1955, the United States responded with an ambitious scheme to establish a complete internal aviation system within three years, with the help of Pan American World Airways, including the big airport at Kandahar. After the first American technicians arrived in April 1957, the scheme ran into severe problems, including an almost complete lack of the necessary local resources and skilled personnel. Gradually the program changed into a cooperative venture between the United States and Afghan governments and great progress was made. The objectives were refined to suit local conditions, the time was stretched out from three to six years, and the cost estimate was revised from fifteen million dollars to fifty. A good system was eventually developed "not with drama and fanfare, but through patience, persistence and slow but steady forward movement." [4] But even in Afghanistan, where air transport is more practical, even more necessary, than in most land-locked states, it is surface transport, and particularly roads and railroads, that carries the burden of internal development and foreign trade.

One of the prime needs of nearly all land-locked countries in Africa, Asia and South America is the integration of their transport systems with those of their neighbors into regional networks. The role of international highways in Asia is described in a recent detailed and candid critique of ECAFE in this way:

> Unlike Europe, for instance, international highways in Asia are not an obvious response to a large and rapidly growing volume of international traffic. On the contrary, like so many development projects, they have to create their own demand; their role is a promotional one.
>
> Historically, the impact of the West on Asia came from the sea and was most marked in the ports and their environs. It is precisely where it was least felt, namely in the hinterlands, that the consequences of road building could well be far-reaching. The importance of the Asian Highway for land-locked Afghanistan, Laos, and Nepal, for instance, needs no emphasis. The Secretariat [of ECAFE] thinks of it as a modern revival of the ancient caravan routes along which travelled not only goods but peoples and ideas. It is as much for these purposes as for their economic benefits that better and cheaper international communications are sorely needed in the ECAFE region. [5]

Afghanistan fully realizes this and is constructing a portion of the Asian Highway, which when completed will connect Istanbul with Saigon and Singapore, as well as good roads connecting the Soviet and Pakistani systems. These represent only a beginning, though, and more international highways are needed not only in Asia, but in Latin America and Africa as well.

Bolivia has similarly made a beginning with her portion (about 300 kilometers) of the Pan-American Transversal Highway (a branch of the

[4] Hans Heymaan, Jr., "Air Transport and Economic Development: Some Comments on Foreign Aid Programs," in "The Role of Transportation in Economic Development," *American Economic Review*, LII (May, 1962), p. 393.

[5] David Wightman, *Toward Economic Cooperation in Asia; The United Nations Economic Commission for Asia and the Far East* (New Haven: Yale University Press, 1963), p. 221.

Inter-American Highway) which, when completed, will connect Rio de Janeiro, Paranaguá, Asunción, La Paz and Lima. She is also participating in planning and eventual construction of the Carretera Marginal Bolivariana de la Selva (popularly known as "The Marginal"), the highway along the eastern foothills of the Andes suggested originally by President Fernando Belaunde Terry of Peru. When completed, this highway will stretch 6,500 kilometers from Puerto Carreño, Colombia to Corumbá, Brazil, including at least 3,800 kilometers of new road. It is being designed to open up vast areas of potentially productive but isolated territory in the interior of South America. For Bolivia alone, the cost of this massive project is expected to run to about $ 71,800,000, [6] but she is expected to derive both direct and indirect benefits far in excess of this figure, not the least of which will be substantial migration into and development of the Oriente. In fact, of the four countries participating, "only in Bolivia has it become apparent that the Oriente must play a major role if overall standards of living are to be raised." [7] While the highway is expected to make an enormous impact on the economies of all four countries, especially Bolivia,

> [t]he indirect cost of the highway in Bolivia is high. In view of current resources and projected availability of external financing, it is evident that a decision to build all the Carretera Marginal sections within the next 15 years would require a rather complete reassessment of priorities . . . It is probable, therefore, that a beginning on the Carretera Marginal de la Selva in Bolivia cannot be made until the middle 1970's in the absence of substantial changes in national highway planning and availability of sources. [8]

Even if this assessment proves to be somewhat conservative, it illustrates the practical difficulties of constructing a transportation system which, in this case, will increase production in the Amazon, Orinoco and Paraguay basins and make not only more necessary but more feasible Bolivia's access to the Atlantic Ocean by rail, road or river through Brazil. [9]

Uganda was described in Chapter V as a country with reasonably adequate transportation facilities. This is true in a relative sense only, for even her happy circumstance of participating in an area-wide transportation system has not cancelled out the fundamental handicap of a mediter-

[6] Charles J. Stokes, "The Economic Impact of the Carretera Marginal de la Selva," *Traffic Quarterly,* XX (April, 1966), p. 205.

[7] *Ibid.*, p. 211.

[8] *Ibid.*, pp. 221–222.

[9] For additional detailed information on this and related topics, including critical comments both on Bolivia's existing transportation network and the plans for improvement, see ECLA, *El Transporte en América Latina* (E/CN.12/703/Rev.1) (February, 1965).

ranean location. In the words of the United Nations Economic Commission for Africa,

Not a single country in the East-African sub-region, with the possible exception of the Union of South Africa, is adequately provided with transport in its national territory; nor can the situation be deemed satisfactory at the subregional level. The transport picture is, as a matter of fact, characterized by missing subregional links and devious transport routes. [10]

This report goes on to detail the deficiencies of transport in eastern Africa and the reasons for them, concentrating almost entirely on road and rail transport, containing much less on inland waterways and very little on air transport. It also contains a comment on an aspect of transport often overlooked or underestimated in treatments of the subject:

Questions of ports and harbours are also of special importance in a sub-region containing many land-locked countries. Hence, it may be deemed desirable to convene a port and shipping seminar for African countries at some suitable time. [11]

Considerable progress has been made in East Africa since this report was published and both the older and newer portions of the transport system, including ports, are functioning reasonably well under the circumstances. Nevertheless, it is still possible to note the handicaps faced by Uganda because of her location "at the end of the line." Her distance from the sea has greatly affected the location of economic activities within the country and her relationships with her neighbors and her trading partners abroad. As one economic geographer sees it,

Location in relation to the sea is of great importance today, especially in connection with overseas trade, and both Kenya and Tanzania benefit from their coastal position. Uganda correspondingly suffers from its interior location, although a superior endowment of climate and soils, together with the establishment of transport facilities, has enabled it to keep pace with Kenya and Tanzania in economic development. Railways and roads reduce the effects of location but they do not abolish them. [12]

Transit, Access and Outlets

Since free transit is recognized as being vitally necessary for the development, if not the very economic existence, of land-locked states, it

[10] ECA, *East African Transport Problems in Relation to the Promotion of Economic Development (Progress Report)*, (E/CN.14/148) (24 January 1962), p. 2.

[11] *Ibid.*, p. 24.

[12] A. M. O'Connor, *An Economic Geography of East Africa*, p. 214.

behooves us to take a closer look at the specific nature of the problems involved in granting such transit rights and what is meant by the terms "access" and "outlet" to the sea. First, John Fried has summarized much of the commentary on the question of transit which appears both in the writings of publicists and in the debates in the several United Nations conferences and committee sessions on the subject.

All States, whether land-locked or not, require transit

In order to gain further perspective of the realities of world trade and intercourse, we must also look at the actual trade arrangements of countries which do possess sea-ports of their own.

Even a cursory glance reveals that they, too, require transit rights.

Firstly many of their exports and imports move, *not* by sea but by land, through one or two or even more countries. For all such transit the coastal States require transit rights. Logically, for example, the Barcelona Convention and Statute on Freedom of Transit of 1921 does not distinguish between coastal and non-coastal States.

Furthermore, even for much of their *sea* trade, coastal States require transit rights – namely whenever the sea voyage of their imports and exports involve stop-overs or transloading in foreign ports. Even on a single trip, ports of several countries may have to be touched by freighters plying between coastal countries of different continents.

Finally, many goods move between coastal States and far away land-locked States. They require not only port transit but also land transit; after passing through foreign *sea-ports* they must also traverse the *territory* of at least one foreign country – for example, goods moving between a South-East Asian sea-port and any land-locked State in Europe, Africa or Latin America.

None of such trade of *coastal States* could function without use of foreign facilities, without exemption from customs duties in the transit States, without well-functioning rules regarding documentation and inspection, and so on.

In short, coastal States do not only *grant* transit *to* other States but also themselves *use* transit *through* (sea-ports and territory of) other states.

Nor can the fact be overlooked that coastal States serve as transit States, not only for land-locked countries but also for other coastal countries, that is, for *each other* . . .

All this is merely to say that maritime countries (although, in Cicero's phrase, "masters of the sea") are *also* dependent on geographic factors, and *also* require (depending on their location and on the complexion of their trade) transit through other countries – maritime and land-locked.

This is obvious. Yet it may require some emphasis in order to refute, or avoid, a superficial impression or psychological attitude which may influence legal and political attitudes – namely, that only land-locked countries demand transit rights, and that only *their* trade is a "burden" on other States.

Such impression is faulty for two reasons: Land-locked States can, and often do, serve themselves as transit States for maritime countries. Secondly, and more importantly, as we have seen, maritime States also constantly require transit facilities of each other, and frequently of land-locked States.

Hence, *if* transit is considered a "burden", then *all* countries, not only land-locked ones, impose such "burden" upon each other; and *if* transit rights are considered "favours", then *all* countries require them.

But it is truer, and more conducive to harmonious economic development generally, to view the greatest possible facilitation of transit trade not as burden, favour, or concession, but as a mutually beneficial form of solidarity.

The Usefulness of Solidarity

We may end these preliminary basic observations on a philosophical note. One of the most meritorious aims of law (as well as of other social institutions and also of technology) is to rectify or alleviate the untoward consequences of man's environment, of geography and topography, of the inclemency of the elements, and of other hazards that threaten the existence or welfare of people and nations. The world legal order is an essential part of this grand effort, – not because statesmen are sentimentalists but because solidarity is in the mutual interest; while exploitation of such adverse facts to the other's detriment ultimately hurts the exploiter. There is constant need to improve that network of treaties, customs arrangements and common institutions which tends to decrease the adverse effects of the vagaries and hazards of man's environment. This is a continuous task, and a principal message and *raison d'etre* of international law.

The Convention [on Transit Trade of Land-locked States]

If transit trade is important to all states, why is a special Convention needed concerning transit trade of land-locked States? The answer is three fold.

(1) Firstly, however important transit trade may be for all countries, land-locked countries are often in a specially vulnerable position in this respect – the more vulnerable, the smaller their choice of outlets. The legislative history of the Convention indicates clearly that it is based on the "recognition of the need of land-locked countries for adequate transit facilities". The Convention is designed, primarily, to assure to land-locked States those links with the outside world which, under present-day conditions, are indispensable for their economic life, their economic development and, in extreme cases, virtually their right of existence. In other words, the Convention endeavours, first of all, to mitigate the adverse consequences of the coincidences of geography of land-locked States, and their dependence on other countries in maintaining their life line with the outside world. This aim is not without significance for the *interpretation* of the Convention.

(2) At the same time, the Convention safeguards very carefully and very extensively all legitimate interests of transit States – or, to put it more precisely, of the States, coastal or land-locked, through which traffic in transit moves to or from a land-locked State.

(3) Finally, the Convention covers not only transit between land-locked States and foreign sea-ports. It also covers transit *through* land-locked States. This is the potentially far-reaching consequence of the Convention's reciprocity clause (Art. 15). The clause underscores the function, obligation, and willing-

ness of land-locked States to act themselves as bridges between other States, coastal or land-locked alike.

Hence, the title of the Convention must be read to mean: "Convention on the Transit of Goods and Means of Transport to, from, and *through* Land-locked States." [13]

This principle of reciprocity, reasonable as it may seem, was not incorporated into the Convention without long debate. The Soviet delegate asked, for example, "How could a land-locked country extend full reciprocity to a transit country when the basic premise of the Convention was that land-locked countries suffered from fundamental disadvantages in certain important respects?" Paraguay voted against the Argentine amendment to the proposed article 18 of the original draft "because any reciprocity extended by land-locked countries must of necessity be qualified and not unconditional." The delegate of Mali "feared that the amendment would open the way to abuses of the principle of reciprocity by countries which were not of good faith, and had accordingly voted against it." Bolivia also voted against it, "considering it to be unnecessary in the present Convention." The United States, like the USSR, voted for it, "although it shared the doubts regarding its legal aspects expressed by other delegations . . . and it hoped that due allowance would be made, in the application of article 18, for the differences existing between land-locked and transit countries." "Like other delegations, the Afghan delegation thought it inadmissable that land-locked countries should be called upon to grant reciprocal privileges to transit countries."

The vote on the Argentine amendment embodying the principle of reciprocity was 37 in favor, 6 opposed and 6 abstentions. The land-locked states were by no means united against it: Czechoslovakia voted against it, opposing the USSR, but Switzerland, another European land-locked state, voted for it. [14] While many states still have reservations about this rather novel provision of the 1965 Convention, it seems likely to have, as Fried put it, "far-reaching" consequences. As has been noted earlier in this paper, Mongolia, Afghanistan and Uganda already are transit states. Many other land-locked states are now or have been transit states, and Bolivia and most others have the potential of serving in this capacity. Article 15 may yet turn out to be a most important "sleeper" of the 1965 Convention.

Another practical problem of granting free transit for developing land-

[13] John H. E. Fried, *op. cit.*, pp. 12–14. All italics are in the original.

[14] All of the foregoing material on the Conference debate is from TD/TRANSIT/SR.29, pp. 2–4.

locked states, as illustrated by the cases of Afghanistan, Bolivia and even Uganda, is the frequently inadequate transportation and port facilities available for the transit trade of land-locked states within the territory of the littoral states. This problem was neatly summarized by the Pakistani delegation during the debate at the 1965 Conference:

> Pakistan made all possible transport facilities available to its neighbours, despite the sacrifices that such a policy entailed. Pakistan was itself a developing country: its economic infra-structure was still far from adequate, its two ports and its railways could hardly meet domestic requirements, and its roads were few and not built to carry heavy traffic. The maintenance and expansion of those transport facilities involved considerable expenditure of foreign exchange, but storage, transport and related fees for transit goods were collected in local currency. Reference had been made to delays in the transit of goods through the territory of the transit States. When the latter were themselves developing countries those delays were often due to the general inadequacy of transport arrangements. Pakistan could certainly not be accused of causing deliberate delays. [15]

While this observation was only part of a longish and rather self-serving speech, and while Pakistan has, apparently, been guilty of "causing deliberate delays" to Afghan transit trade, the main point is well taken. With the possible exceptions of the Soviet Union and South Africa, the neighbors of all of the developing land-locked states are themselves developing and have insufficient resources to meet their own transportation needs. Moreover, some of these neighbors are themselves land-locked, thus compounding their problems even further. Still, the principles and rules of transit are clear enough that given adequate good will and effort by all parties, transit states, coastal or land-locked, should be able to provide for land-locked states adequate access to the sea. The question remains, though, of just what is meant by "access" or "outlet" to the sea.

In Chapter IV it was pointed out that among the millions of words expended on the subject, Bolivia has never included a precise definition of what she means by a "*salida al mar.*" The literal translation of the Spanish term would be "exit", or "outlet to the sea". As it has been used, however, it could also be interpreted as meaning "access to the sea". For this Bolivia is not entirely to blame, as the terms "access" and "outlet" are often used interchangeably in common usage, and even in some of the legal literature. (Even, occasionally, in this book.) An examination of the literature, debates in the United Nations, and other sources, though, reveals a clear difference in the actual meaning of the two terms.

[15] TD/TRANSIT/SR.8, p. 14.

An *outlet* to the sea implies a physical connection between the land-locked territory and the open sea. This connection may be in the form of an internationalized navigable waterway or a land corridor, both discussed in some detail in Chapter II. If a state has an outlet to the sea via a land corridor, it cannot truly be considered "land-locked," even though, as was recognized in Chapter I, the corridor may be of little value to it and it may, in fact, share all of the transit problems of fully land-locked states. If a land-locked state has the use of an internationalized navigable waterway to reach the sea it clearly has an advantage over those mediterranean states which lack such a route. The advantage is limited, however, not only by geographic factors, but by the lack of complete sovereignty over the waterway. Should the coastal state interfere with the interior state's traffic on the waterway, such action would not necessarily be considered hostile under international law, as it would be if the intrusion were made on land, or across a state's boundary anywhere. In any case, of the developing land-locked States, not one has a reliable, adequate, all-water route to the sea.

Access to the sea implies any kind of approach or route between an interior state and the sea which is used on a more-or-less regular basis on equitable terms. It may include corridors and waterways, but in practice is limited to transit rights and facilities across the territory of a coastal state. These are nearly always the subject of bilateral agreements between the parties, though such agreements are often based on the principles and rules of international law and practice on the subject. This access is often precarious, not only for natural and technical reasons, but also for political reasons. The interior and coastal states must either remain on good terms with one another or agree to respect the transit arrangements in the absence of good relations. In addition, the bilateral agreements are often restricted in nature, falling short of providing "a free and secure access to the sea," and are often of limited duration, necessitating frequent renegotiations in which the transit state generally has the upper hand. Often, too, transit arrangements are only mentioned or sketchily outlined in a trade agreement or some other type of treaty. Nevertheless, access to the sea even on these terms is better than no access at all. Thus, while no developing land-locked state has an *outlet* to the sea, each has at least one route of *access* to the sea.

Afghanistan falls into the category of states whose access to the sea depends entirely upon restricted, short-term, bilateral agreements with her coastal neighbors. This has posed no problem thus far with her transit through the Soviet Union, Iran or India, but Pakistan is quite another matter. Here Afghanistan, in common with many other land-locked states, must rely for her most important access route to the sea on good relations with Pakistan – or on her own strengthening bargaining position based on trade and reciprocal transit rights.

Bolivia, to be sure, has no *outlet* to the sea, but she has the widest choice and the freest use of *access* routes to the sea of any developing land-locked state in the world. Her access, moreover, is based not upon short-term arrangements, but upon treaties or other agreements of unlimited duration. Despite her running feud with Chile since 1879 and long periods without diplomatic relations with her transit states, Bolivia's transit has been unimpeded by any action of the Chilean government or, for that matter, by that of any other country. Nevertheless, Bolivian politicians will always be able to use Chile as a whipping-boy whenever they wish to distract their people's attention from domestic problems simply by heating up the *salida al mar* compaign. Both countries may profit from some concession on Chile's part, a suggestion for which is offered below. Meanwhile, Bolivia has no legitimate complaint about her present and potential *access* to the sea.

Uganda is in a peculiar position among land-locked states, for in truth she has available something approaching a permanent, year-round, non-sovereign, dry land *outlet* to the sea. Technically, her access to the sea derives from her membership in the East African common market and the newly formed East African Community. The Kenya-Uganda border has long since ceased to have much meaning except as an administrative boundary. The tendencies toward nationalism and autarky in East Africa in recent years, noted in Chapter V, are grim reminders that this happy condition is not yet permanent and secure. But the Kenya-Uganda Railway was built to connect Uganda with the sea, and for long it served as a kind of prolongation of the Uganda Protectorate. In many ways it still is, since Uganda has a share in the sovereignty over the railroad. Interference with her traffic on the line might be construed under international law as an infringement of her sovereignty, still a more serious offense in the world community than violation of a mere transit agreement. In many ways, the railroad is like a long, narrow wood and steel corridor of Uganda to the sea and to the harbor of Mombasa – in which she also has a share.

This brings our discussion to the final point concerning transit facilities for land-locked states. It has long been reasoned that if an interior state was entitled to free transit to the sea across the territory of a coastal state and free use of the high seas, it was also entitled to some type of free port facility at the end of the transit route *to* the high seas. Free ports or free zones are quite common around the world. Most states which establish them do so in order to stimulate the transit trade of all other states, not just land-locked states. They are areas within which goods may be landed, stored, manufactured and reshipped without going through the normal customs procedures. The tradition is an old one and there are many such free zones in Europe. There are others in, for example, the United States, Mexico, Malaya, Colombia, Lebanon and Panama, not to mention the most famous of all: Singapore and Hong Kong. Even Ireland established a free zone in 1961 at Shannon, but this one was established at an airport rather than a seaport. Most of those established since World War II, including that at Shannon, have had as their primary objective the encouragement of manufacturing, rather than merely break-of-bulk and storage.

Few land-locked states outside Europe have such free zones reserved for their own use. (Those in Kigoma and Dar es Salaam for Congo, Rwanda and Burundi were discussed in Chapter V.) Some share free zones with all other states, but more commonly they merely have bonded warehouses and associated facilities reserved for their use in seaports and often at intermediate points along their transit routes, particularly at or near the border. Under normal conditions these bonded facilities are adequate. In Mombasa goods bound up country for Uganda are passed through customs in the same manner as goods imported into Kenya and not even inspected again until they reach their destination.

Afghan goods are processed through customs in Karachi, sealed and bonded and only the seals are checked as the goods near the Afghan border. As noted in Chapter III, there is an Afghan Transit Area in Karachi and bonded warehouses in other Pakistani cities for Afghan use. Afghanistan and the other sponsors of the Afro-Asian Draft Convention on Transit Trade of Land-locked Countries included in that draft a provision that

> a free zone should be provided at the ports of entry or exit in the country of transit for transit goods only which should be under the control of the customs authorities of the land-locked country. The establishment of the free zones shall be carried into effect by agreement between the land-locked state and the coastal state. [16]

Dr. Tabibi argued eloquently for this provision of the Conference, but was unsuccessful in having it adopted. The final version of the Treaty says only that "free zones or other customs facilities may be provided

[16] A/5906, Annex II, p. 6.

at the ports . . ." Since this mild phraseology was adopted, enthusiasm for free zones seems to have waned. Now that relations between Afghanistan and Pakistan have improved, for example, so has the efficiency of processing of Afghan goods. Afghanistan is satisfied with the customs procedure for the present and is no longer pressing for a free zone within the port. [17]

Bolivia has similar bonded warehouses in several Chilean, Peruvian and Argentine ports, but only Argentina has so far granted her anything approaching a free port – Barranqueras. This, as was pointed out above, is of very limited value to her. Considering the ill-will generated and perpetuated by Bolivia's *salida al mar* campaign against Chile, it might be wise for Chile to grant Bolivia some small enclave, possibly within the port of Arica or even on the barren coast north of the city, perhaps abutting the Peruvian border. Informed sources indicate that Bolivia may now be willing to settle – permanently – for this and no more. She would not even demand a corridor to the enclave but would continue to use the Arica-La Paz Railroad under existing terms and conditions. Within the enclave she could have not only warehouses and associated transit facilities, but her long-sought tin smelter, manufacturing and assembly plants, a fishing industry and tourist hotels and beaches. She would also have a home port for the Bolivian Navy, which now has an admiral but no ships! Considering the small likelihood that Bolivia alone could finance such an ambitious scheme (The cost of supplying power and fresh water alone would be enormous.), Chile and Peru might be willing to risk more competition for Arica and Tacna and grant the necessary permission for such a Bolivian enclave. The cost to Chile would be small, a tiny bit of pride, perhaps, and it would be a small price indeed to pay for the restoration of harmony and normal relations between the two countries. And Bolivia, even if she gets nothing more out of it, shall once more be able to plant her flag upon the shore of the Pacific Ocean. That should be worth a very great deal to an historical accident trying to become a nation-state.

Before closing this chapter on access to the sea a question should be raised which as yet has no answer and cannot even be discussed within the scope of this study. It is, however, an extension of the present topic and

[17] For a detailed discussion of free zones, see UNCTAD, *Background Paper on the Question of Free Zones with Reference to Article 8 of the Draft Convention on Transit Trade of Landlocked States, (A/5906, Annex II, p. 6)* (TD/TRANSIT/4) (10 June 1965), prepared by the UN Secretariat for the Conference on Transit Trade of Land-Locked Countries. Mance, *op. cit.*, also has a useful section on free zones in Europe, the Middle East and East Africa, pp. 12–18.

deserves more consideration than it has so far received, which is virtually none.

The question is, if the sea is in fact *res communis,* the common property of all, and if even land-locked states have the right to transit freely to and from it and navigate freely upon it (and both concepts are by now well embedded in international law), why should land-locked states not also share in the *resources* of the sea? The coastal states have already divided the resources of their territorial waters and the continental shelf among themselves and the United Nations is currently studying allocation of the resources of the floor of the sea, but one-fifth of the states of the world are being left out of the distribution of the riches of man's last frontier on earth. Surely some formula can be found which would enable the land-locked states to share equitably in the wealth of the sea.

CHAPTER VII

SOLUTIONS TO THE QUESTION OF ACCESS TO THE SEA

The fact that access to the sea for land-locked states in general and the developing ones in particular is a real, vital and continuing need is well enough established so that the international community has deemed it appropriate, even necessary, to conclude a convention on the subject, one "which would last at least twenty-five years," a very long duration for a convention on a practical problem in this period of history. That there is a problem is evident from the numerous actual and threatened interruptions of freedom of transit since World War II, from the very restricted character of many transit agreements, and from the generally tenuous nature of transit agreements between weak interior states and their frequently stronger coastal neighbors. While the principle of "a free and secure access to the sea" has been broadly accepted by all states, there still is little agreement on what this orotund phrase actually means and still less on how it relates to "the sovereignty and territorial integrity of all states." Retaliation on the part of a transit state for real or fancied wrongs committed by a land-locked state may still take the form of cutting off the interior state from the sea. Or the transit trade may be subjected to such restriction, harassment and delay that the interior state may suffer grievously even though in a technical sense her access to the sea remains unimpaired. It seems necessary, therefore, to examine several possible ways to make more free and secure the access to the sea of developing land-locked states.

International Law

"International law," says Fenwick, "may be defined in broad terms as the body of general principles and specific rules which are binding upon the members of the international community in their mutual relations." [18]

[18] Charles G. Fenwick, *International Law* (4th ed.; New York: Appleton-Century-Crofts, 1965), p. 31.

This definition is in conformity with many other modern definitions of international law which no longer stress the "rights" and "obligations" of states as the classical writers did. Today international law is based on equity, on general consent deriving from the recognition of the advantages to be gained by all from mutual cooperation. Admittedly international law has not solved all international problems; it has not brought about the millenium of a prosperous, peaceful, orderly world. Still, it has been most useful in resolving many minor problems, in preventing others from becoming major ones, and in creating a climate conducive to the settling of even major disputes among states. It has even greater potential for usefulness in the future, and the World Peace through Law movement is gathering strength. Its third conference, held in Geneva in the summer of 1967, was more optimistic, yet more pragmatic, than its predecessors had been, despite its occurrence in the shadow of the six-day war in the Middle East in June. The International Court of Justice, the International Law Commission, the United Nations itself and its specialized agencies, are all making great contributions to the codification and progressive development of international law. Even resolutions of the General Assembly, United Nations declarations on social and economic matters, and debates on conventions developed by international conferences, even if the conventions never enter into force, are coming to be accepted as contributions to international law, worthy of respect and consideration by "civilized nations." Philip C. Jessup, in reviewing the first Geneva Conference on the Law of the Sea in 1958, wrote, for example, "Of course no one would have ignored the fact that the action of the Conference did not 'make' international law – or did it?" [19]

This development of international law since World War II illustrates its changing nature; indeed, the necessity for it to change. Fenwick puts it this way:

> The international community must from time to time reaffirm its principles, clarifying them in the light of the objectives to be attained; it must from time to time define its objectives anew, taking into account the needs of its member states and the practical ways and means available for meeting them. Just as in determining the relation of the state to the international community a balance must be sought between national sovereignty and the authority of international law, so in the development of the law itself a balance must be sought between stability and justice. International law must be fixed enough

[19] Philip C. Jessup, "The Geneva Conference on the Law of the Sea; A Study in International Law Making," *The American Journal of International Law*, LII (October, 1958), p. 732.

to assure the continuity of rights and duties; it must be elastic enough to meet the changing conditions of international life and intercourse. [20]

Among these "changing conditions of international life and intercourse," one of the most dramatic and farreaching – and significant for the purposes of this study – has been the more than doubling of the size of the international community since World War II as nearly threescore former colonies and other non-self-governing territories have become sovereign states. What has been their attitude toward international law? If they are unwilling to accept the "general principles and specific rules" developed for the most part by their former colonial masters as valid and binding upon them, then international law must either become obsolete, change radically, or be imposed by force upon the new states. In fact, none of these has happened or is likely to happen, since on the whole, the new states respect, utilize and help develop international law, while objecting to certain aspects of it which they deem contrary to their interests. We may well review a cross-section of the attitudes of the developing countries toward international law taken in chronological order through the period when so many of them became independent and which saw most of the postwar United Nations conferences discussed in Chapter II.

One observer answered the charge that new states reject existing international law because they had no part in creating it with the comment that

they have to a large extent voiced agreement with existing prescriptions, while at the same time the views of some Asian nations on certain controversial matters have added even more uncertainty to the overall confusion. It does not seem justified to expect that these nations will in the near future give up their claims which they regard as being of vital importance to their national interest. In the future difficulties are to be expected in the attempts to balance the exclusive national claims on these matters against the inclusive community claims. [21]

He gives as an example of an attempt at balance the 1958 Cairo meeting of the Asian-African Legal Consultative Committee, saying

that it revealed a great awareness among its members of the importance of further development of international law, as well as of their right and responsibility to contribute to that development. There was no tendency to disregard arbitrarily certain existing prescriptions simply because they have once been adopted without their participation or consent. [22]

[20] Fenwick, *op. cit.*, p. 50.

[21] J. J. G. Syatauw, *Some Newly Established Asian States and the Development of International Law* (The Hague: Martinus Nijhoff, 1961), p. 238.

[22] *Ibid.*, p. 239.

Jorge Castañeda, a well-known Latin American international lawyer, emphasizes the negative but still recognizes the value of international law. "It would not be an exaggeration," he says, "to affirm that there is, among the relatively new countries, less acceptance of the provisions of classic international law than among the older states." [23] He gives a number of examples – boundary disputes, fishing zones, extraterritoriality, etc. – and then says,

> The countries that, generally speaking, can be classified as underdeveloped, and, above all, the countries that became independent relatively late, have an interest in modifying in their favor numerous institutions and rules of international law . . .
>
> It is to the interest of new nations to facilitate and simplify the methods of creating and modifying international law. In particular, a tempering of the extreme position maintained by countries adhering dogmatically to the concept of state sovereignty . . . would especially be to the advantage of new states, although many of them are not yet fully conscious of this fact. [24]

Castañeda does not suggest "radical and immediate" changes in international law, but rather gradual ones brought about by greater participation of the new states in the creation of international law. He deemphasizes treaties and suggests greater use of "the nonconventional declarative code" in "clearly defined instances" and argues that customary rules have "no less juridical value than rules originating in conventions."

A sober view of the attitude toward international law in Latin America, where it occupies a unique position among developing countries, is taken by a North American political scientist:

> The vision of an America regulated by its own unique legal order arose with the achievement of independence. It has inspired, amused, interested and frustrated countless writers and statesmen ever since. Rudimentary bits and pieces of such a legal order soon began to develop as the states in this hemisphere set out to formalize various aspects of their mutual relations. By the middle of the present century a substantial but uncoordinated and confusing pattern had emerged.
>
> In 1948, the American states met at Bogota to consolidate, formalize and improve many of the institutions which had developed in this rather haphazard manner . . .
>
> A decade later one could only say that those currents [of development of law] were rough, muddy and of uncertain direction . . .[25]

[23] Jorge Castañeda, "The Underdeveloped Nations and the Development of International Law," *International Organization*, XV (Winter 1961), p. 40.

[24] *Ibid.*, p. 43.

[25] C. Neale Ronning, *Law and Politics in Inter-American Diplomacy* (New York: John Wiley and Sons, 1963), p. 1.

He goes on to mention many violations of traditional principles in recent years by the United States and Latin American states, but points out that this is not really a new phenomenon, that there is always a conflict in international relations between the desire for order and predictability and the desire for freedom of action.

> In contemporary inter-American affairs there can be no escaping the fact that emphasis is now on freedom of action. It is true, of course, that much sentimental nonsense has been written about the extent to which inter-American relations have been governed by legal norms, in contrast to the evils of power and politics in other parts of the world. Yet, when all this has been relegated to its proper place, the fact remains that many of the important aspects of the relations among American states have for the most part conformed to commonly accepted rules . . . [26]

These expressions of devotion to international law in texts, writings of publicists and United Nations conferences and Assembly sessions are most heartening, but one can only wonder how typical they are of the feelings in the communities the writers and speakers represent. The Carnegie Endowment for International Peace undertook a survey to determine the extent and quality of the teaching of international law in the developing countries. Here is an excerpt from a report by one of the survey members:

> With few exceptions, international studies in general and international law in particular, have, at best, a very low priority as an academic discipline in most African, Asian and Western Hemisphere countries visited. It is definitely not a subject of major interest or concern – again with notable exceptions – to the legal profession or to the governments. In most of the countries visited, the teaching of international law is superficial, of mediocre quality and of narrow scope, seldom expanding beyond the traditional topics; opportunities for advanced study and research are rare and often totally absent. This conclusion does not imply criticism, for the low priority and mild interest accorded to international law in many countries have a rational explanation. [27]

Part of the explanation, of course, lies in just these attitudes of suspicion toward principles and rules developed without their participation or consent; part is cultural; and part is practical: how will the study of international law aid one in earning a living or developing the country? Nevertheless, the Carnegie team found ample evidence of a recognition of the deficiency and of efforts to correct it.

[26] *Ibid.*, p. 2.

[27] Francis Deak, "Observations on International Law in Underdeveloped Areas," *Proceedings of the American Society of International Law*, LVI (1962), p. 56.

Finally, another overall view of the attitudes of developing states toward international law was presented early in 1963, well into this period of active participation by these states in the creation and codification of international law:

The assertion that the newly independent nations are not bound by old norms in the making of which they had no part... does not imply a wholesale rejection of the contents of traditional international law; rather it must be regarded as an expression of the resentment the newly independent nations still feel over their colonial past and as an assertion of their sovereignty and equality. It also serves as a reminder to the older states that the views of the newcomers are not to be disregarded in the formulation and further development of the law of nations . . . [28]

So far as attitudes toward specific norms of international law are concerned, all the evidence points to the conclusion that present interest, rightly or wrongly understood, rather than cultural tradition has been the immediately decisive factor. Differences in the levels of economic and political development lie behind the more extreme differences between legal institutions . . . [29]

But these differences are narrowing as the new countries become more developed (industrialized and Westernized) and the developed countries adopt more "welfare state" principles and accept greater state participation in the economy.

It would be a mistake to discount as mere verbiage the often expressed concern of the less developed nations for the strengthening and development of international law. Weak in material power, these nations must seek protection and assistance in international law and organization . . .

The less developed nations may be expected to use their influence to strengthen the trend toward law-making by multilateral treaties, particularly on subjects of special interest to them . . .

Thus, international law will continue to be "universal" in the sense that there will be a substantial number of concepts and norms understood, invoked, and followed – despite occasional violation – by all states. The scope and complexity of international law, furthermore, will continue to expand, especially in the form of treaties, in keeping with the expansion and complexity of transnational activities and interactions in a shrinking world. [29a]

These comments illustrate the general view that the developing countries, while critical of existing international law, neither ignore it nor violate it wholesale, but try to adapt it to suit their needs. [30] In a detailed

[28] Oliver J. Lissitzyn, "International Law in a Divided World," *International Conciliation*, No. 542 (March, 1963), pp. 54–55.

[29] *Ibid.*, pp. 57–58. [29a] *Ibid.*, pp. 65–67.

[30] A more recent, and excellent, discussion of this topic is by R. P. Anand, "Attitude of the Asian-African States toward Certain Problems of International Law," *The International and Comparative Law Quarterly*, XV (January, 1966). Others are cited in the Bibliography.

case study, an American political scientist, Robert Friedheim, examined this process of adaptation at work at the two United Nations Conferences on the Law of the Sea in 1958 and 1960. Only the first dealt at all with access to the sea for land-locked states, and some of his comments on this subject are included below, but his analysis is based on both conferences and illuminate many of the points made by writers cited earlier in this chapter. His whole study is intended to demonstrate the difficulty of achieving "world peace through world law." [31]

"Not only were the participants split on the question of the substantive content of the law," says Friedheim near the beginning of his article, "but they also differed on the nature of the international system, present and future, and on the proper means of negotiating law in a United Nations-sponsored conference, which is itself a special political arena with distinctive characteristics." [32]

He defines the "dissatisfied" states as being the "have nots;" that is, the developing countries, not all of which were either "new" or "revolutionary." The Latin American states, for example, could not have been considered either new or revolutionary. But, according to Friedheim, they all had this in common: "The key attitude expressed by the dissatisfied States was a strong, conscious, and often expressed belief that the conference process was a *political* process." [33] They used bloc voting and other bloc activities, often with great parliamentary skill, but their effectiveness was reduced by high absenteeism. He cites a remark of Dr. Tabibi of Afghanistan as typifying the attitude of the "dissatisfied" states:

> Besides, many of [the international instruments in question] were very old and an historic conference such as the present should replace them by others which would contribute to the development of international law, particularly since the signatories of the instruments relating to the rights of land-locked countries were mainly European countries. [34]

Friedheim says that *sovereignty* was the most meaningful "of all the juridical concepts developed in the long history of international law" and the dissatisfied states defined it very rigidly.

> Sovereignty to them was a symbol of their independence. The dissatisfied were not, however, concerned with the development of a logical theory about the symbol, but rather with the preservation of the facts for which the symbol stood... They were concerned with the preservation of their own sovereignty even at the risk of impinging upon the sovereignty of other states. [35]

[31] Robert L. Friedheim, "The 'Satisfied' and 'Dissatisfied' States Negotiate International Law: A Case Study," *World Politics*, XVIII (October, 1965).

[32] *Ibid.*, p. 20. [33] *Ibid.*, p. 21. [34] *Ibid.*, p. 27. [35] *Ibid.*, p. 29.

This happened a number of times, as when Afghanistan, Bolivia, Laos, Nepal, Paraguay and fourteen other states introduced a proposal which would give land-locked states an absolute right of transit across the territory of a coastal state, thereby infringing its sovereignty. The dissatisfied states insisted upon the political nature of many proposals they wanted codified, distrusted experts as being identified with colonial powers, and generally found it difficult to communicate with more traditionally law-minded states. But they were not solely to blame. The satisfied states did not understand that today, many legal matters actually *are* political in character and that international conferences sponsored by the United Nations to develop international law are legislative in nature. The need to obtain majorities in voting inevitably leads to politicking and compromise with abstractly ideal legal or administrative formulas. But the satisfied states wanted only to codify existing law, not to create new law. "Little wonder," says Friendheim, "that the satisfied states were unable to cope with problems of negotiating legal subjects at a conference which was, after all, a political arena!" [36] But if we are to achieve a universal rule of law, he feels, the satisfied states must recognize the international conference as a political forum.

Whether by parliamentary, strictly political or juridical means, the development of international law continues at a very rapid rate. And notwithstanding the observations of Philip Jessup and the urgings of Jorge Castañeda, most international law having to do with access to the sea and similar practical matters shall continue to be made by means of formal treaties. Chapter II chronicled the gradual development of attitudes, principles and rules regarding free transit and demonstrated that as the needs for such free transit have grown more urgent and at the same time more difficult to satisfy, nothing less than a full-dress conference of plenipotentiaries and a formal multilateral convention devoted specifically and exclusively to this question could satisfy those "dissatisfied" states which lacked coastlines. This raises the question of whether bilateral treaties between the land-locked and transit states, or multilateral conventions negotiated and signed by a substantial proportion of the world community are the best means of achieving the maximum degree of access to the sea consistent with the needs and security of the transit state.

The case for a multilateral, "self-contained international convention on the subject in place of bilateral conventions" was placed before two ECAFE conferences in 1963 and 1964 (discussed in Chapter II) and at the United Nations Conference on Trade and Development in 1964 by

[36] *Ibid.*, p. 36.

the Asian land-locked states. The first of their reasons was that the Barcelona Convention was not detailed enough to meet modern needs. The others were:

(ii) an international convention on an important subject like transit trade is desirable in order to provide for uniformity in the procedures all over the world in the interest of the smooth and unhampered flow of foreign trade.
(iii) Bilateral conventions on transit are often linked with over-all trade conventions. Thus the essential requirements of transit traffic sometimes become subservient to other considerations.
(iv) Implementation of bilateral conventions cannot be made subject to supervision or check by any independent international body. Provisions of arbitration or appeal to the Permanent International Court of Justice, even when such remedies are laid down in the convention, do not serve the same purpose as an appeal to the sponsoring body of an international convention. [37]

Another United Nations organ, the Economic Commission for Africa, argues, however, that

[t]he principles of freedom of transit, established on an international basis, do not and cannot be expected to provide all the details for day-by-day traffic. This is best achieved by bilateral agreements between interested countries, especially if such agreements take into consideration the principles established by international law. [38]

The ECA goes on to say, however, that since the newly independent African states had no representation at the conferences which produced the Barcelona and other relevant conventions or any voice in making the bilateral agreements concerning transit between the European powers ruling Africa, "most of the newly independent African countries are now reassessing such agreements with a view to ascertaining their advantages and disadvantages." [38a] An example of such a reassessment is Uganda, which

declared that it recognized itself as bound by all conventions and agreements concluded on behalf of Uganda by the United Kingdom only up to the end of 1963; after that date, the Government will decide to which of such conventions and agreements it will consider itself a party . . . [39]

[37] UNCTAD, Committee on Preparation of a Draft Convention Relating to Transit Trade of Land-locked Countries, *Transit Trade of Land-locked Countries of the ECAFE Region* (E/CONF.46/AC.2/5) (22 October 1964), pp. 11–12. This document is an updating of ECAFE/I&T/Sub.4/2 of 29 August 1956. Hubert Thierry, *op. cit.*, pp. 616–617, also makes a strong plea for a specific multilateral convention because of the inadequacy of principles of international law and of Article 3 of the Geneva Convention on the High Seas.

[38] E/CN.14/INR/44, p. 8. [38a] *Ibid.*, p. 17. [39] *Ibid.*

The views expressed in the ECAFE and ECA documents are not necessarily mutually exclusive. Both recognize the importance and the limitations of multilateral conventions. The best solution to the question of access to the sea which can be provided through international law is probably a longterm bilateral agreement detailing procedures for transit which are in conformity with the principles and rules laid down in a modern international convention which deals specifically with the question. Such a convention is the 1965 Convention on Transit Trade of Land-locked States. An examination of the Convention and some evaluations of it may help to determine its adequacy, and hence the adequacy of international law, in dealing with this important and complex question.

First, it must be borne in mind that this Convention is but the latest, and not necessarily the last, step in the long and tortuous process of eliminating, so far as is possible, the differences among states in the modern world which derive from their geographic location. Also, many parallel steps are being taken in other fields toward the same end: in communications, commodity agreements, transportation, etc. Second, no one claims that this convention satisfies everyone; it is manifestly a compromise hammered out during a series of international, regional and bilateral conferences extending over a score of years. One United Nations document prepared by the Secretariat for the 1965 Conference lists side by side and article by article, the provisions of the Draft Convention on Transit Trade proposed by Afghanistan, Laos, Nepal, Mongolia and the African land-locked states; the Draft Convention produced by the preparatory Committee of Twenty-Four for presentation to the Conference of Plenipotentiaries; and the "pending amendments," those proposed amendments to the Afro-Asian Draft upon which the Committee could not agree and submitted as presented by their sponsors to the full Conference. [40] These may be compared also with the final Convention as adopted by the Conference. Third, the eight principles included in the 1965 Convention are *verbatim* those adopted by the 1964 United Nations Conference on Trade and Development, and the Preamble to the 1965 Convention reproduces Article 3 of the 1958 Convention on the High Seas. Both of these statements of principle derive from the Barcelona Convention (even preserving some of its provisions *verbatim*) which, in turn, has its roots deep in international law and custom. Thus, despite all of the modernization and compromise which is incorporated into the new

[40] UNCTAD, United Nations Conference on Transit Trade of Land-locked Countries, *Draft Convention on Transit Trade of Land-locked Countries; Comparative Table of Provisions* (TD/TRANSIT/R.1) (4 June 1965).

Convention, there is still an evident continuity with the past. There is no reason to believe that any future revision of or substitute for the present Convention will be radically different.

The text of the Convention is reproduced in Appendix II. John Fried has analyzed it in great detail, article by article, and there is no need to do that again here. It does seem worthwhile, however, to repeat one comment he made:

> The test of a treaty are [sic] its exceptions. The proof of a treaty pudding is, when it can *not* be eaten. It is the old problem of finding a balance between demands for saving clauses, and the opposite claim that the very value of a treaty depends on its reliability. For land-locked States, conditions under which their outlet to the outside world may be curtailed can of course be crucial.
>
> The Convention declares exceptions permissible for five reasons: (1) certain well-specified reasons of public policy; (2) because of overriding international obligations; (3) emergency in the country of transit; (4) in case of war; (5) protection of its essential security interests. [41]

Fried then goes on to examine each of these exceptions in turn and concludes that there are sufficient safeguards imbedded in the Convention itself or in other provisions of international law to prohibit interference with transit traffic except under the most extraordinary circumstances.

In addition to the Convention, the 1965 Conference included in its Final Act two Resolutions which it had adopted. The first

> [e]xpresses the hope that the Inter-Governmental Maritime Consultative Organization will take appropriate measures within the scope of the abovementioned Convention [on Facilitation of International Maritime Traffic, 1965, discussed in Chapter II of this study] and its annex and resolutions four and five of the Conference on Facilitation of Maritime Travel and Transport, to facilitate the transit trade of land-locked countries. [42]

The second resolution recommends that UNCTAD itself and its organs "should give close and serious attention to the importance of the provisions of the Convention . . ." and that the Secretary-General

> through the technical co-operation organs of the United Nations and through the regional economic commissions should extend assistance in furthering transit trade to the Members of the United Nations, land-locked or transit States alike, upon their request, within the framework of established procedures of the United Nations and its agencies. [42a]

[41] Fried, *op. cit.*, p. 21.
[42] UNCTAD, TD/B/18, p. 7.
[42a] *Ibid.*, p. 8.

These resolutions constitute implicit recognition that neither the Convention alone, nor in combination with any bilateral agreements which may be adopted in accordance with its principles and rules, can resolve all of the problems of access to the sea, and that all international machinery which can be helpful should be brought to bear to help resolve them.

Some evaluations of the Convention by interested parties and outside observers may help to put it in some perspective. Dr. Abdul Hakim Tabibi, the Afghan who was perhaps the single individual most responsible for the Convention, writes,

> In the view of the land-locked countries the legal recognition of their right on a universal level represents a victory for which they had been seeking for more than four decades. The convention . . . not only created an atmosphere and [sic] close co-operation between the land-locked countries and their transit neighbours, but certainly stimulated the foreign trade of the land-locked countries, the majority of which are in Asia and Africa. [43]

His superior in the Foreign Ministry, Dr. Ravan Fahardi, is somewhat less enthusiastic about the Convention, however. He feels that it pleases the littoral states who will not reopen the issue. The land-locked states, while not so pleased with it, are not likely to reopen the issue either, and the Convention "will retain its legal importance as a legal document even if not signed" or ratified by many states. [44] Considering that Afghanistan does not intend to ratify the Convention unless Pakistan does, and then only with reservations, this is a portentious commentary on the modern development of international law.

The Economic Commission for Africa says this about it:

> The ratification of this convention and its entry into force will safeguard the rights of land-locked countries and facilitate the conclusion of bilateral agreements specifying the terms of transit for land-locked states. [45]
>
> The adoption of this Convention by the majority of states on 8 July 1965 calls for further action from African States to secure the prompt implementation of the principles expressed in the Convention. [46]

This is consistent with ECA's view, expressed above, that no matter how comprehensive, multilateral conventions must be supplemented by bilateral agreements.

The International Chamber of Commerce (ICC) was an official non-

[43] Tabibi, *op. cit.*, p. 19.
[44] Interview with Dr. Fahardi, July 5, 1967.
[45] ECA, *Transit Problems of African Land-locked States,* p. 5.
[46] *Ibid.*, p. 72.

governmental observer at the 1965 Conference along with the International Confederation of Free Trade Unions. After considering the results of the Conference, the Council of the ICC adopted this resolution:

> The Convention is considered to be a fair compromise between the views of the land-locked States and those of the transit States and provides a definite advance in the atmosphere in which detailed agreements may be negotiated in the future.
>
> The ICC therefore urges all Governments to sign the said convention and to ratify it as soon as possible.
>
> The ICC recommends transit States to grant all the necessary facilities to the transit trade of land-locked countries with a view to promoting the expansion of world trade and the economic development of all countries. [47]

Harm de Blij takes a less sanguine view of the Convention:

> In many ways the most recent Convention, signed in mid-1965, resembles that of Barcelona. The inescapable fact is that even the present Convention still does not guarantee the land-locked state the freedom of access it desires. We have seen how difficult it is for any state to give up any degree of sovereignty, however small. Real freedom of transit, obviously, demands this. As soon as the coastal state can decide that the goods purchased by, and in transit to, a land-locked neighbor are injurious to its "security," the principle of free transit comes to depend upon the good relations between the two states. When relations deteriorate, the question is likely to become one of power. And here, the coastal state has a great initial advantage. [48]

Claude Palazzoli, legal scholar of Grenoble, France, after a thorough study of the development of international law with respect to land-locked states, concludes wistfully,

> . . . new and bold on many points, the [1965] Convention of New York disappoints on the other hand on some other points, by its gaps, by its timidity; so that one can speak relative to it at the same time of progress and stagnation, and see [actual] regression. [49]

John Fried, while still optimistic, in another article places the new Convention in the context of the United Nations contributions to the development of international law and details some problems which it left unresolved:

[47] UNCTAD, Trade and Development Board, *Text of Resolution Adopted by the Council of the International Chamber of Commerce* (TD/B/NGO/1) (18 January 1966), p. 2.

[48] Harm de Blij, *Systematic Political Geography* (New York: John Wiley and Sons, Inc., 1967), pp. 366–67.

[49] Claude Palazzoli, "De quelques Développements Récents du Droit des Gens en Matière d'Accès a la Mer des Pays Dépourvus de Littoral," *Revue Générale de Droit International Public*, XXXVII (July–September, 1966), p. 734.

We said that the creation of the new Convention was greatly facilitated by, if not altogether due to, the existence of the present world order, which centers around the United Nations and its Charter . . .

[B]ut the U. N. System is not satisfied with having a new Convention signed and registered. It is, as it were, natural for the U. N. now to help to make the Convention a reality . . .

In spite of the best-worded treaty, for example, delays in transit traffic will occur if roads are bad, or means of transport lacking, or procedures of customs administration inadequate. National and international endeavours are required to improve the actual conditions, so that the law can be more fully applied and that, gradually, even better, more ambitious law can be made . . . [50]

This somewhat guarded and hard-headed opinion is echoed in much stronger terms by Etzel Pearcy, like Harm de Blij a political geographer, and one long experienced in the realities of international relations as The Geographer of the Department of State. "In reviewing the various agreements permitting land-locked states to have access to the sea," he said in 1959,

it becomes apparent that the geography of the area concerned stands high as a governing factor. No legal document of consequence may be drawn up which does not lend itself to existing or potential routes. It is indeed unfortunate when legal barriers are so established that natural avenues of communication cannot be used. [51]

While recognizing that international law is vital for the establishment of an atmosphere within which free access to the sea for developing land-locked states is encouraged and for the provision of guidelines for working out the details of such access, one cannot help but feel that it is not adequate, not even the 1965 Convention. One must agree with Pearcy that "no international agreement is capable of permitting an interior state to enjoy the freedom of the seas to the extent it would like" [52] and turn to other possible means of reaching this goal.

Political or Economic Integration

Without any doubt, the only ideal and permanent solution to the problem of access to the sea is for land-locked states to merge politically with their seaboard neighbors, thereby eliminating the boundaries between them. This political integration would (or should) eliminate all political

[50] John H. E. Fried, "The New Convention on Transit Trade of Land-locked States and the Development of Law Under United Nations Auspices," *Journal of the Tribhuban University* (Kathmandu), (1966), pp. 25–26.

[51] Pearcy, *op. cit.*, p. 22.

[52] *Ibid.*, p. 20.

impediments to movement between the coast and the interior and problems of transit would be reduced to problems of transportation. The remaining problems may still be formidable, especially in developing countries, but if the residents of the interior and the littoral have a common interest in resolving them and both share in the political and administrative structures of the country, the problems should be easier to solve. Certainly Bavaria, Szechwan, Mato Grosso and Kansas face no *political* hurdles enroute to or from the distant sea, and we may yearn for the day when *all* land-locked territories will be so fortunate.

Cold reality, however, soon dispels any such dreams, for mergers of sovereign states are rare today and those involving land-locked states are rarer still. The only example of political integration involving a land-locked state since World War II, in fact, was Ethiopia's acquisition of Eritrea, giving her a seacoast for the first time in her history. But Eritrea was not a sovereign state and in truth had little to say about her destiny. The former Italian territory was federated with Ethiopia in 1952 under United Nations supervision and later simply absorbed into Ethiopia as part of a unitary state. But despite the acquisition of a seacoast with the ports of Massawa and Assab, Ethiopia still relies for her foreign trade primarily on the port of Djibouti in French Territory of Afars and Issas (formerly French Somaliland), a territory over which she has no political control. Still, political integration offers hope for reducing the number of land-locked states in the world and bears investigation.

We may assume with some confidence that most if not all of the world's mediterranean countries differ enough from their coastal neighbors in most important respects to rule out any peaceful merger into a unitary state – barring some extraordinary circumstance. What remains then is some form of federation. This seems reasonable enough, even logical, and indeed it has been suggested and even attempted in most parts of the world. The failures outnumber the successes. Central America, Gran Colombia, Peru-Bolivia, The West Indies, Central Africa, Mali, the United Arab Republic, Indo-China, South Arabia, all were unhappy and short-lived arrangements. Other federations have endured only by becoming, in fact if not in name, unitary states, and generally some degree of coercion was involved. Examples are the Soviet Union, Argentina and Indonesia. Mexico, Brazil, Nigeria and Uganda remain federations only by virtue of the most generous interpretation of the term. Finally, there is reason to doubt that the federation of Malaysia will endure any longer than similar jerry-built structures in the past. Federalism, it would seem, is a frail flower that flourishes only in the most ideal conditions. Do these conditions exist in South America, South Asia or East Africa; can federation be a way out – to the sea – for Bolivia, Afghanistan or Uganda?

All things considered, the only reasonable federations which might involve Bolivia would be (a) a revival of the Viceroyalty of the Río de la Plata, rejoining Bolivia with Paraguay and Argentina; or (b) a revival of the Peru-Bolivia confederation. The former would seem to be growing more likely as Bolivia gradually shifts her orientation from the Pacific to the Atlantic. It would very likely, however, amount in time to little more than a "greater Argentina," something which neither Bolivia nor Paraguay would accept with equanimity. The latter possibility would make more sense. History, population distribution, transportation routes, economic and cultural ties, physiography, all would seem to argue for closer political ties between Peru and Bolivia. Candidly, though, this seems most unlikely. The 19th century Peru-Bolivia Confederation developed under the most unusual and transitory circumstances – a weak Peru and a strong Bolivia; it lasted only four years and collapsed ignominiously under the first real stress it faced. For the next century Peru made some progress while Bolivia degenerated, shrank, and nearly disintegrated. The 1952 Revolution has revived her, but the nation-building process still is incomplete. Bolivia will be neither an eager nor an attractive partner in any federation for a long time, and no one has seriously suggested such an arrangement.[53]

Pan-Islamic movements and dreams have long included Afghanistan as a member of a Muslim Commonwealth which would reach from the Atlantic to New Guinea and from Kazakhstan to Northern Nigeria and northeast Kenya. Only less ephemeral than this dream is Pan-Arabism, which in a way has competed with the Pan-Islamic ideal. More germane to our topic and somewhat more realistic is some form of unity of the Muslim world lying between the Arabs and the Malays. Turkey, because of her intensifying orientation toward Europe, is often excluded from this scheme and the core of such an Islamic community comprises Iran, Afghanistan and Pakistan. Some even include Kashmir as a fourth or fifth member, while some exclude East Pakistan because of its geographic and cultural distance from the others.

The urge for Muslim unity was especially strong in Pakistan during her first fifteen years of national existence, when she was weak and struggling.

[53] About a decade ago an American aid official remarked in an unguarded moment, only half facetiously, that the best solution for Bolivia's problems would be her partition among her neighbors. This casual remark was widely publicized; it enraged the Bolivians, delighted the Chileans and embarrassed the Americans. While there was some merit in the suggestion, it appears that Bolivia, muddling through, is here to stay, and may even be building a true nation-state.

In 1958, for example, Feroz Khan Noon, then Prime Minister, talked of a Pakistan-Iran-Afghanistan federation and it was much discussed during the next few years. The Shah of Iran raised the question again during the 1961–63 border closure. At that time Pakistan expressed interest in the idea, but Afghanistan strongly opposed it on the grounds that it would only confuse the Pushtunistan issue and compromise her traditional neutrality by aligning her with two Central Treaty Organization (CENTO) powers. Now that Pushtunistan has subsided as an issue, it would seem logical for the three countries, which have so much in common, to federate. This is still unlikely. CENTO is undoubtedly the biggest single obstacle, though Pakistan's gradual gravitation away from Western military alliances may reduce its importance somewhat. Pakistan's attempt to develop a theocracy, however, is regarded suspiciously by Iran and alienates Turkey. The Pakistani conflict with India over Kashmir and other issues puts the other countries, which want to retain good relations with India, in a difficult position. Memories of invasion and counter-invasion remain vivid. Economic and transportation links, especially between Afghanistan and Iran, are weak. Pakistan is a republic while Iran and Afghanistan are monarchies with deep roots in the past.

One suggested federation is that of Turkey, Iran and Afghanistan, the "Northern Tier." Rouhallah Ramazani has drawn up a "balance sheet" of the "prospects for fusion" of these countries in which he examines the difficulties, obstacles and possibilities in some detail. He concludes optimistically that

> [g]eographical location, historical and political experience and above all the state of the Cold War will probably continue to exert far-reaching effects on the foreign policy of the Northern Tier nations. It is likely also that . . . rapid sociopolitical changes . . . will continue to influence their foreign policy . . . They may well multiply the ties of human contact across national frontiers, encourage free movement of goods and services, construct extensive networks of roads and railways, establish common markets, and undertake many other progressive efforts toward regional cooperation and perhaps eventual political federation. [54]

Perhaps, but there is no evidence that this is actually occurring yet or is likely to very soon. The trend, in fact, seems to be toward closer relations among Turkey, Iran and Pakistan, while Afghanistan remains aloof. Withal, it appears unlikely that any federation involving Afghanistan, however logical it appears at first glance on grounds of religion and

[54] Rouhallah K. Ramazani, *The Northern Tier: Afghanistan, Iran and Turkey* (Princeton: D. Van Nostrand Co., Inc., 1966), p. 130.

contiguity, will occur in the near future. It must for the present be ruled out as a means of assuring Afghanistan a free and secure access to the sea.[55]

Of the three countries examined in the present study, in fact of all the developing land-locked states in the world, the most likely candidate for a political federation would appear to be Uganda. The roots of the present movement toward East African unity may be found in the "Closer Union Movement" of the 1920's, but its character has changed greatly since that earlier effort foundered on the shoals of racism. During the colonial period, as we have seen in Chapter V, only economic cooperation developed among the three territories of British East Africa, and that only slowly, by bits and pieces, and at times with considerable reluctance.[56] By the eve of independence, in the early 1960's, East Africa had one of the most elaborate systems of economic cooperation in the world and the movement for political federation was gaining momentum.

The modern growth of the federation idea may be considered as an outgrowth of Pan-Africanism, fostered by Kwame Nkrumah of Ghana and others, and given great impetus in East Africa by the first meeting of the Pan African Freedom Movement of East and Central Africa (PAF-MECA) in 1958. But while pan-Africanism provided the ideological underpinnings for this organization, its primary goal was independence from colonial rule and practical steps toward any kind of federation were meager. Federation remained muted until Julius Nyerere, nationalist leader of Tanganyika, thrust it into the limelight in a speech to the conference of Independent African States in Addis Ababa in 1960. By 1962 the idea had become so popular that the fourth PAFMECSA Conference, held in February that year in Addis, pledged

> to work relentlessly for a federation of Eastern Africa, i.e. Ethiopia, Somalia, Uganda, Kenya, Tanganyika and Zanzibar, to be established immediately now the colonial territories of Kenya, Uganda and Zanzibar attain their independence . . .[57]

[55] Two good analyses of this proposed federation are by Louis Dupree, "A Suggested Pakistan-Afghanistan-Iran Federation", *AUFS Report,* VII (February, 1963), and by Sisir Gupta in his *India and Regional Integration in Asia* (London: Asia Publishing House, 1964), pp. 143–148.

[56] Throughout this period the idea of federation never died and indeed, as in June 1953 in a speech by the British Secretary of State for the Colonies, cropped up publicly from time to time. Invariably, however, the idea was denounced in Uganda, and expecially in Buganda, as a device for extending Kenya white settler influence throughout East Africa.

[57] Quoted in Carl G. Rosberg, Jr. and Aaron Segal, "An East African Federation," *International Conciliation,* No. 543 (May, 1963), p. 55.

with provisions for additional members as they become independent.

The long delay in Kenya's achievement of independence, however, dissipated much of the enthusiasm for, and perhaps possibilities of, federating the three core territories of East Africa, even as the long Algerian War had dissolved the hopes and dreams of a Mahgreb federation in North Africa. The crest of enthusiasm for federation was reached in June 1963, when the leaders of Kenya, Uganda and Tanganyika pledged to federate, but Kenya did not become independent until December of that year and by then it was already too late. All of the internal strains, disparities and distractions discussed in Chapter V had simply become too great and the three territories were drifting further apart. R. S. Odingo, in his discussion of the "Geopolitics of East African Federation," says, "To the geographer the unity in diversity of the East African environment is very striking." After discussing factors of both unity and diversity, he concludes,

> Whatever fate the ideal of federation meets, the realities of East Africa are not a geographical myth and there will always be some element of cooperation between the three national independent states determined to remain independent. [58]

To this thesis of the "obvious geographical unity" of East Africa, Joseph S. Nye responds that this unity

> is obvious only on a map. The only major geographical feature that the three countries have in common is Lake Victoria . . . In their natural features there seems no reason to believe that any of three levels – the individual countries, East Africa, greater East Africa – is more a natural unit than another. The "obvious unity" of East Africa is man-made. [59]

Another observer questions whether, in fact, federation is a valid approach to the political and social modernization of Africa and strikes at the heart of the arguments for federation both within and among the territories, particularly in East Africa. He sums up his discussion in this manner:

> The real trouble in East Africa is that federalism provides a means whereby different areas can be under their own local governments. It assumes that all the people in each of these areas have the same needs and desires. It is very easy to forget that the time is long past when each part of Africa was populated by a different tribe, which dominated it . . . If tribal cultures are to be preserved, then it cannot be on a territorial basis . . .[60]

[58] Odingo, *op. cit.*, p. 24.

[59] Joseph S. Nye, Jr., *Pan-Africanism and East African Integration* (Cambridge: Harvard University Press, 1965), pp. 61–62.

[60] Philip Whitaker, *Political Theory and East African Problems* (London: Oxford

These last two comments raise two questions which have been hotly debated in East Africa and are relevant everywhere that political integration is considered. First is the question of the "level" or, more properly perhaps, the optimum geographical extent of such integration. Each of the three East African countries is having difficulty creating unity out of diversity within its own boundaries (Tanganyika least of all until 1964; now she is trying to digest Zanzibar.). Should federation wait until such unity has been accomplished and the three nation-states then be united in some way, or would federation make less critical and hence less contentious the reconciling of differences among the various ethnic, political and economic interests in each territory? There is no fully satisfactory answer, but the evidence seems to indicate that Kenyatta's resolution of the land (white settler) problem in Kenya and Obote's action in dissolving the autonomy and breaking the power of Buganda may have eased the path to federation. There is some doubt about the union of Tanganyika and Zanzibar. One professor at Makerere University College in Kampala states flatly that this was "the most decisive blow against federal hopes" because it "opened the eyes of the region as a whole to the difficulties involved in such a venture." [61] And as Nye has said elsewhere,

> One of the shocks of independence has been the lesson that tribalism is not the only threat to unity – that national unity may mean East African diversity. This became increasingly clear after the leaders failed to fulfill their stated intention of creating an East African federation by the end of 1963 and when the threats of neglecting national unity were brought home in a particularly nasty fashion by the army mutinies of January, 1964. [62]

Should the greatest effort be expended on bringing about an East African federation to which other countries may wish to adhere in the future? Or would this lessen the chances of achieving a federation of all of the states from the Sudan to the Zambezi? Or would even the latter achievement, gigantic though it be, destroy all hopes for a unity of all of black Africa and perpetuate the "balkanization" of Africa? One analyst, observing that both movements have developed collaterally, feels that this

University Press, 1964). This is a direct attack on the "federalism on a tribal basis" discussed in Chapter V and is, apparently, concurred in by Uganda's President Milton Obote.

[61] Ali A. Mazrui, "Tanzania Versus East Africa; A Case of Unwitting Federal Sabotage," *Journal of Commonwealth Political Studies*, III (November, 1965), pp. 220 and 222.

[62] J. S. Nye, "Unity and Diversity in East Africa: A Bibliographical Essay," *The South Atlantic Quarterly*, LXV (Winter 1966), p. 105. This article is a comprehensive review of the literature on federation, economic union and national unity in East Africa.

double commitment to regional and to African unity . . . was not only feasible; it was desirable. It was less that the two unities were complementary than that the issue of choice could be temporarily avoided. Such an attitude was recurrent throughout the political struggle for unity in Africa. [63]

Many pan-African leaders, however, had denounced any compromise with all-African unity, pointing to Europe and the difficulties of achieving continental unity there.

The second question is whether political federation or economic union should come first or whether economic union could not even be an adequate substitute for political federation. This dispute over the "functional approach" to federation was evident within the East African Common Services Organization. In a most detailed analysis, Proctor and Krishna point out that

EACSO was, in fact, rather widely thought of as a foundation or starting-point for a federal government; the Authority described it as "a basic framework on which the structure of closer political association could be built." . . . It was argued that federation would evolve gradually and organically as EACSO expanded. [64]

But they go on to point out that

[t]he benefits of EACSO with regard to the movement toward federation must not be exaggerated, however, nor should certain harmful effects of its operations be ignored.

The role actually played by the Organization has hardly been such as to support the claim that it constitutes a steppingstone to political unification. It has been particularly cautious when dealing with matters which might infringe on national sovereignty, and it has confined itself in practice to the routine performance of its few specified functions. There has been no real expansion in its capacity to initiate or execute policies on an East African scale. [65]

They point out also that EACSO was regarded with suspicion by the anti-federalists in East Africa, while many of the federalists feared that a stronger EACSO might become a substitute for federal government: "East Africans should concentrate on going all out for federation and not aim at or settle for half-measures," they argued. [65a] "EACSO has failed to evolve

[63] Immanuel Wallerstein, *Africa: The Politics of Unity* (New York: Random House, 1967), pp. 112–113.

[64] J. H. Proctor and K. G. V. Krishna, "The East African Common Services Organization: An Assessment," *The South Atlantic Quarterly*, LXIV (Winter 1965), p. 537.

[65] *Ibid.*, p. 538.

[65a] *Ibid.*, p. 546.

in the direction of federation," they conclude, "and may even have hindered the attainment of that goal." [65b]

In view of this apparent failure of the gradualist approach, some observers contend that federation cannot be built on a functional basis alone, and that a plunge into political federation may be necessary before even economic unity can be achieved. "All this," says Thomas Franck after reviewing the reasons for the weakening of EACSO and growing autarky in East Africa,

> only underscores that federation alone can provide East Africa with a rational political context within which united East African policies toward trade expansion, foreign policy, and economic planning can be formulated . . . [66]

Joseph Nye concludes that

> the East African experience is mainly useful as a qualification of existing generalizations. It suggests that strategies of integration based on gradualism, group theory, the predominance of economics or a welfare calculus, make little sense in these conditions [of developing countries]. Scholars studying integration in Africa must remember the primacy of politics and not be misled by assumptions natural to "developed" societies . . .
>
> Finally, the East African experience suggests that whether ideology helps or hinders integration, it must be raised from a background condition to the position of a major variable. [67]

Nevertheless, the realities of East Africa seem to have made a great impression on the leaders of the region, and they seem to have become more realistic about the prospects of achieving federation. The dream, however, is not dead.

In July 1966, in a talk before the Royal Commonwealth Society in London, Kenya's High Commissioner there said rather forcefully that Kenya still believes in East African cooperation. "We have said that our intention – and this still remains the goal of the Kenya government – is for a political federation in East Africa," he said. He went on, "Some setbacks have obviously appeared, and we have now come to the position where we must – and are determined to – preserve the common market even if we do not achieve political unification." [68]

Since disposing of Buganda in what may have been a definitive manner and consolidating himself in power, and with an economy growing still stronger, Obote of Uganda has also lost some of his fear of being a most

[65b] *Ibid.*, p. 547.

[66] Thomas M. Franck, *East African Unity Through Law* (New Haven: Yale University Press, 1964), p. 170.

[67] Nye, *Pan Africanism . . .*, p. 250.

[68] J. N. Karanja, "Kenya After Independence," *African Affairs*, LXV (October, 1966), p. 296.

junior partner in a federation, but is still willing only to intensify the "functional approach." Even President Nyerere, consistently the staunchest advocate of East African federation, even while resenting the inequitable distribution of benefits from the East African common market and pursuing autarkic policies at home, was constrained to admit in June 1967 that political union would have to be postponed while economic cooperation was being discussed. [69]

Political integration, then, while highly desirable as a means of assuring a land-locked state her access to the sea, is exceptionally difficult to achieve, even under the most favorable circumstances. But this leaves open the question whether economic integration alone, without political union, may serve the same purpose equally well. Logically it might seem so, but again this matter requires careful investigation.

The literature on economic integration is voluminous and evaluations and opinions of it numerous. No attempt will be made here to review all of it, but only to extract some material which is relevant to our central theme. In the first place, it must be recognized that no land-locked state is going to enter into a common market or free trade association or any other form of economic integration with a transit state solely in order to safeguard its access to the sea any more than it would enter into close *political* union for this reason alone. The *overall* advantages of such a move in terms of economic and social progress must outweigh the inevitable dislocations and inequalities inherent in any degree of integration. In the second place, it must be remembered that we are dealing with underdeveloped countries which, by definition, are agricultural and poor, and it is misleading to assume that what may work well in industrialized and relatively rich Western Europe will be equally successful in Africa, Asia, or Latin America – or work at all, for that matter. Sidney Dell, a British authority on the subject, says flatly, "It simply is not true that free trade and greater competition have much to contribute to the economic growth of underdeveloped countries." [70] Nonetheless, since economic integration *might* help to raise living standards, reduce tensions and increase economic interdependence among the participating states, it might be a way of reducing the land-locked state's reliance upon the goodwill and generosity of the littoral state for her access to the sea.

In a most detailed and perceptive article, Robert W. Gregg has examined the role of the United Nations regional economic commissions in Africa,

[69] *The New York Times*, June 5, 1967.

[70] Sidney Dell, *Trade Blocs and Common Markets* (New York: Alfred A. Knopf, 1963), p. 215.

Asia and Latin America in the movements toward economic integration. While the commissions are not charged specifically with encouraging integration, they have been influential in increasing awareness of possibilities of economic cooperation and aiding their members in reaching that goal. But economic policy is still made at the national level, and "cooperation, not federation, has been the high-water mark reached by the commissions, and much of the cooperation is still in a rudimentary stage." [71] He rates each of the three commissions in terms of its "integrative output," its contribution to economic integration. Not surprisingly, he rates ECLA highest, considering that environmental conditions in Latin America are more conducive to integration than those in Asia or Africa. But ECLA could have fallen into the rut of a more limited role. Instead it has had dynamic internationalist, integrative leadership and has developed several "modest but pioneering projects." He ranks ECAFE second, but says it suffers the handicaps of environmental, political and cultural problems, and "an uncritical attitude toward its own performance." It has displayed some examples of creativity and perseverance, for example the Lower Mekong Project and the Asian Highway, but in general it has "no organizational ideology or comprehensive program for regional growth and development" and its integrative output is low. ECA, the youngest of the commissions, is "even weaker than ECAFE in every respect except image." It has placed greatest stress on subregional organization and development and its integrative output is very low. While some of these evaluations may be somewhat overdrawn or obsolescent, they do in general represent the progress toward economic integration in each region and we shall examine them in the same order, focusing on our case studies.

The Central American Common Market and the Latin American Free Trade Association (LAFTA) were both organized in 1960, only partly in response to the organization of the European Economic Community and the European Free Trade Association. The former has had the higher goals and has made the more rapid progress, but has had fewer obstacles to hurdle. LAFTA has moved perhaps too cautiously and evidence of significant increases in intra-regional trade is slight. The Treaty of Montevideo which established LAFTA made special provisions for the least developed countries in the region – Paraguay, Ecuador and Bolivia. But Bolivia remained aloof, deciding not to join for the time being,

[71] Robert W. Gregg, "The UN Regional Economic Commissions and Integration in the Underdeveloped Regions," *International Organization,* XX (Spring 1966), p. 231.

despite the fact that its own representatives had helped to draft the Treaty, and that a place for Bolivia as a founding member had been kept open by the other signatories. The reason given by the Bolivian government for this decision was that most of Bolivia's exports go to countries outside Latin America and that Bolivia is able to buy better and cheaper manufactured products in North America and Western Europe than it can in Latin America. In other words, Bolivia objected to subsidizing industry in Argentina, Brazil or Mexico in the way that Uganda and Nyasaland have been subsidizing industry in Kenya and Southern Rhodesia, respectively. [72]
The Bolivian dilemma is a genuine one. On the one hand, no doubt Bolivia would like to play a part in the evolution of a prosperous Latin American economy and contribute to the success of the enterprise launched by the Treaty of Montevideo. On the other hand, Bolivia is much too poor a country to be able to sacrifice the living standards of its people to regional ideals, however lofty . . . [73]

Not only is Bolivian trade with her neighbors minimal, as pointed out in Chapter IV, but her communications with all of them but Chile are also poor, and this has contributed to her reluctance to join LAFTA.

Despite the impatience of the leaders of the Latin American republics with the slow course of the Latin American Free Trade Association, and their astute criticism of the formulas laid down in the Montevideo Treaty for the progressive lowering of the intra-zonal trade barriers, the fact remains that there are severe geographical obstacles to economic integration that must be overcome if the South American countries are to follow the path of the European Common Market. [74]

Part of the communications network essential to closer economic ties has already been provided by the identity of language and culture. But a united Latin America will not be realized without an extraordinary effort to plan, organize and finance the principal surface and air connections on which closer regional ties depend. The task is no longer one of looking at the transport needs of each country separately, but of all countries regionally . . . [75]

Despite Bolivia's participation in the Inter-American and Marginal Highway projects and her membership, along with Argentina, Brazil, Chile, Ecuador, Paraguay and Uruguay in the Latin American Association of Railroads (organized in 1964), there has still been nothing like the "extraordinary effort" needed to improve her communications with other countries.

[72] Dell, *op. cit.*, p. 268.

[73] Sidney Dell, *A Latin American Common Market?* (London: Oxford University Press, 1966), p. 115.

[74] Robert T. Brown, *Transport and the Economic Integration of South America* (Washington: The Brookings Institution, 1966), p. 212.

[75] Owen, *op. cit.*, p. 83.

The need for a complete integration of all Latin American economies has long been apparent to many people, notwithstanding the skepticism of some economists, for political and social reasons perhaps as much as for economic reasons. The impatience of the more progressive leaders in South America, notably President Eduardo Frei of Chile, led to a heads-of-state meeting in Bogotá in August 1966. The representatives of Colombia, Chile, Ecuador, Peru and Venezuela (the Andean countries with the conspicuous exception of Bolivia) produced the Declaration of Bogotá in which they declared that

> it is our conviction that these [institutional, economic and social] changes and this economic and social development can only become completely possible through the integration of Latin American nations into a great economic community. [76]

The declaration went on to detail many recommendations for bringing about this integration.

This declaration (and political considerations in the United States) led to the "summit" meeting at Punta del Este in April 1967 (which Bolivia, in a fit of pique, it may be recalled, boycotted) in which those countries represented agreed, *inter alia,* to create a Latin American common market and lay the physical foundation for economic integration through multinational projects. *The Christian Science Monitor* commented,

> The effectiveness of this arrangement depends in large measure upon the continuing spirit of cooperation and urgency which was evident here in the past week . . .
> With a tradition of only partly fulfilled plans and with the massive involvement of the United States in Vietnam and a consequent diversion of attention away from Latin America – both these conditions warn of the problems ahead. [77]

Indeed, since then there has been precious little "spirit of cooperation and urgency" manifested either in the United States or Latin America, and even less in Bolivia, which belatedly and reluctantly joined LAFTA, boycotted the Punta del Este meeting, and has refused repeated offers to reestablish diplomatic relations with Chile.

Even should all obstacles be overcome and Bolivia participate fully in a common market, it would be a very long time before her neighbors became greatly dependent upon her as a market for their goods or as a

[76] The text of this declaration may be found in *Inter-American Economic Affairs,* XX (Winter 1966), pp. 88–96.

[77] *The Christian Science Monitor,* April 19, 1967.

source of products they need, if, indeed, this would ever occur. Therefore, economic integration, whatever its other virtues, may effectively be ruled out for Bolivia as a means of assuring her access to the sea. [78]

The obstacles to development of an Asian common market or even free trade area are much more formidable even than those in Latin America. The opinion appears unanimous among economists, other scholars and political leaders that the time is not ripe for such integration, though all urge greater cooperation among the Asian countries. Besides ECAFE, many other regional and sub-regional groups are trying to promote greater intra-regional trade and cooperation. In December 1961, for example, two significant meetings were held under private auspices for this very purpose. In New Delhi 200 delegates and observers from thirty African and Asian countries attended a four-day conference to discuss the possibility of an Asian common market. It was directed by the Afro-Asian Organization for Economic Co-operation, assisted by the Federation of the Chambers of Commerce and Industry of India. In Karachi the Institute of Development Economics held a Seminar on Asian Trade attended by distinguished economists of Asia and Europe. Both groups made many suggestions – but not for regional integration.

Some idea of the problems involved may be gleaned from these few quotations:

> As contrasted to Europe and Latin America, there is little personal contact between policy makers, much less among the dominant elites, in Asia and no ideological link between Asian political groups. Distances are vast, topographic barriers great, and means of transport limited. Because the countries are poor, very few people can afford to travel across their borders; as a matter of fact, intra-Asian communication is confined to officials when they meet in conferences or to businessmen when travelling on strictly business duties. Very often, Asian conferences are attended by delegates who are strangers to each other and to the host city or even to the host country. The language barrier is so formidable that the Asians . . . must speak a European language; sometimes even that is no help. Obviously, such factors discourage organized cooperation and economic integration. [79]

The outstanding features [sic] of intra-regional trade in the ECAFE coun-

[78] Two very useful compilations of materials on economic integration in Latin America are *La Integración Económica Latinoamericana* (México: Banco Nacional de Comercio Exterior, S. A., 1963); and Miguel S. Wionczek, ed., *Latin American Economic Integration; Experiences and Prospects* (New York: Frederick A. Praeger, Publishers, 1966).

[79] Lalita Prased Singh, *The Politics of Economic Cooperation in Asia; A Study of Asian International Organization* (Columbia: University of Missouri Press, 1966), p. 229. This is an excellent detailed study, replete with statistics, maps and commentary.

tries is that it does not constitute a large part of their total trade. In fact, it has been declining over a number of years. As a percentage of their total trade, intra-regional trade came down from 42% in 1928 to 38% in 1938 and 34% in 1952. This trade which in 1953/54 amounted to 25% of exports and 24% of imports has fallen in 1961/62 to 22% and 18% respectively... Countries like Philippines, Ceylon, India, Afghanistan, Iran and Pakistan contribute only 4 to 16% exports of their total exports in intra-regional trade whereas countries like Iran, Afghanistan, China, Republic of Korea, Philippines and India import the least from countries of this region...[80]
Indeed, the non-availability of skilled and managerial manpower, technical know-how, shortage of capital resources for investment, inadequacy of infrastructure i.e. transport, communication, etc., difficulty in gaining export outlets, lack of active entrepreneurial skills are the real factors which are hampering the growth of these economies. Even if it can be established that a broader market in which economies of scale are possible is provided by an integration plan, there is no assurance that an integrated region will be in a position to exploit this possibility through enlarged investment.[81]

This is already a staggering list of problems, but it goes on and on.[82] An official Afghan view was expressed by Mohammed Sarwar Omar, Afghan representative at the 1964 UNCTAD Conference:

I would now like to say a few words about the implications of Regional Economic Groupings. My country has consistently supported plans for regional co-operation and will continue to do so as long as the nature of the co-operation takes into consideration the varying stages of development of the members of regional groupings...
I wish to voice some reservations that we have against too strong a trend toward regionalism. Does this trend mean that in place of national barriers to trade we shall have new and stronger group barriers? Furthermore, individual countries may be forced by this trend to continue restrictions on trade that could otherwise be liberalized. Should we not at this time pause and consider the desirability of substituting a greater degree of global co-operation in the search for solutions to the problems of world trade rather than relying too much on the more limited goals that may be achieved by regional co-operation?[83]

[80] C. L. Gheevala, "Prospects of Regional Co-operation in Asia," *United Asia*, XVII (May-June, 1965), p. 166.

[81] Mangat Ram, "Regional Integration in Asia," *AICC Economic Review*, XVII (December 1, 1966), p. 31.

[82] Another fine, detailed study on this subject is by R. S. Nigam of Delhi University, "Prospects of Asian Economic Cooperation," *AICC Economic Review*, XVI (October 25, 1964). He recommends, *inter alia*, "Instead of making efforts for materialising the idea of establishing an Asian Common Market, the Asian countries can work out the projects for promoting intra-regional trade and economic cooperation and strengthen their collective bargaining power vis-a-vis the 'inward linking' trade blocs like the European Common Market." p. 11.

[83] UNCTAD, Annex 2 of E/CONF.46/SR.10 (E/CONF.46/STA/42) (31 March 1964), pp. 7–8.

Mr. Omar certainly raised a point worth considering, but the fact remains that Afghanistan's isolation from many regional projects and her refusal so far to consider even a limited sub-regional common market effectively eliminate that possibility of assuring her access to the sea. Without doubt, mutual suspicion and mistrust among the Asians weigh more heavily against integration than all the economic, topographic and cultural barriers together. As Singh puts it,

> The fundamental obstacle to regional intergation in Asia, however, is political in nature. Every other obstacle will give way, given the political volition to cooperate with each other. [84]

Africa suffers rather less from the handicaps which beset Asia when economic integration is being considered, but they are still considerable.

> The colonial past has bequeathed to the continent not only linguistic, political, and cultural divisions but also institutional divisions of a far-reaching nature. It can be said with reason that the destiny of Africa is still in large measure shaped outside Africa, or inside by foreign forces . . . Intra-African trade is virtually nil; harmonization, let alone co-ordination, of external marketing policies absent. All in all Africa largely remains a dissected sphere of foreign economic and political control. [85]

Not only this, but topographic and climatic factors make communications difficult, and this problem is compounded by the fact that most railroads and good highways connect the interior with the coasts and not one country with another. Communications are similarly oriented more toward Europe than from one African country to another.

There have been many attempts at economic integration in Africa and the continent is littered with the wreckage of most of them, from the Mahgreb through former French West and Equatorial Africa and the Central African groupings of Rhodesia-Nyasaland and the Belgian territories to the Economic Community of Eastern Africa. [86] Some have never

[84] Singh, *op. cit.*, p. 232.

[85] Donald Rothchild, "The Meaning of Economic Integration in Africa," *East Africa Journal*, II (December, 1965), p. 24.

[86] The terms of association of the Economic Community of Eastern Africa were signed in Addis Ababa on May 4, 1966 by representatives of Burundi, Ethiopia, Kenya, Malawi, Mauritius, Somalia, Tanzania and Zambia, but not Uganda. The aims were "to promote co-ordinated development of the member states, especially in industry, agriculture, transport and communication, trade and payments, manpower, and natural resources. The community will also aim at progressive reduction of customs and other barriers to trade between the members, and will act together to obtain more favourable terms of trade for their products in world markets." *East Africa Journal*, III (June, 1966), p. 28. Its actual achievements have so far, apparently, been quite limited. The same may be said of the Senegal River Authority and West African Economic Community, though they may grow stronger in time.

gotten beyond the talking stage, some have died a-borning, some have withered after a few years or fragmented into smaller groupings, some survive only in a limited manner or in little more than name. [87] The only really closely integrated economic grouping in Africa is that of Kenya, Uganda and Tanzania, and even this, as we have seen, has had a difficult time hanging together.

The economic interdependence of the East African territories has been demonstrated in a detailed study of their economie geography by T. J. D. Fair. He has produced a series of maps showing clearly how a number of "islands" of what he considers to be high economic potential "stand out as widely separated but deeply driven piles upon which the economic edifice has been built." [88] Among these "islands" the most important are the Kenya Highlands and the Lake Victoria borderlands, the regions connected with the sea by the Kenya-Uganda Railway.

Uganda, to be sure, has little real concern at present about her access to the sea because of this very interdependence and economic integration. There are, however, four weaknesses in this arrangement. First is the necessity to continue the process of integration to produce not only a full common market, but a complete economic community. After several years of faltering, a giant step in this direction was taken in June 1967 when the presidents of the three countries signed the Treaty of East African Cooperation in Kampala. An official American source considers the most important points about the Treaty to be

(i) *First,* that every matter has been most carefully thought about and considered in detail bearing in mind the different national interests of the three countries. Unlike other countries which have rushed into grandiose "decisions" or announcements to form political or economic units, and then attempted to build down from the roof, the East African countries have begun, patiently and pragmatically, to build up from the foundations, and have not called the public in to admire the buildings until it is all finished.
(ii) *Second,* that there will in the future be detailed rules for the running of the Common Market (something which has rather grown up by custom) and

[87] Two good collections of papers on African economic integration are the Proceedings of the African Conference on Progress through Cooperation held at Makerere in May 1965, published as John Karefa-Smart, ed., *Africa – Progress through Cooperation* (New York: Dodd Mead and Co., 1966); and the summary of the International Seminar on Economic Co-operation in Africa held at University College, Nairobi in December 1965 which was published as R. H. Green and K. G. V. Krishna, *Economic Cooperation in Africa, Retrospect and Prospect* (Nairobi: Oxford University Press, 1967).

[88] T. J. D. Fair, "A Regional Approach to Economic Development in Kenya," *The South African Geographic Journal,* LXV (December, 1963), p. 58.

that there will be proper machinery, including the proposed Tribunal, to see that the rules are observed.

(iii) *Third,* that the existing Common Services have all been preserved by the deliberate choice of the three States.[89]

But while the Treaty provides for a transfer tax system, exceptions to the principle of free trade to provide protection for certain industries, an unequal allocation of loans from the new East African Development Bank, and continuation of the present industrial licensing system, all intended to help redistribute the gains from the arrangement more to the benefit of Uganda and Tanzania, there is still no regional economic planning, the second weakness which can be observed.[90] Even the decentralization of the headquarters of the various common services, including the choice of Arusha as the headquarters of the East African Community itself, was almost entirely political and may prove to be a handicap to efficient regional economic organization.

The third weakness in the present arrangement is that it is still rather narrowly based. Seven years ago the Economic Commission for Africa noted:

> One critical question for the future will be the extent to which the degree of economic cooperation and coordination between Kenya, Uganda and Tanganyika can be spread wider to embrace the neighboring countries. Having built up a single market which enables development to take place on a scale which would be beyond the possibilities of the territories' own resources of incomes and population, the next stage should be in the direction of broadening the East African Market on a regional basis.[91]

The new Treaty makes provisions for other states to join the Community or associate with it partially. At a meeting of ten heads of state and two foreign ministers[92] held in Kampala in December 1967, Ethiopia and Somalia officially applied to join the common market, while Burundi applied verbally to join. Zambia had already signified an interest in joining, partly to lessen her dependence upon Rhodesia and Mozambique. Perhaps this weakness is on the way to being rectified.

Finally, what may be the most serious weakness (or perhaps the greatest

[89] Report from an American official to the Department of State, 1967.

[90] See Richard Bird, "The Need for Regional Policy in a Common Market," *Scottish Journal of Political Economy,* XII (November, 1965) for a good discussion of this question.

[91] *Economic Bulletin for Africa,* January 1962, p. B-55.

[92] Represented were Uganda, Kenya, Tanzania, Congo (Kinshasa), Ethiopia, Rwanda, Burundi, Sudan, Somalia, Central African Republic, Congo (Brazzaville) and Zambia, but significantly not Malawi.

strength) of the East African Community is that it still makes no provision for a political union. It may, in fact, even come to be regarded as a substitute for federation. Some observers may be pleased with this, but others are not. The United States Department of Commerce in 1966 took account of the political factor when it warned, as it often does with developing countries,

> Of course, political stability, not only in Uganda but also in Uganda's neighboring countries, particularly Kenya which is an important trading partner and which affords Uganda access to the sea, will be an important element in attracting private investment and promoting economic development. [93]

Aaron Segal points out that most of the benefits of economic integration "are not available unless economic integration is accompanied by a substantial degree of political integration since they are the likely products of regional institutions and policies." [94] The World Bank Mission to Uganda strongly supported the common market. "But a fact of central importance in consideration of interterritorial economic relations," it said in its report, "is that Uganda will find it difficult to share equitably in the gains of economic integration without a substantial degree of political integration." [95] Finally, Nye concluded in 1963 that

> the evidence so far available from the East African experience of economic integration suggests that it is unlikely in underdeveloped areas that economic and administrative unions which stop short of political union will be stable over long periods of time. [96]

This very instability of economic unions without strong political ties has been amply demonstrated in Africa. So has the instability of political federations around the world been amply demonstrated, as was noted at the beginning of this section. But the fact remains that while Uganda is intimately tied to the economy of Kenya and to East Africa in general to a lesser degree, her access to the sea can still be curtailed or cut altogether by a political decision made in Nairobi without consultation, to say nothing

[93] United States, Bureau of International Commerce, *Basic Data on the Economy of Uganda,* (OBR 66–19) (April, 1966), p. 16.

[94] Aaron Segal, "The Integration of Developing Countries: Some Thoughts on East Africa and Central America," *Journal of Common Market Studies,* V (March, 1967), p. 259. In this excellent article, Segal evaluates ECLA much as Gregg did and compares East Africa unfavorably with Central America, where integration is proceeding more rapidly.

[95] IBRD, *The Economic Development of Uganda,* p. 95.

[96] Joseph S. Nye, Jr., "East African Economic Integration," *The Journal of Modern African Studies,* I (December, 1963), p. 502.

of agreement, with Uganda. Nevertheless, Bolivia and Afghanistan would be much more secure in their mediterranean status if they could be as closely linked with their transit states as Uganda is with hers. Since they are not and will not be for some time to come, a lesser order of regional ties might be suitable for them. [97]

Regional Cooperation and Development

In view of the manifold difficulties of organizing a common market or other type of regional economic integration among developing countries, a reasonable alternative might be a high degree of cooperation among a group of "sovereign" states, including both land-locked and transit states, for the purpose of stimulating, planning, financing and guiding the development of regional infrastructure projects for the benefit of all parties. This, of course, is being done to some extent in some parts of the world, but seldom are land-locked states involved to the degree that they should be, if they are at all. The concept of regional cooperation raises no objections so long as it remains only a concept. Even the Soviets practice some degree of cooperation in Eastern Europe and preach it for other parts of the world. Two Soviet economists, for example, strongly urge economic cooperation and regional development in Africa as a means of achieving "economic independence" from Europe. They cite several continental and regional organizations, established, incipient or proposed, but never mention the East African common market or any other examples of successful regional economic cooperation. [98]

In Latin America, ECLA, the OAS, the Inter-American Development Bank and other hemispheric bodies have long urged regional cooperation and have provided the stimulus, guidance and financing for such efforts. As mentioned above, the 1967 hemispheric "summit" conference at Punta del Este also urged multinational infrastructure projects. Besides the Marginal and Inter-American Highways, which involve actual construction, and ALAF (Latin American Railways Association), discussed in Chapter VI, other regional projects are under way or proposed. Of them, we are concerned here only with those involving Bolivia and Paraguay, the two land-locked states of Latin America.

[97] Harm de Blij, *Systematic Political Geography*, has some useful material, including maps and reprinted articles, on political and economic integration. See especially Chapter XVI, "The Federal State" and Chapter XVIII, "Supranationalism: Interstate Relationships." His bibliographies are also most useful.

[98] L. Alexandrovskaya and V. Rybakov, *Africa's Economic Problems* (Moscow: Progress Publishers, [1965]).

In its 1958 study of the Bolivian economy, ECLA strongly urged the increased use of Santos and Rosario as entrepôts for Bolivian foreign trade. Its reasons for making this recommendation at that time were largely based on the congestion in and inadequate transportation to and from the Pacific ports. This study was made, however, before the currency stabilization program, the Triangular Plan, a variety of other reforms, and the beginning of development of the Oriente. All of these improvements in Bolivia's economy together have resulted in the shift of the bulk of Bolivia's foreign trade from the United States and South America to Western Europe which we have noted previously. This shift is likely to continue as Western Europe seeks new markets for its products and as Bolivia produces, from the Oriente, more surpluses of products which are in demand in Western Europe. Atlantic ports would be an asset in handling this increased trade because ships plying between them and Western Europe would have shorter routes than if they relied on Pacific ports. They would also be able to avoid paying the tolls and higher insurance rates involved in transiting the Panama Canal. These ports would also be a form of insurance for Bolivia against the possible closure to her of one or more of the Pacific ports. East coast ports, then, would probably serve Bolivia well.

Brazil is currently encouraging colonization in and development of the region between São Paulo and Corumbá. The Tucuman and Córdoba areas of Argentina, on the main rail line between La Quiaca and Rosario, have grown greatly in economic importance in recent years and appear to be continuing this growth. Hopefully, then, Argentina and Brazil will be able, in the near future, to generate enough traffic along these rail lines to make them profitable and worth maintaining properly. Meanwhile, Bolivia, Brazil, Paraguay, Argentina and Uruguay are beginning to cooperate in the development of the Paraguay-Paraná-Plata basin.

This, as with so many other developments described in this book, is not a new idea. The Argentine dream of a "greater Argentina" approximating the old Viceroyalty of the Río de la Plata is well known but has been little more than just that – a dream. Nevertheless, in 1941 the five Plata basin states met in Montevideo and agreed on a resolution expressing their aspirations for regional development. Nothing more was done about it until after Brazil, Paraguay, Argentina and Bolivia all turned their attention to development of the region drained by the Paraguay and the Paraná Rivers in the late 1950's. Then, as described above, Bolivia began making more bilateral arrangements with Argentina and Brazil; Paraguay did the same. Uruguay has long been closely associated with Argentina and Brazil, the two states for whom she acts as a convenient buffer. Finally, in December 1966 the generals ruling Bolivia and Argentina met in Buenos Aires and agreed on a variety of bilateral cooperation projects in transportation, culture, welfare, etc. General Onganía even offered to designate either Santa Fé or Rosario as a free port for Bolivia, aid Bolivia to develop ports on the Bolivian portion of the Paraguay River and help develop a Bolivian merchant fleet for use both on the river and on the high seas. In a most expansive mood, the Argentine President referred to the Argentine coastline as "Bolivia's littoral." [99] But more importantly, at this meeting the two presidents agreed to seek the cooperation of the three neighboring riparian states in developing the basin as a whole.

At their initiative, representatives of the five states met at Buenos Aires in February 1967, shortly before the Punta del Este meeting, to plan this development cooperation. Another meeting was held there in April, after the Punta del Este meeting which Bolivia had snubbed. They "established an intergovernmental coordinating committee to prepare a target program – shipping and other transport, port and power development, flood control and industrialization." [100] Many bilateral projects in these areas have already been completed or are now under way; financing for others is now being sought. All five states stand to gain enormously in a great many ways from cooperative development, Bolivia not the least of all, for her access to the Atlantic would be not only more secure but more practical and economic than at present. But this development will not be easy.

> On the map or from the air integration seems an inviting and magnificent challenge. But down among the forests, the jungle swamps, and the winding river tributaries one begins to appreciate the immense amount of money and labor that will be necessary to clear, drain, and construct the infrastructional industry of which magazine journalists write and diplomats speak so glowingly. [101]

The same writer had begun his article of the previous December with these phrases:

> Land-locked Bolivia, long oscillating between Pacific and Atlantic, has turned definitely eastward and thrown in its lot with Argentina via the tributary outlets of the River Plate.
>
> This veering eastward has been consistently advocated for Bolivians under the presidential leadership of Air General René Barrientos Ortuño . . .
>
> A grouping of five River Plate "basin" powers has begun . . .[102]

[99] *The Christian Science Monitor,* December 30, 1966.
[100] *The Christian Science Monitor,* April 11, 1967.
[101] *Ibid.*
[102] *The Christian Science Monitor,* December 30, 1966.

In view of the sheer physical magnitude of the task involved, plus the Latin American record of unfulfilled dreams and uncompleted projects, this estimate seems premature at best. Moreover, by coincidence the leaders of all five countries happened to be generals, active or retired, when the agreements were made and planning begun. One of them, the President of Uruguay, has since died. No one may be certain how long any of the rest will remain in power or if their successors will be so anxious to cooperate. While we may applaud this regional cooperation for many reasons, a healthy skepticism seems in order. For that reason alone, and because for a long time Bolivia will continue to depend on her Pacific outlets, she must not turn her back on Chile and Peru. Bolivia might do well to consider a regional development program in cooperation with Chile and Peru.

We have already discussed what has come to be a widely accepted principle in resource development – that of planned, rational development of a river basin as a whole, rather than scattered limited-use projects on individual rivers. The same principle can be applied to an entire region in which the water resources are unevenly distributed. As barren as it is, the Altiplano-Atacama region can be made productive. More water is needed, to be sure. Power is needed, and flood control. Improved waterways could ease the strain on overburdened rail and road facilities in Bolivia. Eventually, recreation and tourism could become important economic factors, perhaps even forestry. We have archaeological and historical evidence that this land was once far more productive than it is now. It can be again. One need only look at Israel or Arizona or the Helmand Valley to see the desert bloom. CORFO has a thriving agricultural experiment station outside the city of Antofagasta raising many good crops on pure desert land.

There is water in this region, in the lakes, rivers and snowfields and under the surface of the pampa. There is no need for Lake Titicaca to remain virtually untapped, nor for the heavy rains of "Bolivian winter" to rush unchecked down the *quebradas* from the Altiplano to pour wasted into the ocean. Given a measure of goodwill and cooperation among the three states involved, a massive development scheme could be undertaken with outside aid.

The idea is not inconceivable; it has been suggested by Chile and supported by the United States. Peru is currently studying possibilities of diverting Lake Titicaca water into her own coastal desert. Even Fellman offered at one point to let Chile use water from five additional (unnamed) international rivers in the Andes in exchange for a port. Chile is apparently interested in water from the Río Caquena. The Rivers Mauri, Uchusuma and Lauca have already been tapped for successful irrigation schemes. Hydroelectric plants have been built or planned on the Mauri and the Lauca. There is no practical reason why all of these projects could not be consolidated and expanded by the inclusion of Lakes Poopó, Uyuni and Coipasa in Bolivia and Caritaya in Chile, and the Rivers Desaguadero, Sajama and Sama and perhaps others. It would cost a great deal of money, to be sure, and require many years to accomplish a project of this magnitude, but it can be done. [103]

There is one major political stumbling block, however, besides the Bolivia-Chile dispute. Bolivia and Peru share Lake Titicaca, the key to the whole scheme, under a "condominium" established by a series of treaties and agreements dating back at least to 1926. Under this arrangement, each country has absolute sovereignty over its share of the lake, but each must consult with the other about any proposed project which might change the lake level or otherwise affect the other state. In 1957 the two countries signed a treaty which would establish a "perpetual condominium" over the lake. This provision would require the express consent of the other party for the disposal in any way of any water from the lake by one party to a third party. (This could only refer to Chile.) This treaty was ratified promptly by the Peruvian Government, but it has not yet been submitted for approval to the Bolivian Congress.

There are certainly many problems – economic, technical, financial and political – involved in even beginning negotiations over such a scheme. Not the least of them is just this question of an outlet to the sea for Bolivia. Ideally, the two matters should be kept separated, for they are only indirectly related and inflamed passions over one might imperil success of the other. It does not appear, though, that Bolivia would permit them to be negotiated separately. What kind of arrangement, then, can improve Bolivia's access to the sea sufficiently to induce her to consent to a regional development scheme which would, in turn, automatically resolve the Río Lauca question?

Just as with the Río Lauca, it seems that the real answer lies, not in the development of international law on the subject, but in an immediate, broad approach, encompassing both economic and political factors. The minimum prerequisite for the beginning of negotiations in good faith on

[103] One observer has even suggested construction of a ship canal from Lake Titicaca to the Pacific with associated hydroelectric facilities. Letter to Fellman dated April 16, 1966 from Anthony Essex De Soto, author of a small monograph called "Bolivia's Right to an Access to the Sea." A project of this nature, however, is both impractical and unnecessary.

such an approach is the immediate cessation of Bolivia's propaganda campaign and the reestablishment of diplomatic relations between Bolivia and Chile.

At no time during the past sixty years has Bolivia clearly established that she needs any kind of "sovereign outlet" for economic reasons. She has never demonstrated how such an outlet would, in practice, aid the economic development of the country. For this reason, if for no other, Chile is most unlikely to grant Bolivia any major concession – a strip of coast, an enclave around a port, a corridor to the sea, or any similar transfer of territory (and people). What Chile probably could offer, in exchange for access to the waters of the Altiplano, is a sovereign Bolivian enclave *within* one or more Chilean ports or, as suggested in Chapter VI, an enclave on the coast north of Arica. (In effect this would be, as one Bolivian writer expressed it, an exchange of "salt water" for "sweet water".)

This enclave need consist of no more than a pier or piers with associated rail and dock facilities, warehouses, and offices. Such an arrangement would, of course, entail safeguards against smuggling, harboring of criminals and other offenses. Or it can be more elaborate as described in Chapter VI. If such an enclave is granted within the Province of Tarapacá, as would seem logical, it would probably be construed by Peru as a transfer of territory and thereby require her consent under the protocol to the Treaty of Santiago. Peru has already invoked this protocol, in 1951, and might do so again. Her interests must therefore be taken into consideration.

The enclave would be of little value to Bolivia unless it were accompanied by a modernization and appropriate expansion of port facilities in all of the major ports used by Bolivia in both Chile and Peru. The railroad between Puno and Guaqui should be completed quickly and perhaps the railroad between Arica and Tacna reopened. The projected road between La Paz and Ilo would benefit both Peru and Bolivia. It might result in increased use of this port, which would be of further benefit to both countries. Modernization of the Antofagasta-Bolivia Railroad and the Arica-La Paz Railroad would also be necessary, and probably the construction of the roads from Arica to La Paz and from Iquique to Oruro which Chile has already offered Bolivia. All of these improvements, financed in part by the three governments and in part from foreign sources, could make a package which, together with the enclave, would probably meet whatever need Bolivia might feel for an outlet to the sea. They would also be of great benefit to the desert areas of Peru and Chile which would need improved transportation facilities under the development scheme proposed above. Whether they would also satisfy the Bolivian people is impossible to say. Perhaps the experienced Bolivian propaganda machine could be usefully employed in this connection.

While both the Atacama-Altiplano and Plata Basin projects would be enormously expensive, they would put access to the sea where it truly belongs, as just one of many factors affecting the economic development of small, poor, weak, interior states. They would take much of the political fire out of the issue and reduce the degree of contention too often assumed by land-locked and transit states. The same principle may also be applied in Asia, where similar developments are under way.

While, as we have seen, political or economic integration may be ruled out for the immediate future, at least, as a means of linking most land-locked and transit states, regional cooperation is not quite so difficult to achieve. Asians, like Latin Americans, have long been cooperating in a number of ways. ECAFE has been the major instrument for stimulating cooperation; others have been the Colombo Plan and the new Asian Development Bank. They have cooperated in the Asian Highway and Lower Mekong projects. There are and have been several other regional and sub-regional groupings designed to foster cooperation and regional development, such as the Association of Southeast Asia and the Asia and Pacific Council. These, like their African counterparts, have generally been long on enthusiasm and propaganda and short on durability and concrete achievements. ECAFE describes this situation more diplomatically:

> In the ECAFE countries, although the advantages of regional cooperation are recognized, the progress towards establishing projects requiring multilateral action between different nations has been rather limited. In particular, projects which impinge upon the economic and financial policies of individual countries have not proved very attractive . . . [104]

One new sub-regional organization, however, appears to be more solidly based than most of the others and may offer Afghanistan a viable alternative to her present role of "splendid neutralism" if not complete isolation. This is the Regional Cooperation for Development.

Following the lead of the United Nations Conference on Trade and Development in Geneva in the spring of 1964, which stressed in its Final Act the importance of regional cooperation, the foreign ministers of Turkey, Iran and Pakistan met in Ankara in July 1964 to prepare grounds

[104] ECAFE, *Economic Survey of Asia and the Far East 1965* (Sales No. 66.II.F.1) (Bangkok: ECAFE, 1966), p. 202.

for greater cooperation among them than was possible through CENTO, designed primarily as a military alliance. Immediately following, the heads of state of the three countries met in Istanbul and established the Regional Cooperation for Development (RCD). The RCD was to promote trade among the members (still less than 2% of their total trade), improve transportation and communications among them, cooperate in a wide range of cultural activities, and undertake similar regional projects. It has a Council of Ministers, a Regional Planning Council, fourteen permanent committees, and a Secretariat (located in Tehran with a Secretary General) which produces large numbers of publications about and for RCD in five languages.

Meetings of the RCD have been held since then in Tehran, Islamabad and Ankara and there have been seminars and special meetings on various topics in Karachi, Istanbul, Tehran and elsewhere. A joint Shipping Conference and Shipping Services have already been formed. So has an RCD Chamber of Commerce and Industries. Many other regional projects are being studied or are in process of organization, including petrochemical industries, banking and insurance, tourism, public administration and family planning. Studies are also under way on the feasibility of economic integration. [105] All is not entirely well with RCD, however. Besides the expectable problems resulting from history, geography, economics and politics, RCD has two features which, though distinct, are really intertwined and directly involve Afghanistan. They are its relationship to CENTO and the provision for new members.

Louis Dupree comments that the members consistently deny "any conflict of interests between the military aspects of CENTO and the economic cooperation to be engendered by the RCD. Much of the infrastructure which will eventually contribute to the success of the RCD (if it succeeds) can be directly attributed to CENTO." [106] He goes on to remark that despite the press support for RCD in all three countries (except for East Pakistan) and the great activity of the Secretariat, "the Turks feel ill at ease in the company of 'Asians' (Even Pakistan lists Turkey under 'Europe' in its economic trade statistics!), and Iran turned cool when Pakistan enthusiastically sought to include Indonesia in a greater Asian RCD." [107] Pakistan has also been trying since 1964 to induce Afghanistan

[105] For a detailed but uncritical survey of RCD, see Nurul Islam, "Regional Cooperation for Development: Pakistan, Iran and Turkey," *Journal of Common Market Studies,* V (March, 1967).

[106] Louis Dupree, "Pakistan: 1964–1966 Part IV: The Regional Cooperation for Development," *AUFS Report,* X (November, 1966), p. 4.

[107] *Ibid.,* p. 9.

to join RCD. In that year President Ayub Khan went to Kabul for that purpose. There are many strategic and economic considerations involved, of course, but basically the Pakistanis like the Afghans and feel benevolent toward them when they are not actually disputing Pushtunistan or some other issue.

Afghanistan has no objection to regional cooperation in principle. In February 1966, for example, she proposed a Regional Transport Conference which would include Turkey, Iran, India, Pakistan and the USSR, as well as herself. The first three approved the idea, but Pakistan refused to sit at the same table with India and the project was dropped, at least temporarily. But RCD is another matter. According to Dr. Fahardi, Afghanistan is *not* against RCD and wishes it all success, but will not join. She considers it "another page of the same book" as the proposed Iran-Pakistan-Afghanistan federation discussed earlier in this chapter. Even worse, the similarity in membership and even activities between RCD and CENTO is too obvious to ignore. Afghanistan feels she would compromise her neutrality if she were to join since, as Dr. Fahardi put it, "We do not know where CENTO ends and RCD begins."

Afghanistan would undoubtedly profit from membership in a regional development group. Her extensive high-grade iron ore deposits in the Haji Gak area, for example, could feed a steel mill in Pakistan which could supply all the iron and steel needs of the RCD region. The transportation and communications possibilities need no further elaboration. Any Afghan association with these countries would, of course, have to be satisfactory to the Soviet Union. It probably would be if and when, as seems likely now, Turkey turns definitely toward Europe and Pakistan withdraws from CENTO, possibly to be followed by Iran. This would leave Iran and Pakistan in RCD without the complicating factor of Turkey and without the albatross of CENTO around its neck. Afghanistan should then feel able to join, thus creating a truly meaningful regional grouping which could maintain links with Europe (through Turkey) and eastern and southeastern Asia (through East Pakistan). It would certainly facilitate regional cooperation for development and make more secure Afghanistan's access to the sea through Pakistan. It might also open new access routes for her through Iran, and, conceivably, lead to political cooperation as well, even if not quite the type of federation advocated by Iran.

In summary, it may be said that while international law must provide the atmosphere, establish the framework, and set the minimum requirements for the provision of access to the sea for developing land-locked states, it cannot alone assure such access. Political integration of interior and littoral states can do this best, but since this is so difficult to achieve and rather unlikely until nationalism declines as a motive force in the world, economic integration is more feasible and perhaps just as efficacious. It has worked well in the case of Uganda and has possibilities elsewhere, particularly in West Africa. Where neither economic nor political integration is practicable, a solution to the question of access to the sea for the land-locked states of Africa, Asia and South America must be sought in regional economic cooperation and regional development programs.

This is very much in keeping with the spirit of our times, for now it is economic development that is being stressed in international councils and no longer "natural rights" or "obligations." The new emphasis has been evident since the 1958 Conference on the Law of the Sea and even more so since the 1964 United Nations Conference on Trade and Development. Still a long way from achievement, but still necessary to work toward, is the goal expressed in Principle IV adopted by UNCTAD and incorporated into the Preamble of the 1965 Convention on Transit Trade of Land-locked States:

> In order to promote fully the economic development of land-locked countries, the said countries should be afforded by all States, on the basis of reciprocity, free and unrestricted transit, in such a manner that they have free access to regional and international trade in all circumstances and for every type of goods.

APPENDIX I

CONVENTION AND STATUTE ON FREEDOM OF TRANSIT, BARCELONA, 20 APRIL 1921

A. CONVENTION

Article 1

The High Contracting Parties declare that they accept the Statute on Freedom of Transit annexed hereto, adopted by the Barcelona Conference on 14 April 1921.

This Statute will be deemed to constitute an integral part of the present Convention. Consequently, they hereby declare that they accept the obligations and undertakings of the said Statute in conformity with the terms and in accordance with the conditions set out therein.

Article 2

The present Convention does not in any way affect the rights and obligations arising out of the provisions of the Treaty of Peace signed at Versailles on 28 June 1919, or out of the provisions of the other corresponding Treaties, in so far as they concern the Powers which have signed, or which benefit by, such Treaties.

Article 3

The present Convention, of which the French and English texts are both authentic, shall bear this day's date and shall be open for signature until 1 December 1921.

Article 4

The present Convention is subject to ratification. The instruments of ratification shall be transmitted to the Secretary-General of the League of Nations, who will notify the receipt of them to the other Members of the League and to States admitted to sign the Convention. The instruments of ratification shall be deposited in the archives of the Secretariat.

In order to comply with the provisions of Article 18 of the Covenant of the League of Nations, the Secretary-General will register the present Convention upon the deposit of the first ratification.

Article 5

Members of the League of Nations which have not signed the present Convention before 1 December 1921 may accede to it.

The same applies to States not members of the League to which the Council of the League may decide officially to communicate the present Convention.

Accession will be notified to the Secretary-General of the League, who will inform all Powers concerned of the accession and of the date on which it was notified.

Article 6

The present Convention will not come into force until it has been ratified by five Powers. The date of its coming into force shall be the ninetieth day after the receipt by the Secretary-General of the League of Nations of the fifth ratification. Thereafter the present Convention will take effect in the case of each Party ninety days after the receipt of its ratification or of the notification of its accession.

Upon the coming into force of the present Convention, the Secretary-General will address a certified copy of it to the Powers not Members of the League which are bound under the Treaties of Peace to accede to it.

Article 7

A special record shall be kept by the Secretary-General of the League of Nations, showing which of the Parties have signed, ratified, acceded to or denounced the present Convention. This record shall be open to the Members of the League at all times; it shall be published as often as possible in accordance with the directions of the Council.

Article 8

Subject to the provisions of Article 2 of the present Convention, the latter may be denounced by any Party thereto after the expiration of five years from the date when it came into force in respect of that Party. Denunciation shall be effected by notification in writing addressed to the Secretary-General of the League of Nations. Copies of such notification shall be transmitted forthwith by him to all the other Parties, informing them of the date on which it was received.

The denunciation shall take effect one year after the date on which it was notified to the Secretary-General, and shall operate only in respect of the notifying Power.

Article 9

A request for the revision of the present Convention may be made at any time by one-third of the High Contracting Parties.

B. STATUTE ON FREEDOM OF TRANSIT

Article 1

Persons, baggage and goods, and also vessels, coaching and goods stock, and other means of transport, shall be deemed to be in transit across territory under the sovereignty or authority of one of the Contracting States, when the passage across such territory, with or without trans-shipment, warehousing, breaking bulk, or change in the mode of transport, is only a portion of a complete journey, beginning and terminating beyond the frontier of the State across whose territory the transit takes place.

Traffic of this nature is termed in this Statute 'traffic in transit".

Article 2

Subject to the other provisions of this Statute, the measures taken by Contracting States for regulating and forwarding traffic across territory under their sovereignty or authority shall facilitate free transit by rail or waterway on routes in use convenient for international transit. No distinction shall be made which is based on the nationality of persons, the flag of vessels, the place of origin, departure, entry, exit or destination, or on any circumstances relating to the ownership of goods or of vessels, coaching or goods stock or other means of transport.

In order to ensure the application of the provisions of this Article, Contracting States will allow transit in accordance with the customary conditions and reserves across their territorial waters.

Article 3

Traffic in transit shall not be subject to any special dues in respect of transit (including entry and exit). Nevertheless, on such traffic in transit there may be levied dues intended solely to defray expenses of supervision and administration entailed by such transit. The rate of any such dues must correspond as nearly as possible with the expenses which they are intended to cover, and the dues must be imposed under the conditions of equality laid down in the preceding article, except that on certain routes such dues may be reduced or even abolished on account of differences in the cost of supervision.

Article 4

The Contracting States undertake to apply to traffic in transit on routes operated or administered by the State or under concession, whatever may be the place of departure or destination of the traffic, tariffs which, having regard to the conditions of the traffic and to considerations of commercial competition between routes, are reasonable as regards both their rates and the method of their application. These tariffs shall be so fixed as to facilitate international traffic as much as possible. No charges, facilities or restrictions shall depend, directly or indirectly, on the nationality or ownership of the vessel or other means of transport on which any part of the complete journey has been or is to be accomplished.

Article 5

No Contracting State shall be bound by this Statute to afford transit for passengers whose admission into its territories is forbidden, or for goods of a kind of which the importation is prohibited, either on grounds of public health or security, or as a precaution against diseases of animals or plants.

Each Contracting State shall be entitled to take reasonable precautions to ensure that persons, baggage and goods, particularly goods which are the subject of a monopoly, and also vessels, coaching and goods stock and other means of transport, are really in transit, as well as to ensure that passengers in transit are in a position to complete their journey, and to prevent the safety of the routes and means of communication being endangered.

Nothing in this Statute shall affect the measures which one of the Contracting States may feel called upon to take in pursuance of general international Conventions to which it is a party, or which may be concluded hereafter, particularly Conventions concluded under the auspices of the League of Nations, relating to the transit, export or import of particular kinds of articles, such as opium or other dangerous drugs, arms or the produce of fisheries, or in pursuance of general Conventions intended to prevent any infringement of industrial, literary or artistic property, or relating to false marks, false indications of origin, or other methods of unfair competition.

Any haulage service established as a monopoly on waterways used for transit must be so organized as not to hinder the transit of vessels.

Article 6

This Statute does not of itself impose on any of the Contracting States a fresh obligation to grant freedom of transit to the nationals and their baggage, or to the flag of a non-Contracting State, nor to the goods, nor to coaching and goods stock or other means of transport coming or entering from, or leaving by, or destined for a non-Contracting State, except when a valid reason is shown for such transit by one of the other Contracting States concerned. It is understood that for the purposes of this Article, goods in transit under the flag of a Contracting State shall, if no trans-shipment takes place, benefit by the advantages granted to that flag.

Article 7

The measures of a general or particular character which a Contracting State is obliged to take in case of an emergency affecting the safety of the State or the vital interests of the country may in exceptional cases, and for as short a period as possible, involve a deviation from the provisions of the above Articles; it being understood that the principle of freedom of transit must be observed to the utmost possible extent.

Article 8

This Statute does not prescribe the rights and duties of belligerents and neutrals in time of war. The Statute shall, however, continue in force in time of war so far as such rights and duties permit.

Article 9

This Statute does not impose upon a Contracting State any obligations conflicting with its rights and duties as a Member of the League of Nations.

Article 10

The coming into force of this Statute will not abrogate treaties, conventions and agreements on questions of transit concluded by Contracting States before 1 May 1921.

In consideration of such agreements being kept in force, Contracting States undertake, either on the termination of the agreement or when circumstances permit, to introduce into agreements so kept in force which contravene the provisions of this Statute the modifications required to being them into harmony with such provisions, so far as the geographical, economic or technical circumstances of the countries or areas concerned allow.

Contracting States also undertake not to conclude in future treaties, conventions or agreements which are inconsistent with the provisions of this Statute, except when geographical, economic or technical considerations justify exceptional deviations therefrom.

Furthermore, Contracting States may, in matters of transit, enter into regional understandings consistent with the principles of this Statute.

Article 11

This Statute does not entail in any way the withdrawal of facilities which are greater than those provided for in the Statute and have been granted, under conditions consistent with its principles, to traffic in transit across territory under the sovereignty or authority of a Contracting State. The Statute also entails no prohibitions of such grant of greater facilities in the future.

Article 12

In conformity with Article 23 (e) of the Covenant of the League of Nations, any Contracting State which can establish a good case against the application of any provision of this Statute in some or all of its territory, on the ground of the grave economic situation arising out of the acts of devastation perpetrated on its soil during the war 1914–1918, shall be deemed to be relieved temporarily of the obligations arising from the application of such provision, it being understood that the principle of freedom of transit must be observed to the utmost possible extent.

Article 13

Any dispute which may arise as to the interpretation or application of this Statute which is not settled directly between the parties themselves shall be brought before the Permanent Court of International Justice, unless, under a special agreement or a general arbitration provision, steps are taken for the settlement of the dispute by arbitration or some other means.

Proceedings are opened in the manner laid down in Article 40 of the Statute of the Permanent Court of International Justice.

In order to settle such disputes, however, in a friendly way as far as possible, the Contracting States undertake, before resorting to any judicial proceedings and without prejudice to the powers and right of action of the Council and of the Assembly, to submit such disputes for an opinion to any body established by the League of Nations, as the advisory and technical organization of the Members of the League in matters of communications and transit. In urgent cases, a preliminary opinion may recommend temporary measures intended, in particular, to restore the facilities for freedom of transit which existed before the act or occurrence which gave rise to the dispute.

Article 14

In view of the fact that within or immediately adjacent to the territory of some of the Contracting States there are areas or enclaves, small in extent and population in comparison with such territories, and that these areas or enclaves form detached portions or settlements of other parent States, and that it is impracticable for reasons of an administrative order to apply to them the provisions of this Statute, it is agreed that these provisions shall not apply to them.

The same stipulation applies where a colony or dependency has a very long frontier in comparison with its surface and where in consequence it is practically impossible to afford the necessary Customs and police supervision.

The States concerned, however, will apply in the cases referred to above a regime which will respect the principles of the present Statute and facilitate transit and communications as far as practicable.

Article 15

It is understood that this Statute must not be interpreted as regulating in any way rights and obligations *inter se* of territories forming part or placed under the protection of the same sovereign State, whether or not these territories are individually Members of the League of Nations.

APPENDIX II

CONVENTION ON TRANSIT TRADE OF LAND-LOCKED STATES

(Adopted by the United Nations Conference on Transit Trade of Land-locked Countries at its 35th plenary meeting)

PREAMBLE

The States Parties to the present Convention,

Recalling that Article 55 of its Charter requires the United Nations to promote conditions of economic progress and solutions of international economic problems,

Noting General Assembly resolution 1028 (XI) on the land-locked countries and the expansion of international trade which, "recognizing the need of land-locked countries for adequate transit facilities in promoting international trade", invited "the Governments of Member States to give full recognition to the needs of land-locked Member States in the matter of transit trade and, therefore, to accord them adequate facilities in terms of international law and practice in this regard, bearing in mind the future requirements resulting from the economic development of the land-locked countries",

Recalling article 2 of the Convention on the High Seas which states that the high seas being open to all nations, no State may validly purport to subject any part of them to its sovereignty and article 3 of the said Convention which states:

1. In order to enjoy the freedom of the seas on equal terms with coastal States, States having no sea-coast should have free access to the sea. To this end States situated between the sea and a State having no sea-coast shall by common agreement with the latter and in conformity with existing international conventions accord:

(a) To the State having no sea-coast, on a basis of reciprocity, free transit through their territory; and

(b) To ships flying the flag of that State treatment equal to that accorded to their own ships, or to the ships of any other States, as regards access to seaports and the use of such ports.

2. States situated between the sea and a State having no sea-coast shall settle, by mutual agreement with the latter, and taking into account the rights of the coastal State or State of transit and the special conditions of the State having no sea-coast, all matters relating to freedom of transit and equal treatment in ports, in case such States are not already parties to existing international conventions.

Reaffirming the following Principles adopted by the United Nations Conference on Trade and Development with the understanding that these Principles are interrelated and each principle should be construed in the context of the other Principles:

Principle I

The recognition of the right of each land-locked State of free access to the sea is an essential principle for the expansion of international trade and economic development.

Principle II

In territorial and on internal waters, vessels flying the flag of land-locked countries should have identical rights, and enjoy treatment identical to that enjoyed by vessels flying the flag of coastal States other than the territorial State.

Principle III

In order to enjoy the freedom of the seas on equal terms with coastal States, States having no sea-coast should have free access to the sea. To this end States situated between the sea and a State having no sea-coast shall, by common agreement with the latter, and in conformity with existing international conventions, accord to ships flying the flag of that State treatment equal to that accorded to their own ships or to the ships of any other State as regards access to seaports and the use of such ports.

Principle IV

In order to promote fully the economic development of the land-locked countries, the said countries should be afforded by all States, on the basis of reciprocity, free and unrestricted transit, in such a manner that they have free access to regional and international trade in all circumstances and for every type of goods.

Goods in transit should not be subject to any customs duty.

Means of transport in transit should not be subject to special taxes or charges higher than those levied for the use of means of transport of the transit country.

Principle V

The State of transit, while maintaining full sovereignty over its territory, shall have the right to take all indispensable measures to ensure that the exercise of the right of free and unrestricted transit shall in no way infringe its legitimate interests of any kind.

Principle VI

In order to accelerate the evolution of a universal approach to the solution of the special and particular problems of trade and development of land-locked countries in the different geographical areas, the conclusion of regional and other international agreements in this regard should be encouraged by all States.

Principle VII

The facilities and special rights accorded to land-locked countries in view of their special geographical position are excluded from the operation of the most-favoured-nation clause.

Principle VIII

The principles which govern the right of free access to the sea of the land-locked State shall in no way abrogate existing agreements between two or more contracting parties concerning the problems, nor shall they raise an obstacle as regards the conclusions of such agreements in the future, provided that the latter do not establish a regime which is less favourable than or opposed to the above-mentioned provisions.

Have agreed as follows:

Article 1 Definitions

For the purpose of this Convention,

(a) the term "land-locked State" means any Contracting State which has no sea-coast;

(b) the term "traffic in transit" means the passage of goods including unaccompanied baggage across the territory of a Contracting State between a land-locked State and the sea when the passage is a portion of a complete journey which begins or terminates within the territory of that land-locked State and which includes sea transport directly preceding or following such passage. The trans-shipment, warehousing, breaking bulk, and change in the mode of transport of such goods as well as the assembly, disassembly or reassembly of machinery and bulky goods shall not render the passage of goods outside the definition of "traffic in transit" provided that any such operation is undertaken solely for the convenience of transportation. Nothing in this paragraph shall be construed as imposing an obligation on any Contracting State to establish or permit the establishment of permanent facilities on its territory for such assembly, disassembly or reassembly;

(c) the term "transit State" means any Contracting State with or without a sea-coast, situated between a land-locked State and the sea, through whose territory "traffic in transit" passes;

(d) the term "means of transport" includes:

(i) any railway stock, seagoing and river vessels and road vehicles;

(ii) where the local situation so requires porters and pack animals;

(iii) if agreed upon by the Contracting States concerned, other means of transport and pipelines and gas lines

when they are used for traffic in transit within the meaning of this article.

Article 2. Freedom of transit

1. Freedom of transit shall be granted under the terms of this Convention for traffic in transit and means of transport. Subject to the other provisions of this Convention, the measures taken by Contracting States for regulating and forwarding traffic across their territory shall facilitate traffic in transit on routes in use mutually acceptable for transit to the Contracting States concerned. Consistent with the terms of this Convention, no discrimination shall be exercised which is based on the place of origin, departure, entry, exit or destination, or on any circumstances relating to the ownership of the goods or the ownership, place of registration or flag of vessels, land vehicles or other means of transport used.

2. The rules governing the use of means of transport, when they pass across part or the whole of the territory of another Contracting State, shall be established by common agreement among the Contracting States concerned, with due regard to the multilateral international conventions to which these States are parties.

3. Each Contracting State shall authorize, in accordance with its laws,

rules and regulations, the passage across or access to its territory of persons whose movement is necessary for traffic in transit.

4. The Contracting States shall permit the passage of traffic in transit across their territorial waters in accordance with the principles of customary international law or applicable international conventions and with their internal regulations.

Article 3. Customs duties and special transit dues

Traffic in transit shall not be subjected by any authority within the transit State to customs duties or taxes chargeable by reason of importation or exportation nor to any special dues in respect of transit. Nevertheless on such traffic in transit there may be levied charges intended solely to defray expenses of supervision and administration entailed by such transit. The rate of any such charges must correspond as nearly as possible with the expenses they are intended to cover and, subject to that condition, the charges must be imposed in conformity with the requirement of non-discrimination laid down in article 2, paragraph 1.

Article 4. Means of transport and tariffs

1. The Contracting States undertake to provide, subject to availability, at the points of entry and exit, and as required at points of trans-shipment adequate means of transport and handling equipment for the movement of traffic in transit without unnecessary delay.

2. The Contracting States undertake to apply to traffic in transit, using facilities operated or administered by the State, tariffs or charges which, having regard to the conditions of the traffic and to considerations of commercial competition, are reasonable as regards both their rates and the method of their application. These tariffs or charges shall be so fixed as to facilitate traffic in transit as much as possible, and shall not be higher than the tariffs or charges applied by Contracting States for the transport through their territory of goods of countries with access to the sea. The provisions of this paragraph shall also extend to the tariffs and charges applicable to traffic in transit using facilities operated or administered by firms or individuals, in cases in which the tariffs or charges are fixed or subject to control by the Contracting State. The term "facilities" used in this paragraph shall comprise means of transport, port installations and routes for the use of which tariffs or charges are levied.

3. Any haulage service established as a monopoly on waterways used for transit must be so organized as not to hinder the transit of vessels.

4. The provisions of this article must be applied under the conditions of non-discrimination laid down in article 2, paragraph 1.

Article 5. Methods and documentation in regard to customs, transport, etc.

1. The Contracting States shall apply administrative and customs measures permitting the carrying out of free, uninterrupted and continuous traffic in transit. When necessary, they should undertake negotiations to agree on measures that ensure and facilitate the said transit.

2. The Contracting States undertake to use simplified documentation and expeditious methods in regard to customs, transport and other administrative procedures relating to traffic in transit for the whole transit journey on their territory, including any transhipment, warehousing, breaking bulk, and changes in the mode of transport as may take place in the course of such journey.

Article 6. Storage of goods in transit

1. The conditions of storage of goods in transit at the points of entry and exit, and at intermediate stages in the transit State may be established by agreement between the States concerned. The transit States shall grant conditions of storage at least as favourable as those granted to goods coming from or going to their own countries.

2. The tariffs and charges shall be established in accordance with article 4.

Article 7. Delays or difficulties in traffic in transit

1. Except in cases of *force majeure* all measures shall be taken by Contracting States to avoid delays in, or restrictions on, traffic in transit.

2. Should delays or other difficulties occur in traffic in transit, the competent authorities of the transit State or States and of the land-locked State shall cooperate towards their expeditious elimination.

Article 8. Free zones or other customs facilities

1. For convenience of traffic in transit, free zones or other customs facilities may be provided at the ports of entry and exit in the transit States, by agreement between those States and the land-locked States.

2. Facilities of this nature may also be provided for the benefit of land-locked states in other transit States which have no sea-coast or seaports.

Article 9. Provision of greater facilities

This Convention does not entail in any way the withdrawal of transit facilities which are greater than those provided for in the Convention and which under conditions consistent with its principles, are agreed between Contracting States or granted by a Contracting State. The Convention also does not preclude such grant of greater facilities in the future.

Article 10. Relation to most-favoured-nation clause

1. The Contracting States agree that the facilities and special rights accorded by this Convention to land-locked States in view of their special geographical position are excluded from the operation of the most-favoured-nation clause. A land-locked State which is not a Party to this Convention may claim the facilities and special rights accorded to land-locked States under this Convention only on the basis of the most-favoured-nation clause of a treaty between that land-locked State and the Contracting State granting such facilities and special rights.

2. If a Contracting State grants to a land-locked State facilities or special rights greater than those provided for in this Convention, such facilities or special rights may be limited to that land-locked State, except in so far as the withholding of such greater facilities or special rights from any other land-locked State contravenes the most-favoured-nation provision of a treaty between such other land-locked State and the Contracting State granting such facilities or special rights.

Article 11. Exceptions to convention on grounds of public health, security, and protection of intellectual property

1. No Contracting State shall be bound by this Convention to afford transit to persons whose admission into its territory is forbidden, or for goods of a kind of which the importation is prohibited, either on grounds of public morals, public health or security, or as a precaution against diseases of animals or plants or against pests.

2. Each Contracting State shall be entitled to take reasonable precautions and measures to ensure that persons and goods, particularly goods which are the subject of a monopoly, are really in transit, and that the means of transport are really used for the passage of such goods, as well as to protect the safety of the routes and means of communication.

3. Nothing in this Convention shall affect the measures which a Contracting State may be called upon to take in pursuance of provisions in a

general international convention, whether of a world-wide or regional character, to which it is a party, whether such convention was already concluded on the date of this Convention or is concluded later, when such provisions relate:

(a) to export or import or transit of particular kinds of articles such as narcotics, or other dangerous drugs, or arms; or

(b) to protection of industrial, literary or artistic property, or protection of trade names, and indications of source or appellations of origin, and the suppression of unfair competition.

4. Nothing in this Convention shall prevent any Contracting State from taking any action necessary for the protection of its essential security interests.

Article 12. Exceptions in case of emergency

The measures of a general or particular character which a Contracting State is obliged to take in case of an emergency endangering its political existence or its safety may, in exceptional cases and for as short a period as possible, involve a deviation from the provisions of this Convention on the understanding that the principle of freedom of transit shall be observed to the utmost possible extent during such a period.

Article 13. Application of the convention in time of war

This Convention does not prescribe the rights and duties of belligerents and neutrals in time of war. The Convention shall, however, continue in force in time of war so far as such rights and duties permit.

Article 14. Obligations under the convention and rights and duties of United Nations members

This Convention does not impose upon a Contracting State any obligation conflicting with its rights and duties as a Member of the United Nations.

Article 15. Reciprocity

The provisions of this Convention shall be applied on a basis of reciprocity.

Article 16. Settlement of disputes

1. Any dispute which may arise with respect to the interpretation or

application of the provisions of this Convention which is not settled by negotiation or by other peaceful means of settlement within a period of nine months shall, at the request of either party, be settled by arbitration. The arbitration commission shall be composed of three members. Each party to the dispute shall appoint one member to the commission, while the third member, who shall be the Chairman, shall be chosen in common agreement between the parties. If the parties fail to agree on the designation of the third member within a period of three months, the third member shall be appointed by the President of the International Court of Justice. In case any of the parties fail to make an appointment within a period of three months the President of the International Court of Justice shall fill the remaining vacancy or vacancies.

2. The arbitration commission shall decide on the matters placed before it by simple majority and its decisions shall be binding on the parties.

3. Arbitration commissions or other international bodies charged with settlement of disputes under this Convention shall inform, through the Secretary-General of the United Nations, the other Contracting States of the existence and nature of disputes and of the terms of their settlement.

Article 17. Signature

The present Convention shall be open until 31 December 1965 for signature by all States Members of the United Nations or of any of the specialized agencies or Parties to the Statute of the International Court of Justice, and by any other State invited by the General Assembly of the United Nations to become a Party to the Convention.

Article 18. Ratification

The present Convention is subject to ratification. The instruments of ratification shall be deposited with the Secretary-General of the United Nations.

Article 19. Accession

The present Convention shall remain open for accession by any State belonging to any of the four categories mentioned in Article 17. The instruments of accession shall be deposited with the Secretary-General of the United Nations.

Article 20. Entry into force

1. The present Convention shall enter into force on the thirtieth day following the date of deposit of the instruments of ratification or accession of at least two land-locked States and two transit States having a seacoast.

2. For each State ratifying or acceding to the Convention after the deposit of the instruments of ratification or accession necessary for the entry into force of this Convention in accordance with paragraph 1 of this article, the Convention shall enter into force on the thirtieth day after the deposit by such State of its instrument of ratification or accession.

Article 21. Revision

At the request of one-third of the Contracting States, and with the concurrence of the majority of the Contracting States, the Secretary-General of the United Nations shall convene a Conference with a view to the revision of this Convention.

Article 22. Notifications by the Secretary-General

The Secretary-General of the United Nations shall inform all States belonging to any of the four categories mentioned in article 17:

(a) of signatures to the present Convention and of the deposit of instruments of ratification or accession, in accordance with articles 17, 18 and 19;

(b) of the date on which the present Convention will enter into force, in accordance with article 20;

(c) of requests for revision, in accordance with article 21.

Article 23. Authentic texts

The original of the present Convention, of which the Chinese, English, French, Russian and Spanish texts are equally authentic, shall be deposited with the Secretary-General of the United Nations, who shall send certified copies thereof to all States belonging to any of the four categories mentioned in article 17.

IN WITNESS WHEREOF the undersigned Plenipotentiaries, being duly authorized thereto by their respective Governments, have signed the present Convention.

DONE at the Headquarters of the United Nations, New York, this eighth day of July, one thousand nine hundred and sixty-five.

AGREEMENT BETWEEN THE GOVERNMENT OF THE USSR AND THE ROYAL AFGHAN GOVERNMENT ON TRANSIT QUESTIONS

The Government of the Union of Soviet Socialist Republics and the Afghan Government, in view of the existing friendly relations between the two countries, and also in conformity with and as a consequence of Article VI of the Soviet-Afghan Friendship Treaty of 28 February 1921, have agreed as follows:

Article 1

The Union of Soviet Socialist Republics grants to Afghanistan the right of free transit of goods through its territory on the same conditions applicable to transit of goods belonging to third countries through the territory of the Union of Soviet Socialist Republics. This right is extended to all categories of goods, regardless of their origin or destination, and which are not prohibited under the law regulating transit through the territory of the Union of Soviet Socialist Republics.

Article 2

Afghanistan, on its part, grants to the Union of Soviet Socialist Republics the right of free transit of goods through its territory on the same conditions applicable to transit of goods belonging to third countries through the territory of Afghanistan. This right is extended to all categories of goods, regardless of the country of their origin or destination, and which are not prohibited under the law regulating transit through the territory of Afghanistan.

Article 3

The Contracting Parties shall not collect any dues, taxes, and levies, regardless of whether the transiting goods are sent directly, or are unloaded, transloaded, warehoused, packaged or re-packaged for transport. The transport and consignment dues for transit goods shall be calculated on the territory of each Contracting Party according to the lowest tariffs applicable at the sites where despatching and consignment of goods are carried out.

Article 4

Payments for transit of goods and their handling shall be carried out, under the present Agreement, according to the Soviet-Afghan agreements in force, on commodity circulation and payments by delivery of goods, which shall be specified by the Parties at the conclusion of annual Protocols on commodity-circulation.

Article 5

The relevant Soviet Union economic organizations, on the one hand, and the transport bodies and organizations of Afghanistan, on the other, shall conclude agreements concerning operations connected with transit of goods through the territory of the USSR or Afghanistan. Disputes which may arise in the course of the implementation of the aforementioned agreements shall be settled through the procedure provided for by Article 12 of the Soviet-Afghan Agreement on commodity-circulation and payments of 17 July 1950.

Article 6

Unaccompanied private property of citizens of the two countries also shall be allowed to transit through the territory of each Contracting Party under the provisions of the present Agreement.

Article 7

Customs formalities for transiting goods shall be reduced to their minimum on the territory of each Contracting Party. The Parties shall provide all relevant facilities in this respect.

Article 8

The present Agreement is subject to ratification. It shall acquire legal validity on the day of exchange of ratification papers and shall remain in force for 5 years. The exchange of ratification papers shall take place in Kabul. If none of the parties notifies six months prior to the expiry of the present Agreement its desire for a cancellation, it shall remain in force for another five-year period. The present Agreement was drawn up in Moscow on 28 June 1955 in two copies each in the Russian and Persian languages. Both texts are equally authentic.

AGREEMENT BETWEEN THE 'SOVFRAKHT' (OF THE USSR) AND 'TRANSIT CO' (OF AFGHANISTAN) CONCLUDED PURSUANT TO THE CONVENTION ON TRANSIT QUESTIONS BETWEEN THE TWO GOVERNMENTS

Pursuant to the Convention on transit questions concluded between the Government of the USSR and the Royal Government of Afghanistan, and signed on 28 June 1955, the All-Union Association "Sovfrakht", represented by Mr. N. I. Obozov and referred to hereafter as "Sovfrakht", on the one hand, and the joint-stock company for transport and transit of goods "Transit", represented by Mr. Sedik Khan Tarzee and referred to hereafter as "Transit Co", on the other, have concluded the present agreement concerning the following:

Upon instructions from "Transit Co", "Sovfrakht" shall undertake the shipping from the ports of entry of Kushka and Termez of Afghan goods transiting the USSR from Afghanistan to third countries and in the opposite direction. In pursuance of this undertaking, 'Sovfrakht" shall carry out the following transport and shipment operations:

1. Receive from the representative of "Transit Co" goods in transit from Afghanistan. The following procedure shall be applied:

(a) the reception of goods sent via the port of entry of Kushka shall take place at the frontier trans-shipment warehouse, where a receipt and delivery certificate shall be drawn up and signed by the representatives of both parties; from there freight shall be sent by "Sovfrakht" to Kushka railhead by motor transport;

b) the reception of goods sent via the port of entry of Termez shall take place on the Afghan bank of Amu-Darya River, and "Transit Co" shall ensure their loading with its own means. "Sovfrakht" shall carry out the transport of the freight across the Amu-Darya River to Soviet wharves and from there by motor transport to Termez or Ooch-Keezyl railheads.

Freight shall be checked at reception by the number of specified units and tentatively, the weight indicated by the "Transit Co." in the bill of lading. The weight of goods shall be rechecked at the Soviet trans-shipment warehouse at the port of entry and a receipt and delivery certificate shall be drawn up and signed by the representatives of both parties.

2. Ensure the further transport of freight in transit by railway to points of destination. Ensure also the reception and delivery in ports (Klaypeda, Batumy, Baku, etc.) of freight shipped by sea and its trans-shipment to points of destination.

3. Receive from railways and sea ports consignments of goods purchased by Afghanistan and shipped from third countries; make all necessary payments for transport charges, and deliver the freight to the representative of "Transit Co."

4. Deliver to the representative of "Transit Co." the freight received for Afghanistan. The procedure shall be as follows:

(a) the freight received at Kushka railhead shall be delivered at the frontier trans-shipment warehouse;

(b) the freight sent via Termez shall be delivered to the representative of "Transit Co" on the Soviet bank of Amu-Darya River; then "Sovfrakht" shall ensure its crossing by barges to the Afghan bank, and "Transit Co" shall ensure the unloading with its own means;

(c) the reception of goods according to the number of specified units and the weight is recorded in a receipt and delivery certificate, signed by the representatives of both parties.

5. On its part, "Transit Co" shall observe in all loading and unloading operations the loading and unloading norms established in USSR, namely 15 tons per hour.

6. "Sovfrakht" shall ensure the storage of freight at Kushka, Termez and Ooch-Keezyl railheads pending its further shipment. If the storage has been necessary for reasons depending on "Transit Co", its cost above the legal allowance of 15 days shall be covered by "Transit Co" at the rate of US $ 0.06 the gross ton (metric) a day.

7. Upon request from "Transit Co", "Sovfrakht" shall make for "Transit Co" all necessary payments for shipment charges by sea via ports of Caspian, Black and Baltic Seas.

8. "Sovfrakht" shall control the movement of Afghan freight in transit on the territory of the USSR and inform "Transit Co" as appropriate.

9. Upon request from and in the name of "Transit Co", "Sovfrakht" shall insure the Afghan freight with Ingostrakh State Corporation for Insurance Abroad, or else with the Soviet insurance companies "Blackbulsey" in London and "Shostafag" in Berlin.

10. Upon request from "Transit Co", "Sovfrakht" shall carry out all customs formalities on Soviet territory, as well as other shipment operations.

11. "Transit Co" shall inform "Sovfrakht" in Moscow 20 days before the beginning of every month of the freight which shall be sent during the month from Afghanistan via the ports of entry of Kushka and Termez.

12. "Transit Co" shall inform in advance "Sovfrakht" in Moscow of the shipment of every concrete consignment of freight in transit and ask for the conditions and cost of shipment. In its shipment notice, "Transit Co" shall point out: the name and address of the consignor, the denomination, volume and weight of the freight, the time of arrival at the port of entry, the place of destination and the name of the addressee, the particulars concerning the shipment papers and the insurance of the consignment, the kind of transport to be used, etc. Once "Sovfrakht" has confirmed that the said consignment has been duly received for shipment and has submitted to "Transit Co" the corresponding bill, the latter shall open with the Administration of Foreign Operations of the State Bank in Moscow a letter of credit in favour of "Sovfrakht", to the amount indicated by "Sovfrakht" and valid for 60 days; at the same time, it shall entrust "Sovfrakht" with the responsibility of shipping the said consignment.

13. "Transit Co" shall present freight to "Sovfrakht" in good packing condition, adequate for further transportation by rail as well as by waterways, and shall provide all necessary shipment papers: specifications, certificates, packing invoices. Whenever "Sovfrakht" shall receive untransportable goods or goods without the necessary papers, it shall not accept them for shipment and shall indicate the reasons for the rejection in the bill of lading.

14. The payments for services rendered in connection with transit transportation of freight via Soviet territory shall be made in American dollars through clearing of the letters of credit opened in favour of "Sovfrakht" with the State Bank of the USSR in Moscow. The payment under the letters of credit shall be made against "Sovfrakht" accounts, with indication of the dates and numbers of the receipt and delivery certificates drawn up at Termez or Kushka.

The questions concerning the payments of premiums for insurance of freight shall be settled separately.

"Sovfrakht" and "Transit Co" shall be economically responsible to each other for any possible breach or undue fulfillment of the present Agreement.

16. Any possible dispute concerning the implementation of the present Agreement or in connection with it shall be settled according to the procedure established in Art. 12 of the Trade and Payments Agreement of 17 June 1950.

17. The present Agreement shall remain in force for one year after

the date of its signature (i.e. from 11 October 1955 to 10 October 1956).

If none of the parties notifies three months prior to the expiry of the present Agreement its desire for cancellation or revision, the Agreement shall be considered as remaining in force for another year.

18. The present Agreement was drawn up in two copies, each in Russian and Persian languages; both texts are equally authentic.

19. Legal addresses of both parties concerned:

"Sovfrakht" – Moscow, Smolenskaya-Sennaya Plostchad, 32/34.

"Transit Co" – Kabul.

AGREEMENT BETWEEN THE GOVERNMENT OF THE KINGDOM OF AFGHANISTAN AND THE GOVERNMENT OF THE ISLAMIC REPUBLIC OF PAKISTAN FOR REGULATION OF TRAFFIC IN TRANSIT

The Government of the Kingdom of Afghanistan and the Government of the Islamic Republic of Pakistan being desirous of strengthening the economic ties between their two countries on a mutually advantageous basis, improving the facilities now available for transit trade, and removing the difficulties in the movement of goods through the two countries, and having taken into consideration the present volume and future development of transit trade have decided to conclude an Agreement and to this end have appointed their Plenipotentiaries as under:

The Government of the Kingdom of Afghanistan
Mohammed Sarwar Omar, Minister for Commerce
The Government of the Islamic Republic of Pakistan
Wahiduzzaman, Minister for Commerce

who having exchanged their full powers, found in good and due form, have agreed to the following Articles:

Article 1

The Contracting Parties undertake in accordance with the provisions of this Agreement to grant and guarantee to each other the freedom of transit to and from their territories.

No distinction shall be made which is based on the flag of vessels, the place of origin, departure, entry, exit or destination or any other circumstances relating to the ownership of goods, of vessels or of other means of transport.

Article 2

Goods including baggage, and vessels and other means of transport shall be deemed to be in transit across the territory of a Contracting Party, when the passage across such territory with or without trans-shipment, is only a portion of a complete journey beginning and terminating beyond the frontier of the Contracting Party across whose territory the traffic passes. Traffic of this nature is termed in this Agreement "Traffic in Transit".

Article 3

The transit routes shall be:

1. Peshawar-Torkham and vice versa.
2. Chaman-Spin Boldak and vice versa.

Additional routes may be agreed between the Contracting Parties from time to time. Goods moving via these routes shall be entered at the proper Customs post prescribed by each Party. Adequate transit and other facilities shall be provided by the Contracting Party concerned at these posts.

Article 4

No customs duties, taxes, dues, or charges of any kind whether national, provincial or municipal regardless of their names and purposes, shall be levied on traffic in transit except charges for transportation or those commensurate with the administrative expenses entailed by traffic in transit or with the cost of services rendered.

With a view to achieving simplification of existing Customs practices and procedures, the Contracting Parties agree to adopt at points of entry and exit the procedures laid down in the Annex to this Agreement.

Article 5

Without prejudice to the generality of the provisions contained in Article 3, the Government of the Islamic Republic of Pakistan shall earmark sheds and open spaces in the Karachi Port Area, to be known as Afghan Transit Area for the goods in transit to and from Afghanistan. For hazardous and awkward goods separate arrangements for storage will be made as indicated in the Annex.

Article 6

The two Contracting Parties, recognizing the importance of the Kabul-Torkham-Peshawar transit route, have decided to examine all matters pertinent to the development of this route, including further consideration of the extension of the railway from Landi-Khana to Torkham.

Article 7

The Government of the Islamic Republic of Pakistan undertake to meet in full the requirement of wagons for transit traffic on both Karachi-Spin Boldak and Peshawar-Karachi routes.

Article 8

Each Contracting Party shall appoint Liaison Officers in their respective territories to look into the working of this Agreement and to refer, for expeditious solution, to the appropriate authorities in their own country and to the Liaison Officer in the other country, any question arising from the operation of the Agreement. The two Liaison Officers will meet as often as necessary and the Contracting Parties shall provide them with the necessary facilities.

Article 9

The Contracting Parties agree that railway freight, port and other dues shall be subject to the most sympathetic consideration and shall be no less favourable than those imposed by either Party on goods owned by its own nationals.

Article 10

Nothing in this Agreement shall be construed to prevent the adoption and enforcement by either Party of measures necessary to protect public morals, human, animal or plant life or health and for the security of its own territory.

Article 11

The Contracting Parties shall meet and consult each other once a year to review the working of this Agreement.

Article 12

The Contracting Parties agree to resolve any differences relating to the interpretation of this Agreement, by mutual negotiation and in the event of failure to reach a settlement, to refer the matter to an arbitrator acceptable to both Parties, whose decision shall be binding.

Article 13

Nothing in this Agreement or its Annexes will affect in any way the political stand of the two countries or the political differences existing between them, and the Contracting Parties fully reserve their rights with regard to these subjects.

Article 14

This Agreement shall be ratified and the Instruments of Ratification shall be exchanged at Rawalpindi. The Agreement shall come into force from the date of the exchange of the Instruments of Ratification and shall remain in force for five years from the date it comes into force. Unless notice of termination is given in writing by either Contracting Party to the other six months before the expiration of the five years' period, the Agreement shall be automatically renewed for a further period of five years. It can thereafter be terminated by either Party at any time provided six months' notice of termination is given by either Party.

Article 15

The present Agreement is drawn in duplicate in the Dari and English languages, both texts being equally valid.

IN WITNESS THEREOF, the undersigned, being duly authorized by their respective Governments, have signed the present Agreement.

Done in duplicate in the Dari and English languages at Kabul on 2 March 1965.

ANNEX ON THE CUSTOMS AND OTHER PROCEDURES TO THE AGREEMENT SIGNED ON 2 MARCH 1965 BETWEEN THE ROYAL AFGHAN GOVERNMENT AND THE ISLAMIC REPUBLIC OF PAKISTAN FOR REGULATING TRAFFIC IN TRANSIT

I. *Customs and other procedures in respect of goods and passengers' unaccompanied baggage entering Pakistan for transit to Afghanistan*

1. On arrival of the goods the owner or his agent shall at the time of entering them at the Customs House:

(a) declare that the goods are intended for such transit;

(b) furnish in quadruplicate an invoice of the goods so declared in the prescribed form specifying therein by which of the two authorized routes the goods are intended to be transported via:

1. Peshawar-Torkham,
2. Chaman-Spin Boldak;

(c) on compliance with the above provisions the documents will be completed on the basis of exemption from duty, sales tax and import trade control regulations after such inspection as may be considered necessary.

2. The further procedure in respect of goods arriving through Karachi will be as follows:

The goods will be sealed with Customs seal and removed from the Karachi Port Trust transit sheds, under Customs supervision, to the Afghan transit sheds specially set apart for the purpose under Customs physical control. Heavy goods such as machinery and iron or steel, etc. will be removed from the Karachi Port Trust transit areas under Customs supervision and stored in enclosed open spaces, specially provided for the purpose, under Customs control. Explosives and hazardous goods and heavy cargo exceeding five tons in weight for which special storage arrangements have been provided by the Karachi Port Trust will not be removed to the transit shed or open space set apart for Afghan transit goods.

3. The goods will be loaded under Customs supervision into railway wagons, exclusively provided for in-transit goods, which will be sealed by the railway. In the case of open wagons loading heavy articles such as cars, trucks, machinery, iron and steel etc., sealing may be dispensed with. The original copy of the invoice duly checked and completed by the Customs will be handed over to the owner or his agent. At the same time the duplicate and triplicate copies of the invoice will be dispatched by the Customs House to the Afghan Customs at Spin Boldak.

4. On receipt of the invoice from the Pakistan Customs, the Afghan Customs at Spin Boldak will retain the duplicate and return the triplicate copy to the Customs House of dispatch in Pakistan with appropriate endorsements certifying the arrival of the goods.

5. The procedure in respect of goods dispatched by the Peshawar-Torkham route from Karachi will be the same as detailed up to and including paragraph 3 in respect of Spin Boldak. The procedure thereafter will be that the Customs House will dispatch the duplicate and triplicate copies of the invoice to the Customs Officer at Peshawar. On

receipt of the invoice from the Karachi Customs the Customs Officer at Peshawar shall retain the duplicate and forward the triplicate copy to the Customs Officer at Torkham. On arrival at Peshawar such goods will be carried to a transit shed or area under Customs control or transferred directly to a road transport under Customs supervision. Road transports in which the goods are carried forward to Afghanistan will, where possible, be sealed with Customs seal.

6. Goods which require repacking after arrival at Peshawar will be allowed repacking facilities at the transit shed or area under Customs control. The Customs Officer at Peshawar will check the goods with the original copy of the invoice and compare the latter with the duplicate copy received from the port of entry. If the seals are intact and the goods correspond with the description in the invoice, the Customs Officer shall allow the goods to be repacked and resealed under his supervision, shall endorse on each copy of the invoice details of any changes in the number or description of the packages involved by such repacking, shall where possible seal the road transport in which the goods are loaded for final transport to Afghanistan, return the original copy of the invoice so endorsed to the owner or his agent and forward the duplicate copy to the Customs Officer at Torkham. On arrival at Torkham the goods must be presented to the Customs Officer along with the duplicate copy of the invoice for inspection and final clearance. The Customs Officer shall note the repacking particulars, if any, on the reverse of the triplicate copy and return the duplicate to the Customs Officer at Peshawar.

7. In the case of goods entering Pakistan at Lahore the procedure will be the same as detailed above in respect of Karachi except the provisions of paragraph 2 above.

8. The procedure in respect of goods moving into Spin Boldak will be enforced only when the railway-line has been extended up to that point. Until then the formalities provided for in respect of Peshawar-Torkham route will apply *mutatis mutandis* to Chaman and to the Customs post opposite Vesh.

9. Afghan goods or passengers' unaccompanied baggage arriving in transit by sea at Karachi if moving by air to Afghanistan from Karachi Airport, will be transported under Customs seal to Karachi Airport and placed on board the oncarrying aircraft under Customs supervision. The documentation in respect of such goods will be similar to that for goods dispatched by rail, with appropriate modifications.

II. *Procedure in respect of goods and passengers' unaccompanied baggage moving in transit from Afghanistan to foreign countries through Pakistan*

1. On entry of the goods at the Land Customs Stations at Torkham-Peshawar or at Chaman until such time as the railway-line is extended up to Spin Boldak and Torkham, the Afghan exporter or his agent shall declare that the goods are in transit to a third country or overseas and furnish in quadruplicate an invoice in the prescribed form.

2. The Government of Pakistan may require certain specified goods dispatched in transit from Afghanistan to foreign countries to be sealed by the Afghan Customs before their dispatch out of Afghanistan. A list of such goods will be furnished to the Government of Afghanistan from time to time.

3. On compliance with the above provisions the seals on the goods will be checked and the goods removed under Customs supervision to the transit shed or area at the Pakistan railhead at Peshawar or Chaman under Customs control. Repacking facilities will be allowed at these transit sheds or areas as well as at the transit shed in the Karachi Port Area.

4. The goods will be loaded under Customs supervision into railway wagons exclusively provided for in-transit goods which will be sealed by the railway. The original copy of the invoice duly checked and completed by the Customs will be handed over to the owner or his agent. At the same time, the duplicate and triplicate copies of the invoice will be forwarded by the Frontier Customs Officer at the Pakistan railhead to the Collector of Customs, Karachi, if the goods are to be exported by sea or to the Land Customs Officer at the Land Customs Station through which the goods are to be exported by land to India. The quadruplicate copy will be retained by the Frontier Land Customs Officer for his record. The Customs Officer, who supervises the loading of goods into the railway wagons, will record on all copies of the invoice the number of the wagons in which the goods have been dispatched.

5. (a) In the case of goods to be exported by sea from the Port of Karachi, the goods will on arrival at Karachi Railway Station be unloaded from the wagons under Customs supervision after verifying that the seals are intact. They will then be carried under Customs supervision to the Afghan transit shed specially set apart for the purpose in the Port area, under Customs control. The goods will remain in Customs control until they are duly exported on filing of an export shipping bill. The goods will

be inspected and examined if necessary, before shipment is allowed under Customs supervision.

NOTE: Goods of hazardous nature such as cotton which are in transit from Afghanistan to foreign countries cannot be stored in the transit shed along with other goods and the present arrangement of storing such goods will continue.

(b) In the case of goods to be exported by land to India, the wagons will on arrival at the Land Customs Station, be inspected by the Customs. Detailed examination of the goods will be dispensed with if the seals on the wagons are intact. The Customs Officer will satisfy himself that the seals are intact and that the numbers of the wagons correspond with those entered in the invoice. If the duplicate and triplicate copies of the invoice have not been received from the Frontier Customs Officer, he will not detain the goods but will pass them after entering the verified particulars of the wagons and if necessary enter the goods in a register and on the original copy of the invoice produced by the owner or his agent. On receipt of the duplicate and triplicate copies of the invoice, he will make the necessary endorsements on the basis of the particulars recorded in his register.

6. After the goods have been duly shipped for export by sea or handed over to the railway authorities for onward transmission by land, the Customs Officer will certify on each copy of the invoice that the goods have been duly shipped or exported. The original copy of the invoice will be returned to the owner or his agent, the duplicate copy will be sent to the Frontier Customs Officer at Peshawar or Chaman as the case may be, and the triplicate copy will be retained for record by the Customs House, Karachi, or the Land Customs Station of export, as the case may be.

7. As soon as the railway line is extended to Spin Boldak and Torkham the documentation and sealing of packages in respect of such goods will be the responsibility of the Afghan Customs, the sealing of wagons being done by the railway, the detailed procedure respecting which will be drawn up by mutual consultation by representatives of the two Governments.

PROTOCOL ANNEXED TO TRANSIT AGREEMENT SIGNED BETWEEN THE GOVERNMENT OF THE KINGDOM OF AFGHANISTAN AND THE GOVERNMENT OF THE ISLAMIC REPUBLIC OF PAKISTAN DATED 2 MARCH 1965

In accordance with the provisions of the Agreement signed in Kabul between the authorized representatives of the Contracting Parties on 2 March 1965, regulating Traffic in Transit to and from Afghanistan, the signatories, in order to regulate the transport of goods by lorries from Peshawar to Kabul and from Chaman to Kandahar and vice versa, until such time when extension of railroads is completed, have agreed as follows:

Article 1

The two Governments agree that there shall be open competition for all transporters for carriage of all categories of goods to and from Afghanistan irrespective of ownership of goods.

Article 2

The two Governments agree to accord to transporters and clearing and forwarding agents from either country national treatment.

Article 3

Determination of freight rates shall be left to market conditions for goods of all descriptions and denominations. No discrimination shall be made by the authorities of either Government in the matter of allocation of freight as between the transporters of either country.

Article 4

Each Government agrees that no taxes shall be levied by it on transport vehicles registered in the territory of the other country except by prior consultations and on the basis of equality.

Article 5

The two Governments agree that:

(a) Route permits shall be issued by the country in which the vehicles are registered;

(b) Driving licences and certificates of fitness in respect of transport vehicles covered by this protocol issued in one country shall be valid in the other country; vehicles carrying petroleum and petroleum products shall continue to be governed by existing practice regarding certificates of fitness; and

(c) The period for which vehicles of one country may stay in the other on each trip shall be fixed on a uniform reciprocal basis.

Article 6

The two Governments agree to grant to transporters multiple entry visas valid for a period of six months at a time.

Article 7

The two Governments agree to grant to transport vehicles road permits valid for a period of six months at a time.

Article 8

The two Governments shall consult each other with a view to adopting necessary measures to facilitate the flow of traffic between the two countries and shall seek all possible means within their power to remove any factors which may damage the normal accomplishment of the operation foreseen in the Protocol.

Article 9

This Protocol shall come into force simultaneously with the Agreement on Traffic in Transit signed on 2 March 1965.

Done in duplicate in English and Dari, both texts being equally authentic, in Kabul on 2 March 1965, corresponding to the 12 of Hoot, 1343.

BIBLIOGRAPHY

Public Documents

Afghanistan. Royal Afghan Embassy, London. *Afghanistan News,* November 1961.

Afghanistan. Ministry of Commerce, Statistical Department. *A Summary of Afghanistan's Foreign Trade in 1344 (March 21, 1965 through March 20, 1966).* Kabul, August 1966.

Afghanistan. Ministry of Commerce, Planning Department. *Business and Investment Opportunities in Afghanistan.* Kabul: The Government Press, April 1967.

Afghanistan. Pazhwak, Rahman. *An Article on Pakhtunistan; A New State in Central Asia.* London: Royal Afghan Embassy, 1960.

Afghanistan. Pazhwak, Rahman. *Pakhtunistan; The Khyber Pass as the Focus of the New State of Pakhtunistan.* London: Afghan Information Bureau, n.d.

Bolivia-Chile. *Gestión Directa Para la Revisión del Tratado de 1904.* La Paz, 1923.

Bolivia. Bedregal, Guillermo, *La Revolución Boliviana: Su Realidad y Perspectivas dentro del Ciclo de Liberación de Latino América.* La Paz: Dirección Nacional de Informaciones de la Presidencia de la República, 1962.

Bolivia. *Bolivia's International Policy.* Washington: The Bolivian Legation, 1925.

Bolivia. Ministerio de Relaciones Exteriores y Culto. *Informe Sobre el Río Lauca.* La Paz, 1962.

Bolivia. Ministerio de Relaciones Exteriores y Culto. *La Desviación del Río Lauca (Antecedentes y Documentos)* [The Red Book]. La Paz, 1962.

Bolivia. Ministerio de Relaciones Exteriores y Culto. *Rumbo al Mar; Documentos Trascendentales.* La Paz, 1963.

Bolivia. Ministerio de Relaciones Exteriores y Culto. *¿Por Qué Bolivia no está presente en Punta del Este?* La Paz, 1967.

Chile. Ministerio de Relaciones Exteriores. *Chile Responde al Presidente de Bolivia.* Santiago, 1967.

Chile. Ministero de Relaciones Exteriores. *Discursos y Documentos; Relationes Entre Chile y Bolivia.* No. 1 Santiago, March 28, 1963.

Chile. Ministerio de Relaciones Exteriores. *Facilidades de Libre Tránsito Que Chile Otorga a Bolivia.* Santiago, 1963.

Chile. Ministerio de Relaciones Exteriores. *La Cuestión del Río Lauca* [The White Book]. Santiago, 1963.

Chile. *Tacna-Arica Arbitration: The Case of the Republic of Chile.* n.p., n.d.

East Africa High Commission. *Report upon the Possibilities of Developing Dar es Salaam into a Major Port.* Nairobi, March 1949.

The East African Common Services Organization. *Annual Report 1965.*

East African Railways and Harbours. *Annual Report 1966.* Nairobi, 1967.

East African Railways and Harbours. Hill, M. F., *Permanent Way; The Story of the Kenya and Uganda Railway.* Nairobi, 1950.

East African Railways and Harbours. *Report on an Engineering Survey of a Rail Link Between the East African and Rhodesian Railway Systems.* Nairobi, June 1952.

Great Britain. Colonial Office Command Paper 1279. *East Africa: Report of the Economic and Fiscal Commission.* London: HMSO, February 1961.

Great Britain. Hawkins, E. K. *Roads and Road Transport in an Underdeveloped Country; A Case Study of Uganda.* Colonial Research Studies No. 32. London: HMSO, 1962.

Great Britain. *Kenya: Report for the Year 1962.* London: HMSO, 1964.

Great Britain. *Tanganyika under United Kingdom Administration.* Part II Statistics. London: HMSO, 1961.

Great Britain. *Uganda: Report for the Year 1961.* London: HMSO, 1963.

Great Britain. Reference Division, Central Office of Information. *Zambia.* London: HMSO, 1964.

India. Department of Commercial Intelligence and Statistics. *Bilateral Trade Statistics 1965–1966 and 1966–1967.* Calcutta.

India. Department of Commercial Intelligence and Statistics. *Monthly Statistics of the Foreign Trade of India.* Vol. I, Exports and Re-exports; Vol. II, Imports. Calcutta, December 1966, March 1967.

India. Minister of Commerce and Industry. *India's Trade Agreements with Other Countries.* Delhi: Government of India Press, 1957.

Kenya. Statistics Division, Minister of Economic Planning and Development. *Economic Survey 1965.*

Kenya. Statistics Division, Minister of Economic Planning and Development. *Statistical Abstract 1965.* Nairobi: The Government Printer, 1965.

Pakistan. Department of Films and Publications. *Papers Read at the RCD Colloquium on Common Problems of Economic Growth, Karachi, 28–30 June, 1965.* Karachi, n.d.

Uganda. Statistics Division, Ministry of Planning and Community Development. *1965 Statistical Abstract.* Entebbe: Government Printer, 1965.

Uganda. Statistics Division, Ministry of Planning and Economic Development. *Uganda Quarterly Digest of Statistics No. 4.* September, 1966.

United States. Bureau of the Census. *Statistical Abstract of the United States,* 1963.

United States. Bureau of International Commerce. *Basic Data on the Economy of Afghanistan.* Overseas Business Reports. OBR 66–34. June 1966.

United States. Bureau of International Commerce. *Basic Data on the Economy of Bolivia.* OBR 63-126, October, 1963.

United States. Bureau of International Commerce. *Basic Data on the Economy of Tanzania.* OBR 66–4, February 1966.

United States. Bureau of International Commerce. *Basic Data on the Economy of Uganda.* OBR 66–19. April 1966.

United States. Department of State, Bureau of Intelligence and Research. "Uganda's Administrative Divisions," *Geographic Note.* GE-29. 30 September 1966.

United States. Department of State, Office of Media Services. *Background Notes,* 1964–1967.

United States. Department of State, The Geographer. "Afghanistan-USSR Boundary." *International Boundary Study* No. 26. 30 December 1963.

International Bank for Reconstruction and Development. *The Economic Development of Kenya.* Baltimore: The Johns Hopkins Press, 1963.

International Bank for Reconstruction and Development. *The Economic Development of Tanganyika.* Baltimore: The Johns Hopkins Press, 1961.

International Bank for Reconstruction and Development. *The Economic Development of Uganda.* Baltimore: The Johns Hopkins Press, 1962.

Organization of American States. *Proceedings of Fourth Meeting of Consultation of Ministers of Foreign Affairs.* Conferences and Organization Series No. 12. Washington: Pan American Union, 1951.

Organization of American States. Council Series. Washington: Pan American Union.
OEA/Ser. G/II C-a-444. 3 May 1962.
OEA/Ser. G/V C-d-1018. 4 September 1962.
OEA/Ser. G/V C-d-1107. 18 June 1963.

Pan American Union. Department of Economic Affairs. *A Survey of Factors Which Affect Transportation Cost.* Washington, 1964.

Regional Cooperation for Development. The Secretariat. *RCD Anniversary Publication.* Tehran, 21 July 1965.

Regional Cooperation for Development. The Secretariat. "Report on First Two Years of RCD", *RCD Mirror,* Vol. 1 No. 2, 21 July 1966.

Regional Cooperation for Development. The Secretariat. *Economic Reconstruction of Iran, Pakistan and Turkey.* Tehran, 1966.

United Nations Conference on the Law of the Sea.
Official Records, Preliminary Conference of Land-locked States. A/CONF. 13/C.5/L.1. 28 February 1958.
Official Records, Vol. VII (Fifth Committee-Question of Free Access to the Sea of Land-locked Countries). A/CONF.13/43 24 February–27 April 1958.

United Nations Conference on Trade and Development.
Activities of the Economic Commission for Asia and the Far East Related to the United Nations Conference on Trade and Development. Prepared by ECAFE. E/CONF.46/87 21 March 1964.
Problems of Land-locked Countries; Note Submitted by Afghanistan, Laos and Nepal to UNCTAD. E/CONF.46/88.
Statement Delivered by the Representative of Afghanistan, Mohammed Sarwar Omar, Geneva, 30 March 1964. E/CONF.46/STA/42 (Annex 2 to E/CONF.46/SR.10). 31 March 1964.
Statement Delivered by the Representative of Uganda, Jehoosh S. Mayanja-Nkangi, Minister of Commerce and Industry, Geneva, 3 April 1964. E/CONF. 46/STA/88 (Annex 5 to E/CONF.46/SR.18). 7 April 1964.

United Nations. Office of Public Information. Press Release.
EC/TR/148 (CTD/E/21). 29 April 1964.
EC/TR/191 (CTD/E/34). 11 May 1964.
EC/TR/258 (CTD/E/45). 25 May 1964.

United Nations Conference on Trade and Development.
Final Act and Report. E/CONF.46/141, 1964.

United Nations. UNCTAD. Committee on Preparation of a Draft Convention Relating to Transit Trade of Land-locked Countries.
[*Recommendation by UNCTAD, Principles adopted by UNCTAD and Draft Convention proposed by Afro-Asian Land-locked Countries.*] E/CONF.46/AC.2/1. 23 September 1964.
Texts of International Instruments and Certain Recommendations Relating to Transit Trade. E/CONF.46/AC.2/2. 25 September 1964.
Various Questions Affecting the Preparation of a Convention Relating to the Transit Trade of Land-locked Countries. E/CONF.46/AC.2/3. 1 October 1964.
Transit Trade of Land-locked Countries of the ECAFE Region. E/CONF.46/AC.2/5.
Summary Records. E/CONF.46/AC.2/SR.1–30. 1 December 1964–7 January 1965.

United Nations. UNCTAD. Conference on Transit Trade of Land-locked Countries.
Draft Convention on Transit Trade of Land-locked Countries, Comparative Table of Provisions. TD/TRANSIT/R.1. 4 June 1965.
[*Afghanistan-Pakistan transit agreement*]. TD/TRANSIT/R.2. 10 June 1965.
Note by the Observer of the Inter-Governmental Maritime Consultative Organization. TD/TRANSIT/R.3. 10 June 1965.
Background Paper on the Question of Free Zones... TD/TRANSIT/4. 10 June 1965.
List of Conventions and International Agreements (Multipartite and Bilateral) Relating to Questions of Transit. TD/TRANSIT/6. 15 June 1965.
Summary Records. TD/TRANSIT/SR.1–36. 11–13 October 1965.

United Nations. UNCTAD. Trade and Development Board, Second Session. *Report on the United Nations Conference of Plenipotentiaries on Transit Trade of Land-locked Countries.* TD/B/18. 1965.

United Nations. UNCTAD. Trade and Development Board, Third Session. *Text of Resolution Adopted by the Council of the International Chamber of Commerce.* TD/B/NGO/1. 1966.

United Nations Economic Commission for Africa.
Economic Bulletin for Africa. Vol. II No. 1. January 1962.
East African Transport Problems in Relation to the Promotion of Economic Development (Progress Report). E/CN.14/148. 24 January 1962.
Transit Problems of Eastern African Land-locked States. E/CN.14/INR/44. 6 November 1963. Also UNCTAD, E/CONF.46/AC.2/4. 16 October 1964.
Transit Problems of African Land-locked States. E/CN.14/TRANS/28. 2 February 1966
United Nations Conference on Trade and Development; Activities and Recommendations. E/CN.14/WP.1/9 also OAU/TRAD/8. 23 March 1966.

United Nations Economic Commission for Asia and the Far East.
Problems of Trade of Land-locked Countries in Asia and the Far East. ECAFE/I&T/Sub.4/2. 29 August 1956.
Regional Economic Cooperation in Asia and the Far East; Report of the Ministerial Conference on Asian Economic Cooperation, Manila, 3–6 December 1963. E/CN.11/641, 1964.
20th Session of ECAFE, Tehran, March 1964. E/CN.11/657. 15 March 1964.
Report of the Second Ministerial Conference on Asian Economic Cooperation, Manila, 29 November–2 December 1965. E/CN.11/716. 15 December 1965.
Economic Survey of Asia and the Far East 1965. Sales No. 66.II.F.1. Bangkok, 1966.

United Nations Economic Commission for Latin America. *Análisis y Proyecciones del Desarollo Económico. Vol. IV. El Desarollo Económico de Bolivia.* E/CN.12/430 y Add. 1/Rev. 1. México, 1958.
Boletín Económico de América Latina. Vol. VII. No. 2. Suplemento Estadístico. Sales No. 63.II.G.9. Santiago, December, 1962.
El Transporte en América Latina. E/CN.12/703/Rev.1. New York: February 1965.
Economic Survey of Latin America 1965. E/CN.12/752/Rev.1.

United Nations. General Assembly. *Provisional Verbatim Record of the 1137th Plenary Meeting of the United Nations General Assembly, 17th Session.* A/PV. 1137. 28 September 1962.

United Nations. Secretariat. *Status of Multilateral Conventions in Respect of Which the Secretary-General Acts as Depositary.* Supplement No. 4. ST/LE 6/3/Rev.1. 1964.
ST/LEG/3/Rev.1. 7 July 1967.

United Nations. Security Council.
S/5562. 25 February 1964.
S/5564. 27 February 1964.
S/5567. 29 February 1964.
United Nations. Statistical Office of the United Nations, Department of Economic and Social Affairs. *Statistical Yearbook 1961 and 1966.*

Books

Akademiia Nauk SSSR. Institut Narodov Azii. *Afganistan (spravochnik).* Moskva: Izdatelstvo "Nauka," 1964.
Akademiia Nauk SSSR. Institut Narodov Azii. *Voprosy ekonomiki Afganistana.* Moskva: Izdatelstvo vostochnoi literatury, 1963.
Akers, Charles Edmond. *A History of South America.* 3rd ed. London: John Murray, 1930.
Alexandersson, Gunnar, and Norström, Göran. *World Shipping; An Economic Geography of Ports and Seaborne Trade.* New York: John Wiley and Sons, 1963.
Alexandrovskaya, L. and Rybakov, V. *Africa's Economic Problems.* Moscow: Progress Publishers, [1965].
Arnade, Charles W. *The Emergence of the Republic of Bolivia.* Gainesville: University of Florida Press, 1957.
Avery, Peter. *Modern Iran.* New York: Frederick A. Praeger, Publishers, 1965.
Bennett, George. *Kenya; A Political History, The Colonial Period.* London: Oxford University Press, 1963.
Berber, Friedrich Joseph. *Rivers in International Law.* Translated by R. K. Batstone. London: Stevens and Sons, Ltd. and New York: Oceana Publications, Inc., 1959.
Bowman, Isaiah. *Desert Trails of Atacama.* New York: American Geographical Society, 1924.
Brown, Robert T. *Transport and the Economic Integration of South America.* Washington: The Brookings Institution, 1966.
Bulnes, Gonzalo. *Chile and Peru: The Causes of the War of 1879.* Santiago: Imprenta Universitaria, 1920.
Butland, Gilbert J. *Chile: An Outline of its Geography, Economics and Politics.* London: Royal Institute of International Affairs, 1956.
Carrasco, José. *Bolivia's Case for the League of Nations.* London: Selwyn and Blount, 1920.
Carter, Gwendolen M. (ed.). *National Unity and Regionalism in Eight African States.* Ithaca, New York: Cornell University Press, 1966.
Cressey, George B. *Crossroads: Land and Life in Southwest Asia.* Chicago: J. B. Lippincott Company, 1960.
de Blij, Harm J. *A Geography of Subsaharan Africa.* Chicago: Rand McNally and Co., 1964.
–. *Dar es Salaam; A Study in Urban Geography.* Evanston: Northwestern University Press, 1963.
–. *Systematic Political Geography.* New York: John Wiley and Sons, Inc., 1967.
Dell, Sidney. *A Latin American Common Market?* London: Oxford University Press, 1966.
–. *Trade Blocs and Common Markets.* New York: Alfred A. Knopf, 1963.
Dennis, William Jefferson. *Tacna and Arica: An Account of the Chile-Peru Boundary Dispute and of the Arbitration by the United States.* New Haven: Yale University Press, 1931.

Escobari Cusicanqui, Jorge. *El Derecho al Mar.* La Paz: Editorial Juventud, 1964.

Evans, Henry Clay, Jr. *Chile and its Relations with the United States.* Durham, North Carolina: Duke University Press, 1927.

Eyzaguirre, Jaime. *Bolivia – An Isolated Country?* Santiago: Empresa Editora Zig-Zag, S.A., 1965.

Fenwick, Charles G. *International Law.* 4th ed. New York: Appleton-Century-Crofts, 1965.

Fletcher, Arnold. *Afghanistan; Highway of Conquest.* Ithaca: Cornell University Press, 1965.

Franck, Thomas M. *East African Unity Through Law.* New Haven: Yale University Press, 1964.

Fraser-Tytler, W. K. *Afghanistan; A Study of Political Developments in Central and Southern Asia.* 2nd ed. London: Oxford University Press, 1953.

Fromm, Gary (ed.). *Transport Investment and Economic Development.* Washington: The Brookings Institution, 1965.

Galdames, Luis. *A History of Chile.* Translated and edited by Isaac Joslin Cox. Chapel Hill: University of North Carolina Press, 1941.

Ginsburg, Norton (ed.). *The Pattern of Asia.* Englewood Cliffs, New Jersey: Prentice-Hall, Inc., 1958.

Green, R. H., and Krishna, K. G. V. *Economic Co-operation in Africa; Retrospect and Prospect.* Nairobi: Oxford University Press, 1967.

Greve, Ernesto. *Informe Sobre la Demarcación de los Paralelos de los Grados 23 y 24 de Latitud Meridional, Elevado a la Superintendencia del Salitre.* Santiago: La Ilustración, 1932.

Gupta, Sisir. *India and Regional Integration in Asia.* London: Asia Publishing House, 1964.

Gutiérrez G., Mario R. *Alegato Histórico de los Derechos de Bolivia al Pacífico.* La Paz: np., 1962.

Hagras, Kamal M. *United Nations Conference on Trade and Development; A Case Study in UN Diplomacy.* New York: Frederick A. Praeger, Publishers, 1965.

Hazelwood, Arthur. *Rail and Road in East Africa; Transport Co-ordination in Under-developed Countries.* Oxford: Basil Blackwell, 1964.

Hooson, David J. M. *The Soviet Union.* London: University of London Press Ltd., 1966.

Humlum, Johannes. *La géographie de l'Afghanistan.* Copenhagen: Gyldendal, 1959.

Hunter, Holland. *Soviet Transportation Policy.* Cambridge: Harvard University Press, 1957.

Instituto de Investigaciones Históricas y Culturales de La Paz, *Mesa Redonda Sobre el Problema del Litoral Boliviano.* La Paz: Honorable Municipalidad, 1966.

Ireland, Gordon. *Boundaries, Possessions and Conflicts in South America.* Cambridge: Harvard University Press, 1938.

James, Preston E. *Latin America.* 3rd ed. New York: The Odyssey Press, 1959.

–., and Jones, Clarence F. (eds.). *American Geography; Inventory and Prospect.* Syracuse, New York: Syracuse University Press, 1954.

Karefa-Smart, John (ed.). *Africa – Progress Through Cooperation.* New York: Dodd Mead and Co., 1966.

La Integración Económica Latinoamericana. México, D.F.: Banco Nacional de Comercio Exterior, S.A., 1963.

Legum, Colin (ed.). *Africa: A Handbook to the Continent.* Revised and enlarged edition. New York: Frederick A. Praeger, Publishers, 1966.

Leonard, Olen E. *Bolivia: Land, People and Institutions.* Washington: The Scarecrow Press, 1952.

London, Kurt (ed.). *New Nations in a Divided World.* New York: Frederick A. Praeger, Publishers, 1963.

Low, D. Anthony, and Pratt, R. Cranford. *Buganda and British Overrule 1900–1955.* London: Oxford University Press, 1960.

McBride, George McCutchen. *Chile: Land and Society.* New York: American Geographical Society, 1936.

McDougal, Myres S., and Burke, William T. *The Public Order of the Oceans; A Contemporary International Law of the Sea.* New Haven: Yale University Press, 1962.

Mance, Brig. Gen. Sir Osborne. *Frontiers, Peace Treaties, and International Organization.* London: Oxford University Press, 1946.

Markham, Clements R. *The War Between Peru and Chile 1879–1882.* 4th ed. London: Sampson Low, Marston, Searle and Rivington, 1883.

Massel, Benton F. *East African Economic Union: An Evaluation and Some Implications for Policy.* Santa Monica: The RAND Corporation, December 1963.

Meneses, Rómulo. *El Imperativo Geográfico en la Mediterraneidad de Bolivia.* La Paz: Editorial Renacimiento, 1943.

Moraga, Oscar Espinosa. *Bolivia y el Mar 1810–1964.* Santiago: Editorial Nascimento, 1965.

–. *La Cuestión del Lauca.* Santiago: Editorial Nascimento, 1964.

Nye, Joseph S., Jr. *Pan-Africanism and East African Integration.* Cambridge: Harvard University Press, 1965.

O'Connell, Daniel Patrick. *International Law.* Vol. I.. Dobbs Ferry, New York: Oceana Publications, Inc., 1965.

O'Connor, A. M. *An Economic Geography of East Africa.* New York: Frederick A. Praeger, Publishers, 1966.

–. *Railways and Development in Uganda.* Nairobi: Oxford University Press, 1965.

Osborne, Harold. *Bolivia; A Land Divided.* London: Royal Institute of International Affairs, 1954.

–. *Indians of the Andes; Aymaras and Quechuas.* Cambridge: Harvard University Press, 1952.

Owen, Wilfred. *Strategy for Mobility.* Washington: The Brookings Institution, 1964.

Peñaloza, Luis. *Historia Económica de Bolivia.* Vol. II. La Paz: n.p., 1954.

Prescott, William H. *The Conquest of Peru.* Partly abridged and revised by Victor W. Von Hagen. Originally published by Harper Bros., Boston, 1847. Mentor edition published by The New American Library, New York, 1961.

Puente Arnao, Juan Angulo. *Historia de los Límites del Perú.* 2nd ed. Lima: Intendencia General de Guerra, 1927.

Ramazani, Rouhollah K. *The Northern Tier: Afghanistan, Iran and Turkey.* Princeton: D. Van Nostrand Co., Inc., 1966.

Reyes, Federico Nielsen. *¡Del Lauca Al Mar!* La Paz: n.p., 1963.

Ríos Gallardo, Conrado. *Chile y Bolivia Definen Sus Fronteras 1842–1904.* Santiago: Editorial Andrés Bello, 1963.

Robinson, Edward Austin Gossage (ed.). *Economic Development for Africa South of the Sahara.* New York: St. Martin's Press, Inc., 1964.

Ronning, C. Neale. *Law and Politics in Inter-American Diplomacy.* New York: John Wiley and Sons, Inc., 1963.

Russett, Bruce M. *World Handbook of Political and Social Indicators.* New Haven: Yale University Press, 1965.

Saavedra, Abdon S. *Reivindicación Marítima.* La Paz: Honorable Municipalidad, 1966.

Siddiqi, Aslam. *Pakistan Seeks Security.* Lahore: Longmans, Green and Co., 1960.

Singh, Lalita Prasad. *The Politics of Economic Cooperation in Asia: A Study of Asian International Organizations.* Columbia: University of Missouri Press, 1966.
Stamp, L. Dudley. *Africa: A Study in Tropical Development.* 2nd ed. New York: John Wiley and Sons, Inc., 1964.
Stevens, Roger. *The Land of the Great Sophy.* London: Methuen and Co. Ltd., 1962.
Steward, Julian H., and Faron, Louis C. *Native Peoples of South America.* New York: McGraw-Hill Book Co., Inc., 1959.
Syatauw, J. J. G. *Some Newly Established Asian States and The Development of International Law.* The Hague: Martinus Nijhoff, 1961.
Tayyeb, Ali. *Pakistan; A Political Geography.* London: Oxford University Press, 1966.
The Economy of East Africa; A Study of Trends. London: The Economist Intelligence Unit, October 1955.
Urquidi, Victor L. *Free Trade and Economic Integration in Latin America.* Berkeley and Los Angeles: University of California Press, 1964.
Vidaurre P., Juan José. *Puerto Para Bolivia; Antecedentes Diplomáticos; Basis de Negociación.* La Paz: Editorial Universo, 1950.
Von Hagen, Victor W. *Realm of the Incas.* New York: The New American Library, 1957.
Wallerstein, Immanuel. *Africa: The Politics of Unity.* New York: Random House, 1967.
Wambaugh, Sarah. *Plebiscites Since the World War.* Vol. I. Washington: Carnegie Endowment for International Peace, 1933.
Whitaker, Philip. *Political Theory and East African Problems.* London: Oxford University Press, 1964.
Wightman, David. *Toward Economic Cooperation in Asia; The United Nations Economic Commission for Asia and the Far East.* New Haven: Yale University Press, 1963.
Wilber, Donald N. *Afghanistan.* New Haven: HRAF Press, 1962.
–. *Contemporary Iran.* New York: Frederick A. Praeger, Publishers, 1963.
–. *Pakistan.* New Haven: HRAF Press, 1964.
Wilde C., M. Fernando. *Historia Militar de Bolivia.* La Paz: n.p., 1963.
Wionczek, Miguel S. (ed.). *Latin American Economic Integration; Experiences and Prospects.* New York: Frederick A. Praeger, Publishers, 1966.
Zondag, Cornelius H. *The Bolivian Economy, 1952–1965; The Revolution and its Aftermath.* New York: Frederick A. Praeger, Publishers, 1966.

Articles

"Afghan Supplement," *Eastern World,* XIX (December, 1965).
Ahsanullah. "Economic Relationship of Karachi with its Hinterland Regions," *Geografia* [Karachi: Pakistan Institute of Geography], III (Winter 1964), 99–109.
Anand, R. P. "Certain Problems of International Law," *The International and Comparative Law Quarterly,* XV (January, 1966), 55–75.
–. "Role of the 'New' Asian-African Countries in the Present International Legal Order," *The American Journal of International Law,* LV (April, 1962), 383–406.
Ballis, William B. "Recent Soviet Relations with Afghanistan," *Institute for the Study of the USSR Bulletin,* XIII (June, 1966), 3–13.

Banfield, Jane. "Federation in East Africa," *International Journal,* XVIII (Spring 1963), 181–193.

Bartlett, Captain LeRoy, Jr. "Bolivia and the Arica-Santos Railway," *The Military Engineer,* XXXIII (July-August, 1941), 301–307.

Birch, A. H. "Approaches to the Study of Federalism," *Political Studies,* XIV (February, 1966), 15–33.

Bird, Richard. "The Need for Regional Policy in a Common Market," *Scottish Journal of Political Economy,* XII (November, 1965), 225–242.

"Bolivia and Chile Disagree," *The Inter-American,* II (July, 1943), 8.

Caroe, Sir Olaf. "Afghan Highways," *The Geographical Magazine,* X (Winter 1956), 43–59.

Castañeda, Jorge. "The Underdeveloped Nations and the Development of International Law," *International Organization,* XV (Winter 1961), 38–48.

Cliffe, Lionel. "East Africa – Unity and Diversity," *Current History,* L (March, 1966), 147–152.

Crist, Raymond E. "Politics and Geography; Some Aspects of Centrifugal and Centripetal Forces Operative in Andean America," *The American Journal of Economics and Sociology,* XXV (October, 1966), 349–358.

Deak, Francis. "Observations on International Law in Underdeveloped Areas," *Proceedings of the American Society of International Law,* LVI (1962), 54–63.

Dean, Arthur H. "The Geneva Conference on the Law of the Sea: What Was Accomplished," *The American Journal of International Law,* LII (October, 1958), 607–628.

Declaration of Bogotá, 16 August 1966, *Inter-American Economic Affairs,* XX (Winter 1966), 88–96.

"Development of Uganda's Communications," *Spear,* V (October, 1962), 244–250.

Dutta, R. "Uganda; A Geopolitical Study," *Modern Review* (January, 1965), 17–28.

East, Gordon W. "The Geography of Land-Locked States," *Transactions and Papers, The Institute of British Geographers,* Publication No. 28. (London: George Philip and Son, Ltd., 1960), 1–22.

"The Economic Community of Eastern Africa," *East Africa Journal,* III (June, 1966), 28–30.

Edelmann, Alexander T. "Colonization in Bolivia: Progress and Prospects," *Inter-American Economic Affairs,* XX (Spring 1967), 39–54.

Eltezam, Z. A. "Afghanistan's Foreign Trade," *The Middle East Journal,* XX (Winter 1966), 95–103.

Etienne, Gilbert. "L'economie de l'Afghanistan," *Tiers-Monde,* VI (October-December, 1965), 934–957.

Fair, T. J. D. "A Regional Approach to Economic Development in Kenya," *The South African Geographic Journal,* LXV (December, 1963), 55–77.

Feygin, L. Ya. "Problems of Improving Inter-Regional Productive Relationships of the Central Asian Economic Region," *Izvestiya Akademii Nauk SSSR,* seriya geograficheskaya, No. 1 (1964), 44–51. In *Soviet Geography: Review and Translation,* VI (June, 1964), 3–11.

Fifer, J. Valerie. "Arica: A Desert Frontier in Transition," *The Geographical Journal,* CXXX (December, 1964), 507–518.

–. "Bolivia's Boundary with Brazil: A Century of Evolution," *The Geographical Journal,* CXXXII (September, 1966), 360–372.

–. "Bolivia's Pioneer Fringe," *The Geographical Review,* LVII (January, 1967), 1–23.

Franck, Peter G. "Economic Progress in an Encircled Land," *The Middle East Journal,* X (Winter 1956), 43–59.

–. "Problems of Economic Development in Afghanistan," *The Middle East Journal,* III (July, 1949), 293–314.

Fried, John H. E. "The New Convention on Transit Trade of Land-locked States, and the Development of Law under United Nations Auspices," *Journal of the Tribhuban University,* Department of Political Science, (Kathmandu, 1966), 16–29.

–. "The 1965 Convention on Transit Trade of Land-locked States," *Indian Journal of International Law,* VI (1966), 9–30.

Friedheim, Robert L. "The 'Satisfied' and 'Dissatisfied' States Negotiate International Law: A Case Study," *World Politics,* XVIII (October, 1965), 20–41.

"From the Chilean Desert," *Américas,* VIII (June, 1956), 25–28.

Ghai, Dharam. "Territorial Distribution of Benefits and Costs of the East African Common Market," *The East African Economics Review,* XI (June, 1964), 29–40.

Gheevala, C. F. "Prospects of Regional Cooperation in Asia," *United Asia,* XVII (May-June, 1965), 165–169.

Gladden, E. N. "The East African Common Services Organization," *Parliamentary Affairs,* XVI (Autumn 1963), 428–439.

Gochenour, Theodore S. "A New Try for Afghanistan," *The Middle East Journal,* XIX (Winter 1965), 1–19.

"Good Scope for Tyres, Tubes Exports to Afghanistan," *The Journal of Industry and Trade,* XVI (New Delhi: Directorate of Commercial Publicity, Ministry of Commerce, Government of India, December, 1966), 1469–1470.

Gregg, Robert W. "The UN Regional Economic Commissions and Integration in the Underdeveloped Regions," *International Organization,* XX (Spring 1966), 208–232.

Guha, Amalendu. "Economic Development of Afghanistan – 1929–1961," *International Studies,* VI (April, 1965), 421–439.

Harrod, Sir Roy. "Economic Development and Asian Regional Cooperation," *The Pakistan Development Review,* II (Spring 1962), 1–22.

Hartshorne, Richard. "The Functional Approach in Political Geography," *Annals of the Association of American Geographers,* XL (1950), 95–130.

Hasan, Khursid. "Pakistan-Afghanistan Relations," *Asian Survey,* II (September, 1962), 14–19.

Hasan, Zubeida. "The Foreign Policy of Afghanistan," *Pakistan Horizon,* XVII (First Quarter 1964), 48–57.

–. "South Asia as a Region," *Pakistan Horizon,* XVII (Second Quarter 1964), 161–167.

Hauberg, C. A. "Challenge in Bolivia," *Current History,* XXXVIII (March, 1960), 155–164.

Hazelwood, Arthur. "The East African Common Market: Importance and Effects," *Bulletin of the Oxford University Institute of Economics and Statistics,* XXVIII (February, 1966), 1–18.

–. "The 'Shiftability' of Industry and the Measurement of Gains and Losses in the East African Common Market," *Bulletin of the Oxford University Institute of Economics and Statistics,* XXVIII (May, 1966), 63–72.

Hoyle, B. S. "The Proposed Tanzania-Zambia Railway," *The East African Geographical Review,* (April, 1965), 51–52.

Jessup, Philip C. "The Geneva Conference on the Law of the Sea; A Study in International Law-Making," *The American Journal of International Law,* LII (October, 1958), 730–733.

Johns, David H. "East African Unity – Problems and Prospects," *The World Today,* XIX (December, 1963), 533–540.

Kain, Ronald Stuart. "Bolivia's Claustrophobia," *Foreign Affairs,* XVI (July, 1938), 704–714.

Karanja, Dr. J. N. "Kenya after Independence," *African Affairs,* LXV (October, 1966), 289–296.

King, J. W. "Nile Transport in Uganda," *The East African Geographical Review,* (April, 1966), 25–36.

Kristof, Ladis K. D. "The Nature of Frontiers and Boundaries," *Annals of the Association of American Geographers,* IL (1959), 269–282.

Land, Thomas. "Back Door to Zambia," *Atlas,* X (December, 1965), 376–377.

Lauterpacht, E. "Freedom of Transit in International Law," *Transactions of the Grotius Society,* XLIV (1958–1959).

Lissitzyn, Oliver J. "International Law in a Divided World," *International Conciliation,* No. 542 (March, 1963).

Lomas, P. K. "The Report of the East Africa Economic and Fiscal Commission," *The East African Economics Review,* VIII (June, 1961), 14–23.

Malik, Rashid A. "Pakistan's Intra-Regional Pattern of Transportation," *The Journal of Geography,* LXI (May, 1962), 209–214.

Mazrui, Ali A. "Tanzania Versus East Africa; A Case of Unwitting Federal Sabotage," *Journal of Commonwealth Political Studies,* III (November, 1965), 209–225.

Michel, Aloys A. "Foreign Trade and Foreign Policy in Afghanistan," *Middle Eastern Affairs,* XII (January, 1961), 7–15.

Newlyn, Walter T. "Gains and Losses in the East African Common Market," *Yorkshire Bulletin of Economic and Social Research,* XVII (November, 1965), 130–138.

Nigam, R. S. "Prospects of Asian Economic Cooperation," *AICC Economic Review,* XVI (25 October 1964), 7–13.

Nye, Joseph S., Jr. "East African Economic Integration," *The Journal of Modern African Studies,* I (December, 1963), 475–502.

–. "Unity and Diversity in East Africa: A Bibliographical Essay," *The South Atlantic Quarterly,* LXV (Winter 1966), 104–123.

O'Connor, A. M. "New Railway Construction and the Pattern of Economic Development in East Africa," *Transactions, Institute of British Geographers,* No. 36 (June 1965), 21–30.

Odingo, R. S. "Geopolitical Problems of East Africa," *East Africa Journal,* II (February, 1966), 17–24.

"Pakistan – Relations with Afghanistan," *The Round Table,* LII (December, 1961), 81–84.

"Pakistan's Trade with the Afro-Asian Countries," *Pakistan Trade,* XIV (December, 1963), 3–10.

Palazzoli, Claude. "De Quelques Développements Récents du Droit des gens en matière D'Accès a la Mer des Pays Dépourvus de Littoral," *Revue Générale de Droit International Public,* LXXVII (July-September, 1966), 667–735.

Pavlenko, V. F. "The Transport-Geography Situation and Inter-Regional Links of Central Asia," *Geografiya i Khozyzystvo,* No. 12 (1963), 43–48. In *Soviet Geography: Review and Translation,* IV (November, 1963), 27–34.

Pearcy, G. Etzel. "Geographical Aspects of the Law of the Sea," *Annals of the Association of American Geographers,* IL (March, 1959), 1–23.

Pounds, Norman J. G. "A Free and Secure Access to the Sea," *Annals of the Association of American Geographers,* IL (September, 1959), 256–268.

Proctor, J. H., Jr. "The Effort to Federate East Africa: A Post Mortem,' *The Political Quarterly,* XXXVII (January-March, 1966), 46–69.

–., and Krishna, K. G. V. "The East African Common Services Organization: An Assessment," *The South Atlantic Quarterly,* LXIV (Autumn 1965), 526–548.
Qureshi, S. M. M. "Pakhtunistan: The Frontier Dispute Between Afghanistan and Pakistan," *Pacific Affairs,* XXXIX (Spring-Summer 1966), 99–114.
Ram, Mangat. "Regional Integration in Asia," *AICC Economic Review,* XVIII (1 December 1966), 29–32, 44.
Ramazani, R. K. "Afghanistan and the USSR," *The Middle East Journal,* XII (Spring 1958), 144–152.
"RCD News," *Pakistan Trade,* XVI (September, 1965), 5–10.
"The Rectification of East African Trade Imbalances," *International Legal Materials; Current Documents,* III (November, 1964), 3–12.
Reyes, Salvador. "Oases in the Atacama Desert," *Américas,* XV (September, 1963), 10–16.
"The Role of Transportation in Economic Development," *American Economic Review,* LII (May, 1962), 386–415.
Rosberg, Carl G., Jr., and Segal, Aaron. "An East African Federation," *International Conciliation* No. 543 (May, 1963).
Rothchild, Donald. "The Meaning of Economic Integration In Africa," *East Africa Journal,* II (December, 1965), 23–28.
Rudolph, William E. "Sulphur in Chile," *Geographical Review,* XLII (October, 1952), 562–590.
Segal, Aaron. "The Integration of Developing Countries: Some Thoughts on East Africa and Central America," *Journal of Common Market Studies,* V (March, 1967), 252–282.
–. "The Tanganyika-Zambia Railway Project," *Africa Report,* IX (November, 1964), 9–10.
Sinha, S. Prakash. "Perspective of the Newly Independent States on the Binding Quality of International Law," *International and Comparative Law Quarterly,* XIV (January, 1965), 121–131.
Sorensen, Max. "Law of the Sea," *International Conciliation* No. 520 (November, 1958).
Spencer, D. L. "The Role of Oil in Soviet Foreign Economic Policy," *The American Journal of Economics and Sociology,* XXV (January, 1966), 91–107.
Stokes, Charles J. "The Economic Impact of the Carretera Marginal de la Selva," *Traffic Quarterly,* XX (April, 1966), 203–226.
Stokes, William S. "The 'Revolución Nacional' and the MNR in Bolivia," *Inter-American Economic Affairs,* XII (Spring 1959), 28–40.
Thierry, Hubert. "Les Etats Privés de Littoral Maritime," *Revue Générale de Droit International Public,* LXII (October–December, 1958), 610–617.
Tretiak, Daniel and Lois Dougan. "Moscow's Trade with Asia," *Far Eastern Economic Review,* LI (3 February 1966), 204–208.
Urbanski, Edmund G. "The Development of Andean America," *Current History,* XLII (February, 1962), 96–105, 115.
van Dongen, Irene S. "Mombasa in the Land and Sea Exchanges of East Africa," *Erdkunde,* XVII (July, 1963), 16–38.
Vasey, Sir Ernest. "The Common Market in East Africa; Dangers of the drift towards separate fiscal and commercial policies,' *East African Trade and Industry,* VI (September, 1959), 89–91.
Wilber, Donald N. "Afghanistan, Independent and Encircled," *Foreign Affairs,* XXXI (April, 1953), 486–494.
Wionczek, Miguel S. "Latin American Free Trade Association," *International Conciliation,* No. 551 (January, 1965).

Wood, R. N. "The East African Common Market: A Reassessment," *Bulletin of the Oxford University Institute of Economics and Statistics,* XXVIII (November, 1966), 273–280.

Periodicals

Asian Recorder. 1955–1967.
The Christian Science Monitor. 1962–1968.
El Diario (La Paz, Bolivia). 1964.
The Economist. 1939–1967.
Hispanic American Report. 1962–1964.
The Kabul Times. 1967.
Keesing's Contemporary Archives. 1967.
La Nación (La Paz, Bolivia). 1963–1964.
The New York Times. 1962–1968.
Presencia (La Paz, Bolivia). 1964.
The Times (London). 1965–1966.
The Wall Street Journal. 1965–1967.

Unpublished Sources

Bahadur, Prakash. "Free Access to the Sea of Land-locked Countries in International Law and Practice." Unpublished Master's thesis, Cornell University, 1959.
Chile, Corporación de Fomento de Industria y Comercio (CORFO). Untitled and unpublished report. Santiago, September 29, 1961.
Fischer, Eric. "Landlocked Countries of Africa." Paper read before the Association of American Geographers in Denver, Colorado, September, 1963.
Glassner, Martin Ira. "Bolivia and an Access to the Sea." Unpublished Master's thesis, California State College at Fullerton, August, 1964.
Moscoso, Teodoro. Address before the Coordinating Committee of International Activities of Private Enterprise, Mexico City October 26, 1962. (Mimeographed.)
Spain, James W. "Pakistan's North-west Frontier: Political Problems of a Borderland." Unpublished Ph. D. dissertation, Columbia University, 1959.
United States, International Cooperation Administration. "Inspection of Ports and Rail Facilities for Discharge and Shipment of Economic Aid and Technical Assistance, Supplies and Equipment." Unpublished report, La Paz, October 16, 1956.

Other Sources

DeSoto, Anthony Essex. *Bolivia's Right to an Access to the Sea.* Pasadena: Jensen Publishing Company, 1962.
Dupree, Louis. "Afghanistan: 1966," *American Universities Field Staff Report, South Asia Series* (*AUFS Report*), X July, 1966.
–. "Afghanistan's Big Gamble," *AUFS Report,* IV May, 1960.
–. "Pakistan: 1964–1966 Part IV: The Regional Cooperation for Development." *AUFS Report,* X November, 1966.

–. " 'Pushtunistan': The Problem and Its Larger Implications," Part I *AUFS Report,* V November, 1961.
Ibid., Part II, November, 1961.
Ibid., Part III, December, 1961.
–. "A Suggested Pakistan-Afghanistan-Iran Federation," *AUFS Report,* VII February, 1963.
Letter from Office of the General Manager of East African Railways and Harbours, Nairobi, August 1967.
Encyclopaedia Britannica. 1965 edition. Volumes I, IX, and XXII.
–. *Book of the Year 1967.*
The Gallatin Annual of International Business 1965, R. W. Greenebaum, editor. New York: The American Heritage Publishing Company, 1965.
Goode's World Atlas. 12th ed. Chicago: Rand McNally and Co., 1964.
The Kabul Times Annual. Kabul: The Kabul Times Publishing Agency, 1967.
Kenya. London: Barclay's Bank D.C.O., 1967.
Koebig and Koebig, Inc., *Report on Transportation Facilities of Afghanistan and Pakistan.* Los Angeles, October 1957.
Patch, Richard W. "Bolivia's Developing Interior," *American Universities Field Staff Reports Service, West Coast South America Series* (*AUFS Report*), IX (April, 1962).
–. "Bolivia Today," *AUFS Report,* VIII (March, 1961).
The Statesman's Yearbook, 1967–1968. New York: St. Martin's Press, 1967.
Tabibi, Dr. Abdul Hakim. "The Right of Free Access to the Sea." n.p., 1966.
Tanzania. London: Barclay's Bank D.C.O., 1965.
Uganda. London: Barclay's Bank D.C.O., 1967.
World Bank Atlas. Washington: International Bank for Reconstruction and Development, September, 1967.

INDEX

Made in the USA
Monee, IL
18 October 2026

66037583R10175